James Hildyard

The Ingoldsby letters

1858-1878

James Hildyard

The Ingoldsby letters
1858-1878

ISBN/EAN: 9783337283056

Printed in Europe, USA, Canada, Australia, Japan

Cover: Foto ©ninafisch / pixelio.de

More available books at **www.hansebooks.com**

THE

INGOLDSBY LETTERS,

(1858—1878)

IN REPLY TO

THE BISHOPS IN CONVOCATION, THE HOUSE
OF LORDS, AND ELSEWHERE,

ON THE

Revision of the Book of Common Prayer.

BY THE
REV. JAMES HILDYARD, B.D.,
RECTOR OF INGOLDSBY, LINCOLNSHIRE.

VOL. I.

"Nonumque prematur in annum,
Membranis intus positis."—HOR., *Ars Poet.*, 388.
"Let them not come forth
Till twenty rolling years have proved their worth."
FRANCIS.

Fourth Edition,
REVISED AND ENLARGED;
BRINGING THE REVISION MOVEMENT DOWN TO
THE PRESENT TIME.

CASSELL PETTER & GALPIN:
LONDON, PARIS & NEW YORK.
1879.
[ALL RIGHTS RESERVED.]

To

WILLIAM PARKER, Esq.,

OF HANTHORPE HOUSE, NEAR BOURN, LINCOLNSHIRE,

THE UNFLINCHING ADVOCATE, BOTH BY PRECEPT AND EXAMPLE,

OF SOUND PROTESTANT AND RELIGIOUS PRINCIPLES

THROUGH A LONG AND USEFUL LIFE,

THIS FOURTH EDITION OF

THE INGOLDSBY LETTERS,

PUBLISHED AT HIS SPECIAL REQUEST AND CHIEF COST,

IS DEDICATED

BY HIS ATTACHED AND GRATEFUL FRIEND,

THE AUTHOR.

The following notice of the THIRD EDITION of the Letters appeared in the *Church Standard*, August 15, 1868:—

It is not often that anonymous letters written to newspapers attract more than a passing notice. These, however, by "Ingoldsby" have not only been collected in two handsome volumes, but have reached a third edition. This unusual success is to be explained, in the first place, by the nature of the subjects treated; and in the next by the fact that their author is really so well known that he can, and does, repudiate the idea of writing from behind a mask. The topic is a REVISION OF THE LITURGY; and the writer, the Rev. James Hildyard, Rector of Ingoldsby, Lincolnshire, is one of the most eminent scholars of the day, having obtained the highest classical honours at Cambridge; and who would, it is said, have been Master of Christ's College certainly, and probably a Bishop, if he had not shown, even in early life, that free spirit which breathes throughout his pages and makes them so refreshing.

What he wants is a ROYAL COMMISSION charged to inquire whether reforms are needed in the Book of Common Prayer: and it is evident that he looks for a settlement more truly comprehensive than that which, while it retained those who have expanded into Mackonochies and Littledales, nevertheless excluded those 2,000 Puritans whose wrongs and sufferings have been so eloquently recorded by Mr. Mountfield, of Newport. We have only to add that Mr. Hildyard has thrown his whole heart into the work; that he has brought to bear on his opponents innumerable and most apposite classical allusions and quotations, close arguments, keen irony, sharp wit, and caustic ridicule, showing himself more than a match for the Bishop of Oxford, and capable of breaking a lance with the mighty Bishop of St. David's. We had marked many passages deserving to be extracted, but, good as they are by themselves, they read so much better when joined with the context, that we resolved not to injure them by citation.

PREFACE
TO
THE FOURTH EDITION.

> "Veluti pueris absinthia tetra medentes
> Quom dare conantur, prius oras pocula circum
> Contingunt mellis dulci flavoque liquore,
> Ut puerorum ætas improvida ludificetur
> Labrorum tenus,—interea perpotet amarum
> Absinthi laticem, deceptaquo non capiatur,
> Sed potius tali tactu recreata valescat:—
> Sic ego nunc." Lucret., Lib. i. 937—44.

Twenty years have gone over the head of the Author of these Letters since the bulk of them were written, and published in various London and Provincial Newspapers of the day. His hair has grown grey in the interval, and he has witnessed much of the changes and chances of this mortal life;—but nothing that he has seen or heard in all those years (and they have been not uneventful ones, whether in Church or State) has tended in the slightest degree to shake any one of the opinions expressed in the course of the following pages;—nay, rather, he is abundantly confirmed in all he has written by everything he has in the meanwhile noticed passing around him.

The position, under the good Providence of God, which he has been permitted to hold during that long period in the life of man, in the very prime of manhood and presumed maturity of judgment, has enabled him to look around and witness calmly what was occurring elsewhere, without being himself in any way mixed up with the strife of tongues.

This was a rare opportunity;—and he has availed himself of it to review at leisure, from time to time, the sentiments put on record when the question of a REVISION OF THE BOOK OF COMMON PRAYER was more before the public than it is at the present moment.

He has seen an active and earnest section in the Church striving continually for the mastery,—setting the Law and the Bishops at defiance,—while they shelter themselves behind certain words in the unreformed Prayer-book, which they defy their opponents to remove, or, if not removed, to interpret against them.

He has witnessed, on the other hand, an *Imperium in Imperio* established under the title of "The Reformed Episcopal Church in England," which threatens in time to develop into a serious schism, analogous to that which lately shook the Church of Scotland to the centre.

He has seen, and partly himself experienced, a growing disinclination on the part of the more talented youth of the country to enter the Church as a profession; while a daily increasing demand is felt for their services.

He has seen the Church in Ireland robbed and disestablished; at the same time that Popery in that Country has been encouraged and endowed with a portion of the spoil.

He has seen in England, through the length and breadth of the land, the Education of the rising generation handed over to Board Schools, from which the Church Catechism and the distinctive teaching of the Clergy of the Establishment is excluded.

He has seen Church Rates abolished; and an internecine struggle carried on in Parliament for the surrender of the churchyards to those who never set foot within the church.

All this, and more, he is inclined to attribute to the fact that the intelligence of mankind in the latter part of the nineteenth century refuses to be governed by a Law passed in the middle of the seventeenth; and which Law it has been, and is, a main part of the object of THE INGOLDSBY LETTERS to get either repealed or revised.

He therefore hesitates not, at the earnest desire of an old and valued friend, to commit them again to the Press, with such annotations and observations as the experience of twenty years enables him to bring to bear upon them.

A new generation of Clergy, and an almost entirely different Bench of Bishops, have come upon the scene since the LETTERS were originally written. No offence, therefore, can reasonably be taken (as none is intended) at any of the seemingly severe remarks made upon a few individuals in the course of the following pages.

Finally, as to the vein of banter, or humour, which more or less pervades the whole,—the Author begs here once for all (as he has done elsewhere) to state, that he adopted that course *designedly* from the beginning, after the example— though at a humble distance—of the learned Erasmus, and the genial Canon of St. Paul's, in order the better to attract public attention to a subject from which the natural man is too much disposed to turn aside,—but in which all, from the highest to the lowest, have in reality the deepest concern.

He has, in short, imitated, as closely as he was able, the cunning practice of the old physician in his motto. He has sweetened the rim of his cup with as much sugar and honey as he could command, in order to induce to the swallowing of a potion, intended to effect a radical cure in the admittedly disorganised condition of the Body Corporate of the Church.

Ingoldsby Rectory, Dec. 21st, 1878.

PREFACE TO THE THIRD EDITION.*

ONLY a few words are needed in explanation of the different form the Letters now assume to that in which they have previously appeared. The subject having become one of far more extended interest than was the case when the Letters were originally commenced, they have insensibly increased in number, and become greatly enlarged in their scope. The question now embraces, not only the Abridgment, and re-arrangement to a certain extent, of the Church Services, with consequent alteration of the Rubric and Calendar, but also the much wider department of an examination into the doctrine of the Prayer-book.

On this last point there is naturally much difference of opinion; but it is clear that it cannot be any longer ignored by those to whom the task of Revision shall be committed. The Author has all along maintained that a ROYAL COMMISSION

---

* The Author may be excused introducing this Edition in the words of an unknown Reviewer of a former one:—

"Ingoldsby's task is not without difficulties: he has to contend against the powerful influence of the most wealthy hierarchy in the world, and to arrest the attention of an age decidedly averse to theological controversy. He succeeds, by means of a light and pleasant style, in interesting us in a subject, not attractive, however important it may be. We think that Ingoldsby is fully justified in using this vivacious style; had he not done so, we are quite sure that he would not have had a tithe of his present readers. The grave sober treatises, which our forefathers read and digested, find no favour with people of the present day. This is Ingoldsby's own experience. He did his utmost in the way of solid arguments upon the subject for upwards of two whole years, consuming all his living in printing, advertising, letter-writing, reviewing; and had the satisfaction for his pains of finding that he convinced none but those who were convinced already. He has, therefore, resorted to another method of warfare, the success of which is shown by the circulation of these letters."—*London Morning Paper.*

is the only safe, as well as constitutional, method of undertaking the preliminary steps of INQUIRY and SUGGESTION. To that view he still adheres. Nor can he conceive a fitter time for the purpose of issuing such Commission, than when parties are so nicely balanced both in Church and State, that it is reasonable to conclude all sentiments would be fairly represented, and all representations fairly entertained.

This, it is well known, was far from being the case on the last Review of the Prayer-book. Whereas the recent debate in the House of Lords on the Act of Uniformity Amendment Bill shows a present disposition not only on the part of the Government, but also on that of a portion of the hierarchy, to enter on the question without heat and without partiality. The fact, too, of the year 1862 being the Bicentenary of the last Review, appears remarkably to coincide with other signs in fixing upon the present time as the most appropriate one for grappling with this great work.

In conclusion, the Author would express his earnest hope that the matter may be temperately handled by all whom it concerns; and that neither jealousy of those who are without the pale of the Church, nor differences of opinion amongst those who are within, may prevent the harmonious working of the Commission, should Her Majesty be advised to issue one. Their task, under the most favourable auspices, will be an arduous one; but no difficulty is insuperable where there is a willingness to co-operate cheerfully in the single desire to promote the glory of God, and the well-being of his people.

Ingoldsby Rectory, July 1st, 1862.

P.S.—A COMMISSION was, indeed, issued; but so limited in its scope, and so unsatisfactory in its original constitution, that it proved a *fiasco*,—as was anticipated from the beginning by those who had been most anxious for its appointment.

Dec. 21st, 1878.

TABLE OF CONTENTS TO VOL. I.

LETTER		PAGE
I.	Convocation of February, 1858	1
II.	The Upper House of Convocation	6
III.	Petition of the Lincolnshire Clergy	12
IV.	Bishop of Lincoln (Jackson) and the Prayer-book	19
V.	The Length of the Morning Service	25
VI.	Abridgment of the Morning Service	32
VII.	The Length of the Church Services	37
VIII.	Charity thinketh no evil	44
IX.	The Occasional Services of the Church	50
X.	This is not the Time	57
XI.	The Bishop of Oxford (Wilberforce), No. 1	65
XII.	The Commission of 1689	74
XIII.	Lord Ebury's Motion, May 6, 1858	82
XIV.	The Bishop of Oxford again, No. 2	90
XV.	The Bishop of St. David's (Thirlwall), No. 1	99
XVI.	The Deanery of York and Church Patronage	106
XVII.	Anonymous Letter-writing	117
XVIII.	The Bishop of St. David's, No. 2	124
XIX.	Ridicule will frequently prevail	130
XX.	Strike while the iron is hot	137
XXI.	Debate on the State Services	146
XXII.	Suggestions for a Royal Commission	153
XXIII.	The Many-headed Monster, Liturgical Reform	160
XXIV.	Insufficiency of Supplemental Rubrics	167
XXV.	The People's Call for Revision	168
XXVI.	There is a Lion in the Path	176
XXVII.	The Bishop of St. David's again	183
XXVIII.	George III. on the Length of the Church Service	189
XXIX.	The Bishop of St. David's once more	194
XXX.	Rev. C. Girdlestone and Church Patronage	200
XXXI.	The Bishop of Winchester (Sumner)	204
XXXII.	The Rev. C. Girdlestone and the Bishops	209
XXXIII.	The Bishop of Oxford, No. 3	215
XXXIV.	The State Services Expunged	221

TABLE OF CONTENTS.

LETTER		PAGE
XXXV.	The Bishop of London (Tait)	226
XXXVI.	The Bishop of London's Primary Charge	233
XXXVII.	The Bishop of Lincoln's Charge, Oct., 1858	238
XXXVIII.	The Archdeacon of Lindisfarne	246
XXXIX.	The Bishop of Lincoln's Charge, continued	250
XL.	The Bishop of Lincoln's Charge, concluded	264
XLI.	Re-assembling of Convocation, Feb., 1859	270
XLII.	The Burial Service of the Church	276
XLIII.	Adjournment of Convocation, Feb., 1859	282
XLIV.	Bishops of St. David's, Llandaff, and St. Asaph.	286
XLV.	Bishop of St. David's and Occasional Services	291
XLVI.	Dissolution of Parliament, April, 1859	296
XLVII.	The Liturgical Reformers and the Elections	302
XLVIII.	Election of Proctors for Lincoln Diocese	309
XLIX.	Bishop of Llandaff on the Morning Service	313
L.	Archdeacon Musgrave's Charge, May, 1859	319
LI.	The Bishop of St. Asaph on the Prayer-book	324
LII.	Rev. Vowler Short, Student of Christ Church	328
LIII.	Hereford, Bath and Wells, and Chichester	334
LIV.	The Convocation of Canterbury	339
LV.	Postponement of Lord Ebury's Motion, 1859	343
LVI.	The Archbishop of Canterbury (Sumner)	347
LVII.	The Dean of Norwich (Pellew) on Revision	351
LVIII.	The Rector of St. George's-in-the-East, 1859	354
LIX.	Lord Lyttelton and Lord Ebury	358
LX.	Lord Ebury and the *Morning Post*	363
LXI.	Bishop of Salisbury (Hamilton) on Revision	366
LXII.	The *Times* and Bishop of Chester (Graham)	371
LXIII.	Liturgical Revision and Church Reform	375
LXIV.	Disturbances at St. George's-in-the-East (1859)	379
LXV.	Morning Service at St. George's-in-the-East, (1).	386
LXVI.	Morning Service at St. George's-in-the-East, (2).	392
LXVII.	Rev. C. H. Davis on Liturgical Revision	400
LXVIII.	Dr. C. Robinson's Church Questions	405
LXIX.	Apology for the Ingoldsby Letters, 1859	411
	Dublin Review of the Ingoldsby Letters	419
Appendix A.	The Ritual Commission, 1867-70	426
" B.	The *Times* Newspaper on Convocation, 1872	428

"*Audi Alteram Partem.*"

REPLY TO THE BISHOPS IN CONVOCATION

AND IN THE

HOUSE OF LORDS

ON THE

Revision of the Book of Common Prayer.

The *following Letters appeared originally in various London and Provincial Newspapers at the date attached to each.*

LETTER I.

THE CONVOCATION OF FEBRUARY, 1858.

" I ask why the Civil State should be purged and restored by good and wholesome laws, made in every third or fourth Parliament, providing remedies as fast as time breedeth mischiefs, and contrariwise, the Ecclesiastical State should continue upon the dregs of time, and receive no alteration?"—LORD KEEPER BACON.

To THE EDITOR, &c.

SIR,—The liberal and independent tone your journal has uniformly adopted leads me to believe that whatever your individual opinion may be on the question of a Revision of the Book of Common Prayer, you will not refuse admission to the remarks of one who has devoted much time and attention to this important subject.

I am tempted to address you at this moment, in consequence of your observations on the subject of Convocation: its revival, its powers for good or ill, its real or assumed

B

character as the arbiter of the discipline, doctrine, and practice of the Church. Upon these matters you appear to take a large and unprejudiced view; and, while doing so, I have little doubt of your receiving the support of all that influential portion of the clergy who are unwilling to be trammelled by more restrictions than the already sufficiently straitened nature of their profession has imposed upon them. I confess myself to be of this number; and while no one would acquiesce more readily than I should in any decision of the *National* Legislature, consisting of Queen, Lords, and Commons, I cannot help protesting against the attempted revival, at this period of the world's history, of a *Church* Legislature, an *imperium in imperio*, an exclusive jurisdiction of equals over equals; or, at the best, a class legislation, where the absence of the voice of the laity* renders all opinion one-sided, to say the least of it, if not narrow and intolerant.†

With these short preliminary remarks, I will, with your permission, proceed to make a few observations upon the session of Convocation, which took place at Westminster, on Wednesday, the 10th of February, 1858; and having no other information on the subject, I presume I shall be in order if I accept as authentic the report of their proceedings as given in the *Times* newspaper of the following morning.

---

* See the opinion of the late Bishop of Gloucester and Bristol (Baring) on the authority of Convocation.—*Guardian*, March 20, 1861.

† See Dr. Arnold on "the *general* spirit which has marked Convocations of the Clergy."—*Hist. of Rome*, ii., p. 155.

In the Life of Gregory Nazianzen we read, that being summoned to attend a Council at Constantinople A.D. 382, "he utterly refused to comply with it, or indeed to be present at any synod whatsoever. This he signified by an epistle written on the occasion, wherein he tells them he had sufficient experience how little benefit one might expect from synods, which *commonly make breaches wider rather than cement them;* adding that such assemblies are usually full of brawls and clamours, more like a flock of geese or cranes than a convention of sage prelates."—*Biographia Eccl.*, ii. 327.

If that report is a partial one (of which I think there is strong internal evidence), the blame will fairly rest with those by whom it was supplied, and not, I trust, with one who, in common with others in all parts of the world, is thus alone made acquainted with the sayings and doings of that august body.

To commence, then, with the preamble. We are informed that "yesterday morning (*i.e.*, February 10th) the members of both Houses, composing the Convocation of the Province of Canterbury, assembled at Westminster, in pursuance of a Royal writ, *for the consideration of urgent business in connection with the Church*. The recent *passing* of the *Divorce and Matrimonial Bill*, the *attempt* which is being made to bring about a *Revision of the Liturgy*, and the measures which are being taken to extend episcopal and missionary operations in India, imparted more than ordinary interest to yesterday's proceedings."

Now, I would ask, *in limine*, is it seemly that the first important "business" to be taken in hand by this Church Legislature should be the impugning an ACT of Parliament, which received the Royal assent so lately as last year, after the most mature and patient deliberation in both Houses? If such is to be a sample of the *modus operandi* of Convocation (and it is only necessary to refer to the proceedings in the Lower House on the day named to see that I am not misjudging them), I can hardly conceive anything more calculated to lead to its speedy suppression. That the clergy, in solemn synod, should be the portion of the community that first sets the example of openly defying the acts of the Imperial Legislature,* is a bad omen of either their ability or temper to discuss calmly the affairs of the Church.

---

* How this was subsequently done in the case of the Public Worship Bill is too notorious to require note or comment. See *Times*, July 11, 1874.

But, as my immediate concern is not with the Divorce and Matrimonial Act, but with the proposed Revision of the Book of Common Prayer, I shall pass on to that; only noticing, as necessary to my future remarks, the constitution of the two Houses on this particular occasion.

The Prelates composing the Upper House, we are told, "assembled in the large apartment of Queen Anne's Bounty Office." And here I may be allowed to make one observation in passing. It occurs to me—and I am far from being singular in that opinion—that the unequal division of the two Houses of Convocation is a radical defect in its composition, and utterly fatal to the efficiency of the whole body as a legislative corporation. Who would bear that the House of Lords should consist only of dukes and marquises, to the number of two or three score, and that their *fiat* should override a House of Commons containing upwards of 650 representatives of the people? Whereas, constituted as the Upper House of Parliament now is, of about 450 members, thus forming a reasonable and just proportion to the numbers of the House of Commons elected by the people, nothing can be more salutary than the check it imposes on too rapid legislation; while the wisdom it has occasionally shown in timely yielding to the loudly expressed popular will—as in the case of Catholic Emancipation, the Reform Bill, and the Repeal of the Corn Laws—has only established its authority more firmly in the hearts of the wise among the people. The hasty and the violent may, indeed, raise their voice against its supposed disposition to resist reasonable reforms, but their cavils fall powerless to the ground; and the glorious Constitution of England—Sovereign, Lords, and Commons—is still (and may it ever be!) the envy and admiration of the world.

Now turn we to the *Church Parliament*, as it has been called by some of the advocates for revived Convocation. How different the case! Supposing *all* the Bishops and one Archbishop of the province of Canterbury congregated in the " large apartment" of Queen Anne's Bounty Office, there would be but *twenty-one* individuals assembled to control, check, and in a manner to override, the opinion expressed or understood of the *hundred and fifty* members of the Lower House; and these the so-called representatives of the Church! How, again, these latter are collected together; how it is altogether a "*packed assembly;*"* how the voice of the clergy at large is all but stifled in even their own House, is too notorious to need my dwelling upon here; † and I fear I have already exceeded the limits of an ordinary letter. Judging, however, the above prefatory remarks to be necessary towards establishing my future position, I hope you will excuse my so far digressing

---

* " A view of the composition of this anomalous assembly will show the unreality of its pretence to represent even the Clergy. In the Upper House sit, under the Presidency of the Archbishop of Canterbury, the twenty Bishops of his Province, all of them nominees of the Crown. In the Lower House sit twenty-three Deans, also nominees of the Crown; fifty-six Archdeacons, nominees of the Bishops—making a total of seventy-nine *ex-officio* members out of the 143 of which the House consists; while of the sixty-four elected Proctors, twenty-two at least are representatives of Cathedral Chapters, and only forty-four represent the parochial clergy. Forty-four out of 143! But this is not all. In most dioceses curates are not permitted to vote, and parishes which are not included in any Archdeaconry are shut out from a share in a representative; a large portion of the East of London, comprehending nearly the whole borough of the Tower Hamlets, is in this position. To call a body so constituted a representative assembly, is a mere farce; to argue whether it may or may not be entrusted with the general interests of the Church is grave nonsense."—*National Standard*, vol. iii., p. 134. To this may be added the circumstance of the Irish branch of the Church of England not being represented at all, which, of course, is utterly fatal to the body as a representation of the *United* Church, to say nothing of the Colonies.

† " I must needs wish," says Bishop Kennett, "that the parochial clergy in England were more equally and more fully represented; that their Proctors in the Lower House might at least be a balance to the other dignified presbyters, and not be exceeded by them more than one-half."

on this occasion. In my next I shall proceed to notice the observations made on the subject of Revision of the Prayer Book by such of the prelates as are reported to have taken any part in the debate. Meanwhile, I have the honour to remain,
        Yours obediently,
February 18, 1858.   " INGOLDSBY."

LETTER II.

THE UPPER HOUSE OF CONVOCATION.

" Una maraviglia dura *tre giorni.*"—*Italian Proverb.*

SIR,—Most people are familiar with the saying of "*a nine days' wonder.*" Some few limit the duration of marvels to a still shorter period, and adopt the Italian proverb in preference to the English one—which, in the case to which I am about to refer, appears to be the more accurate of the two; and, sooth to say, quite enough of so good a thing as CONVOCATION has *hitherto* proved itself to be.*

When I last wrote to you, I anticipated a lengthy Spring Session of the "two Houses," and wishing not to be wearisome to your readers, I proportioned the length of my first letter to the expected number of them. I cannot say that I am otherwise than agreeably disappointed at finding my task so speedily

---

 * The Convocation of February, 1860, produced indeed two reports; one on Dilapidations, under the guidance of the Dean of Norwich, the other a schedule of additional Services for special occasions. The Convocation of March 14, 1861, even entertained the Dean of Norwich's motion for a Revision of the Prayer Book—*but how?* Practically, Convocation has done nothing for the benefit of the clergy or the Church in general, and, to judge by all outward appearances, *never will.* See *Times* leader, January 12, 1866:—"There will never be two rival Parliaments in this country, either in secular or spiritual affairs. The House of Commons will not abdicate any portion of its inheritance, so let the clergy come to it for what they want, and not waste their prayers upon such a helpless idol as Convocation."

and happily abridged, by the precipitate breaking up of the *Church Parliament* after three days' session. Let me be allowed, however, to congratulate the Church at large upon the first-fruits of its labours; the solitary practical result, I believe, up to this time, of its six years' adjourned debates. The working clergy have henceforth the privilege—recommended by an archbishop, and endorsed by one of the highest of the suffragan bishops—to omit the Lord's Prayer before their sermons, even at the risk of being supposed "to have an objection to the Lord's Prayer altogether."*

I trust the priests and deacons of the empire will duly appreciate the boon thus extorted from "the authorities" by the pressure from without. For my own part, having for some years disused that beautiful and Divine prayer at that portion of the service, owing to the law of the land having already forced me to repeat it so often, I feel no obligation whatever to the Upper House of Convocation for the above concession, and shall therefore, I hope, not be considered as very ungrateful if I proceed to comment freely on their proceedings, notwithstanding this novel and curious illustration of the *Mons Parturiens*.

On the occasion referred to, it appears his Grace the Archbishop of Canterbury (Sumner) presided in "the Upper House," assembled in the "large apartment" of Queen Anne's Bounty Office. To occupy the remainder of the spacious chamber there were present, we are told, the Bishop of London (Tait), the Bishop of Winchester (C. R. Sumner), the Bishop of Bath and Wells (the Right Hon. Baron Auckland), the Bishop of Chichester (Gilbert), the Bishop of Llandaff (Ollivant), the Bishop of Hereford (Hampden), the Bishop of Lincoln (Jackson), the Bishop of Oxford (Wilberforce), the Bishop of St. Asaph (Short), and last,

---

* See speech of the Bishop of London (Tait) on the occasion.

though not least, the Bishop of St. David's (Connop Thirlwall)—in all, ten bishops and one archbishop.

I am the more particular in noting down the *names*, as well as the *titles*, of the prelates assembled on this occasion, as it will become hereafter matter of history who were the individuals who took part in a proceeding, the object of which evidently was to stifle in the birth *all attempts at inquiry* into the present working of the Church Services and Rubrics—a system, be it observed in passing, which dates from 1662, and is consequently two hundred years old, and whose fruits appear in the admitted fact, that, after so long a trial, the various denominations of Dissenters (including Roman Catholics) considerably outnumber the members of the Established Church in England and Wales.*

But having mentioned those of the prelates who were present on this memorable occasion, and on whose supposed—but by no means proved—*unanimity* much stress has been laid, it may be as well to call attention in this place to the names of those prelates who were absent, since it will sometimes happen—as in the case of the statues of the great Roman patriots—that more honour is due to those who do not take part in certain ceremonies than to those who do. I find, therefore, amongst the absent prelates of the province of Canterbury, the following names, most of whom will be allowed to be as distinguished for learning, piety, liberality, and judgment, as any of those above-mentioned :—The Bishop of Bangor (Bethell), the Bishop of Ely (Turton), the Bishop of Exeter (Philpotts),† the Bishop of Lichfield (Lonsdale), the

---

* See a Tract by the Rev. Isaac Taylor, M.A., of Trinity College, Cambridge, entitled "The Liturgy and the Dissenters." (Hatchard and Co., Piccadilly, 1860. Second Edition.) See also an able work by the Rev. D. Mountfield, of Oxon, Salop, entitled "Two Hundred Years Ago." (Second Edition. Kent and Co., Paternoster Row, 1862.)

† See, however, next Letter, No. III., p. 13, where it will be seen that the

Bishop of Norwich (Pelham), the Bishop of Peterborough (Davys), the Bishop of Rochester (Murray), the Bishop of Salisbury (Hamilton), the Bishop of Worcester (Pepys), and the Bishop of Gloucester and Bristol (Baring).

I may possibly, in my ignorance of the antiquarian lore of Convocation, have here set down the name of some prelate belonging to the northern Province of York, whose Convocation is prevented by the present occupant (Musgrave) of the archiepiscopal chair in that portion of the kingdom from exhibiting before the world those scenes which have occasionally displayed themselves in the council chamber of their southern sister. But, lest I should thus be charged with taking an undue advantage of my reader's ignorance, while pleading my own, I will further set down the names of all the remaining prelates of the English Bench; and it will then appear with what degree of fairness the public have been led to believe (as I have myself seen it stated in several papers) that "THE BISHOPS have declared *unanimously* against the Prayer-book being touched!"

There remain, therefore, the venerable and respected Archbishop Musgrave, of York, the Bishop of Durham (Longley), the Bishop of Carlisle (Villiers),* the Bishop of Chester (Graham), the Bishop of Manchester (Prince Lee), the Bishop of Ripon (Bickersteth), the Bishop of Sodor and Man (Powys). None of these last seven—nor, as far as I am aware, of the other ten absent prelates—have as yet publicly expressed their sentiments on the important subject of the Revision of the Book of Common Prayer. What they may have said or written privately is another matter.

Bishop of Exeter was present, though, as it would appear, silent. This eminent prelate died September, 1869, æt. ninety-two.

* The Bishop of Carlisle (afterwards of Durham) openly gave in his adhesion to the side of Revision even at "this present time." The Bishop of Chester's Charge, and the *Times*' remarks upon it, had not then appeared.

Perhaps some of them may have spoken somewhat more favourably of the expediency of at least "inquiry" being instituted, than those who took part in the Upper House conclave of February 10. But of that hereafter: our concern now is with the reported observations of those who were present on that occasion; foremost among whom appears the Bishop of Lincoln. Observe, however, that for *eleven* prelates *present*, we have *seventeen absent*, without reckoning the Irish bishops and archbishops, among whom one at least —the eminent and learned Dr. Whately*—is understood, both by his writings and by his expressed sentiments, to be far from unfavourable to a temperate consideration of the question at issue; while another,† the pious and able Bishop of Limerick, has in his published Charge of last autumn distinctly avowed himself a Liturgical Reformer.

After a petition had been presented by the Bishop of

---

* The Archbishop of Dublin said in the House of Lords, 1840,—
"He was for remedying those changes of that great innovator Time, who, as it was said by Lord Bacon, was insinuating imperceptibly many alterations, and was changing things for the worse if they were not changed for the better; and he would ask whether, in the alterations made by the first Reformers, they intended that their amendments should never be changed—whether they were like the laws of the Medes and Persians, unalterable—and whether it were their intention that the door should be locked, and the key buried and lost for ever?" See also Charge by Archbishop Whately, 1860. (See Vol. II., Letter LXXXVIII.)

† The Lord Bishop of Limerick (Griffin), in a Charge delivered in the year 1857, observed:—
"Such are my reasons for considering that the time has now arrived when increased knowledge, increased intelligence, and, in consequence, increased spirit of inquiry, have rendered such a revision necessary, seeing it may fairly be hoped that discussion may now be conducted with calmness and forbearance, which, if discontents be allowed to gather, might end in a disruption of that amity of spirit which alone can impart vitality in the connection between our Church and its Blessed Head, with Him, who will in vain have broken down the wall of partition between His followers if our own discussions and divisions were to rear it up again."—*Lord Ebury's Speech before the House of Lords, May*, 1858.

St. Asaph (Short), for the laudable purpose of a sub-division of the enormous diocese of Calcutta, rendered vacant by the death of the justly-lamented bishop, Daniel Wilson—

The Bishop of Lincoln (Jackson) said: "He had a Petition signed by 200 of the clergy of his diocese relative to the proposed Revision of the Liturgical Services of the Church; and it was one of no ordinary importance, for he believed it represented the opinions of a great majority of members of the Church of England. Although much had been said of the length of the Sunday Services in the Church, the general opinion of members of the Church was strong in opposition to any material alteration. He was quite sure that there was no sympathy on the part of the great body of the clergy and laity of the Church of England with those crude attempts to shorten her services which had been witnessed of late by entire omissions, and by bringing together different parts of different services, in total forgetfulness of the true and deep meaning which ran through each service, and of the immemorial traditions of the Church of Christ in each of those separate services. The Sunday Morning Service, exclusive of the sermon—which was a subject resting entirely with the minister—did not last more than an hour, or an hour and ten minutes, and the Afternoon Service from half an hour to forty minutes: making two hours out of that day set apart for special worship, to be spent in social service; less than two hours out of the 168 hours of each week spent by most members in the church, some from necessity, some from habit. The main reason why the services appeared long, unhappily, to large numbers of their congregations was that they had not formed habits of devotion. But he apprehended that it was the intention and the duty of the Church not to lower the tone of her devotions to the low pitch of her weakest members, but to keep them to the higher pitch, so as to provide for the wants of her more faithful members, and also to raise others to the same standard. With regard to occasional services, the case was entirely different."

The above is copied, verbatim, from the *Times* newspaper; as to whose report, if it does not convey the exact words spoken by the right reverend prelate, we at least know on the authority of the Bishop of Oxford (Wilberforce) that "somehow or other it had contrived to be marvellously correct." So in my future observations upon this speech, I shall, unless otherwise advised, take it for granted that it more or less accurately represents the sentiments then and there delivered by the Bishop of Lincoln on the subject of the proposed Revision of the Book of Common Prayer.

But as my remarks, though I study brevity, must necessarily extend to a much greater length than the speech itself which forms my thesis, you will allow me to reserve a portion of them for future communication; in the meanwhile, I have the honour to remain,

Yours faithfully,

February 25, 1858. "INGOLDSBY."

LETTER III.

THE PETITION OF TWO HUNDRED AND FIFTEEN LINCOLNSHIRE CLERGY.

"Men who have grown old under a system learn to look at all parts of it as equally essential to its existence: they cannot distinguish with any accuracy the sound from the unsound, the substance from the accident; and they regard the moss upon the branches of the tree of life as no less sacred than the fruit."—ANON.

SIR,—Before pursuing our observations on the late meeting of Convocation, I must here state, that a copy of the *Guardian* newspaper has been put into my hands since the two former letters were written; and as that paper is generally understood to give the most authentic version of what takes place in Convocation, it will henceforth form my text-book in place of the report given in the *Times*.

The only material correction I have so far to make is that it appears the Bishop of Exeter (Philpotts) was present, in addition to the prelates named in the *Times*, making, accordingly, *twelve* prelates out of the twenty-one forming the Upper House (or " House of Bishops," as it is styled in the *Guardian*), and leaving, therefore, nine prelates of the province of Canterbury, and the whole seven of the province of York—in other words, *sixteen* in all of the English bishops—hitherto uncommitted on the question at issue; even assuming, which by no means appears, that the whole of the above-named dozen were *unanimous* on the point.* The speech of the Bishop of Lincoln is in substance much the same in both reports; but in quoting it in detail I shall make use of the *Guardian* version, for the reason given above, being most anxious to avoid the smallest appearance of misrepresentation or misconception in so grave a matter.

Perhaps I am presumptuous enough in expressing an opinion at all, seeing that I do not possess the magic "two or three thousand a year"—(much less the Episcopal £5,000) which Sydney Smith has wittily designated as the Englishman's "Knight's Census," the qualification giving the franchise to write, speak, or think for oneself.† But at any rate I will be as careful as I can to keep within the strict bounds of truth; to take nothing for granted which I cannot prove; and to deal that measure of justice to others which I should expect to be extended to myself in a like case.

---

* It will be borne in mind, throughout, that the "LETTERS" themselves were written *twenty years ago;* the NOTES have been added since at various intervals of time.

† I hold, however, the inestimable privilege " et sentire quæ velim, et quæ sentiam dicere," with my living of gross £700 per annum.

The *Guardian* report, then, is as follows :—

"LEGISLATIVE INTERFERENCE WITH THE BOOK OF COMMON PRAYER :—The *Bishop of Lincoln* :—' I have another petition to present—to which I would request particular attention—proceeding from a number of clergymen throughout the diocese of Lincoln. To this petition are appended the signatures of 215 clergymen of great respectability and standing in that diocese, and representing no one particular part or section of the Church. The petition is on the subject of the alteration of the Liturgy, and runs thus :—

"'To the Most Rev. the Archbishop, the Right Rev. the Bishops, and the Rev. the Clergy of the Province of Canterbury, in Convocation assembled :—The humble petition of the undersigned clergy of the diocese of Lincoln, Showeth,—That your petitioners have reason to know that efforts are being made in divers quarters for the Revision of the Book of Common Prayer, with the professed view of abbreviating the ordinary services of the Church; that they believe that the announcement made by many of your lordships, of your willingness to allow the use of the Litany in certain cases as a separate service, is calculated to lead to such abbreviation as may sometimes be desirable; that they feel the value of the suggestions offered in the report of the Committee of Convocation on Church Services in the Session of 1854, and various occasional offices, such as thanksgiving offices, penitential offices, offices for children, and others, to be used with the permission of the bishop of the diocese; that while they deprecate most strongly any fusion of the three offices of our usual Morning Services into one, by the omission of portions of each or any of them, they would rejoice that every facility should be afforded for the use of all these offices separately when desirable. But, considering the many difficulties and hazards which beset the question, your petitioners earnestly pray that your venerable body will strenuously oppose any attempt at legislative interference with, or alteration of, the Book of Common Prayer itself.'

"The Right Rev. Prelate then observed:—'I have much pleasure in presenting this petition, because I believe that in the main it represents the sentiments of a very large number of (I may say, the *great majority of*) *the members of the Church of England.*'"

Why, this is out-Heroding the three tailors of Tooley Street!—" WE, THE PEOPLE OF ENGLAND!"—" *We*, 215 Lincolnshire clergymen, being, or representing the sentiments of, 18,000 clergy—of whom we form a *ninetieth* part—do hereby enter our solemn protest against any and every *attempt* to interfere with, alter, revise, or otherwise amend, directly or indirectly, either by omission, addition, subtraction, variation, purification, or in any other way whatsoever, a certain book, commonly called the Book of Common Prayer, as appointed to be read in all churches and chapels of England, Wales, and Ireland, in obedience to an Act passed in the second year of the reign of his late Majesty King Charles II., of blessed memory, known by the name of an 'Act for the Uniformity of Public Prayers, and Administration of Sacraments, and other Rites and Ceremonies; and for establishing the form of making, ordaining, and consecrating bishops, priests, and deacons in the Church of England:' and your petitioners will ever pray," &c.

Now, observe, the diocese of Lincoln is, next to that of Norwich, the largest in the kingdom in respect of the number of its clergy. By a return I have before me, and which I presume to be official, being published under the sanction of the Society for Promoting Christian Knowledge, the number of benefices in the diocese of Lincoln is 797, the number of curates 309; aggregate number of benefices and curates, 1,106. And though some few of these benefices are still, no doubt, held in plurality, yet, making allowance for the *unattached* clergy, who are to be met with in every diocese, schoolmasters in orders, and the like, I think it not unreasonable to infer that there are *at least* 1,000 clergy in the diocese of Lincoln, *one-fifth* part of whom, or *one-ninetieth* part of the clergy of the kingdom at large,* appear to have signed the above petition; and this infinitesimal portion of the clerical community is to be pronounced as " representing the sentiments of the *great majority* of the *members* of the Church of England!"

How large a body *this last* may be I have no means of ascertaining; but the same statistical paper to which I have already referred gives upwards of seventeen millions as the united population of the English dioceses alone, without reckoning the Welsh or Irish, or such " members of the English Church" as may happen to dwell in our vast Colonial Empire, and other parts of the world. By what process of calculation, therefore, the bishop has arrived at his conclusion, I am at a loss to conceive. Possibly his lordship may be possessed with so exalted a notion of the relative importance of " *my* diocese " † as compared with all other dioceses, as to lead him somewhat hastily to multiply these five loaves and two small fishes in the fens of Lincolnshire into the personification of a *majority of the whole Church of England.*

I speak with reverence, for this is no matter for trifling;‡ but I assert that something more than the mere *ipse dixit* of any man is required before the people of this nation are

---

* There is reason to believe that the clergy of the United Kingdom amount in round numbers to no less than 23,000.

† Sydney Smith on " Persecuting Bishops," *Ed. Review*, 1822. Works, vol. ii., p. 20.

‡ I have the greatest possible respect for Bishop Jackson (now of London), who perhaps after twenty additional years' experience as a bishop is not as averse to Revision as he was in 1858.

to be gulled into the belief that the "large majority of the Church" are wholly opposed to all *inquiry even* into the present working of the Prayer-book, as laid down by an Act of Uniformity "always of questionable expediency, and passed two centuries ago."* I quote the words of one of the most talented of our English prelates, and one, too, who was present at, and took part in, the discussion of which I am now treating, and who is yet, by some extraordinary manipulation, assumed to have joined in the alleged *unanimity* of his brethren on that occasion.

But to return "to the loaves and fishes." Had these nothing to do with the getting up of this petition? How many of the 309 *curates* had the boldness to refuse to sign such a document when hawked about, as I am well advised it was, for many weeks, in all parts of a diocese, the bishop of which has upwards of *seventy livings in his gift*, and was known to have expressed himself not unfavourable to the prayer of the memorialists? How many of the seventy incumbents of those said livings declined to sign?—how many of the rural deans, all under the nomination and direction (I trust not the dictation) of the bishop?—how many of the clergy of Lincoln, *cum adjacentibus?*—how many of the dignitaries (alas! the *honorary* dignitaries, all of whom are nominated by the bishop, and are in honour bound —as Lord Palmerston said of the bishops—to reverence their Maker, and generally, as a rule, are known to do so) of that noble cathedral? I find, by the Clergy List for 1858 that, besides some seventy-eight other pieces of preferment, the patronage of the Bishop of Lincoln includes also "the *canonries*, the *precentorship* of the cathedral, with the prebend of Kilsby or Kildesby annexed; the *chancellorship* of

---

* Charge by Bishop Thirlwall to the Clergy of St. David's, 1857. See more of this hereafter, Letters xv., xxv., cvi

C

the cathedral, with the prebend of Stoke annexed; the
subdeanery of the cathedral; the three *archdeaconries*; *all
the prebends*, except those of Corringham, Buckden (annexed
to the bishopric), and Sanctæ Crucis." Are there no beneficed clergy in and about Lincoln, or otherwise distributed
throughout that vast diocese, whose mouths water at reading
this list (which is in the hands of almost every clergyman);
and is it probable that they should all be so stoical and
self-denying as to refuse their signatures to a simple
PETITION that " can do no harm," the object of which is
only to " let well alone," at the request of some proctor of
the " Lower House," *known to be in the confidence of the
bishop*—or some " rural dean," known as his *nominee* and
confidant, the recipient from time to time of his lordship's
" strictly private and confidential " communications? But
enough of this. I know not what conclusions other people
may draw from these premises; but, for my own part, so far
from being surprised or cast down because I heard that 215
of the Lincolnshire clergy had thus petitioned, and that
their petition had been accepted and endorsed by their
diocesan, I must confess I was only astonished that the
whole 1,000 clergy, or at least nine-tenths of them, had not
rushed forward instantly, with their " pens up to the feather
in ink," to attach their names:—

> " *Curramus præcipites, et*
> Dum jacet in ripâ calcemus Cæsaris hostem (*i.e.*, " Ingoldsby ") :
> *Sed videant servi, ne quis neget.*"

But I must conclude for the present, hoping that I have
said enough to caution *your* readers, at any rate (whatever
conclusion the readers of the *Guardian* and *Clerical Journal*
may arrive at), against being too hastily led away by the
notion, so industriously and gratuitously circulated, that
" the *great majority* of the members of the Church of
England " have hitherto expressed any opinion whatever

on the expediency of Her Majesty's issuing a Royal Commission for the purpose of inquiring into (and possibly revising) the Book of Common Prayer.

I am, Sir, yours very obediently,
March 5, 1858. " INGOLDSBY."

LETTER IV.

THE BISHOP OF LINCOLN (JACKSON), AND REVISION OF THE PRAYER-BOOK.

"What would I give to see our Liturgy amended! But our Bishops cry, 'Touch not! meddle not!' till indeed it will be too late to do either."
—*Arnold's Letters*, No. lxxxiv., 1834.

SIR,—In my last I took the precaution of warning your readers that the petition of the 215 Lincolnshire clergy was so far from being a reflex of the sentiments of the "great majority of the members of the Church of England," that there was, on the contrary, a *primâ facie* probability, amounting almost to demonstration, that it represented little else than the views of the individual bishop by whom the petition was presented.

Now, I am not prepared to say, nor even to insinuate, that his lordship of Lincoln (of whom, both for his zeal and courtesy, I would wish to speak with the utmost respect) had the smallest hand in promoting or getting up that petition; or that he was even necessarily aware that such a document was being promoted by others. I simply assume that the bishop's sentiments on the subject were not unknown to the 215 clergy who signed the paper, out of the 1,000 who go to make up that extensive diocese.

A city placed on a hill is not so easily hid; especially a city like Lincoln, with its commanding cathedral, proudly

overlooking the fenny district, from which it rises like the
pyramids in the plains of Egypt, and whence it issues its
mandates with an air, as who should say,

> "I am Sir Oracle,
> And when I ope my lips, let no dog bark."

And when the bishop expresses himself so decisively in
the Upper House of Convocation against *all attempts at
touching* the Book of Common Prayer, as he proceeds to do
in the speech accompanying the presentation of the above
petition, I ask, is it probable that his sentiments on the
subject had been suppressed up to that moment—

> "Molemque et montes insuper altos Imposuit?"—

Is it reasonable to suppose that his lordship had reserved
his long-digested and carefully-hoarded opinions for the
special benefit of the "House of Bishops," and had concealed them previously from his chaplains, his candidates
for orders, archdeacons, and rural deans? Be that as it
may, certain it is that but one-fifth part of the clergy of
the diocese are found to echo the voice of their diocesan in
this momentous matter, notwithstanding all the inducements,
direct and indirect, to recommend themselves to "the powers
that be," which I endeavoured to set forth in my former
letter.* Moreover, it must not be forgotten that the question
of Liturgical Revision, if it did not originate in the diocese
of Lincoln, had at least been more vigorously agitated there
for the previous three years than in any other part of the
kingdom. The clergy of that district, therefore, were not
taken by surprise; it was not "a new thing" upon which

---

* It is but fair to add here that many more of the Lincolnshire clergy
afterwards signed the manifesto of the "Ten Thousand;" but the above was
written two years before the appearance of that curious State paper, of
which more hereafter.

they were now asked to express their opinion. Many of them were fully aware that a petition, signed by 320 members of the Established Church, had been got up in less than three weeks, last summer, by a solitary clergyman of that diocese,* acting without the assistance of any one, with the single aid and appliance of the penny-post, and by the issue of but 500 circulars. As, however, that petition will not have been seen by the bulk of your readers, it may be as well to furnish you with a copy, that they may have an opportunity of comparing it with that of the 215 Lincolnshire clergy. The petition in question was presented to the House of Commons by Lord Robert Grosvenor (now Lord Ebury), on the 28th of July, 1857, and was to the following effect :—

" *To the Honourable the House of Commons in Parliament Assembled.*

"The humble Petition of the undersigned Members of the Established Church of England and Ireland, showeth—

"That your petitioners are of opinion that the Book of Common Prayer, as at present used in the Churches of England and Ireland, is capable of such modification in its arrangement and Services as to render it far more profitable than it now is for the religious instruction and edification of the people.

"That your petitioners believe that a Royal Commission is the safest and least objectionable mode of dealing with the consideration of that book with a view to its revision.

"Your petitioners therefore humbly pray your Honourable House to move that Her Most Gracious Majesty may be pleased to grant such Commission, with sufficient time and powers for the full and mature weighing of the matters which shall be submitted to them in this behalf.

"And your petitioners will ever pray," &c.

---

* The Rector of Ingoldsby, to wit.

The late period of the session, and the engrossing topic of the Indian Mutiny, then first announced, prevented his lordship from proceeding at that time with the motion of which he had given notice, the object of which was to promote the prayer of the petitioners; but it is well known that, in his capacity of a Peer of the Upper House of Parliament, Lord Ebury has already signified his intention of again bringing the subject before the public after the Easter recess. The terms of his lordship's motion are as follows:—
"That Her Majesty will be pleased to grant a Commission to revise the Liturgy of the Church of England, with a view to such re-arrangement of the Services as shall obviate needless repetitions, and curtail the length of a portion of them; and also with a view to such other alterations as may suggest themselves in the course of the inquiry, and which may tend to render the services more efficient for the religious edification of the people at large."

It is worthy, therefore, of consideration by whom the above petition was signed; and as the signatures have since been printed through the favour of one of the London journals, it can be no secret who the petitioners were, nor is there any reason why they should wish their names concealed. I find accordingly amongst them—not indeed "the authorities of the Church" (bishops, deans, and archdeacons)—but doctors and bachelors of divinity, learned professors in both universities, fellows and tutors of colleges, lawyers, schoolmasters, physicians, prebendaries, magistrates, country gentlemen, rectors, curates—in short, men of *every class* competent to form an opinion upon this important matter, in which all (especially, perhaps, the laity) are alike interested. And though I am far from presuming to affirm that these 320 independent gentlemen, acting without concert, or dictation from any one, without fear of cold looks or hope of smiles from those in power, represent the sentiments of the "great majority of the members of the Church of England," yet, I am bold to say, that, all circumstances considered, they have at least as much pretension to do so as the 215 Lincolnshire clergy, who have (I suspect much against their will) had that honour so unexpectedly thrust upon them.

I have dwelt longer than I intended on the subject of this latter petition; not that I attach the slightest importance to such a document, manufactured through such machinery, but because I think it most material that others, who are liable to be caught by first appearances, and who may not have leisure to go to the bottom of the matter, should see it in its true light, as an undoubted attempt to throw dust in the eyes of the unwary, and to stifle inquiry before the public is fully alive to the real merits of the question.

I suspect, too, that the Lincolnshire petition* is only the forerunner of a host of similar ones,—

"Nati natorum, et qui generantur ab illis,"

---

* That I was justified in anticipating a swarm of similar PETITIONS, got up under Episcopal suggestion (not to say dictation), will appear from the following communication made last summer to the Rural Deans of the diocese of Lincoln; and which, as we know in one instance at least, from the Rev. F. Massingberd, was responded to (as one would expect under the circumstances) by 12 out of 14 of the clergy of *his own* Deanery *in the affirmative!*

(Copy.) " Riseholme, June 20, 1859.

" Rev. and dear Sir,—I beg to suggest a few subjects which, I think, may usefully be submitted to the consideration of the clergy of your deanery when you call them together in Chapter. 1. Night Schools. 2. Farm Servants. 3. REVISION of the LITURGY.

"On this last subject there may possibly be some difference of opinion; but should the clergy of your deanery consider that such a revision of the Prayer-book is undesirable as could be effected only by the intervention of Parliament, as would trench on the doctrinal expressions of the Liturgy, and as would therefore provoke controversy, and probably result

destined in due time to be showered upon the devoted head of Lord Ebury, when he brings forward his threatened and justly dreaded motion in the Lords. Cuddesdon, I am told, is up in arms;—the word of command has gone forth: PETITION, PETITION, PETITION! and we all know how readily the orders of the dictator are obeyed in that quarter.

It has been said that,

"Regis ad exemplar totus componitur orbis:"

which, however true it may be of kings or queens, is certainly found practically true of most bishops and their dioceses. Let the steersman, therefore, between the banks of the Isis but cry out lustily "Back water," and it needs no prophet to tell us with what rapidity, precision, and unity of purpose, the whole of that well-trained crew, from the heavy stroke to the light No. 1, will obey the signal, and what a total stagnation will instantaneously ensue to the onward progress of the ecclesiastical vessel.

Ab uno disce omnes. Wherever there is a High-Church bishop, there will be plenty of followers with the same cut coat and collar, and the same type of petition, clad in the uniform of Lincoln green; and though a few Low or Broad-Church divines may be caught unawares in the comprehensive net,* and so give colour for the assertion of the bishop that the petition "represents no one particular part or section of the Church," I need only refer

---

in schism, *it would be well to Petition both Houses of the Legislature, if any attempt should be made to procure such revision.*—Yours faithfully,
"J. LINCOLN."

We have reason to know that a similar document issued from head-quarters in many other dioceses, probably with a kindred response.

* For example, Canon Stowell, and Sir Henry Thompson, as signing the Westminster Manifesto of December, 1859; the consequence being that the resistance to revision was represented as proceeding from *all parties* in the Church.

to the list of Petitions presented to the House of Commons last session by Mr. A. J. B. Hope, in opposition to Lord Robert Grosvenor's motion, to prove to the satisfaction of all who are "not ignorant of their devices," the class of persons from whom obstinate resistance to all inquiry into the present working of the Act of Uniformity is most likely to emanate.

Having now done with THE PETITION, and *all Petitions* of which it may prove the prolific parent, I shall, in my next, proceed to discuss the further remarks made by the Bishop of Lincoln, upon presenting the said document to the "House of Bishops" on the 10th of last month, and remain, meanwhile,

Yours very obediently,

March 12, 1858. " INGOLDSBY."

LETTER V.
THE LENGTH OF THE MORNING SERVICE.

"By long expense of time the King and the Queen shall peradventure wax so weary at the beginning, that they shall have small delight to continue throughout to the end."—*Todd's Life of Cranmer,* i. 140.

SIR,—The Bishop of Lincoln is reported to have next stated, that, "notwithstanding much that has been said with respect to the length of our Services, the *general opinion of the members of our Church is so strongly against* any material alteration in our Sunday services, that they will be very unwilling that *any* legislative interference should take place, or *any* interference that should make *any* material alteration in those services."

When, I would ask with all deference, and by what process, did his lordship arrive at this comprehensive view of the "general opinion of the members of our Church?" It is a strong statement; and, as coming from one of the prelates of that Church, will no doubt have its due weight with the "inferior clergy, the priests and deacons," if not with the vast bulk of the laity who make up the body which *we* call, and which I presume the bishop calls, "The Church."

But *when* and *how*, I ask, did his lordship arrive at this conclusion?—and first, for the *when?* If *before* the signing of the petition, then it is pretty clear his lordship's own sentiments could not have been unknown to the 215 petitioners, out of the 1,000 and more clergy of his diocese; and all the arguments made use of in my third letter must tell with double force, and the bare 215 names must be received as point-blank evidence in contradiction of the assertion that such *is* the *general* feeling. If *after* the petition was signed, then how comes it that, out of the millions of members of the Church of England, but 215 Lincolnshire clergy have been found, up to this time, to petition at all on the subject?*

But *how* is this knowledge of the "general sentiments of the members of the Church" ascertained? Is it by the number of publications on the subject? I have before me, at this moment, a list of some three or four dozen pamphlets, or tracts, calling earnestly for a REVISION of the LITURGY, in every variety of shape, size, and price, all published *within the last three or four years*,† one of them having already reached a fourth edition. On the other hand, I find but two *replies* to these, in the shape of two

---

* The so-called Ten Thousand Clergy, it is true, afterwards petitioned against any revision at *this present time;* but even they did not make up *one half* of the whole body *even of the clergy*, nor did they venture to affirm that a revision *in the abstract* was not needed.

† A list of these was printed by the Association for Promoting a Revision of the Liturgy, 17, Buckingham Street, Adelphi, and may still be had on inquiry.

sixpenny pamphlets, one of them from the pen of the somewhat notorious author of the "Directorium Anglicanum."*

Is it, then, from the daily or weekly press?—the great organ of public opinion?—the alone recognised vehicle of the sentiments of Englishmen all over the world? I can produce articles, and letters without number, from many of the Reviews, and almost every London newspaper, from the *Leviathan Times* down to the *Penny Star*, in which this subject has been more or less favourably handled, from 1834 to 1858; and if I were to add to these the list of *provincial* papers in which the same view has been taken, their number is legion :—

"quorum si nomina quæras
Promptius expediam, quot * * *."—

To set off against these there are certainly (if they may be called in any sense exponents of public opinion) the *Clerical Journal* and the *Guardian*, and, in a modified degree, the *English Churchman*. So that I leave your readers again to measure the balance of probabilities (as in the case of the 215 Lincolnshire petitioners), and ask if it be not proved, almost to demonstration, which way the real bent of the "general" sentiments of members of the Church of England inclines.

One thing, however, must be clear to the simplest comprehension, that the persons who are so satisfied that they have the "great majority of the members of the Church of England" with them, have no occasion to shrink from Lord Ebury's motion for a *Commission of Inquiry*,†

---

* The Rev. John Purchas, of Brighton; who died in 1872, and—
  "Left a name at which his friends grew pale,
   To point a moral and adorn a tale."

† Such was the argument very properly made use of in the House of Commons, March, 1862, in reply to those who objected to the appointment of a Committee of Inquiry into the doings of the Ecclesiastical Commission.

which would speedily set that matter at rest. They who maintain the *negative*, on the contrary, are most thankful to his lordship for thus boldly coming forward as their champion, by demanding a commission of moderate men— a commission composed exclusively of neither the *Guardian* nor the *Record* School of Church Politics, but one which would patiently collect the real sentiments of the Church at large, and publish them in a report to be seen and read of all men. Such was the course adopted in the case of the two universities, notwithstanding the most strenuous opposition of "the authorities" in those venerable seats of learning; and the fruit is already manifest in a visible increase of their efficiency, with a considerable relief from many oppressive burdens under which they previously laboured.*

But to proceed with our own more immediate object.

The next clause is as follows:—" Still less, I am sure, is there any sympathy on the part of the *great body of the laity* and the clergy of the Church of England, with those crude attempts to shorten the services, which we have of late so frequently seen, by omissions, and by bringing together different parts of different services, in total forgetfulness of the true and deep meaning which runs through each service; and also of the immemorial tradition of the Church of Christ in its services."

This is a long sentence, and requires some digestion to prevent the remarks that may be made upon it seeming "crude;" but I will, nevertheless, make bold to "rush in" where, possibly, I shall be told I ought in prudence to have "feared to tread."†

---

* Among these may be mentioned the removal, in some instances (under certain regulations), of that remnant of Popish times, the celibacy of Fellows of Colleges; thus doing away, it is to be hoped for ever, with a class of persons who were formerly the incubus and disgrace of their respective colleges.

† Let me again repeat that the following observations were made in

We have here again a positive assertion. "*Still less I am sure!*" and again, an assumed knowledge of the sentiments "of the *great body* of the laity and the clergy of the *Church of England*." Assertions are not proofs; and I am simple enough to fall back upon my undergraduate training, and to say, with Professor Vince,* "This is all very well, Sir, but it *proves* nothing."

But *where* have these "crude attempts to shorten the services" been *so frequently seen?* I am glad to hear from the bishop's mouth that there *are* clergy who are bold enough to make these attempts. Few laws are altered till they have been "frequently" broken with impunity; and if that be really the case with the Act of Uniformity (which no man who has had his eyes and ears open for the last twenty years can possibly deny), then is the most convincing argument furnished to those who call for its legislative repeal; or who at least join in the cry, with Lord Ebury's petitioners, for a COMMISSION of INQUIRY into its present working.

As for "bringing together parts of different services, in total forgetfulness," &c. &c., if that be done, the fault rests with those who persist in maintaining the *tria juncta in uno*, the three single services rolled into one†—Morning Prayer, Litany, Communion Service,—in indissoluble bonds; with a "total disregard" of the infirmities to which flesh and blood are liable—the sick, the weak, the young, the old, "the fidgety" (*vide Morning Post*), and, last not

---

the spirit of an anonymous Reviewer, and in perfect good-will and kind feeling toward the object of them, a further knowledge of whose character the Author has since had the opportunity and the satisfaction of acquiring.

* Plumian Professor of Astronomy at Cambridge from 1796 to 1821.

† On this junction of the three services and its inseparable evil, see Paley, "Moral Phil.," B. v., Ch. v., p. 288. Letter VII., p. 38.

least, the officiating clergyman himself, who has to get up in the pulpit and appeal *earnestly* to the feelings, the passions, the hopes, the fears, of his audience; to awaken their lethargy, to excite their piety, to evoke their gratitude, to inflame their devotion; with lungs and frame already more than half-exhausted by the hour and ten minutes which have been (by the Bishop of Lincoln's scanty admission) already devoted to reading the Prayers, Psalms, Lessons (often 120 verses, or more, together),* Litany, and Communion Service!—Perhaps his lordship forgets that, while he reposes in all the *otium cum dignitate* of lawn sleeves in his arm-chair at the Cathedral Church (where there are several different orders of Clergy appointed to the different portions of the service), himself no doubt taking part by reading the Ten Commandments and the Gospel for the day, and giving the benediction, and even occasionally preaching†—his lordship, I say, seems to forget, or to ignore the fact, that there are in his vast diocese, thickly scattered with rural churches, some 600 or 800 clergy who have all this and more to perform single-handed for the fifty-two Sundays in the year, with a second duty closely following, of which his lordship is a rigid and (in most cases justly so) conscientious enforcer.

I say nothing of how much of his time and breath the said solitary rector or vicar—aged, perhaps, infirm, delicate from hard study at college, or accidentally invalided, it may

---

* See Tract by the Rev. Ashton Oxenden, some time Proctor for the diocese of Canterbury, now Bishop of Montreal, on the Abridgment of the Morning Service: 1855. This gentleman afterwards distinguished himself by an able speech in support of the Dean of Norwich in Convocation on this subject; March, 1861.

† It is right here to note, that no Prelate on the bench was more indefatigable in this important part of his office than the Bishop of Lincoln but still the argument in the text holds unanswerable where there is *only one* officiating minister for all this.

be—has previously given, or will give, in the course of the Sunday, to superintending the Sunday-school, or conducting private devotion in his family, or to any of the other numerous occupations which fall to the lot of the "working clergy" on that day of *sacred rest;* but I maintain that the three-fold junction of the so-called "Morning Service," as it now stands, is too much for *any man*, be he who he may, to discharge with that efficiency throughout the year which the solemn nature of its object requires; and I attribute very much of the dissent, and indifference to the Church system, which has so long been steadily gaining ground in this country, to the absurd regulation which has thus put more than a due burden on the back of the clergy, and then has expected of them more than it is in human nature to perform.*

I could speak volumes on this branch of my subject, for I feel it is the turning-point of the whole, as far as the Abridgment portion of Revision is concerned, and, being physically not strong myself, I enter here into the feelings of others. But I am transgressing the bounds you so liberally allow me; so for the present I shall conclude with a quotation from the clearest-headed, and most kind-hearted, writer that ever devoted his talents to advocating the independence of the inferior clergy: "The fact is," says the admirable Sydney Smith, "a man is thrown into the Church with both his hands tied behind him, and then is bid to swim: he does well if he contrives barely to keep his head above water."—I remain, yours faithfully,

March 19, 1858. " INGOLDSBY."

---

* The well-known phrase of "*doing* the duty" is very expressive of the manner in which the duty is too frequently *done* under the circumstances enumerated in the text.

LETTER VI.

ABRIDGMENT OF THE MORNING SERVICE.

"Piety stretched beyond due limits is the parent of impiety."
SYDNEY SMITH.

SIR,—The Bishop of Lincoln proceeds:—"In point of fact, it can hardly be said that our Sunday Services *are long.*" Assertion number *three.* And now for the *proof:* —"I am not, of course, now speaking of the sermons, but of the morning service, with the usual amount of chanting or metrical psalmody. The morning service may be said to occupy an hour, or an hour and ten minutes, and the afternoon service from half an hour to forty minutes; that is to say, that out of that day which God has set apart for His special service not more than two hours are spent by His people in the work of social worship."

Now, I had always hitherto been taught to believe that the golden rule for all things was NON QUAM MULTUM, SED QUAM BENE: and I had been led to think that half an hour, or even less, say a quarter of an hour or ten minutes, of deep, and earnest, and heartfelt prayer, were of more real value to the soul's health than the *opus operatum* of an hour and a half spent *in the church;* to what *profit* I leave those to explain who deliberately give it as a *reason* for repeating the Lord's Prayer "five, six, or seven times in the same service," that if their thoughts wander at one part of the service they may be able to collect them by the next time the prayer is read.*

---

* See the Dean of Norwich's reply to this argument in his speech before Convocation, March, 1861. Hatchard, Piccadilly. This *reason* was actually given to *myself,* in justification of the frequent repetition of the Lord's Prayer, by the Hon. and Rev. Richard Cust, at that time Rector of Belton, Lincolnshire, and Rural Dean!

Why, I ask, do their thoughts wander?—why, but because they are *wearied out* with the same unvaried routine of our unelastic Liturgy? No doubt there is a "deep and hidden meaning which runs through all these several parts of the service." But *quotus quisque*—How many, I ask, of the millions who *ought* to attend the public worship of God in the church are capable of penetrating below the surface, and entering fully into this "deep and hidden meaning?" Is the preacher to be continually dwelling upon the hidden mystery of the various parts of our Liturgy, in order that his hearers may be alive to its esoteric beauties and excellencies, and duly appreciate them as they severally arise? I apprehend this is hardly fulfilling our Saviour's precept, "The poor have the *Gospel* preached to them;" and without such reiteration, most undoubtedly all this "deep and hidden meaning, which runs through each service," is utterly lost, and will for ever be so, to the great bulk of those who should be worshippers in the House of God.

When our Saviour entered the synagogue on the Sabbath-day, we do not hear of His reading a service of an hour and ten minutes' length, but of His "opening the Scriptures and *finding a place*"—not reading the one unvarying chapter "appointed for the day." And what was the passage He found? Why, that in which His divine mission is distinctly set forth in prophecy; the prominent feature thereof being "to *preach* the *Gospel to the poor.*" And yet the Bishop of Lincoln, in his reverence for the stereo-typed hour and ten minutes of set service in the church, takes no notice of this corner-stone of religion; at least he would appear to treat it as of quite secondary consideration. "I am not now, of course (says his lordship), speaking of the *sermons.*"—What if the sermon be on such a text as that I have just referred to? What preacher, of the smallest ability in rightly dividing the

Word of Truth, could possibly compress his discourse on such a subject, so as to do it full justice in less than half an hour or forty minutes? Some preachers would hardly exhaust it in an hour. What then becomes of an argument based on the assertion that "not more than two hours are spent in social worship out of that day which God has set apart for His special service?"

Where is the afternoon service which is to follow this morning one, already two hours long? Where the evening service, so universally popular among the middle and lower orders, no doubt partly because the sermon is then made a more prominent feature than at any other hour? Why are Westminster Abbey and St. Paul's crowded almost to overflowing at that hour, when a preacher of ordinary capacity for his work occupies the pulpit? Try throwing the Abbey open to the public for morning prayer, including psalms, chanting, lessons, litany, anthem, Communion Service, sermon, offertory sentences, prayer for the church militant, possibly followed by the administration of the Holy Communion, and see how many of the poorer classes will attend. No doubt, as experience tells us, many of the more educated among the people will be always attracted by the gorgeous and histrionic character of the Cathedral service, with its accompaniments:—

"Where through the long-drawn aisle and fretted vault,
    The pealing anthem swells the note of praise:"

and by help of these adjuncts to devotion, and excitements to the imagination, the devout or even the careless worshipper may not feel the two hours or more of service so very wearisome; especially if (as is often the case with our Cathedrals) the congregation does not consist regularly of the same individuals, the *habitués* of the place, but is formed chiefly of strangers, paying an occasional visit to this attractive shrine.

But what is there to supply the place of all this pomp and ceremony to the thousands of village churches, with their congregations of some one or two hundred worshippers, or less; or the district churches of our populous towns, with their scanty endowment of £150 or £200 per annum? And are we to ignore this vast proportion of the churches in the land, because the Cathedral, or *quasi* Cathedral, can maintain a sufficient interest throughout the whole length of a two hours' service? But I deny that they do so. I was myself present at one of the Westminster Abbey services of January last; and it was impossible not to notice the evident listlessness and inattention that pervaded the bulk of that enormous assembly, while the preliminary form of prayers, psalms, lessons, &c., was gone through.* It was impossible, on the other hand, not to be struck by the comparative zest with which the same congregation joined, as with one accord, in singing, immediately before the sermon, the magnificent 100th Psalm; and the earnestness with which they addressed themselves to hear the words proceeding from the mouth of the preacher of the day—a preacher, observe, coming fresh to his task, not jaded and half worn-out by an hour's rehearsal of the previous service!

This I venture, with all respect, to tell the Bishop of Lincoln, is the thing "wanting" to give life and unction to our Church system. Not the "deep and hidden meaning which runs through each service,"—but a reasonable and wholesome variety to secure attention; a judicious brevity to prevent weariness; the liberty occasionally to expound the Lessons as read; and, above all, a preacher who understands his mission, and whose powers have been husbanded

---

* The Puritans, not without reason, called our stereotyped form of Prayer "the Lethargy of Public Worship." (Southey, "Book of the Church," vol. ii., p. 441.)

for the great business of the day; not exhausted and consumed upon a long routine of ceremonious worship, which, however excellent in detail, is oppressive by its weight, and defeats its own ends by the attempt to do too much at once. There is an old Greek proverb which tells us that "*half is better than the whole;*" and never did it find a truer illustration than in the overloaded services of our Church. "*Voluptates commendat rarior usus,*" says another proverb:—

> "When they *seldom* come they wished for come,
> And nothing pleaseth but rare accident,"

says our own great dramatist. Of course I shall be told (as, indeed, I have been) that Hesiod, Juvenal, and Shakespeare were no divines; but a man may be a good judge in these matters, though he be not a D.D. And, for my own part, I would rather have one ounce of common sense, even when applied to the solemn matter of public worship,[*] than I would all the musty folios of patristic divinity, carefully hoarded in the precincts of Lincoln Minster, or all the precedents of "immemorial tradition," if found *practically* to fail in the object they should have in view, the bringing millions within the reach of the sound of the Gospel, and so promoting the salvation of souls.

But is it *true*, again, that "immemorial tradition" does sanction these lengthy services? I opine not. Surely a bishop does not need to be told that our Prayer-book services have swelled by repeated and considerable accretions, from the first book of Edward VI. down to the last revision under Charles II.

The first Liturgy of Edward VI., the bishop must surely be aware, commenced with the *Lord's Prayer*, and ended

---

[*] See an excellent pamphlet entitled "Common Sense about the Church," by a High Churchman. Hatchard and Co., 1860.

with the third collect for grace. To this "reasonable service" have been added by various revisions, and at sundry times, "the opening sentences, the exhortation, the confession, and the absolution, the Litany ordered to be used in the *Sunday Service;* the Decalogue introduced into the Communion Service; the prayers for the Queen and clergy; and, finally, the prayer for all sorts and conditions of men, and the general thanksgiving!"*

"Piety," says our motto, "stretched beyond due limits, is the parent of impiety;" and an argument founded on a false hypothesis is apt to be the parent of something akin to irreverence, if nothing worse. "Immemorial tradition," if an argument for anything, is an argument for *changing* and *amending* the Liturgy of the Church; not for obstinately retaining everything as it is, merely because it is so.† But as I shall have occasion to enter more at large on this portion of our subject, when I come to examine the Bishop of Oxford's remarks in support of the Bishop of Lincoln, I will for the present conclude; and remain yours,

Very faithfully,

March 26, 1858. " INGOLDSBY."

LETTER VII.

THE LENGTH OF THE CHURCH SERVICES.

"Let all things be done unto edifying."—1 Cor. xiv. 26.

SIR,—It is consolatory to find the bishop, in the next paragraph of his speech, so far making concession to the

---

* See "Abridgment of the Sunday Services," by the Rev. Ashton Oxenden. Wertheim and Macintosh (1855), p. 6. Also the Dean of Norwich's Speech before Convocation, March 14, 1861, p. 13 Hatchard, Piccadilly.

† " Morosa morum retentio res turbulenta est æque ac novitas."—BACON

cry for a revision of the Liturgy, as to admit that, in *some cases*, the present services of our Church may be found too long. That his lordship is not singular in this opinion will readily be allowed by most of your readers. It is not many weeks ago since you favoured us with a letter from a correspondent, who is apparently driven to adopt the feigned signature of " U. G. O.," in order to escape the abuse so freely lavished on *known* Liturgical reformers, by certain of the High Church organs. In that letter it was shown to *what class* of persons the present Church Service is irksome or tedious, while even in the case of the *most spiritually-minded*, there is reason to believe that it not unfrequently tends to exhaust their powers of devout and earnest attention.* I will not attempt to go over ground that has been so well occupied, but will content myself with referring your readers to the letter itself, and will confine myself to the matter we have more immediately in hand.

The *Guardian* report of the Bishop of Lincoln's speech proceeds as follows:—"Of course I am not prepared to say that our services, even in the present state, are not felt to be too long by many members of our congregations. But

---

* Nearly one hundred years ago this defect in our much vaunted Liturgy was noticed by the celebrated Archdeacon Paley. See " Moral Philosophy," B. v., Chap. v. :—

"The too great length of Church services is more unfavourable to piety than almost any fault of composition can be. It begets in many an early and unconquerable dislike to the public worship of their country or communion. They come to church seldom, and enter the doors when they do come under the apprehension of a tedious attendance, which they prepare for at first, or soon after relieve, by composing themselves to a drowsy forgetfulness of the place and duty, or by sending abroad their thoughts in search of more amusing occupation. Although there may be some few of a disposition not to be wearied with religious exercises, yet when a ritual is prolix, and the celebration of Divine service long, no effect in general is to be looked for, but that indolence will find in it an excuse, and piety be disconcerted by impatience."

this, I apprehend, arises not from any fault in the services themselves, but from causes *principally in the worshippers*, which are themselves removable."

This, if not assertion number *four*, is, at any rate, not a very "charitable hypothesis," to say the least of it. Are, then, the "many worshippers in our congregations" to be blamed because they cannot, in the middle of this rapidly-moving nineteenth century, duly appreciate the accumulated form of prayer which we showed in our last had rolled together like a snow-ball during the troublous ecclesiastical period between Edward VI. and Charles II.; a period in which (as is well known) there was a constant struggle going forward between the Romanising party on the one hand and the Puritan or Reforming party on the other; and when the homilies, sermons, and other controversial writings of the day, show that *verbosity* and *repetition* were the essential characteristics of the age? There are, unfortunately a few members *in* our Church, though hardly *of* it, who would revive that struggle now. But I trust the little countenance they have found from the good sense of the British public will do something to check their ardour, and pour oil on the troubled waters of the Church.

To return to our bishop:—" It is worthy of considera- tion, I think," his lordship proceeds, "whether some feelings of weariness and tediousness may not be produced by the careless manner in which those services are sometimes read by *ourselves."*

These remarks were addressed to the "House of Bishops." How many of these, I would ask, are in the habit of reading the services at all, or *any part of them*, in church, except (as I before said) possibly the Ten Commandments, and the short and (for the most part) admirably-selected Gospel of the day? It is an easy matter to round your periods, to vary the intonation of your voice, to modulate your accents to every ear, when delivering that most beautiful part of our service, and *that alone*, from the north side of the communion-table, relieved as you are by the pealing organ, and the distant choir taking up the response at alternate intervals. But it is *not so easy* to sustain the same reverential and measured tone, when rehearsing from the reading-desk the whole of the preceding service, of "an hour and ten minutes' duration," consisting of words in great part of *human* composition; "the Scripture moveth us in sundry places;" the five-times repeated Lord's Prayer; the Psalms of various length, and of very miscellaneous and often incongruous matter; the lessons amounting together to a hundred and more verses, and selected *by no means always* for special edification; not to mention other anomalies in the service, which it is needless to dwell upon.

I tell his lordship, with all submission, it is taking an unfair advantage of his position to impute to *any* of his clergy (for it is to *them* clearly the observation is intended to apply, though addressed to "the House of Bishops")—to impute, I say, to the working clergy—his inferiors in rank in the profession which they have chosen for its own sake, and which many of them adorn with talents and zeal not inferior to those of the bishop of *any* diocese—to impute to such men "carelessness," because they find it physically *impossible* to maintain the same impressive tone throughout the whole length of the accumulated services of our Church.

I speak as I feel, as I have long felt, and as thousands, I know, feel with me:—

"Haud ignara' mali miseris succurrere disco:"—

I am a clergyman, the son of a clergyman, the brother of five clergymen; and from peculiar circumstances, into which it is unnecessary to enter, am acquainted with the sentiments of more of the clergy in all parts of the kingdom than the Bishop of Lincoln has in his whole diocese;* and I maintain, and am prepared to prove it, that I speak the mind of a very large number of these, when I assert that more duty is exacted of them, in the above way, than they are able faithfully to discharge; and many, there is reason to believe, have sunk under the pressure of the unequal burden.

It would occupy more of your space than I feel justified in appropriating, were I to attempt giving extracts from the mass of evidence upon which the above conviction is founded. But, as some set-off against the 215 Lincolnshire petitioners, I may be allowed to observe, that I have received upwards of 1,600 letters from various correspondents, the bulk of them clergymen, more or less complaining of the evil of our present lengthy Church service, and this within the space of two years; while, had more pains been taken to collect them, there is reason to infer that the number might have been multiplied fourfold.†

One of these letters, from a clergyman of long standing in the diocese of Lincoln,‡ I may be excused producing, as the tone of piety which pervades it will at least exempt the writer from the charge of "carelessness in his manner of reading the services of the Church."

"Having," says this septuagenarian, "for more than forty years read, *with the utmost devotion and care in my power*, our beautiful and incomparable Liturgy to rural,

---

* My correspondence on this subject was spread over many years, and extended to all parts of the kingdom, including largely Wales and Ireland.

† At the date at which I am now writing (1862) the number of letters I have received on the subject of a Revision of the Book of Common Prayer amounts to 3,500: not one of the writers, that I am aware of, being otherwise than favourably disposed to *this* branch of the subject.

‡ The Rev. Mr. Rawnsley, of Halton Holgate, near Spilsby.

but partly well-educated congregations, I have still to lament that *the length and repetitions* of the morning service waste and dull through long continuance that vigilant and erect attention of mind which in prayer is so necessary, and without which, I fear, it degenerates into a mere form, if not a mockery."

Another, from the diocese of York,* observes :—" The abridgment of the morning service is what I have desired for many years. My conviction, from eighteen years' experience in a district containing above 10,000 souls, is, that the length of the morning service is one of the chief reasons why so many keep away from church altogether. Their inmost thought is, 'Oh, what a weariness is this!' On Communion Sundays, who, of all the congregation, can enjoy from first to last a service of more than three hours? I have above 160 communicants (out of a population of 10,000!—*Why*, I ask, is the proportion so small?), and it is two o'clock before we separate. The service commences at eleven. I usually preach twenty-five minutes on days when the Communion is administered. In heaven we shall not weary; but on earth 'the spirit indeed is willing, but the flesh is weak.'"

The writer of the above has been known to myself for upwards of twenty years; and so far from being obnoxious to the above imputation of "carelessness," I would appeal to his own congregation to say whether a more devoted, earnest, and self-denying minister could be found to adorn the Church of Christ, or one less likely to evade any part of his duties from indolence or neglect. These are, however, but human testimonies, and may possibly be confronted by conflicting evidence from men of iron mould and superhuman power of lungs—to whom it is a matter

---

* The Rev. John Deck, of St. Stephen's, Hull.

of indifference to preach, or to pray, or to speak for two or three hours' continuance, and who marvel that any one should tire while either "sitting under them" or endeavouring to imitate their voluble example. It is a sound saying, however, that "*exceptio probat regulam;*" and for one such prodigy—one of such spiritual gift of tongue in high place—such

"Ingenium velox, *audacia perdita, sermo
Promptus*, et *Isæo torrentior*"—

I could produce from the rank and file of "the inferior clergy" a thousand to whom the full morning service of our Church (if conducted single-handed, as it is in nine-tenths of the rural churches) is a sore travail—yea, at times a heavy burden to the flesh.*

I will conclude by citing a passage which not even a bishop will venture to impugn, and which if it be not applicable to our present object, I see not to *what* it was intended to apply:—" Woe unto you, Scribes and Pharisees, hypocrites! for ye devour widows' houses, and *for a pretence make long prayer;* therefore ye shall receive the greater damnation." With these memorable words, speaking volumes to the wise, I will take leave of this portion of my subject, and remain,

Yours obediently,

March 31, 1858.   "INGOLDSBY."

---

* In the Life of Martin Luther, by Henry Worsley, M.A., Rector of Easton, Suffolk, vol. ii., p. 19, it is said: "With regard to divine service generally a chapter of the Old Testament and of the New should be read, *one* in the morning, the *other* in the afternoon, with an exposition from the minister. A *large discretionary power is allowed the minister* in the selection of the chapter to be read and the Psalms to be used, and it is specially enjoined that needless wearying of the congregation be avoided."

LETTER VIII.

CHARITY THINKETH NO EVIL.

" You tell me that you apprehend
My words may touchy folks offend;
For though nor this nor that be meant,
Can we another's thoughts prevent?"—GAY.

SIR,—It is with reluctance that we pursue our present theme. But our duty is clear, and at all risks the *truth* must be spoken, especially where the matter at issue is one of such high and holy interest as that on which we are engaged. All we can say is, that it is neither our intention nor our wish to give offence to any man.

"Carelessness in reading the Church Service" is not the only charge brought against the clergy by the Bishop of Lincoln. There is, *secondly,* and "still more" than the former, "that—I must call it most un-English—habit of monotonously mumbling through the service; the only recommendation for which, that I can understand, being one which ought to condemn it, its approximation to one of the bad practices of the Church of Rome."

Allow me, by the way, to commend this paragraph to the conductors of the service at St. Paul's, Knightsbridge; St. Barnabas, Pimlico, Margaret Street Chapel; St. George's-in-the-East, *et id genus omne.*

One thing, however, may be said in defence of this "un-English habit"—that it has certainly no tendency to *prolong* the service; and, therefore, I hardly see how it can be charged with *producing*, though it is quite possible it may *increase*, that sense of "weariness and tediousness" which is laid to its score. It would appear to derive its origin from the ancient habit of mumbling through the Roman Breviary—so called, like the lawyer's *brief*, from its wearisomeness; and a consciousness of which inherent defect no doubt led to the "mumpsimus" class of mediæval divines adopting this method of getting over the ground as quickly as they could. I have nothing to say in defence of the practice; but certainly it does appear hard to charge it with *producing* that which it was evidently intended to obviate or to mitigate. A wiser course, if not a more charitable, would surely be to remove both the cause and the effect together, by reducing the too lengthy service within reasonable bounds.

But a *third* charge remains; and alas! this, though addressed to the "House of Bishops," is directly referred, by the Bishop of Lincoln himself, to the hapless, inoffensive, and wholly unconscious congregation.

"The *main reason*, doubtless, why the services appear long, is, that unhappily a *large number of our congregations* have not themselves formed habits of devotion."

This is a most sweeping accusation against a numerous class; and one that ought to rest on very conclusive proof before it should ever have been made. However, "*nescit vox missa reverti;*" and though I am willing to hope this charge may have been inconsiderately uttered, my business is, as undertaking the *defensio populi Anglicani* on this occasion, to rebut it if I can.

In the first place, who is to be the judge in this matter? Who is authorised to enter into other people's hearts, and to decide summarily that "a large number of our congregations have unhappily not formed habits of devotion?"

Charity thinketh no evil; and unless strong proof were given to the contrary, I should be inclined to judge, from the outward appearance of the bulk of English congregations with which I have been acquainted (in the course of a life somewhat longer, and not, I believe, less active or observant than that of the bishop), that "habits of devotion" are very fairly attributable to such of the English people as go to church at all. Certainly, as compared with the whole of the continent of Europe (including every province, with the exception of Spain, Russia and Norway, which I have not visited), I should contrast favourably the devotional appearance and conduct of our English congregations on a Sunday with the best specimen that could be produced from other countries. And as I presume that neither America, nor either of the remaining continents, will be held up as exhibiting devotional habits superior to those of England, the conclusion is that "habits of devotion" are the exception, not the rule, *even with professed church-goers* throughout the world—a conclusion I confess I should be very unwilling myself to draw. For if such be the case with "the green tree, what shall we say of the dry?" If church-goers have not habits of devotion, what are we to say of the millions who never attend church at all?

It is true the people of Scotland present a more earnest appearance in their churches than some of our English congregations; but may not the difference be attributed to the more flexible nature of their service, the greater variety, the extempore prayer, the avoidance (so to speak) of the *red tapism* of our Liturgy, beautiful as it is upon the whole? So true is this, that the service of the Kirk, though in some respects *longer in point of time* than our own, does not appear so tedious and wearisome to the habitual worshippers. The inference one would be disposed to draw from the above premises is, that the fault, supposing the charge to be founded on fact, is inherent in the nature of the *service itself*, rather than in the *congregation*; especially when we bear in mind how many of the worshippers have been accustomed to the same unvarying form of words from their childhood; several of them under the awe of the master's ferule; and at a time of life when it was utterly impossible that they could have the most remote appreciation "of the true and deep meaning which runs through the whole."

But the bishop thinks (and so far well, if it were feasible) that it is our business to teach the people better things, if they have not already been taught them during the two hundred years that our present service-book has been the text of the Church.

"Now, I apprehend," his lordship proceeds, "that it is the intention, and ought to be the duty, of our Church, not to lower the tone of her devotion to the low pitch of her weakest members, but to keep them at a higher pitch, both in order to provide for her more faithful members provision for their souls' needs, and also, by God's help, to raise others up to the same standard."

To *lower* to *low*, and to *provide provision*, may be Hebraisms, though they certainly are not very elegant phrases; but doubtless here the reporter is at fault—these shorthand writers will be so very careless! But what the "higher pitch" is, I am at a loss to conceive, unless it has its prototype in some ideal form of worship, after the most approved Cuddesdon fashion, with its "Hours" and Antiphons," of which we have of late heard so much, and which stand condemned even before their own partial tribunal.* The expression "high and low pitch," by the way, thus used by the Bishop of Lincoln, in connection with the administration of divine worship, reminds me of an anecdote told by the late Bishop of London (Blomfield), in reference to "screwing up" and "screwing down" a certain pulpit, to suit the doctrine of the Arminian or the

---

* Ritualism was then in its infancy, but rapidly developed itself under the fostering care of Bishops and Prime Ministers.

"Parva metu primo; mox sese attollit in auras,
Ingrediturque solo, et caput inter nubila condit."

Calvinist occupant, as the case might be, and which may possibly have been heard by the present Bishop of Lincoln at Dr. Blomfield's table, and have accordingly suggested the above idea. For my own part, I plead guilty to thinking the Liturgy of our Church screwed full "high" enough already; and have no sympathy with those who would continually tighten her cords, and straiten her stakes, to the repelling of thousands who might be disposed to enter within her pale. True policy would recommend comprehension, rather than exclusion; true charity would aim at embracing the largest possible number within the bounds of the Church; not seek to narrow its limits by insisting on carrying out to the letter a code whose Draconian character has been sufficiently proved by its having long ceased to be observed.*

But who *are* "the weakest members," whose low pitch we are bid to eschew? Not, surely, the "large number of our congregations!" But be they who they may, is it so very unreasonable that "the more faithful members" should make allowance for those whom the will of Providence, or their position in life, has not furnished with such an exalted "pitch" of righteousness as others happily possess? The humble publican was accepted, in that he smote upon his breast, saying, "God be merciful to me a sinner." The "high standard" above exacted would drive such feeble members of the Church to despair, by holding up to them a model of perfection, which, with all their desire, they feel themselves incapable of attaining.

<blockquote>
"It is excellent
To have a giant's strength; but tyrannous
To use it like a giant."
</blockquote>

---

* See, in proof of this, the 9th, 10th, 11th, 12th, and other Canons of the Church, with the constant breaches of the letter of the Rubric in all parts of the Prayer-book.

St. Paul's rule—himself a giant in devotional capabilities, —was, " We that are strong, ought to *bear with the infirmities of the weak.*" And again, "To the weak became I *as weak*, that I might *gain the weak;* I am made all things to all men, that I might by all means save some." But our severer occupant of the *Cathedra Petri* at Lincoln says, or would seem to say, "Wherefore do ye, Liturgical Reformers, let the people from their tasks?—get you unto your burdens. Let there be more work laid upon the men, that they may labour therein; and let them not regard vain words. For they be idle, therefore they cry."

But cry they do, and cry they will, notwithstanding the late attempt of the "House of Bishops," headed by the Bishops of Oxford and Lincoln, to stifle all inquiry into this *gravamen* of the inferior and working clergy. That other and even weightier reasons move many to join in the cry, it is useless to deny. But my present concern being with this particular question—the undue length, the repetitions, and the unvarying character of the Morning Service of our Church—I do not wish to mix up with it other changes that may be involved,* and may be not less desirable.

Your columns, Mr. Editor, sufficiently show that an extensive feeling of dissatisfaction does exist, and has long existed, with the "Prayer-book as it is." And as it will always, I trust, be the privilege of Englishmen "*et sentire quæ velint, et quæ sentiant dicere*"—I, for one, am thankful to you for the permission you have so long given me, as the feeble organ of thousands, to express unreservedly what we think on this, to us important, subject; and I remain,
    Yours faithfully,
April 8, 1858.   " INGOLDSBY."

---

* More is said of these in the following Letters.

LETTER IX.

THE OCCASIONAL SERVICES OF THE CHURCH.

Bishop of Lincoln (Jackson).—"I had one Ordination Service which lasted *three hours.*"
Bishop of London (Tait).—"I am sorry to say that one of mine occupied *four* hours." REPORT OF CONVOCATION, 1858.

SIR,—I am glad to see that in his next paragraph the Bishop of Lincoln is a little more tolerant towards the advocates for a revisal of the Prayer-book. He admits that, "with respect to the *occasional services* the case is *entirely different.*"

I don't, however, quite understand what are here meant by "the occasional services." Does the bishop allude to confirmations, visitations, ordinations, consecrations?—services in which the officiating bishop bears a conspicuous and often a very laborious part, and where, therefore, it is not unnatural that he should feel some of that "weariness" which the working clergy experience on the fifty-two Sunday mornings of the year. I infer this from the fact, that in administering the rite of Confirmation the Bishop of Lincoln limits the service for the day (albeit in contradiction, as it appears to some of the inferior clergy, to the letter of the Act of Uniformity, and the spirit of the Fourteenth Canon) to the reading the Litany, a short hymn or psalm, and the imposition of hands, followed by an exhortation of about ten minutes; and at his Visitation omits the customary sermon, to make way for a *charge* of an hour's duration. The Bishop of London also appears to object to the length of the Ordination Service,[*] which is one of the defects in our Prayer-book, as

---

[*] See his lordship's observations before Convocation in 1858.

at present arranged, and which has been long ago pointed out by those whose minds have been directed to the subject. And yet, strange to say, neither of these prelates is prepared with a remedy for what they each admit requires alteration; on the contrary, they seem rather to set themselves to resist those friendly efforts which have been perseveringly made by others towards obtaining that very relief which they themselves appear to desire.

However, the Bishop of Lincoln can hardly be referring to these offices (except possibly Confirmation) in his present remarks, as he proceeds to say: "These are intended specially for the class of persons to whom I have just alluded, who have not formed habits of devotion, but require, more or less, to be gathered in to the fold of Christ. For them shorter services are desirable, and this has been in a great measure provided for, by *permission* to use the Litany in such cases." This is very considerate, no doubt; but I must still profess my ignorance as to what these special occasions are, or with whom rests the power to give *permission* to violate an Act of Parliament, or who are those other individuals who (*in addition to* "the large number of our congregations") have not as yet formed habits of devotion. And as for "gathering in to the fold of Christ," I apprehend that the advocates for a Revision of the Prayer-book will hold that something more than mere shorter "occasional services" is required to accomplish that object which every liberal Christian must have at heart.

The bishop proceeds:—"It is a matter well worthy of consideration whether it is possible, without legislative interference, by availing ourselves of our present Rubrics and the provisions of our Prayer-books, to form other short services, not *of course* for Sunday services in our Church, but for *special occasions;* and I should be very glad myself if it were found possible to order for the daily prayers of the Church a shorter service than that which is now appointed."

We have no objection to make to the above clause, except so far as it distinguishes between the Sunday and the daily service. I had always understood that, *Omne majus continet in se minus*. Surely, therefore, if the service be found long when confined (as on the six days of the week) to the Prayers, Psalms, and Lessons (the Litany only occurring on Wednesdays and Fridays), *à fortiori* it must appear long when, as on the Sunday morning, the Litany is superadded, with a sermon of from twenty to forty minutes, the reading of the Communion Service, offertory sentences, prayer for the Church militant, and occasional administration of the Holy Communion—now not uncommonly celebrated *weekly* (at the instance of some Bishops) even in country parishes—to say nothing of the previous exhaustion of a part of the congregation by the attendance in Sunday-schools, which the Bishop of Lincoln would hardly wish to dispense with. So that the conclusion to be drawn from the above paragraph would be, that what we have been advocating is *secretly* admitted by his lordship, whatever reason he may have for arguing against his convictions and the common-sense view of the matter.

"I believe," the bishop proceeds, "there are hundreds and thousands of the laity who would willingly attend the daily service, if, instead of half or three-quarters of an hour, it were to last not more than ten minutes or a quarter of an hour."

Why, is not this the very thing that the Liturgical Reformers have been urging for this last two years and upwards, *usque ad nauseam*, till they have incurred the imputation by the *Clerical Journal* of being "gone mad" upon the subject? Such persons may well say, with the Apostle, "I am not mad," most learned doctor;* "but speak," and have long spoken, "the words of truth and soberness;" and if, at last, I have obtained a hearing, it is only by persevering in that species of madness which brought about the Reformation in Luther's day, and Catholic Emancipation and Parliamentary Reform in our own. Such madness it was which accomplished, after many years' struggle, the annihilation of rotten boroughs; the enfranchisement of towns like Birmingham, Manchester, and Liverpool; the repeal of the corn laws; and every other measure for the relief of mankind, which has ever been achieved by the devoted zeal and unwearying patience of a handful of determined men—men of the stamp of Luther, Cromwell, Russell, and Cobden; content to bear much personal obloquy, much malignant abuse, much calumny and misrepresentation, provided they are conscious to themselves of the soundness of their views, and the honesty of their intentions.†

Such men will not be deterred from their purpose by arguments like those we have had to deal with; still less will they yield to any attempt to stifle their fearless expression of opinion by an exercise of authority, which was never conferred for this purpose, and which deceives

---

* The Editor of the Journal at that time was the celebrated Dr. Burgess, who lived, however, to modify his views very considerably on this point.

† To men like these it is not flattery to apply the lines of Horace:—
> "Justum et tenacem propositi virum
> Non civium ardor prava jubentium,
> Non vultus instantis tyranni
> Mente quatit solida; neque auster,
> Dux inquieti turbidus Adriae:
> Nec fulminantis magna Jovis manus:
> Si fractus illabatur orbis
> Impavidum ferient ruinae."

itself if it thinks to carry matters in the middle of the nineteenth century with the high hand and spirit of a Laud.

If a reform is *needed* in this matter, why should it be refused? What is there in our profession to preclude us from making our grievances heard as well as other members of the State? It is usual for the cry of "Reform the Church" to proceed from *without;* why should it not be heeded when it proceeds from *within* the pale? Is it the *clerical oath,* as it is called, that binds us? By the same argument Colleges and Universities would have remained unrelieved to this day from their oppressive restrictions. We seek not revolution, but reform; not destruction, but renovation. We seek the same amount of attention and internal repair which has been conceded to corporations, courts of justice, public schools, charitable institutions—every establishment, in short, that dates its existence beyond the present century. "If a man," says Sydney Smith, "were to wear the same coat now which was worn by his grandfather, the very pug dogs in the street would bark at him." And is there any such charm in the particular form and arrangement of all the accidents of public prayer (designed upwards of 200 years ago) as to exempt it from this universal law of humanity?*

"We live," says Lord Derby, "in an age of constant progress, moral, social, and political,"—why not add *religious?* What is there in that word to imply stagnation more than in any of the other three? Why are

---

* "Everything human," says Burke, "must yield to the great *law of change,* the most powerful and the most uncontrollable of all Nature's laws."

"All human institutions are liable to abuse, and require continual amendment," says the great historian Hume (vol. vi., p. 67).

the laws which regulate the devotional services of the country to stand for ever upon an Act bearing date 1662, when the "moral, social, and political" administration of the State has undergone, during the same period, an endless series of change and improvement?

"Constant progress," continues the same high authority, "constant progress—improving upon the old system, *adapting our institutions to the altered purposes* which they are intended to serve, and by *judicious changes* meeting the increased demands of society"—these are the principles which, if true of the State, are not less true of the Church. And never will I believe, till I hear it from his own lips,* that one who can give utterance to such sentiments will refuse the demand that will shortly be made by Lord Ebury, in the name of a body of Church Reformers, for a COMMISSION OF INQUIRY into the working of our ecclesiastical system, with a view to adapt it to the exigencies of the times we live in.

To what more accurately than to the Church do the following words apply?—is it not "the result of a series of perpetual changes?"—like the venerable old country houses of England, has it not been "formed from time to time by successive occupants, with no great regard to architectural *uniformity*, or regularity of outline, but adding a window here, throwing out a gable there, and making such fresh accommodation in another place as might appear to suit, not the beauty of the external structure, but, *what is of more importance, the convenience and comfort of the inhabitants?*" And is it conceiv-

---

* Alas, that this hope should have been expressed in vain! So true is Paley's remark on the aversion of "Ministers of State" to touch "Liturgical Reform" with one of their fingers.—See Paley's Life, by Meadley, Appendix, p. 45.

able that 200 years of the most rapidly moving phase of the world's existence shall have gone by, and have left the Church Service the only unimproved, unimprovable, feature on the scene? To affirm this is a libel on the profession to which we belong. It is tantamount to saying that law, physics, politics, arts, arms, machinery, roads, buildings, anything, everything, can be improved, and have been so within the last fifty years; but that there is something about the Church so impracticable, so exceptional, so unmanageable, that no one either cares or dares to meddle with it.

Meanwhile, dissent and indifferentism, and we might add infidelity, multiply. Church-rates must be repealed to satisfy the demands of those who take advantage of our weakness and internal divisions. A spirit of disaffection towards those in authority spreads within our ranks; while the Right Reverend the Bishops, who should be looked up to as our natural leaders in the march of improvement, are regarded with mistrust or suspicion, as evincing a disposition to stifle inquiry and the free expression of opinion; a desire, in short, to retain abuses and to perpetuate defects in our system which they either cannot or will not see.*

In my next I shall have done with the Bishop of

---

* "A little *common sense* is what we so much want. We should bo no less Scriptural or Apostolical if we pushed a few of our traditions aside, and cast off some of our habits. The old black stocks were done away with in the Army some time ago; and if we had a little less starch in our ties, and a little more breadth of mind inside our coats, probably we shouldn't be any worse parsons, and we should do our people a deal more good. Let us give reasonable services; let us not whine instead of speaking; let us suit our people's time and convenience as much as possible; let us be strictly Scriptural and simple; and if we will just use common sense in all these matters. we shall help ourselves wonderfully in helping others, and do the best possible service to the Church of England."

See "*Hints on Common Sense for Clergymen, by one of Themselves.*"
W. J. Johnson, 121, *Fleet Street, E.C.* 1878.

Lincoln, whose speech, being first on the list, has detained me longer than will be the case with any other of the prelates who took part in the debate of February last. I shall, however, with your permission, briefly notice the remainder, avoiding as much as possible all vain repetitions: and am, meanwhile,

Yours obediently and obliged,

April 17, 1858.   " INGOLDSBY."

LETTER X.

THIS IS NOT THE TIME.

' R usticus expectat dum defluat amnis ; at ille
  Labitur, et labetur, in omne volubilis ævum."—HOR.

" Waits till the river pass away; but lo,
  Ceaseless it flows, and will for ever flow."—FRANCIS.

SIR,—The Bishop of Lincoln concludes as follows:—
" I entirely agree with the petition which I have just presented, that we should use our utmost endeavours to prevent, if possible, legislative interference *at this present time.*" *

At this present time! Can his lordship name *any time*, from the days of Luther to the moment at which we are now arrived, when such has not been the watch-word of anti-Reformers?† At this present time! Why, if the thing

---

* See Charge by the Bishop of Bath and Wells, April, 1861.

† Such was the argument made use of by the Oxford Let-well-aloners a century ago. Thus at least writes one of their number in 1774:—" There are some things in our Articles and Liturgy which I should be *glad to see amended, many* which I should be *willing to give up to the scruples of others;* BUT . . . we had better *wait for more peaceable times,* and be contented with our present constitution, until a fairer prospect shall appear of changing it for the better."—*Answer, &c.;* by Thomas Randolph, D.D., President of C.C.C., Lady Margaret's Professor of Divinity, and Archdeacon

is worth doing at all, no time like the present. If it is
not worthy of being done, then the time can never come
that shall make it so. But the fact is, they who use this
argument seek delay as the surest method of shelving the
question. Let but the present excitement on the subject
be allowed to subside, it will take another century before
such a resolute assault on the strongholds of "let well
alone" can be again got up. Another Russian war,*
another Indian rebellion, another Reform Bill, a change of
Ministry, a famine, a cholera, a thousand things may happen
to divert the public mind into fresh channels, if we can
but stave off the *present time!* If we can but stop Lord
Ebury's mouth for this session, it may not be so easy for
the Liturgical Reformers to find another champion equally
able and willing to undertake their cause.† Now, therefore, or never, "let us use our utmost endeavours"—a
long pull, and a strong pull, and a pull all together against
the stream.

But why all this fear, my excellent Lord Bishop?
Why all this determined and united resistance to "the
People's call?"‡ What is it you are alarmed at? *Unde
hæ lacrymæ?*

You shall be allowed to speak for yourself : " We cannot,

---

of Oxford, 1774. See also John Newton (Life of Bishop Blomfield, vol. i.,
ch. vii., p. 190) : "As to our Liturgy, I am far from thinking it incapable
of amendment; though when I consider the temper and spirit of *the present
times*, I dare not wish that the improvement of it should be attempted, lest
the remedy should be worse than the disease."

* How truly this vaticination has been fulfilled need hardly be pointed
out (1878).

† Lord Ebury's motion was announced to come on in the House of Lords
the following May.

‡ The author of these letters had recently published a pamphlet bearing
the title of "The People's Call for a Revision of the Liturgy, in a Letter
to Lord Palmerston," 1857.

of course, be ignorant of the fact, that there are a great
many persons who, conceiving that our Liturgy contains
passages not consistent with the Word of God, are most
anxious to have it altered to what they consider the
standard of truth."

So, so; the murder is out at last! It is the Fishero-
phobia that possesses his lordship! Because a certain
barrister in the North has published a μέγα Βιβλίον, a thick
crown 8vo, of some 600 pages, entitled "Liturgical Purity
our Rightful Inheritance,"* which has drawn forth the
wrathful denunciation of the Bishops of Bangor (Bethell),
Exeter (Philpotts), and St. David's (Thirlwall), therefore
the Bishop of Lincoln must take up the alarm, and call
aloud to arms, to arms! "resist legislative interference by
all means—at this present time!" Surely one would have
thought it a wiser course and a more manly to *answer* the
book than to denounce it; to silence one man, and that
a layman, by a straightforward honest reply, than to try
by force of authority to stop the mouths of some thousands
of clerical reformers, who have never read the book, and
are never likely to read it.

Mr. Fisher may be right, or he may be wrong. Lawyers
are no more infallible than popes or bishops; but lawyers
have a claim to be *heard* in their *own* defence, as well as
in the defence of their clients, if they have any. And if
Mr. Fisher, being a lawyer, and finding leisure for the
purpose, chooses, as *amicus curiæ*, to volunteer the defence
of the clergy, common justice requires that he should
have a hearing, an open and impartial tribunal, and a
verdict of acquittal or condemnation. This is all he asks
—this all the Liturgical Reformers as a body ask—a Com-

---

* London: Hamilton, Adams, & Co., 33, Paternoster Row. 1860.

mission of Inquiry. Can anything be more harmless? It is granted every day upon some one's request.* Sir John Pakington has got his Commission of Inquiry into National Education; another honourable gentleman has got his Commission of Inquiry into the way in which the soldiers are fed in barracks; another, as to how many acres are sown yearly in beans, turnips, or mangel wurzel; and yet the whole machinery of the "House of Bishops" is to be set in motion to resist *totis viribus* a Commission of Inquiry into Mr. Fisher's book! Why, the thing would be simply ridiculous, if it were not too serious. Our churches are to remain half filled;† half our should-be congregations are to stop at home; half those who go to church (or, according to the bishop, the *majority* of those who go) are to grow up with "habits of indevotion;" to fall asleep over the Litany; to compose themselves to absence of mind at the commencement of the sermon; to rush out of church when it is ended, with faces gleaming with delight, like schoolboys let out to play; to forget as quickly as possible the text, and all that was said upon it; to vote the Morning Service a bore; to refuse church-rates; to abuse the clergy;—and all this simply because Mr. Fisher has "written a book" —and *therefore* it is not safe, advisable, or expedient to entertain the question of Liturgical Revision "at this present time."

I do not blame Mr. Fisher. The bishop does not blame him; nay, his lordship goes further, and says "he

---

* Mr. H. Seymour had just got, and not before it was needed, his Commission of Inquiry into the Ecclesiastical Commission.

† "While we are freezing common sense for large salaries in stately churches, amidst whole acres and furlongs of empty pews, the crowd are feasting on ungrammatical fervour and illiterate animation in the crumbling hovels of Methodists."—*Sydney Smith*, Works, Vol. i., 85.

There *must* be *something* wrong here: explain it who will.

is quite right." "Of course, they are perfectly right. They have the right to use every effort to obtain such alterations as they think necessary."

But it is not an equal *sequitur* that, because one class of Reformers seeks the alteration of the Baptismal Service,* or objects to an ambiguous phrase or two in the Catechism, therefore *all* legislative interference is to be suspended, and the Church is to crawl along upon her old turnpike road, with the signposts and milestones of 1662 as her guide, half obliterated as they are by time, overgrown with moss and lichens, battered by passengers, occasionally broken down, or rendered useless by the diversion of traffic into newer and more commodious routes. Why, this is to refuse to hear of a new Reform Bill because Mr. Bright will be satisfied with nothing less than the ballot,† or Mr. Williams considers "universal suffrage" the "rightful inheritance" of the British public.

But *what* is the Bishop of Lincoln afraid of? His lordship should particularise his fears. Mr. Fisher is definite and specific enough; his impugners should not deal in generals.

Who can make anything of the concluding paragraph of his lordship's speech?—"But we, who hold that our Reformers have built upon the framework of Apostolic order what we consider to be the pure truth of the Gospel, have occasion to dread, I think, lest our Legislature, composed as it is at present, should take into its hands the Prayer-book; and should have even the pretext of altering it according to what its members—ill-informed sometimes,

---

* Surely it is not absolutely necessary that this one *crux* should stand in the way of other reforms upon which all parties are agreed.

† And yet even this last bugbear of Reform was ultimately granted by a *Conservative* Ministry; while, alas! the Act of Uniformity of 1662 remains *in statu quo*.

hasty often—may consider an improvement upon it."—" Our Legislature, composed as it is *at present—ill-informed sometimes—hasty often!*" Are bishops never hasty? Are they, as a matter of course, well informed on all subjects? —We hope these words proceeding from the mouth of a churchman, will recommend the Church in the eyes of the Non-Cons.; but we can hardly expect them to deal the more tenderly with the Prayer-book, should the opportunity be offered them, in return for such a courteous advance on our part. Probably some of them have not yet forgotten the summary manner in which 2,000 of their forefathers were ejected from their occupation on Bartholomew's day, 1662. Sound policy, one would think— not to say Christian charity — should suggest the most delicate forbearance towards those who may feel that the Act of Uniformity bears somewhat hardly upon them.

But we are not asking for "Legislative interference at this present time." We are not seeking to submit the Prayer-book to the handling of a Parliament, "ill-informed sometimes, and hasty often." It is not even proposed to refer the matter to a Parliamentary Committee, still less to a Committee of the whole House.

What Lord Ebury's 320 petitioners ask for, as contrasted with the 215 Lincolnshire clergy, is, a ROYAL COMMISSION OF INQUIRY *into the working and wording* of the Prayer-book, from beginning to end—such a Commission as has been granted before for the same purpose, and which it is an undoubted prerogative of the Crown to issue;* nay, which even the Bishop of Lincoln is known not two years ago to have defined, as "the *only practicable mode* of carefully revising the Liturgy." Why,

---

* See a Letter to the Archbishop of Canterbury on the "Special Services," by the Very Rev. G. Elliot, Dean of Bristol. Bristol, 1860.

then, does his lordship shrink from this mode of undertaking it now? The petitioners do not, however, ask for a Commission composed wholly or chiefly of bishops. They would have their lordships *fairly* represented in such Commission,* but no more; not, at least, in such proportion as to swamp the opinions and views of the other members of the Church. They would have all classes of the clergy represented, and they would especially wish the voice of the laity to be heard. They ask that the Commissioners be persons in whom the public would have confidence; men not committed to any extreme views, and who have given their minds to the examination of the subject; men who have not pronounced *ex cathedrâ* that no reform is needed, or that THIS IS NOT THE TIME for entertaining the question; men who are *willing* to undertake the labour of collecting, arranging, and digesting the various materials that will be offered for their consideration; not too hasty, from youth and inexperience; not too cautious, from age and constitutional timidity; not too many—(the last Commission consisted of thirty, an unmanageable number)—lest in the multitude of counsellors there should be confusion; not too few—the Commission of 1558 consisted only of eight—lest all classes be not duly represented.†

Such a Commission appointed for a period of *not less than two years*, with full powers for receiving evidence from all quarters, could hardly fail to make a report which would give satisfaction to reasonable men. And were the

---

* Some such Commission was at length extorted from the Powers that be; but it was so partial in its construction that the result was (after interminable delay) a Report hardly worth the paper on which it was printed: but more of this hereafter.

† Probably about fifteen Commissioners would be found practically the best number for work, five to form a quorum, eight a majority.

clergy *properly* represented in Convocation * (*which they are not*), it is more than probable such report would be endorsed by the majority of that body.

Be that as it may, such is our confidence in the wisdom, the impartiality, and the moderation of the two Houses of Parliament, that we do not anticipate from them, *as a body*, any material interference with the scheme which a Commission so constituted would offer for their acceptance.

That, finally, her Most Gracious Majesty the Queen would hail the occasion of sanctioning with her approval a measure that has been loudly called for at various intervals during the last two centuries, and in which the honour of God and the welfare of her people are intimately concerned, all will, I think, readily allow.

May we express a hope, that as the reign of Elizabeth, of famous memory, stands forward most conspicuous for the part then taken in the matter of the Reformation, so in future ages, the reign of Victoria, amidst all its other glorious acts, may not be least renowned for having grappled with this difficulty; relieving, to some extent, the consciences of Dissenters; disarming all *legitimate* grounds for dissatisfaction with the established form of public worship; rendering, in fine, the Book of Common Prayer as nearly perfect as may be; and thus causing it to become *indeed*, what it is now *in name*, the brightest jewel in the Sovereign's crown?

Having at length brought to a conclusion our observations on the Bishop of Lincoln's speech, we will in our

---

* See Letter i., p. 5; on the Composition of Convocation. Bishop Blomfield (a great authority) very wisely objected to the revival of Convocation "under its present constitution." See his Life by his Sons, vol. i., ch. vii., p. 198.

next make a few remarks upon such parts of the Bishop of Oxford's address, which follows, as differ materially from the former. Of course it will not be expected that we should travel over the same ground again. Those, therefore, of your readers who have not seen the preceding letters will take it for granted that, should any of the latter prelate's arguments appear to be passed over with undue brevity, it is because we consider them sufficiently replied to in our previous remarks.

I remain, yours very obediently,

April 22, 1858. " INGOLDSBY."

LETTER XI.

THE BISHOP OF OXFORD (WILBERFORCE).—NO. I.

"Larga quidem, Drance, semper tibi copia fandi,
Tunc cum bella manus poscunt; Patribusque vocatis,
Primus ades." VIRGIL, Æn. xi. 378.

"Ingenium velox, audacia perdita, sermo
Promptus, et Isæo torrentior." JUV., Sat. iii. 74.

SIR,—Once upon a time, says Æsop, a monkey, having lit on a bag of raw chestnuts, and being minded to roast the same for his eating, was at his wits' end how to compass his object without burning his fingers. By chance a cat passing by at this instant, Pug immediately seized her, and, using her fore-paws for tongs, inserted the chestnuts, one by one, between the bars of the grate until all were roasted, and by the same process plucked them out again, with a grin of satisfaction at the cleverness of his device.

The Bishop of Lincoln having resumed his seat, the Bishop of Oxford* next addressed the right reverend prelates,

---

* The Right Rev. Samuel Wilberforce; translated to Winchester in 1869 on the resignation of Bishop Sumner; and killed by a fall from his horse near Dorking, Surrey, July 19th, 1873, ætat. sixty-eight.

assembled in the large apartment of Queen Anne's Bounty Office; and is reported to have spoken as follows:—

"I am very thankful that, in presenting this petition, my right rev. brother has brought this matter under the notice of your Grace and my right rev. brethren. . . ."

Now, far be it from me, a humble country parson, to make any offensive application of the above familiar fable; but I cannot deny that, upon first reading the Bishop of Oxford's address, and being not unaware (as which of us is?) of the odour in which a certain party in the Church is supposed to stand with the public;—I cannot deny that the thought did occur to me at the moment (and I have seen no reason since to alter my opinion), how very clever it was to put my brother of Lincoln in the front of this fire, and so to forward my own views under shelter of his petition.

A document signed by two hundred and fifteen *Oxfordshire* clergymen might "at this present time" have been looked upon with suspicion. No one could reasonably take exception at so many Lincolnshire divines expressing their opinion on a matter that has been for years in fierce agitation in that part of the kingdom.

Of course I am mistaken; and I am well aware that I ought to think no evil; but it is as difficult sometimes to control one's thoughts as it is to conceal one's intentions, however much art be used for the purpose. And certainly there can be no mistake as to the *animus* with which the *second* speaker (who is not wont to occupy the background) enters upon the business in which his more retiring brother of Lincoln has hitherto borne the brunt, and in which, to the distant spectator, both the right rev. prelates *appear* to take an equally warm interest.

Unfortunately, brevity forms no part either of the soul or the wit of the Bishop of Oxford. One stands paralysed and confounded before the following sentence—if sentence it can be called:—

"We, of course, cannot shut our eyes to the fact that there is a movement on foot for introducing direct changes into the Prayer-book; and leaving for a moment quite out of sight the grave considerations which the Bishop of Lincoln has urged, which would leave us to believe that those alterations might possibly be most dangerous in themselves, and in the present temper of men's minds might lead to our losing many important views of truth, I entirely agree in what my right reverend brother has said on another ground which I shall be glad if my brethren will attentively consider; and that is, not only that in our Prayer-book we have a precious inheritance of truth from Catholic times—from the earliest Catholic times—and with the revision of our own Reformers—so that we have really given us back again the old jewel, well cleansed from all the injuries and defacements and mists which one after another had in some measure clouded and tarnished its brightness; not only have we that inheritance, great as it is, but the Book of Common Prayer of the Church of England is the common standing-place between those persons in our Church, who, from the natural condition of men's minds, or the effects of early education, do, to a certain allowed and permitted degree, take different views of divine truth."

Well, thank goodness we have come to the end of it at last; the only thing wanting to qualify it for the prize being that the orator should have delivered it *stans pede in uno*. But as that notion might suggest undignified recollections of the celebrated Cambridge epigram,* we will say no more about it. No wonder his lordship is an

---

* Οὐκ ἐστὶν χηνῶν οὕτις ὃς οὐ δύναται.
"There is not a goose in the land who could not do as much."

advocate for retaining all the "vain repetitions" in our Morning Service, when we have here, in *a single sentence* of his own, "Prayer-book" three times repeated, "truth" three times, "views of truth" twice, "men's minds" twice, "inheritance" twice, "Catholic times" twice, "Church" twice, "injuries and defacements," "clouded and tarnished," "allowed and permitted." I have heard it said that the Bishop of Oxford is the only speaker on the Bench of Bishops worthy of the name; and certainly, unless the adage hold good, that

> "Words are like leaves, and where they most abound
> Much fruit of sense beneath is rarely found,"

or that other:

> "My tongue within my lips I rein,
> For who speaks much must speak in vain;"

it would be difficult to conceive any one more entitled to the above praise.* At the same time, I suppose an Oxford Second-class man will allow some authority in the art of speaking to one who has laid it down as a law in composition that,

> "Est brevitate opus, ut *currat sententia*, neu se
> Impediat verbis lassas onerantibus aures."

> "Close be your language; let your sense be clear;
> Nor with a weight of words fatigue the ear."

Such is not the style of Lord Derby's nervous harangues, nor such of Disraeli's addresses to the House. Verbosity may confound, but it does not convince. The Bishop of Oxford's speeches remind one too painfully of our nursery

---

* It was said by some one in praise of Epaminondas, that "he had never met with a man who knew more and spoke less." Cowper has also well defined such wordy eloquence in the following couplet,—

> "Like quicksilver, the rhetoric they display;
> Shines as it runs, but grasp'd it slips away."

days, when we were trained to rehearse at a breath the astonishing adventures of Peter Piper and his peck of pickled pepper.* There is something in them (to adapt our simile more to the dignity of the subject) that conjures up the mighty spirit of Demosthenes on the shores of the Piræus, fulmining out his exercises to the roaring Ægean *ore rotundo*, with pebbles in his mouth.

It was not without reason that, *apropos* of this last-mentioned orator, the satirist bitterly observed,—

"Torrens dicendi copia multis
Et sua mortifera est facundia."

But, alas! the curse does not light only on the speaker. He entails the like misfortune on his unhappy audience:—

"Occidit miseros crambe repetita."

Vain repetitions are as painful to listen to in a speech as they are in a set form of prayer. They also throw no small difficulties in the way of the hapless reviewer who undertakes to analyse such an harangue. He never seems to get any nearer the close of the story. It is like a recurring decimal: *Labitur et labetur;* never ending, still beginning. Would that I had at hand some convenient Grimalkin, whose paws to make use of instead of my own for this disagreeable, not to say dangerous operation!

It is currently reported that everybody, from the humblest curate in his diocese to the Prime Minister for the time being, is *afraid* of the Bishop of Oxford; and that the real secret of the alleged unanimity of the "House of Bishops" on the 10th of February last, was, that none of their lordships dared to contravene the dictum of their

---

* What was afterwards well said of another by Lord Beaconsfield might be applied equally in this case, "a sophisticated rhetorician inebriated with the exuberance of his own verbosity." (1878.)

Superior.* I see accordingly small prospect of any *Deus ex machinâ* descending to my aid on this occasion.

CONTRA AUDENTIOR ITO

must, therefore, I suppose, be again my motto, as it has been before now. I must buckle on my armour, though it consist but of a sling and a stone. And as fortune is known to favour the bold, I may chance to escape with the empty threat of having my flesh given to the fowls of the air and the beasts of the field.

To have done at length with these *præludia pugnæ*, and to enter upon the task lying before us—who shall define the meaning of that expression "*the present temper of men's minds?*"†

---

* The present Bishop of Durham (Dr. Baring) is a conspicuous exception to this rule. See Report of Convocation, March 14, 1861; with the *Guardian's* comment on the occasion. But even he at last appears to have succumbed to the difficulties thrown in the way of all Liturgical Reformers, high or low.

† A certain writer, comparing the attempt at Revision in 1762 with that now made, observes:—

"The answers of Anglican Church Governors to all demands for a Revision of the Liturgy have at all times a remarkable identity, and might be formulated for Episcopal use. The grounds of the petition may be denied, and the Liturgy regarded as perfect; or, granting imperfections, it may be alleged that every human composition must have imperfections; or, granting that the imperfections complained of ought to be removed— *men's minds are so excited*—there would be such strifes about it—no moderation in effecting it; or, men's minds are *not* excited about it—it would be a sad pity to set them by the ears.

"The formula, 'THIS IS NOT THE TIME—too excited,' is the commonest, because a bishop will not usually answer at all unless there is a general interest on the subject, and this general interest is 'excitement.'

"I happened to stumble on the sermon which an Archbishop of Canterbury (Secker) wrote to preach before Convocation in 1761. It would do exactly for 1858—at least on the point of Revision. The excitement argument is thus put:—

"'Ornatior quidem, *accuratior*, plenior, *brevior*, et *potest* ea [Liturgia scil.] fieri et *debet:* sed modestâ tractatione, sed *tranquillis* hominum animis

Language, says Talleyrand, was given to disguise thoughts; and as the present Bishop of Oxford has evidently no lack of words, it is possible he may occasionally make use of them to conceal his esoteric views. To say simply, as so many do, "*this* is not the time," is to concede the principle, which we suppose the Bishop of Oxford is not exactly prepared to do. To name any *other* time, we imagine, is equally foreign to his intention.

Can it then be that the present temper of men's minds is inclining towards Romanism? And that, *therefore*, it is, at this present time, highly inexpedient to meddle with that "jewel, the Prayer-Book," lest we should loosen from their settings some of those additions which we owe to "the revision of our own Reformers," and thus incur the danger of "losing many important views of truth?"

Or can it be, that the notion uppermost in the Bishop's mind is, that "the present temper of men's minds" is, for some cause or other, a good deal set *against* Popery in all its branches, *open or concealed?*—that the high day of Tractarianism is on the wane—the Star of Protestantism in the ascendant; that many fearless Reformers have of late years sounded the trumpet loudly, and with no uncertain blast, against the secret practices of those who would draw us on blindfold to the edge of a precipice, whence to retreat in safety is hardly possible? Does the Bishop of Oxford flatter himself that, if we wait a little longer—if Lord Ebury and his petitioners can but be silenced for a few years—these Rylands and Tyndales, these Girdlestones and Gells, these Powyses, Hulls, Fishers, Davises, Mountfields, Binghams, Neviles, Milnes,

---

non temerariis, qualia vidimus et videmus, ausis; non inter media *dissidia* mutuasque suspiciones.'—SECKER'S WORKS, Vol. v., p. 517.

"How often have we heard this in English in our day?" See Letter x.

Trails, Nihills, Taylors, *et id genus omne,** will have dropped into their graves (like the Gorhams and other importunate protesters in their day), unpitied, unregretted, *unpromoted;* while their places may be supplied by hopeful disciples of the Bennett, Denison, Liddell, Poole, Mackonochie, West, Randall, Bryan King, Lee, Lowder, Purchas, Tooth, Lavington, Cuddesdon, Boyne Hill, and East Grinstead school; men duly alive to the importance of forms and ceremonies—tenacious of rubrics 300 years old—not disposed to concede one inch to popular outcry—deaf, as rocks to the drowning mariner, at the call of "common sense"† or expediency — prepared to die at the stake sooner than surrender a single gem from that compound "*jewel,*" the Prayer-book, or run the remotest risk (in any efforts to improve it) of sacrificing a tittle of that "precious inheritance which they have derived from Catholic times—from the earliest Catholic times?"‡

My question, I am aware, is somewhat lengthy. But prolixity is catching; verbosity, like silence, is infectious. Nevertheless, an explanation is needed, and I pause for a reply. *Davus sum non Œdipus.* I am no expounder of riddles.

The words mean something, or they mean nothing. And until a more satisfactory answer is given by the only competent authority, the petitioners, of course, are at liberty to put their own construction upon the possible meaning of an expression calculated to throw dust in the eyes of the unwary,

---

* A list of some five hundred of these may be seen as Members of the Association for Promoting a Revision of the Prayer Book, No. 17, Buckingham Street, Adelphi, W.C.

† See a Tract with this title, by a "High Churchman." Hatchard: 1860.

‡ In illustration of the remark in the text, read the speeches of Archdeacon Denison and the Rev. John Jebb, in Convocation, upon the Dean of Norwich's (Pellew) Motion for certain alterations in the Prayer-book, March 14th, 1861.

and make the innocent public believe that some awful catastrophe is impending; that "men's minds" are on fire; "the Church in danger;" and that their only hope of safety is to rally as one man round the Bishop of Oxford.

Such, I must candidly confess, is the impression produced on my own mind by these enigmatical words; and I imagine others are not unlikely to draw from them a similar inference. For, as for supposing the Bishop of Oxford really expects, or that any man in his senses expects, the time will *ever* come when "the temper of men's minds," especially of High Churchmen, shall be sufficiently calm and composed to entertain with equanimity a proposition for revising the Liturgy, we should as soon look to see an elephant at the top of St. Paul's, or a certain nameless prelate safely installed in the archiepiscopal throne at Canterbury.

The fact is, as I said in my last, "the present time" is objected to simply BECAUSE it IS THE PRESENT TIME. It is the old story over again; there is a lion in the path; it is the "*Rusticus expectat*"—the more convenient season!—the season that always *was* looked for, and always *will* be, by men who meant to do nothing, and mean to do nothing. But we trust there is a spirit abroad that will no longer submit to be put off by this stale artifice, but will demand a hearing with a louder and yet a louder cry—a cry which no torrent of words in the House of Bishops can drown, no "decided vote in another place" silence or put down.

But it is time, Mr. Editor, that I brought this letter to a conclusion. The theme is a tempting one, but I must rein in. And should it seem to you, or to any of your readers, that I have dwelt longer than needful on the preamble to my present subject, let them remember how large a portion of the public is ever liable to be led away by the voice of authority speaking in high places; how few have leisure or inclination *approfondir une matière;* how essential, therefore, it is to the establishment of "the truth" to brush away all mystification at the very outset, and make it appear to the meanest apprehension that words are not necessarily arguments, nor assertions proofs. I have the honour to remain,

Yours faithfully,

April 29, 1858.   " INGOLDSBY."

LETTER XII.

THE COMMISSION OF 1689.

" How often a great truth must come forth into light, and be revived and overborne, and lapse back into obscurity, before it receives a general acceptation! What a strange variety of champions and opponents it finds before it obtains the one powerful friend that calls forth the general acclaim and lands it in success!"—*Times Newspaper.*

SIR,—Since I commenced my reply to the Bishop of Oxford, my attention has been called to Canon Wodehouse's* republication of Archbishop Tenison's Discourse on the Ecclesiastical Commission of 1689. That Commission failed in its object from several concurrent causes, which have now in great measure been removed. But had everything else been favourable, there was an inherent defect in the constitution of the Commission, calculated to be fatal to its success from the very outset. It was too cumbersome; † the elements of which it was composed were too discordant; they were as vinegar and oil in the same vessel—

> " Frigida pugnabant calidis, humentia siccis,
> Mollia cum duris, sine pondere habentia pondus."

Like the Lower House of Convocation in our own day, the

---

 * Of the part enacted by this gentleman, as connected with the Revision of the Prayer-book, see Chapp. LXXIII., CVI.

 † Exactly the same mistake, intentionally or unintentionally, was made with the Commission of 1867, under the presidency of Archbishop Longley.

Commission of 1689 defeated its own ends by the incongruity of its materials. Much talking and little work must always be the result of a Council so constructed. The opposite sides of the equation cancel one another, and the product is NIL. *Some* of the recommendations, however, of that Commission are well worth attending to; and since they have been made public by order of the House of Commons,* it is impossible not to admit (with Bishop Burnet) *of several of them*, that while they were calculated in great measure to conciliate and bring the Dissenters into communion with the Established Church,† they were of themselves desirable, even though there were not a Dissenter in the nation.

Precisely, however, as Lord Ebury's proposal for a ROYAL COMMISSION in 1858 is denounced by certain worthy individuals, so was the Commission of 1689 by the Let-well-aloners of that date. Amongst others, one under the assumed title of the Quærist was loud in his protestations, laying particular stress on the fact that the passions of men were, *at that time*, in such a vehement state of perturbation.

Tenison's reply (for he was then neither a bishop nor an archbishop) was, " That is true which the Quærist says; and in part he makes it good by his own manner of writing, that the passions of men are in a vehement fermentation; but it is so always in all revolutions; and 'tis one great business of the Parliament and Convocation to *allay our heats;* but he that would abate the fever may stay too long if he forbears to prescribe till the blood is quiet."

"True wisdom would not delay what is necessary or expedient to be done beyond the due season of action. Those, therefore, in my opinion, do not give wholesome advice who

---

* Seeley and Jackson, Fleet Street, London, 1855.
† Such was the earnest wish of Archbishop Sancroft, as well as of Tillotson, Burnet, and many others of not less note.

say, *Do nothing now, or as little as may be. Little* or *much* is not the business, but as much as is fit. And if the opportunity be neglected, it may discourage the Powers that offer it from vouchsafing another." *

---

* To those who, while admitting the need of Revision, plead for postponement till a more convenient season, we would earnestly commend the following remarks of Archbishop Whately, though not originally penned with reference to this particular subject:—

"It is far from being sufficient, as seems to be the notion of some persons, to show that the present is not the *fittest conceivable* occasion for taking a certain step. Besides this, it is requisite to show, not merely that a better occasion may be *imagined*, or that a better occasion is *past*—that the Sibylline books might have been purchased cheaper *some time ago;* but that a more suitable occasion is likely to arise *hereafter*, and *how soon;* and also, that the mischief which may be *going on during the interval* will be more than compensated by the superior suitableness of that future occasion; in short, that it will have been worth waiting for. And in addition to all this, it is requisite to show also the probability that when this golden opportunity shall arise, men will be more *disposed to take advantage* of it than they have heretofore appeared to be; that they will not again fall into apathetic security, and fondness for indefinite procrastination.

"This last point is as needful to be established as any; for it is remarkable that those who deprecate taking any step *just now*, in these times of extraordinary excitement, did not, on those former occasions, come forward to propose taking advantage of a comparatively calmer state of things. They neither made any call, nor responded to the call of others.

"And, indeed, all experience seems to show—comparing the apathy on the subject, which was so general at those periods, with the altered state of feeling now existing—that a great and pressing emergency, and *nothing else*, will induce men to take any step in this matter; and that a period of discussion and perplexing difficulty is, though not *in itself* the most suitable occasion for such a step, yet, constituted as human nature is, the best, because the *only* occasion on which one can hope that it will be taken. A season of famine may have been, in some respects, a bad occasion for altering the corn laws; but experience showed that nothing less would suffice.

"Who can say that a large proportion of those who are now irrecoverably alienated from the Church might not have been at this moment sound members of it, had timely steps been taken, *not by any departure from the principles of our Reformers*, but *by following more closely the track they marked out for us!*"—BACON'S ESSAYS, with Annotations, &c., by Archbishop Whately. Essay xxiv., Of Innovations, pp. 271, 272, edit. London; 1860.

These appear to me the words of sound sense and good policy. I wonder whether Tenison was charged by the *Morning Post* of his day with being a "fidgety man," or whether the *Clerical Journal* of 1689 gave out that "a certain amiable Archdeacon in the diocese of London has gone mad on the subject of Liturgical Revision."

Very likely; for it appears nothing came of his recommendations; and, like Cassandra of old,* he is only found out to be a prophet when it is too late. Meanwhile Dissent, which was then in its infancy, has multiplied a hundred-fold; † and, what is worse, the Church is torn with internal strife;

"Illiacos intra muros peccatur et extra;"

and all attempts to heal its divisions show too clearly that the seat of the disease is radical—in short, that all laws of *human* origin, however excellent in their primary institution, *must bend* to times and circumstances, or *break* from the too great strain upon them. In other words, common sense will have its way. The world *will move along*, as well as go round. The blood will circulate. George Stephenson's engines will persist in running forty miles

---

* "Ora, dei jussu, non unquam credita Teucris."—VIRGIL, Æn. ii. 247.

† "The census of 1851 brought to light three facts, of deep, and, to Christian Churchmen, painful interest. 1st, that between six and eight millions of the people, chiefly of the labouring classes, uniformly abstain from attending any place of religious worship; 2ndly, that *the number of Nonconformists* in England and Wales is *equal* to that of the members of the Established Church; and, 3rdly, that this double process of alienation from the established worship, and presumed hostility to all religion, has wrought with increasing accelerated force during the present century, as compared with any previous period of the history of our country. The time has therefore come when it behoves the true friends of the Church to inquire into the causes of this miscarriage, and to labour for their removal."—T. N. BENNETT, *Plymouth*, 1854. See also "The Liturgy and the Dissenters," by the Rev. Isaac Taylor. Hatchard: 1860.

an hour. Hahnemann's disciples will prefer infinitesimal globules of sugar of milk to black doses, boluses, and blisters. And, in spite of the Bishop of Oxford, sensible laymen will recalcitrate at being compelled to listen to the damnatory clauses of the Athanasian Creed thirteen times a year; and little children will tumble off their benches in the gallery, if compelled to sit out the length of our present Morning Service.

But *is it a fact* that "men's minds" are at present in such a violent state of perturbation? I am disposed to question it; and I do not speak without some knowledge of the matter. My own opinion, as opposed with all due deference to so high an authority as that of the Bishop of Oxford, is that "men's minds" never contemplated the subject of Liturgical Revision with more calmness and self-possession than they do at present.* I am far from saying that there is *no* excitement abroad (that day I never expect to see), but I think that the bulk of the people, while taking a decided interest in the present struggle, look on nevertheless rather with the quiet indifference of spectators, than with the ardour and passions of partisans. Here and there, indeed, one hears of a

---

* It may not be amiss to record here the reply of the Rev. Charles Girdlestone to the Dean of Westminster (Trench), Jan. 25, 1860. "Dear Sir,—In reply to a circular signed by yourself and others, inviting me to join in deprecating the revision of the Prayer-book '*at the present time,*' I take the liberty of asking at what time, past or future, you and they would judge it more expedient than now? For my own part, I think the present the best time that ever was or ever will be. My reasons for so thinking are as follows:—First, it never was so obvious as now that our Liturgy, in its present state, *admits of being interpreted in harmony with that spurious Christianity called Popery, against which the Church of these realms is pledged to protest.* Secondly, the danger never was so imminent as now, that if temperate revision be frustrated we shall have in its stead a sweeping revolution. For such a calamity I dare not in anywise make myself responsible by signing the proposed declaration."

"Rupture in the Church," as the certain result of any *attempt* to tamper with the Liturgy. "Touch the Prayer-book, and we go," says another. "Expect from me the most unmitigated opposition," says the eccentric member for Maidstone.* But a fair examination of the relative strength of parties at this moment would, I think, show a very small minority on the side of these uncompromising gentlemen, whose zeal one cannot help respecting, though we may not admit that it is always exercised according to knowledge or discretion—knowledge, at least, of human nature and the general feelings of mankind; discretion as to the probability of their cause being recommended by this stern refusal to redress even admitted evils.

OMNIA DAT QUI JUSTA NEGAT:

and probably no surer way could be devised for the ultimate *concession of everything*, than the course pursued by these worthies, including the Right Reverend Prelates, of resisting *inquiry into anything*.

The real fact I believe to be, that there never was a period when so much sober reasoning and temperate discussion was put forth by the advocates for Revision; while it is undeniable that their object has been pursued of late with an unprecedented degree of perseverance and determination. The only way of accounting for this is, the supposition that the petitioners feel they have truth and public opinion on their side—two mighty and irresistible allies—which, they are well assured, *must* and *will* prevail

---

* A. J. B. Hope, afterwards M.P. for the University of Cambridge, who, nevertheless, in spite of these pronounced opinions, by the irony of fate, was made, along with the Bishop of Oxford (Wilberforce), a member of the "Rubrical Commission of Inquiry" of 1867.

in the long run. Very different this to the tone of the remonstrants from the Feathers Tavern Association in 1772. We hear nothing now of the "whining, canting, snivelling generation."* It does not even appear that the Dissenters, as a body, are taking any active part in the present movement. It has originated with members of the Church, and been carried forward by the consenting voices of several of the clergy, supported by influential laity both in and out of Parliament. And if moderation and sobriety in urging their views are not to command attention, what is this but to set a premium upon violence and agitation? Can any one conceive a more suicidal policy on the part of the powers that be, whether in Church or State? Is it not tantamount to giving out that we will yield to the gridiron of a Cobbett, or the raw head and bloody bones of an O'Connell, what we persist in withholding from the quiet and peaceful demands of the real friends of the Church?

But what business, it is asked, have these last (the clergy in particular) to make their voices heard at all in this matter? Have not they given their unfeigned "assent and consent" to the Book of Common Prayer just as it is, with all its contents, for better, for worse?† I reply, No; THEY HAVE NOT. They have *not* pledged themselves to "love its faults." They have nowhere and never said that they considered it perfect and incapable of improvement. They have *not* bound themselves, either by the declaration in the thirty-sixth Canon or otherwise, to resist all attempts to adapt that book to the advanced intelligence of the

---

* See Burke's speech on the occasion; Works, vol. x.

† On "the unfeigned assent and consent to all and everything," see more hereafter, Letters LXVIII., CII. It was to relieve the clergy from that oppressive enactment that Lord Ebury introduced his Bill of 1862, which afterwards became the law of the land and of the Church.

people; any more than a judge or magistrate, who is sworn to administer the laws, is thereby pledged to resist all amendment or repeal of the same.

Surely a clergyman, as well as a layman, may be content to admire generally the Prayer-book as it is, and yet be allowed to see the blemishes which deform it, and seek to remove them. If the authority of one living prelate be good for *upholding* the acknowledged defects in the Liturgy, the authority of another must be equally valid in maintaining that the clergy, by having signed their declaration of conformity, have bound themselves no further than to "use in *general that form* in the administration of the Church Services." Such a declaration never was, and never could be, intended to require of any man that he should, "with more than Chinese exactness, make a point of conscience to adopt every expression, and implicitly to follow every direction, therein contained, notwithstanding any changes which altered modes of thinking may have rendered expedient."* This would be binding the clergy for all time more severely than even the recipients of the good Lady Margaret's bounty at Christ's College, Cambridge; whose oath, previous to the late visitation by Royal Commission, was as follows:—" Hæc omnia in me recipio, et hoc jurejurando confirmo; neque ullam dispensationem ab hoc jurejurando meo impetrabo, *nec impetratam ab aliis acceptabo ullo modo.*" And yet such is the tyranny these sticklers for the Rubric, and PRAYER-BOOK AS IT IS—(the Book, the whole Book, and nothing but the Book)—would seek to impose upon the vast body of the clergy; to the certain encouragement of hypocrisy among many, and the more sure repulsion from the Church of hundreds of high-

---

* Charge to the Clergy of the Diocese of Worcester, by the Right Rev. Henry Pepys, D.D.

minded Christians, whose enrolment would have added strength and vitality to the Establishment.*

I hope I shall not be thought to have gone out of my way to introduce these remarks here. They are essentially connected with the question at issue, and therefore cannot be too early or too frequently insisted on. Let but *the clerical oath*† (as it is erroneously called) be once exhibited in its true light, and thousands of the clergy who now stand aloof would be found ready to come forward in support of a temperate revision of the Prayer-book.

I have the honour to be, Sir, yours faithfully,

May 5, 1858. "INGOLDSBY."

LETTER XIII.

THE BISHOP OF OXFORD.—NO. II.
LORD EBURY'S MOTION IN THE HOUSE OF LORDS, MAY 6, 1858.

SIR,—

"Sicelides Musæ, paullo majora canamus:
Non omnes arbusta juvant humilesque myricæ,"

which, being interpreted, means that there are more important things in the world than "the House of Bishops;"

---

* A fair writer upon the Savoy Conference of 1660 remarks:—

"The unbending temper of the bishops made no discrimination between the different classes of objections. . . . If the winning over so large and respectable a body of men as that headed by Baxter and Calamy was an object worthy of the least sacrifice, these men did not ask too much in proposing such an enlargement of the mode of worship as would comprehend their usages and views. The party existed, and claimed consideration for its numbers and influence. It comprised multitudes of the most sincere and correct professors of Christianity in the realm, with not a few individuals of distinguished name."—BAIRD on Liturgies, 1856, p. 165.

See also a pamphlet by the Rev. Dr. Muhlenberg, of New York, entitled "What the Memorialists Want." R. Craighead, New York, 1856.

† See a pamphlet with this title by the Rev. R. M. Milne. Partridge, 1858. This gentleman is one of that unnoticed army of martyrs who have felt compelled to leave the profession "for conscience' sake."

and that when prime ministers and other noble lords come upon the stage, even the Bishop of Oxford must hide his diminished head, and be content that the light of Convocation pale for a while before the more attractive luminaries that now occupy the scene.

It was my purpose to have troubled you with a few more comments on the Bishop of Oxford's speech in Convocation on the 10th of February last; so far as the said speech was not a "vain repetition" of himself, or of the Bishop of Lincoln who preceded him.

For instance, I might have shown, as Mr. Fisher has done, that from "Catholic times"—yes, from "the earliest Catholic times," our Book of Common Prayer had been ever subject to *alteration;* that *variety rather than uniformity,* change rather than permanency, had been the characteristics of Liturgies from the very beginning; and that they are, and ever were, "wholly destitute of those distinguishing peculiarities which invest the sacred Canon with its high prerogative of immutability." Even Archbishop Laud, an authority to whom the Bishop of Oxford will surely bow, has observed, that "the true reason why we cannot show the exact primitive forms is, because they were continually *subject to alterations* both in times and places."* And the conclusion I was prepared to draw from these premises was, that it was little short of the ludicrous to set up, in the middle of the nineteenth century, a plea for immutability on behalf of a document of human institution, which had not been claimed for it from the beginning of the third to the end of the sixteenth.

My next idea was to have said something about "*cleansing* the old jewel from all the injuries, and defacements, and *mists,*

---

* Such, too is the case with the Romish Ritual, and even the Order of the Mass, to this very day.—BAIRD on Liturgics, chap. ix., p. 166.

which, one after another, had in some measure clouded and
tarnished its brightness."* And it occurred to me, that if
ever " mists " did " tarnish a jewel," they might by possibility do so again; and that 200 years of the world's history
was a tolerably long period to admit of such a deteriorating
process going on. Methought that there had been occasional
intervals during the last two centuries in which the sun
of the Church had not shone forth in its greatest possible
splendour; and that it was within the range of probability
that the progress of education and general enlightenment,
which has been witnessed so remarkably of late years,
might have dispersed a few fogs that still hung about here
and there, and intercepted some stray rays of light from
our eyes. I fancied in my simplicity, that, whatever might
be the wisdom, the learning, the judgment, or the discretion
of the hierarchy at the two respective epochs, there were
certain unmistakable signs of the inferior clergy, the priests
and deacons of the Church, *now* exhibiting (as a body) more
independence of character, and greater general capacity and
intelligence, than Macaulay has been pleased to attribute to
them about the period of the last Revision of the Liturgy.
It appeared to me, therefore, not surprising that some of
them should display a little uneasiness at being still held
fast in the leading-strings of the seventeenth century; and
not unnatural that they should occasionally play the truant
and the rebel in thinking, speaking, and acting for themselves.

It is true the fashion of making schoolmaster-bishops
(if it existed 200 years ago) has not yet become obsolete;†
but that is no reason why the class of vicious rectors and

---

* Bishop of Oxford's Speech in Convocation, Feb. 10, 1858. Letter
XI., p. 67.

† A remarkable instance of the Nolo Episcopari on the part of one
of this class has been lately exhibited (in the case of Dr. Vaughan, late

naughty-boy curates should go on for ever; and it is to be hoped that the race is gradually disappearing, and that in the next generation it will be clean put out. Rectors and curates, there is reason to believe, have at length learned to respect themselves as well as their bishop; and the latter, methinks, will act wisely not to attempt too rudely to unteach them that wholesome and salutary lesson.

So clear, in short, were these general conclusions to my mind, that it seemed to me (to borrow an expression of the Bishop of Oxford) a "special miracle," or "little short of a miracle," that the bulk of the clergy had not learned this lesson long ago. But a good deal has been done by the railroads, during the last quarter of a century, towards opening men's eyes, as well as equalising ranks; a good deal of useful knowledge has been diffused by the penny post, and the repeal of the newspaper stamp; and let but the paper duty be also taken off, as it will be one of these days,* who can foresee the pitch of self-reliance at which all classes of Her Majesty's subjects may at length arrive, from the tiny urchin who now trembles at the shadow of Mr. Squeers's cane, to the most deferential curate in the extensive dioceses of Lincoln, Salisbury, and Oxford.

The next paragraph in the bishop's speech that had attracted my attention was this:—"And that, not because we do not agree on fundamental truth, but that fundamental truth being stated there, is stated fully and fairly on all its sides, so that those whose minds incline to one view of the truth, and those whose minds incline to the

---

Head Master of Harrow), not perhaps altogether to be regretted, bearing in mind the adage,

"Quo semel est imbuta recens servabit odorem
Testa diu."

* The removal of this most impolitic tax was a prominent feature in Mr. Gladstone's budget for 1861.

other view of the truth, each find their own view fully and fairly stated in that book;" and when I had got to the end of it, thought I to myself, What, are there *two* views of truth—a true view of truth and a false view of truth; and are they both "fully and fairly stated" in the Prayer-book? Well, I suppose it is so, for the Bishop of Oxford says it is, and no doubt he knows much better than I do. So, methought I would leave that long sentence to Mr. Fisher and Mr. Davis* (who don't mind long stories) to settle between them; and I passed on rapidly to the next paragraph, with a view to enter my protest against the *necessary consequence* it assumes as the result of Lord Ebury's motion being acceded to.

"If either party were called upon to modify the statements in that book, they would, AS A MATTER OF COURSE, endeavour to introduce such alterations as would make *their own truth* appear more plainly and distinctively; and in making *that truth* so appear, they would do it in such a way that the opposite side would, probably, not be able to acquiesce in the *common statement of truth*."

It is just possible it might be so; but as I hope and believe that neither Lord Derby, Lord Palmerston, nor any other Prime Minister would be so ill-advised as to put upon the Commission any one known to hold such *extreme* "views of truth" on one side or the other, I have myself none of these apprehensions, and can afford to dismiss them, at least for the present, without being "over-exquisite to cast the fashion of uncertain evils."

I meant next—if your readers' patience were not exhausted, and you did not interdict the appearance of any more of these "Ingoldsby Legends," lest they should

---

* Mr. C. H. Davis is well known as a frequent contributor to the *Record* and *Rock*, and a voluminous writer upon Liturgical Reform.

ruin the sale of your independent and valuable journal*
—I meant next to have disputed with his lordship the
position that "thousands of minds" *did* "*now rest
satisfied* with the English Prayer-book;" or rather I
proposed to show, and indeed to prove, that *as many*
thousands, if not more, were *dissatisfied* with it, to at
least the extent of believing it capable of very considerable
amendment.† It appeared therefore to me, that supposing
the result of the projected Commission were to be, as
assumed by the bishop, to "unsettle men's minds"—(a
supposition which I am disposed to question)—it would
but be *actum agere*, or, in other words, to leave things *in
statu quo*; as it would be next to an impossibility, or
" little short of a miracle," to bring "men's minds" into
a condition of more " hopeless and injurious strivings one
with another" than they are at present.‡

Lastly—after observing *en passant* that "at this
moment" was synonymous with " at this present time,"
and that both of them apparently meant in the bishop's
mind the same thing (videlicet, NEITHER NOW, NOR EVER),
—I should have proceeded to analyse the next paragraph,
which is as follows:—" Upon this ground, if there were

---

* It is an undeniable fact that many clergymen withdrew their subscriptions, in consequence of the publication of these Letters in the journal in which they first appeared.

† A petition to this effect from 10,000 inhabitants of Liverpool and the neighbourhood was presented to Parliament in 1859.

‡ " There never was a period," says Bishop Stanley, " of our Church history with so little harmony within the pale, and so fearful a prospect of fiercer and wider dissensions."—*Life*, by A. P. Stanley, p. 83.

These remarks were made just forty years ago; and who shall say that the prospect of dissension within the Church is less apparent now? Will the time *ever* come when the rulers of the Church shall see that the way to calm these dissensions is not to shut the eye to the cause of them, but to probe it to the bottom, and remove for ever the root of the evil?

no other, it is of the utmost importance *at this moment*, when there is a tendency amongst *good men on the one side*—who think that this great inheritance received from our fathers may be perfected by striking out this, and putting in that, and modifying the other—it is of the utmost importance that we should take this ground, and say, that while the Book of Common Prayer is *no more perfect* than any *other work of man*, yet that to have it as a common ground, *with all its imperfections (!)*, is a boon so great, that we do not think it desirable to strive to remove any possible errors, at the great cost of losing it as the bond of unity between ourselves and our brethren."*

This sentence I was proceeding to dissect, and indeed had got so far as "the good men on *the one side*"—and I looked naturally, though in vain, for the good men (or at least men good or bad) on *the other side*. Having been educated in my early days under a most excellent schoolmaster (who made afterwards, by-the-bye, but a very indifferent bishop), the late Dr. Butler of Shrewsbury, one of my first lessons in Latin composition was something about a *protasis* and an *apodosis*; a lesson, no doubt, very valuable, as everything proceeding from the mouth of that eminent scholar was, as far as related to the laws which regulate the dead languages, and not less valuable to all living writers or speakers; and though I am afraid I have almost forgotten the rule, as I have too many of the instructions of that worthy man, yet the impression remains vivid upon my mind that every proposition which

---

* To the Bishop of Oxford's wordy rhetoric might be applied, by a slight parody, the lines of Horace (Od. IV. ii.)—
"Monte decurrens velut amnis, imbres
Quem super notas aluere ripas,
Fervet, inmensusque ruit profundo
Samuel ore.'

has a *first* dependent clause, should, in due course, have a *second* to correspond to it; or, in other words, if " good men" were brought forward " on *the one* side" of an argument, *something like* " good men" would, by the laws of grammar, be required on the other, to balance the equation. So I went back to the sentence, and read it carefully over and over again, as I should have done some thirty years ago a crabbed passage in Aristotle or Thucydides; but I again and again stuck at the " good men on the one side;" and, still floundering on in the dark, I

"Found no end in wandering mazes lost."

Well, thought I to myself, I must be very stupid to-day, so I will shut up the speech, and try my hand at it another time.

Just at this moment the letter-bag of the morning was put into my hands, containing a copy of the *Times of Friday, May 7th;* wherein, to my joy, I discovered that Lord Ebury's long-threatened motion had come off in the House of Lords the previous evening; thus effectually setting the matter of Liturgical Revision before the bar of PUBLIC OPINION.

That Lord Ebury's speech on the occasion was unanswerable I do not presume to say; but that it was *unanswered*, will, I venture to assert, be the judgment of ninety-nine out of every hundred sensible men who read what was said on both sides of the question in the House that night.* There the subject may, therefore, be safely allowed to rest for the present; and as I have already trespassed more than usual on the space you so

---

* The Speech was subsequently published, and rapidly passed through three editions.

liberally allow me, I will conclude with thanking you for the part you have taken in assisting to dissipate the vast amount of misapprehension and misstatement which has for years overlaid this important matter.

         Yours obediently,
May 10, 1858.   " INGOLDSBY."

LETTER XIV.

THE BISHOP OF OXFORD AGAIN.—NO. III.

"Ecce iterum Crispinus:—et est mihi sæpe vocandus
In partes."   JUVENAL.

WHAT, not done with the Bishop of Oxford yet? I thought you told us in your last, that Prime Ministers and other lay lords having come upon the stage, you meant to change your ground and sing a loftier strain. Well, so I did, and so I intended, and so I still intend. But it would be hardly fair upon you, Mr. Editor, who have for the last three months so courteously allotted me a very considerable portion of your independent journal—it would be hardly fair upon you (to say nothing of your readers, many of whom, you assure me, are pleased to take an interest in this controversy) were I to suddenly withdraw from the undertaking in which we have embarked, and which is, as yet, very far from being brought to a satisfactory conclusion.

Though, therefore, Lord Ebury has made an admirable speech upon the expediency of revising the Liturgy "at this present time;" and though he has been more or less supported by the Lords Grey, Granville, and Abinger; and though an English archbishop, and a Welsh and Irish bishop have replied to (not answered) his lordship; and though the Premier (Lord Derby) has thought fit to cast in his lot with the non-movement party,* I see no reason why I should make such an invidious distinction between the eleven prelates who expressed their opinions in "the House of Bishops" in February last, as to select only two of them for the purpose of review, leaving it to be inferred, as it possibly might be, that the remainder were considered either above or beneath criticism. The latter of these conclusions I should be sorry to give the remotest handle to, seeing the eminence of the individuals in question. The former assumption I should be still more unwilling to sanction, as tending to disparage the cause we have in hand, and which I trust is able to stand in its own strength against any amount of artillery that can be brought to bear upon it by the united brigade of the Bench of Bishops.

Concluding then, to-day, as I hope to do, with the Bishop of Oxford, I shall, in my next, proceed to make a few comments upon the speech of the third prelate who addressed their lordships on the 10th of February last—the right rev. and right learned the Bishop of St. David's (Thirlwall).

Recurring to the concluding paragraph of my last letter, I found myself, after all, obliged to give up that hard sentence in despair; and so, to waste no more time, we come next to "the great inheritance received from our fathers," which is the same thing as we have had *twice before* in this short speech, under the title of "a precious inheritance of truth," and "that inheritance great as it is."

Now, as I am not fond of tautology, I will not dwell upon this further than to make two passing observations. Can it be that this idea is so deeply impressed on the bishop's mind,† by studying Mr. Fisher's "Liturgical

---

* See Letter IX., p. 55.
† Curious that the same expression should be adopted by the Bishop of Salisbury in his Charge of August, 1858.

Purity, our Rightful Inheritance?" If so, is it not surprising that all that author's other arguments and conclusions are passed over so lightly in his lordship's speech as to leave no trace of his ever having read or seen the book?

Secondly, have we received no *other* "precious inheritance from our fathers," besides "the Prayer-book as it is?" If then our laws, our constitution, our liberties, our press, and other temporal institutions, are all equally "inherited," and have all been indefinitely improved during the last 200 years, is it so very unreasonable that we should seek further to embellish "the precious inheritance" of a book which professes to be our guide in things eternal?

But the bishop says we should *not* improve it, by "striking out this, and putting in that, and modifying the other;" and yet such I apprehend is the process, by which, at various periods, improvement of that book has been made or attempted before, "from Catholic times— from the earliest Catholic times." I can see, therefore, no reason why the same thing should not be done or attempted again, with an equal probability of improvement being the result; or at least an equal absence of any serious danger—especially as his lordship admits that "the Book of Common Prayer is no more perfect than any other work of man."

But then it appears to be "of the utmost importance" that we should consider this book, "*with all its imperfections*," as "a boon so great" that we are not to "think it desirable to strive to remove any possible errors at the great cost of losing it as the bond of unity between ourselves and our brethren."

Oh, for a memory to carry one back just eight-and-twenty years! How it would recall the image of a Prime

Minister, the hero of Waterloo, in all his glory hurled suddenly from the very pinnacle of power, because he could not conceive it possible to improve the British Parliament by enfranchising Birmingham and Manchester "*at the great cost of losing*" the venerable Gatton and Old Sarum!

FELIX QUEM FACIUNT ALIENA PERICULA CAUTUM.*

Methought that lesson would hardly so soon have lost its influence upon educated men, who had then reached, as I had, the mature age of one-and-twenty years; and the Bishop of Oxford is, I believe, but six years older than myself. Did not the support which "the united Bench of Bishops" then gave to the noble duke cost the right reverend prelates their wigs, and therewith no small portion of their prestige and dignity?† Were they not afraid to appear in public for some months, or to *vote at all* upon the second reading of THE BILL?

I am far from saying that the British public take up, or are likely to take up, the present question with the same determination that they did "the Bill, the whole Bill, and nothing but the Bill;" but I do say, and maintain, that it is at all times (especially in quiet ones) a perilous course to enter on, to refuse all INQUIRY into an ADMITTED EVIL, lest some imaginary mischief should ensue from the process. And I warn the right reverend prelates, in all the honesty of as sincere a well-wisher to the Church as any of their number, that so far from doing it a kindness by their over-solicitude for its welfare in this matter, they

---

* "Be warned in time by others' harm,
    And you shall do full well."
                        Ingoldsby Legends.

† "On this day (Feb. 22, 1832), following the example of almost all the bishops, left off my wig."—*Bishop Coplestone's Diary.* (*Life, &c.*, p. 151.)

are taking the surest course towards imperilling its very existence and their own.*

But the Bishop of Oxford, in his greater knowledge of the feelings of the people, is persuaded that "the vast mass of the less educated poor in England receive the English Prayer-book, next to the Bible, as God's special gift and blessing to them; and anything that might induce them to think you could alter this or that, or that one thing in it may be left out, and another thing may be put in, would shock their simple feelings of devotion, and do a mischief the extent of which no man can conceive."

What a picture of rural or episcopal simplicity is here! How many, I would ask, of "the less educated poor" in England—ay, or in Wales or Ireland, since a Welsh and Irish prelate have denounced the idea of *touching* the Prayer-book—how many of those, I would ask, can read that book at all; or, as they say in the calendar of Quarter Sessions, read it "perfectly or imperfectly?" How many are there to whom these simple lines of our sweetest bard do still, and may they ever, apply—

> "Their name, their years, *spelt* by the *unlettered* Muse,
> The place of fame and elegy supply;
> And many a holy text around she strews,
> That teach the rustic moralist to die?"

---

* Hear Bishop Stanley in his speech on Subscription, May, 1840:—"I am confident that the time will come when this alteration—this privilege —will be allowed and acquiesced in. It is for us, the heads of the clergy, to meet the difficulties of the case; for I am persuaded that if we do not, the time may come when, under other powers, under another pressure, *we may be forced to do that* which we may now do quietly, which it is now in our power to do voluntarily; and we may be compelled to adopt measures opposed to our feelings, and to which we should all object."

"Scilicet et tempus veniet"—

He being dead, yet speaketh;—shall he still speak to the deaf adder?

How many to whom the text of the sermon is the principal, if not the only thing, they carry away with them from the church? And well if they always do that. How many of the Lincolnshire, ay, or of the Oxfordshire bumpkins, in spite of the leavening influence of its renowned University, and not less renowned Theological College, are able to follow "the officiating minister," or to "find the places," as he leads them backwards and forwards through the intricate mazes of our present lengthy Morning Service? I am fully aware that there is much in the argument of OMNE IGNOTUM PRO MAGNIFICO. And it is quite possible that, as in "Catholic times—the earliest Catholic times," the sacrificing priest found no difficulty in persuading the ignorant and gaping multitude, *as he turned his back upon them*,* that he "verily and indeed" transmuted the material elements of bread and wine into the body and blood of Christ their Saviour; so now a well-tutored priest of the Cuddesdon school may possibly succeed, in some remote parts of the country, though not in the suburbs of our great metropolis, in making "the *less educated* poor" believe that there is something holy and mysterious in every syllable of their unintelligible Prayer-book; and that to attempt to meddle with the hallowed volume is an act of profanation paralleled only by touching the ark, and certain to bring down plague or destruction on the presumptuous head of him that attempts it.

But "I apprehend," says the *Bishop of Lincoln*, "that it is the intention, and it ought to be the duty of our Church, *not* to lower the tone of her devotion to the low pitch of her *weakest* members, but to keep them at a

---

* See proceedings at St. George's-in-the-East, November, 1859.—Letters LVIII., LXIV.

higher pitch, both in order to provide for her more faithful members provision for their souls' needs, and also, by God's help, to raise up others to the same standard."

Who shall decide when bishops disagree? The Bishop of Oxford is all for "the *less educated* poor;" the Bishop of Lincoln is for raising the pitch of Church membership to some imaginary standard of excellence, which I fear there is small prospect of "the less educated poor" in our day arriving at, by all the aids and appliances to be obtained from the most rigid adherence to the Rubric and the Canons of the Church.

For my own part, I must confess that I am so far from anticipating all the terrible consequences which are prefigured to the large organ of ideality of the Bishop of Oxford, from our "putting in this, and taking out that, and modifying t'other," that I should look for about as great a convulsion of nature to ensue in such a case as is usually witnessed when some rural clerk, bolder than common, ventures timidly on substituting the 33rd for the 34th chapter of Genesis on the Second Sunday in Lent, or forgets (accidentally, no doubt) to rehearse the Athanasian Creed instead of the Apostles', should the festival of St. Matthias fall on a Sunday.

The bishop's peroration is as follows:—

"Before we are called upon in another place to give a *decided vote* one way or another, we ought to consider whether we will endeavour to perfect the blessing which God has given us, at the risk of destroying these great advantages which it possesses, in virtue at once of its amount of truth and of our peaceful acceptance of it as a common inheritance; and it would be well that the Church should know that the *desire of the bishops of the Church at this time*, quite uninfluenced by their own peculiar views of truth, is to keep, as one of God's special gifts to us, UNTOUCHED and UNALTERED, our Book of Common Prayer." *

> "Such were the sounds that through the vaulted roof
> Of 'Anne's large chamber' scattered wild dismay:
> Stout Bangor stood aghast in speechless trance;
> 'To arms,' cried Exeter, and couched his quivering lance."

The Bishop of Oxford speaks as if in the name, and we presume with the sanction, of his right reverend brethren. His lordship also appears to be well acquainted with "their peculiar views of truth." Happily, the desired opportunity of giving "a decided vote in another place" was withheld from their lordships by Lord Ebury's withdrawing his motion until his unanswered and unanswerable speech should have had time to work upon the public mind. It is surprising, however, that, notwithstanding the serried phalanx of lawn sleeves which was arrayed over against his lordship on the 6th of May,† the great body of the bishops should have allowed it to be inferred by their silence that they acquiesced in the sentiments expressed by but three of their number.

The inevitable conclusion to be drawn from the speeches of those three is, that the Book of Common Prayer is to remain FOR EVER, as the Bishop of Oxford declares it shall, "untouched and unaltered;" a statute, not of 200 or 300 years old,‡ but as if enacted under Cyrus the

---

* From this moment may be dated the organised and united movement of all classes of Revisionists.

† "It was a most refreshing event to my heart, that when Lord Ebury moved for a Commission, the bishops *were present in great numbers*, and were *unanimous* in opposition to his motion."—*Charge by Walter Kerr Hamilton, Bishop of Salisbury*, August, 1858; p. 53.

‡ The laws of Solon were enacted to continue in force for one hundred years only; and quite enough too.

H

Mede, or Darius the Persian; a book to be handed down to the latest posterity,

"Through every unborn age and undiscovered clime,"

by millions and millions of copies, "with all its imperfections," to be defended, criticised, tolerated, excused, explained, evaded, accepted, or rejected, as the case may be, till time itself shall be no more.

If, as the *Times** expresses it, "*Superis ita visum;*" if bishops and High-Church peers are determined, at all hazards, to have "peace in their time;" if they are resolved, at any rate, to avoid a troublesome controversy, to which they do not feel themselves equal; if they have fully made up their minds to let things, bad enough already, get worse and worse, rather than run the risk of an imaginary religious revolution; then let the responsibility rest with themselves: we know their power, and cannot doubt of their will. Meanwhile, shall age after age increasingly proclaim that SOMETHING IS WANTING to the full efficiency of the Established Church. Then shall it appear more and more conspicuously that we have got ten thousand fairly endowed churches with but half congregations; bishops, priests, and deacons in plenty, but with a very inadequate following, compared to the cost at which they are maintained; generals, in short, in abundance, without an army; while we retain inviolate and inviolable "the precious inheritance" of a Book of Common Prayer, which, though 200 years old, no one dares to amend, no one pretends implicitly to obey, and which the Bishop of Oxford proclaims shall remain "untouched and unaltered" in his day.

If such a consummation is to be desired, so be it. That

---

* In a leader upon Lord Ebury's Speech, May 7th, 1858.

we are drawing towards it, no one, I think, can deny; and I much misread the signs of the times, and the warning voice of all history, if the resistance now offered by those in authority to the most temperate demand of Lord Ebury does not precipitate a " religious revolution " * more certainly, and render it tenfold more radical when it comes, than any present concession of a ROYAL COMMISSION of INQUIRY into the Book of Common Prayer could possibly have done.

I remain, yours obediently,

May 21, 1858. " INGOLDSBY."

LETTER XV.

THE BISHOP OF ST. DAVID'S, THE RIGHT REV. CONNOP THIRLWALL.—NO. I.

"As in a theatre, the eyes of men,
After a well-graced actor leaves the stage,
Are idly bent on him that enters next,
Thinking his prattle to be tedious;
Even so"——
SHAKESPEARE, *Rich. II.*, Act v., Sc. 2.

SIR,—I have often wondered how any human being could have the boldness to rise and address an assembly, whether of bishops or of ordinary individuals, after the Bishop of Oxford had just resumed his seat. How weary, flat, stale, and unprofitable must the arguments of the most accomplished orator of modern times fall on the ear, saturated to overflowing with the torrent of eloquence, a sample of which has been so recently furnished for our admiration.

Yet, so it is; mortals, as I have said before, are still

---

* See Letter of Rev. Charles Girdlestone to the Dean of Westminster (Trench), quoted at Letter XII., p. 78.

found to rush in where angels fear to tread; and as the Bishop of St. David's shrinks not from occupying this unenviable position, my fate, unhappily, is to be dragged along with him into the same predicament. Should, therefore, the ensuing criticisms read to any one somewhat dry and vapid after the effervescence of the previous pages, I trust he will make due allowance for the remarkable difference in the style of the present, compared with that of the last speaker.

A skilful reviewer, according to the poet—

"Reddere personæ scit convenientia cuique;"

and though I am far from arrogating to myself the above honourable title, yet I should be deficient in the very first qualification for my present undertaking, did I not recognise the wide dissimilarity between the ground I am now about to tread, and that on which my small artillery has been hitherto engaged.

Few men, perhaps none on the bench, have a higher claim to our attention than the present Bishop of St. David's.* His antecedents, as they are popularly called, are of the first class. He is, therefore, entitled to speak on any subject to which he may direct his mind, with a degree of authority to which not every one of his right reverend brethren can offer an equal pretension. He is known, both at home and abroad, as "a scholar, and a ripe and good one." He is versed in most of the modern, as well as the dead, languages; and has the rare praise of having made it his business to acquire, late in life, even the Welsh tongue, in order to qualify himself for

---

* Dr. Connop Thirlwall, some time Fellow and Tutor of Trinity College, Cambridge; appointed Bishop of St. David's in 1840, resigned 1874. Died July 27, 1875. R. I. P.

fulfilling the duties of his position in the Principality. He is generally allowed to be a sound and deep divine.* His Charges bear the impress of a liberal and thoughtful mind; and would lead the reader to conclude that he is not attached to either of the extreme parties which divide and harass the Church.

With these recommendations as an arbiter in a case of acknowledged difficulty, had the Bishop of St. David's pronounced firmly and decisively on one side or the other in this controversy, we should have felt almost constrained to follow his lead, and say at once, *Cadit quæstio:* the oracle has spoken—the die is cast—*conclamatum est:* such will be the verdict which PUBLIC OPINION, to which we have all along professed to bow, will ultimately pass upon this matter.

But, unfortunately, for some inexplicable cause or other, we have here the Bishop of St. David's at issue with himself. We have a Court of Appeal giving what sound to us conflicting decisions: a *Janus bifrons*, uttering war and peace from each of his mouths at once; smiling and frowning with his ambi-visage on friend and foe alike; a moral phenomenon, to which all the learned prelate's classic lore can find no parallel. He outdoes, in this instance, even Proteus himself, who, with all his skill, never offered, as far as we have read, to be fire and water, lion and lamb, Liturgical Reformer and Anti-reformer, at one and the same time. As, however, I cannot pretend to keep pace with his lordship here, I shall, to-day, exhibit him simply in the former capacity: begging my readers to bear in mind that the second and third acts of our drama are not (as usual) supposed to follow *consecutively,*

---

* This position, however, was disputed by the Rev. Dr. Williams, late Vice-Principal of Lampeter, perhaps not without reason.

but must be understood as proceeding simultaneously, or as nearly so as may be, with the first.

I do not, of course, presume to charge his lordship with designed inconsistency. I am sure also that the public will acquit him, as I do, of any intentional duplicity. But it is impossible to deny that we have, in what follows, a trumpet giving a most uncertain sound in the war of Liturgical Revision. And one can hardly help feeling that the bishop himself betrays a kind of uneasiness in attempting to occupy the *via media* on this occasion. One detects throughout his speech a sort of consciousness that it requires a steady hand and clear head to reconcile what he has said in his address before Convocation, and in the House of Lords upon Lord Ebury's motion, with what he may have spoken, written, or published elsewhere. Otherwise what need for proclaiming, as his lordship does more than once, that he "does not recede in the slightest degree from any opinion he may have ever expressed upon this subject?" *Qui s'excuse, s'accuse*, says the proverb. No one had accused his lordship of contradicting himself. But it has a tendency to cast a *primâ facie* suspicion upon the sincerity of a speaker, when he finds it needful to preface thus:—"Observe, gentlemen, this is what I have *always* said; I am not in the habit of blowing hot and cold. I have all along maintained that the Liturgical Revisors are right—and that they are wrong."

"There are no tricks in plain and simple faith:"

an Aye or a No is easily said; and there is no mistake about them. But when once men come to splitting hairs; to "letting I dare not wait upon I would;" to sailing N. by N.E. or S. by S.W., one hardly knows where to have them; they are here to-day, and gone to-morrow. And such, I fear, is the judgment which the public, clear-sighted in the main, will be disposed to pass upon the evidence we shall shortly have to produce. Each party will for the moment think to claim the right reverend prelate as his own, and will prepare to rejoice and make merry accordingly. When, hey presto! the bird is flown; the aqueous god has dissolved into his native element; he has vanished into thin air; the chameleon has changed its colour; *elapsa est anguilla;* the animal has quietly slid away while the council of cooks are in warm debate as to whether they should serve him up fried or stewed.*

In what follows we shall deal with the Bishop of St. David's in his three-fold capacity: as bishop in "the House of Bishops;" bishop on the Bench of Bishops; and lastly (though not there least well placed), bishop in the bishop's chair of his diocese in Wales.

The unravelling this three-fold cord will necessarily involve a little difficulty, and require some patience on the part of my readers.† But I will endeavour to thread my way through the labyrinth as carefully as I can; and will, at least, undertake to set nothing down to his lordship's credit but what I find attributed to him as written or spoken at one time or another in connexion with our present subject.

It is not necessary to carry our inquiry further back than the year 1845, when the Bishop of St. David's delivered the second of his many able charges—the one referred to by Lord Ebury in the House of Lords; a Charge which, his lordship justly remarked, derives additional importance from the confirmation it receives from the bishop's δεύτεραι φροντίδες in the autumn of last year.

---

* The Bishop subsequently designated the above remarks as "coarse insinuation and misplaced ridicule;" but he has failed to show that the imputation was not justified by the premises. See Charge by Bishop of St. David's, October, 1860; p. 46.

† See Letters XXVII., XLV., CVI.

The paragraph quoted by Lord Ebury occurs at page 24 of this Charge; but, as many of your readers will not have seen that document, or even the report of the debate of May 6th, I will give the passage at length.

"We are not bound," says the bishop in the bishop's chair, "to shut our eyes to the *need that exists* for a revision of the Liturgy, because it is our duty, *for the present, patiently* to submit to the want of it."

This was in 1845; so the bishop's patience, and the patience of the Liturgical Reformers, which I fear is not quite so exemplary, has been exercised *thirteen years*,* and the cry is still "*for the present* we must patiently submit." Such at least is the inevitable inference, should the voice of the bishops prevail on the present occasion.

The Bishop of St. David's proceeds:—

"We must suspect that the persons who have resisted *all attempts* at change, on the plea that our Liturgy is absolutely perfect, are, *if sincere*, VERY UNENLIGHTENED AND INJUDICIOUS FRIENDS OF THE CHURCH."

I might here rest my case. The force of language can no further go. The "Ingoldsby Letters" have said nothing more severe and cutting than this. But it is due to his lordship to continue the extract a little further:—

"Nor is it true, as has been ignorantly or insidiously alleged, that the clergy have set up any such extravagant pretensions in its behalf. On the contrary, that large body of them, including *a great majority of the whole*, who, about eleven years ago, thought proper to make a solemn joint declaration of their devoted adherence to the doctrine

---

* Now upwards of *thirty* years, and the word is still "not at the present time." See Letter x. Precisely the same argument was made use of by Bishop Blomfield, in a Letter to Archdeacon Lyall, November, 1833. See his Life by his Son, vol. i., chap. vii., p. 190.

and polity of the Church, and their deep-rooted attachment to her Liturgy, earnestly deprecating rash innovation in spiritual matters, nevertheless in the same document disclosed their consciousness that, from the *lapse of years* or *altered circumstances,* some things pertaining to such matters *might require renewal or correction.*"

Why, here is the whole question at issue. It is a plain *concessio principii.* What more have Lord Ebury's petitioners required or demanded? What a pity the Bishop of Lincoln had not heard of this document signed by the "great majority of the clergy" a quarter of a century ago! But *humanum est errare.* Other people besides the House of Commons will occasionally act "hastily,"* and be not "well informed" upon every subject. These clergy —and this, observe, was about the year 1832 or '33, under the pressure of "the Bill, the whole Bill, and nothing but the Bill," when the Bishop of Lincoln and I were reading hard for our degrees—this large body of the clergy, it appears, "expressed their willingness to co-operate with the rulers of the Church in *carrying into effect any measures to supply that want,* should it appear to exist."

Why, then, was not the thing done? Why, at least, was not an inquiry instituted? Were the rulers or the ruled at fault on that occasion? or were the latter lulled to sleep by the potent sop thrown out to them by the former, that it was not expedient to make the attempt "*at the then present time?*" Into this question the Bishop of St. David's declines to enter.† But his lordship proceeds to make a few just observations on the conduct of that numerous body of petitioners, or remonstrants, or whatever they were called. These remarks I must, how-

---

* See Letter x., p. 62.
† So also the Bishop's Charge of 1860. Rivingtons, London.

ever, reserve for my next, having already trespassed greatly on your columns, which I rejoice to see want not my aid to fill the space you usually allot to the interesting question of Liturgical Reform.

I am, Sir, yours obediently,

May 27, 1858.   " INGOLDSBY."

LETTER XVI.*

CHURCH PATRONAGE; THE DEANERY OF YORK.

> "A canon! that's a place too mean:
> No, Doctor; you shall be a Dean.
> Two dozen canons round your stall,
> And you the tyrant of them all."—SWIFT.

SIR,—It will not be inappropriate to our present subject if you allow me for once to interrupt the even

---

* In allowing this Letter to re-appear in the present edition, the author begs most emphatically to declare that he does so on public grounds alone. He has not the smallest personal knowledge, directly or indirectly, of the individual referred to, whose appointment gave rise to much newspaper correspondence at the time. The temporary feeling is, of course, long since allayed; but the *principle* remains, and is deserving of grave consideration, as involving no less than the whole question of scholastic and academical emulation, so far as the clerical profession is concerned.

If amiability of character, personal respectability, and ample pecuniary means, are legitimate grounds for promotion to the few remaining prizes in the Church, away with all motive for exertion, little enough already, but on this principle utterly annihilated! The days of England's greatness as a nation would have long since passed away had such a rule prevailed in the high appointments in the Law, the Army, or the Navy. Under the shelter of examples like that denounced by Mr. Ewart in the House of Commons in 1858, every private patron and every Bishop on the Bench might with equal plausibility defend nepotism of the most glaring magnitude, in defiance of all higher claims for advancement in the Church.

tenor of these Letters, in order to comment upon the following extract from the *Times* of Friday, May 28th:—

"DEANERY OF YORK.

"*To the Editor of the Times.*

"SIR,—I join with 'A Yorkshire Curate' in holding up to public indignation the appointment of the Hon. and Rev. Augustus Duncombe to the Deanery of York.

"This gentleman has held no clerical office of any description for upwards of fifteen years. He had previously held the family rectory of Kirby-Misperton, of the yearly value of £1,000. In 1841 he succeeded to a fortune of which the annual income is believed to be upwards of £8,000, and for the last ten or twelve years he has resided on his own estate in Derbyshire.

"Now, if this piece of preferment had fallen to the gift of Lord Palmerston, and if he had conferred it on a Howard or a Dundas, the appointment would have been scouted as a Whig job of Lord Carlisle or Lord Zetland.

"As it is, the appointment of Mr. Duncombe can only be considered a Tory job* of Lord Feversham.—Your obedient servant, "A YORKSHIRE LAYMAN.

"*May* 26, 1858."

Whether the Premier acted in this case, as in his recent opposition to Lord Ebury's motion, under the advice of the most reverend and right reverend prelates, I will not stop to inquire. But certainly, if the act originated with himself, it would be difficult to conceive how any Commission of Inquiry into the Prayer-book

---

* Exactly a similar offence was perpetrated by the same Minister, Lord Derby, April 1, 1867, in the appointment of the Hon. and Rev. George Herbert to the Deanery of Hereford.

could have done the Establishment more harm—"*for the welfare of which*" Lord Derby was fain to admit "the noble mover's desire was *earnest and undoubted*"—than the principle involved in such an appointment as the one here referred to.

Let it be borne in mind that the so-called Tory party have, with slight intermission, been out of office for many years, and that it is fair to presume there must be, in the ranks of the noble earl's adherents during the period of his adversity, some hundreds of clerical aspirants to high office, of talent and distinction and long service in their profession, who might reasonably have expected to see this first conspicuous vacancy filled by one of their number, and who would have looked upon the favoured individual without envy and without regret—nay, rather with (perhaps qualified) joy that the Church had received such an accession to her strength.

Moreover, it must not be forgotten, that by the operation of the Ecclesiastical Commission—in which, if I am not mistaken, as well as in the confiscation of half the Irish bishoprics, the present Premier had some hand—the "prizes" of the Church have been enormously reduced both in value and number. I am old enough, too, to remember how it was urged, with great plausibility, by the Church Reformers of that day (about 1835-7), that by diminishing the *number* of Church dignitaries there would no longer be room left for jobbing, either through family or political connexions; that *professional eminence* and merit would thenceforth become the sole passports to high ecclesiastical preferment, and that, *in proportion as the dignitaries were few in number, their qualifications would be more closely and narrowly scanned.*

All this sounded very well; and many an honest Church Reformer was caught in the trap, and lent his hand to carrying out the very questionable machinery of the "Ecclesiastical Commission;"* rejoicing that at any rate they had seen the last of bishops' sons and sons-in-law made canons and archdeacons, for no other reason than because they *were* bishops' sons and sons-in-law, and that the Percevals, Liverpools, and Eldons were about for ever to make way for conscientious Prime Ministers and self-denying Lord Chancellors, who would no longer barter the high and sacred appointments in the Church for the base meed of political support, but bestow them as the rewards of merit on the most deserving.

"O vanas hominum mentes. O pectora cœca!"

What a golden age in prospect for the Church militant here on earth had this vision been realised!†

Now turn we to the *Clerical Directory* for 1858—that Army and Navy List of our profession, which shows, or professes to show, the pretensions of its several members to advancement in their order; supposing merit, or length and laboriousness of previous service, or, in fact, *desert of any kind*, to have anything to do now or in future with promotion in the Church.

Under the head of the D's, we find—

---

* Mr. Henry Seymour, M.P. for Poole, succeeded in obtaining a Parliamentary Committee of Inquiry into the misdoings of this body; 1862. See "Notes" by Ecclesiasticus; Ridgway, 1863.

† Hear the sentiments of a Layman on this subject. "It must be evident to the most superficial observer of passing events that a time is rapidly approaching when all appointments, whether in Church or State, are likely to be made upon a principle of selection altogether different from that which has hitherto prevailed, and that, in the department of ecclesiastical labour more especially, none will be suffered to attain the first rank of whom it cannot be said that in all the higher branches of secular acquirement—in literature, science, knowledge of the world, and, above all, in practical acquaintance with the business affairs of life—they are in every respect upon a par with the more advanced intelligence of the age."—*Fisher's Liturgical Purity*, p. 662.

DUNCOMBE, *Honble.* AUGUSTUS, Worc. Coll., Oxon. B.A. 1836; M.A. 1850; Deac. 1837; Pr. 1838; Preb. of Bole in York Cathl. 1841."

Comment is superfluous. Yorkshiremen will henceforth duly appreciate the antecedents of their dean.*

Behold, ye anti-revisionists,—behold the new-born zeal for the Church evinced by your ally, the Prime Minister of England! Rejoice, and be exceeding glad, ye Church dignitaries that have trembled for the last three months under the dread of Lord Ebury's Commission of Inquiry! Rely upon it no COMMISSION OF INQUIRY will receive the sanction of one who can recognise as a sufficient qualification for one of the highest offices in the Church the having already an income of £8,000 per annum, and the having " retired from business" fifteen years ago.

---

* The following is from the *Times*' report of the proceedings in the House of Commons on Friday, June 4th, 1858:—

"THE DEAN OF YORK.

"Mr. W. Ewart, in asking the Chancellor of the Exchequer for what special reasons the recent appointment had been made to the Deanery of York, declared that he was not influenced by any other motive than the interests of the Church, and, through that, of the country. The Church Commisioners, in their report of 1836, said—

"'The advantages resulting to the interests of religion from the existence of this species of preferment, when conferred on clergymen *distinguished for professional merit*, are too obvious to require illustration.'"
And in 1852 that—

"'In considering the employment of deans and canons we are of opinion that it is one distinct purpose of cathedral institutions to make provision for *the cultivation and encouragement of theological learning.*' He thought it rested with the Government to show that they had made the appointment in question in conformity with those recommendations."

The reply of the Chancellor of the Exchequer (Mr. Disraeli) was a complete justification of all that the late Sydney Smith has written of the Ecclesiastical Commission of 1836, but a very insufficient one of the appointment in question; and even this reply, insufficient as it was, has been wholly stultified by the subsequent *doubling of the salary* to the present dean by the Ecclesiastical Commissioners.

Happy, thrice happy, York Minster! destined, for another generation, to drag along your weary chain of the lengthened Morning Service; to witness your desolate stalls occupied by some half-dozen gazers for six days in the week;* your officials dozing, and your choristers playing tricks,† during the Wednesday and Friday intonation of the Litany; and all this because the Premier finds himself supported in rejecting Lord Ebury's proposition by "almost the whole of the episcopal bench, which is not an unimportant consideration in a question of this sort;" while the Bishop of Oxford declares, with oracular authority, that the Prayer-book shall remain UNTOUCHED and UNALTERED in his day.

Turn we from this melancholy picture—this nineteenth-century illustration of *quieta non movere*—turn we with shame from this "to-him-that-hath-shall-be-given" system of bestowing the honours and prizes of the Church, to another not unimportant sign of the times, suggested by a double advertisement which met my eye in the papers the same day on which the above pungent letter appeared in the *Times*.

I find the two following tracts advertised side by side:—

SPEECH OF LORD EBURY in the HOUSE OF LORDS,
May 6th, on Revision of the Liturgy.

PROGRESSIONIST CHURCH TRACTS.
No. I.—On Liturgical Revision.

---

* That this is still the case with too many of our highly endowed Cathedrals cannot be denied by the stoutest admirer of those stately, but, I fear, somewhat useless edifices.

† The writer was eye-witness to this in the summer of 1857. It is but justice to the present occupant of the Dean's seat to add that such scenes no longer occur, and that other important reforms have been effected. Still the *principle* remains unaffected; the same reforms in the Cathedral would, in these days, have been forced upon *any man* by public opinion, while previous claims might at the same time have been duly recognised.

I don't say that the letter on the Deanery of York and the above advertisements have any necessary connexion with one another; they bear, on the contrary, sufficient internal evidence that they have not the smallest relationship to each other; and yet, methinks, the conjunction on this occasion has a not insignificant bearing on the present position of the Church for weal or woe.

Mark the consequences of the bishops' and the Premier's opposition to the "People's call for a Revision of the Prayer-book." Behold the first-fruits of this piece of Conservatism, in the appearance of No. 1. (followed closely by Nos. II., III., and IV.) of a series of "PROGRESSIONIST CHURCH TRACTS,"* which would never, probably, have been heard of, but for the resistance offered to Lord Ebury's motion in the House of Lords, and which cannot but have their influence upon the well or ill being of the Church.

Do I hear some one say, True, these tracts may influence the Church indeed; but will it be for good or for evil? my answer is, I know not; I pretend not to know; I am wholly innocent of their origin, and was only made aware of their existence by receiving No. I. through the post, from an unknown hand, and by subsequently noticing the above advertisement in the paper. But *if for evil*, I charge with the sin, not the author of these tracts, but the determined Oppositionists to *any* revision of the Prayer-book, who have thus called them into existence. It was not my Lords Grey and Russell who accomplished

---

* These were followed by twelve more under the auspices of the Liberation Society. London: H. J. Tresidder, Ave Maria Lane; 1862.

Probably nothing has contributed so much to forward the views of this last-named body as the determined resistance of the bishops to admit of any alteration in the "twin curses of the Church of England, RUBRIC and ROUTINE."

the Reform Bill of 1831-32. The real fathers of that measure, for weal or for woe, were Peel and Wellington and their episcopal and Conservative supporters. And so it is now with the "Progressionist Church Tracts" and whatever they may lead to. The real authors of any ill consequences which may ensue therefrom are my Lords Derby and "almost the whole of the episcopal bench."

I have before said, but I will say it again, at the risk of being charged with "vain repetitions," to which I have a deep-rooted aversion—differing in this respect, as I fear in most others, from the Bishop of Oxford—

OMNIA DAT, QUI JUSTA NEGAT.*

And the rejection, the summary rejection, of Lord Ebury's motion by the Powers that be, bids fair, ere long, to add a remarkable illustration to this well-known and pregnant saying.

His lordship's speech is now published, in a corrected form, under his own hand; and will take its place, probably after passing through several editions (the third, I understand, is already announced), among the permanent literature of the Revisionists, to form a powerful basis for future operations—a lever by which, most assuredly, sooner or later, in spite of all opposition from prelates or premiers, Liturgical Reform WILL BE CARRIED, and become part and parcel of the law of the land.

It is to be regretted that the speeches of the most reverend and right reverend prelates in reply, and that of the Premier, feebly, and, as it were, in a voice not his own, echoing their lordships' fears, are not printed side by side with Lord Ebury's pithy and closely-argued oration. The reformers might then say, with pride, Look on this picture and on that. On the one hand—facts, arguments, proofs;

---

* Letter XII., p. 79.

on the other—fears, misgivings, possible contingencies. The most ardent advocate for Liturgical Reform could not desire a better method for securing his long-deferred hopes.

Then look at the Tracts. Read the title alone. *Dictum sapienti*, I have heard said. And here are three words speaking volumes to the wise, or even the "unwise among the people."

PROGRESSIONIST CHURCH TRACTS.

What a tale does it unfold! What a vision of unborn ages crowd upon one's soul as one listens to the words! Progress of any kind is abomination to some people. But Church progression!—who ever heard of progress in the Church?—Why, it is a contradiction in terms. Perish the idea, and the author together. Refuse him salt and fire, earth and water. Let him be *anathema, maranatha,* to every true-born Conservative Churchman.

But who is at the bottom of all this?—

"Nay, never shake thy gory locks at me! *
Thou canst not say I did it."

You cannot charge Lord Ebury's supporters, in or out of Parliament, with this sin. We charge, and we do it deliberately, Lord Ebury's *opponents* with being the direct or indirect promoters of this impending revolution in the Church. What says his lordship in his memorable Speech of May 6th?—" I have just finished thirty-six years of Parliamentary life, in which I have not been an inattentive observer; and I can most sincerely declare that I have never known a single instance where the *granting of inquiry*

---

* The author of the Ingoldsby Letters was called by the *English Churchman* "the Arch-Agitator of Liturgical Reform," and by the *John Bull* "The *notorious* Prayer-Book Revisionist." The Bishop of Oxford also was understood as hinting as much at the close of his Reply to Lord Ebury in the House of Lords, May 8, 1860. See end of Letter xcvi.

by a fair tribunal has done otherwise than mitigate the mutual asperity of those whose difference of opinion caused the investigation to be set on foot."

CEDE REPUGNANTI, CEDENDO VICTOR ABIBIS.

It needed no ghost, my lord, to tell us that. But there are some minds which will never learn a lesson of wisdom till it comes too late to be of any use. When, on the other hand, people meet with obstinate resistance to a reasonable demand; when their cause appears utterly hopeless so long as they meekly contend under the olive-branch and the myrtle; is it to be wondered at that they unsheath the sword, and fling the scabbard away? It was not till the *Guardian* proclaimed that "Lord Ebury's motion had vanished in smoke," and the *Clerical Journal* advertised its too credulous readers that "they had heard the last of Liturgical Revision for some time to come," that No. 1. of the Progressionist Tracts made its appearance; to be followed, I have little doubt, by others in rapid succession,* till they have at length, by the force of public opinion alone, stormed the feather-bed breastwork of red-tapism in the Church, and opened the way for that freedom under which alone it can permanently and extensively flourish.†

> "Sic ego torrentem, qua nil obstabat cunti,
> Lenius et modico strepitu decurrere vidi:
> At quacunque trabes, objectaque saxa tenebant,
> Spumeus et fervens, et ab objice sævior ibat."

---

* The number of Tracts bearing on Revision that were published within the next five years amounted to near a hundred, and have been continually accumulating ever since, indicating surely a deep sense of *something needed*, though bishops and prime ministers choose to turn a deaf ear to the call.

† In a debate on the subject in the House of Lords the Bishop of London (Tait) said that "his only idea of a National Church was, that it should be rooted in the affections of the people." Feb., 1860.

The pent-up waters, which should have gently irrigated the meadow, have forced their way through the feeble barrier that would stay them. The compressed steam that might have been advantageously directed to some useful end, has burst its iron bonds, and scattered the fragments of its prison-house far and wide into the air; and who shall offer to confine it again?

I see, however, in all this no real cause for alarm. Say, rather, it may be, cause for thankfulness and congratulation to the Church.

> "There is a providence that shapes our ends,
> Rough-hew them how we will;"

and methinks I discern here the agency of a higher power than man's.* No one can deny that there is—that there has long been—SOMETHING WANTING to the full efficiency of the Church system in this country. The efforts of the Tractarians, who first saw and deplored the want, have miserably failed (as the result has shown) to supply the deficiency.

And if the refusal to grant Lord Ebury's modest petition for a Commission of Inquiry into the Prayer-book should lead eventually to the demanding and obtaining something more radical—and possibly, therefore, more advantageous to the Church—no one will more sincerely rejoice at the temporary (for temporary it is and will be) rejection of his lordship's motion than your obliged correspondent,

June 4, 1858. "INGOLDSBY."

---

* "Heaven hath a hand in these events,
To whose high will we bound our calm contents."
SHAKSP., *Rich.* II.

LETTER XVII.*

ANONYMOUS LETTER-WRITING.

"Ardet atrox Volscens, nec teli conspicit usquam
Auctorem." VIRGIL.

SIR,—I am afraid, if I am to run after every ball that is flung at my head, I shall never get to the end of the race on which I have set out. Nevertheless, there are one or two points in the assault made upon me by your correspondent " C. W. T.," whose edge it is expedient I should put aside, or some of my friends may be under serious apprehension for my bodily welfare or peace of mind. The consequence will be, that in addition to my voluminous correspondence on the subject of Liturgical Revision, I shall be deluged with letters of sympathy, condolence, inquiry, indignation, advice, and so forth, which will be quite annoying. I seldom take advice; and I hate to be pitied. I cannot endure it; I never could. It implies a species of mental imbecility that my proud spirit revolts from. I had rather die a hundred deaths, than be pitied for having to die once. So, in the hope of arresting this flood of good nature, which will be utterly thrown away, I wish my friends to regard this epistle as a circular reply to all their kind intentions, and to give themselves no further trouble on this score, either on the present or any future occasion which may arise connected with my perilous adventure.

The only real grievance I feel is, that my antagonist is *anonymous*. I am afraid of no man, not even of a real

---

* This Letter and the XIXth were provoked by torrents of abuse levelled at the Author by *anonymous* writers in two or three Clerical Newspapers of the time.

bishop—a bishop-suffragan or an ex-colonial would alarm few people—with his staff of chaplains, secretaries, archdeacons, and rural deans. But who can fight with a shadow? The coat of darkness proved too much for the lusty giant Blunderbore; and it was in vain he flung about him with his tremendous club, while Master Jack was sneaking all the while in a corner under the bed.*

"Why, you are anonymous yourself," retorts my invisible foe.—Ah! have I you there, my friend? I hear you, though I see you not; but, with all courtesy, I deny the fact. I am *not* anonymous; and I detest the whole system.† All the world knows who "Ingoldsby" is; that is to say, all Liturgical Reformers and Anti-Reformers, which is the same thing. Concealment neither did, nor does, form any part of my plan. I adopted this name advisedly instead of my own, as being more in unison with the light and somewhat satirical‡ tone of these letters, which unfortunately give such offence to "C. W. T.," but in which others, I am told, find considerable entertainment, if not instruction. But who ever heard of "C. W. T.?" He may be a Puseyite priest, or a Methodist parson. C. T. *alone* might have stood for Connop Thirlwall, my remarks upon whom seem to have elicited this cutting rebuke, which was withheld so long as I was engaged with the Bishops of Lincoln and Oxford. But then the W. throws one out, unless it be put in as a blind. Or the initials may stand for the *next* bishop on the list; who,

---

* The above remarks are equally applicable to a sharp newspaper war, carried on against me in 1867, when I stood, *on independent grounds*, a contest for the Proctorship of the diocese of Lincoln.

† See the remarks of Bishop Stanley on anonymous letter-writing in his primary Charge to his clergy, July, 1838. It is not to the credit of the Anti-revisionists that *almost the whole* of their correspondence in the papers has been conducted under the shelter of assumed signatures.

‡ Such is the well-known character of the "Ingoldsby *Legends*," by the Rev. Charles Barham.

standing by, and seeing the manner in which his three right reverend brethren have been handled before him, begins to wince before he is hurt.

"Nam tua res agitur paries cum proximus ardet.
Et sibi quisque timet, quanquam est intactus, et odit."

This shows the extreme unfairness of all anonymous writing, when the letters descend to personalities. As long as they deal in generals, there is no more to be said against them than against a leading article or a review, which are allowed the freedom of criticism on the responsibility of the editor. But, my dear unknown friend, you have no occasion to be alarmed. I have no intention whatever of hurting you or your master, supposing you to be only the chaplain. I am as gentle and playful as a lamb, as all my friends will tell you. And I am convinced that nothing that I have written, shall write, or can write, will injure the right reverend prelates in the slightest degree, if you will but leave them to fight their own battles, or rather to receive my shafts as they have hitherto done in their impenetrable woolsack of dignified reserve.*

I have no wish to be severe. My object is, and has been throughout, "the truth," which the Bishop of Oxford lays such stress upon—the whole truth, and nothing but the truth. And if you are a scholar, which I have no means of ascertaining, except from the internal evidence supplied by your letter, which shows that "*paulo majora*" is not Greek to you: if, I say, you are a scholar, I ask you

"—— Ridentem dicere verum
Quid vetat?"

Why may not my argument be carried on as well with a

---

* A remarkable exception to this general rule was furnished by the Bishop of St. David's in his Charge of November, 1860, p. 46. Rivingtons.

smiling as a frowning face? It is true a man *may* "smile, and smile, and smile, and be a villain;" as said Lord Derby on a memorable occasion to, or of, a certain right reverend prelate.* But I hope every man who smiles is not to be so set down. I would live, if I could, under the sunbeam of a perpetual smile. I once knew at Cambridge a conspicuous doctor of laws† who was never seen without a smile on his countenance, and it was quite refreshing to look upon him: he was like Bacchus, ever fair and young, though in his sixtieth year. Lord Palmerston too, they tell me, and Lord Lyttelton, have always a smile on their face: who ever thinks the worse of them for that? How very cruel of "C. W. T." to seek to rob me of so innocent a gratification! It is the unkindest cut of all I have received. "But," says my opponent, "to make a joke of things serious is not so innocent as I imagine." The "effervescence of those previous critiques" was calculated to do an infinity of mischief, both to the bishops and to the cause I profess to advocate.

My friends in general, I believe, are of a different opinion, and are content to leave me to judge what is most likely to serve our common cause.‡ But as for the bishops, if "C. W. T." thinks they can be injured by attacks like these, he must have a much lower opinion of their lordships' position than I have. The notion reminds one of H. B.'s caricature of the redoubtable Lord John firing off his sixpenny cannon at the Duke of Wellington. The idea of the whole bench of bishops being held up to ridicule by a single country

---

* The Bishop of Oxford, Samuel Wilberforce.
† Professor Geldart of Trinity Hall.
‡ "Take my word for it," says Salmagundi, "a little well-placed ridicule, like Hannibal's application of vinegar to rocks, will do more with certain hard heads and obdurate hearts than all the logic and demonstration of Longinus or Euclid." Certain it is, that till the *argumentum a ridiculo* was brought to bear on the question it was in a state of utter stagnation.

parson is too absurd. Why, I should have been a bishop myself long ere this, or Dean of York at any rate, had I possessed a tithe of that sledge-hammer power which "C. W. T." assigns to me.

"Sed tamen amoto quæramus seria ludo."

Let us endeavour to be grave, and treat this matter as "C. W. T." would have us to do, "in a style more in tune with the subject." He is evidently one of those saturnine individuals who cannot bear a joke; so I will try him with "solid arguments," which I hope will convince him as easily as he thinks they would "the bishops, the clergy, and the people."

Does he wish to see Liturgical Reform carried, or not? One would suppose he does, from more than one passage in his letter; and for this I respect him. But when he says, "The advocates of a reform of the Prayer-book have no need of any but SOLID ARGUMENTS to convince bishops, clergy, and people that they are right in the object they have at heart," I must take leave to differ from him *toto cœlo*. Dear man! I wonder how long ago he took his degree, or whether he is yet *in statu pupillari?* Was he born in Wales, or in Ireland? Where has he lived all his life? Has he ears and eyes? He would be worth something for a show; like a real Protectionist, or a *bonâ fide* Tory, before they were "educated" by Mr. Disraeli.

Do you know, Mr. Editor, I begin to suspect that this letter is a hoax after all; a trick of some Liturgical Reformer in disguise, devised on purpose to draw me out.

What, I should like to know, is Lord Ebury's speech of May 6th, but a tissue of "solid arguments" from beginning to end?—and what the result? Why, that his modest proposition was resisted by the Premier, backed by a dense phalanx of Conservative Peers, and, as Lord

Derby himself tells us, by "*almost the whole of the episcopal bench,*"* "which," he sarcastically added, "is not an unimportant consideration on a question of this sort."

So much for "solid arguments," as far as the bishops are concerned.

And now for the "clergy and the people." Have not they been assailed with solid arguments for the last quarter of a century, till their stomach rises at the sight of such indigestible food? It is like the boiled beef in the Knightsbridge barracks;† they sigh for the garlic of Egypt, a little allspice, something piquant and pungent, curry-powder, cayenne, and the like.

Have not all the writers on Liturgical Reform from 1834 to 1858 plied them with "solid arguments," thick and hard, and cold as hailstones? Riland with an i, and Ryland with a y; Powys, Hon. and Rev.; and Powys, Rev. but not Hon.; Archdeacon Berens, now in his eighty-third year, and "holding the same sentiments with failing eyesight," which he published to the world above thirty years ago;‡ Tyndale the same, in his eightieth year; Hull, Gell, and Nihill, in their seventieth;§ Girdlestone, Wodehouse, Oxenden, Pellew, Davis, Milne, Bingham, Mountfield, Trail, Venables, Taylor, Dayman, Carr Glyn, Lester, Nevile,‖ and last, not least, the learned barrister in the North, Mr. J. C. Fisher;—have not all of these, in their several ways, and

---

* See Charge to the diocese of Salisbury, by Walter Kerr Hamilton, D.D., August, 1858, p. 53, quoted above, Letter xiv., p. 97.

† A question was then before the public respecting the diet of the soldiery in barracks.

‡ This venerable Church Reformer died at Shrivenham, April, 1859.

§ And now the venerable author of the "Ingoldsby Letters" has attained that patriarchal age, holding still the same sentiments he published to the world at *fifty*.

‖ A list of some 500 or more of these is now published by the Association for Promoting a Revision of the Prayer-book; 17, Buckingham Street, Adelphi, W.C.

according to their "peculiar views of truth," tried the force of "solid arguments" in every diversity of expression, till they have exhausted the vocabulary, and rung the changes upon Liturgical Revision to the last conceivable variation? —and *cui bono?* to what effect?—Why, that when their eyes are waxed dim with writing, and their natural strength abated from waiting so long upon the bishops, they have the satisfaction of hearing that their lordships have declared through their mouthpieces in their own proper House, that the Prayer-book shall remain UNTOUCHED and UNALTERED in their day.

But I have a stronger reason still for pursuing the course I am now doing, and which I regret does not meet with the approval of " C. W. T." Is he aware that " Ingoldsby" himself, whose talents in the way of composition he is pleased to admire, did his utmost in the way of "solid arguments" upon this subject for upwards of two whole years without once drawing breath, consuming all his living in printing, publishing, advertising, letter-writing, reviewing; and had the satisfaction for his pains of finding that he convinced none but those who were convinced already; while by the rest he was dubbed fool, ass, madman, idiot, and bid to hold his tongue, and sit at the feet of his betters? So, surely, " C. W. T." has no right to blame him if he retired from that unequal campaign, and resorted to another method of warfare ; with what prospect of success it is as yet premature to decide. But at any rate it can hardly have a worse issue than the former. To have persisted any longer in that line of argument, though he was urged to it by several, would indeed have proved him to be the description of person which those courteous but anonymous gentlemen who write in the *Guardian, Clerical Journal,* and *English Churchman* represent him. He might then truly have had a fair title to wear the cap and bells for the rest of his life; and no one, not even "C. W. T." himself, would have pitied him.*

To whom, Mr. Editor, I beg, through the favour of your columns, to present these "solid arguments" with my best compliments; and if they do not convince him, I am quite sure that nothing which I, or any other Liturgical Reformer, can say will; and I remain,

Yours obliged,

June 11*th*, 1858. "INGOLDSBY."

LETTER XVIII.

THE BISHOP OF ST. DAVID'S.—NO. II.

"Illuc unde abii redeo."—HOR.
"But to return from whence we have digressed."—FRANCIS.

SIR,—It is time we returned to the matter we have in hand, and from which I hope not to be soon again diverted.

When the Court rose it was engaged in hearing the evidence of the Bishop of St. David's on behalf of the Revisionists. The counsel for the defence had just been

---

* It is but fair to give the titles of "Ingoldsby's" *graver* pamphlets on the subject of Revision, as he was invited by "C. W. T." to address himself to "solid arguments" in support of his position.

1. "The Morning Service of the Church, Abridgment of, urged in a Letter to the Lord Bishop of Ely; *second edition:* with an Appendix, exhibiting the proposed changes in detail." London: 1856.

2. "A Revision of the Rubric and Liturgy, urged with a view chiefly to the Abridgment of the Morning Service; *third edition* of a Letter, &c., with Answers to Objectors."

3. "Further Arguments in favour of the Abridgment of the Morning Service; *fourth edition* of a Letter, &c., with a reply to the question, How is it to be done?"

4. "The People's Call for a Revision of the Liturgy, in a Letter to Lord Palmerston, with copious Extracts from Private Correspondence on the subject." 1857

quoting from his lordship's Charge of 1845, in which he referred to a certain statement, made by the "great majority of the clergy" some thirteen years before, that, "*from the lapse of years* or *altered circumstances*, some things pertaining to spiritual matters in the Church might require renewal or correction;* and that they were willing to co-operate with the rulers of the Church in carrying into effect *any measures tending to supply that want*, should it appear to exist; while, at the same time, they declared their devoted adherence to the doctrine and policy of the Church, and their deep-rooted attachment to her Liturgy."

Such I believe to be the sentiments of the "great majority of the clergy" in 1858; such their willingness to co-operate with the rulers of the Church in carrying into effect any *needful* reforms; and such their prospects, humanly speaking, of getting *anything done*, unless they adopt a tone somewhat more defiant, and pursue a course of somewhat sterner determination, than they appear to have done six-and-twenty years ago, when many of the priests and deacons of this generation were yet unborn, and, probably, four-fifths of them had not as yet entered into holy orders.

The bishop proceeds to show that the conduct of those clergy was straightforward and consistent enough. "No reasonable man could contend that there was the slightest inconsistency between such an admission, even if extended (beyond a bare possibility) to *the actual need of amendment* with the previous professions"—alluding to the declaration made by these clergymen of attachment to the Liturgy, notwithstanding an admission of its faults or imperfections. Surely the same credit may now be claimed by Lord Ebury's petitioners, and all that class of Liturgical reformers who seek to make the formularies of our Church more profitable

* See Letter xv., p. 103.

than they now are for the religious instruction and edification of the people, while they have no wish to disturb the general tenor and order of the Prayer-book.

"Rather," proceeds the Bishop in the bishop's chair, "would there have been reason for doubting the sincerity of those professions if they had not been accompanied by such an admission. We may well maintain that our Liturgy is excellent in its parts, and good even as a whole; that is, better suited than any other we know of to the purposes of public devotion, and affording no ground of fair excuse for separation; and *yet believe it capable of some* IMPORTANT IMPROVEMENTS, *and* EARNESTLY DESIRE THAT IT SHOULD RECEIVE THEM."

Such, one is constrained to believe, were the Bishop of St. David's own sentiments at that time; at least, his lordship's Charge of 1845 gives us no reason to think that he differed in opinion from these memorialists; and it is fair to conclude that, had those gentlemen been represented in the House of Peers by any Lord Ebury of the day,* their case would have been supported (or, at least, not opposed) by the voice and vote of the Bishop of St. David's. I am the more inclined to this inference from a significant *note* attached to this portion of the Bishop's Charge of 1845 (pp. 24, 25).

Notes to bishops' charges are like postscripts to ladies' letters; sometimes they tell a great deal in few words; often they tell very little in many words. Of the former class, as might be expected, is the note to which we are now referring, and which runs as follows:—

"If I were to be asked what is my own opinion as to the expediency of attempting any ALTERATION IN THE LITURGY, I should be deficient in candour if I did not

---

* They were supported by Lord Henley, but to no purpose.

acknowledge that I think the Liturgy *capable of improvement*. It would be little short of a miracle were it otherwise; and I know not why I should be ashamed or reluctant to avow an opinion which was entertained by Sancroft, Stillingfleet, Tenison, Wake, Secker, and Porteus. I heartily pray a season may come when the question may be looked at *with calmness and candour.—Bishop of London's Charge*, 1834, pp. 40, 41."

> "Alas! poor Blomfield!—
> I knew him once; he was a goodly bishop.
> He was a man, take him for all in all,
> I shall not look upon his like again."

I was in his diocese when a young divine,* and met with a fair amount of hospitality and courtesy at his hands. But, as a warning to all future revisionists not to put their trust too confidently in bishops, let it be noted here that Bishop Blomfield, from 1834 to 1854, never took any active steps for accomplishing those "alterations in the Liturgy," or those "improvements," which he was "not ashamed to confess" it was capable of; and which sentiments he appears to have prided himself in holding in common with such authorities as Sancroft, Stillingfleet, Tenison, Wake, Secker, and Porteus.

This last was Bishop Blomfield's immediate predecessor but two. We shall come presently, in the course of these Letters, to his immediate successor, Dr. Tait; and shall then see what are *his* sentiments upon the subject of Liturgical Reform. But if there be one name in the above list more than another which it would appear the present Bishop of London is desirous of emulating, it is that of the active and liberal-minded Porteus; a name held to this day

---

* As preacher at the Chapel Royal, Whitehall, 1843-4.

in high honour by the College to which he belonged;* and to whose memory the present writer, as a gainer of one of the Porteus medals in his undergraduate days, takes this opportunity of recording his gratitude and respect.

> "Manibus date lilia plenis:
> Purpureos spargam flores, animamque *sepulti*
> His saltem accumulem donis, et fungar inani
> Munere." †

To return from this digression (which my fellow-collegians will, I am sure, excuse), I would here add a few more names of weight to the cloud of witnesses by which Bishop Blomfield (and apparently the Bishop of St. David's in 1845) rejoiced to find himself encompassed. They are all of them, I believe, of episcopal or archiepiscopal rank, *except two*, whom, *honoris causá*, I take the liberty of inserting in the list, which they will not disgrace by their presence; the one having been prevented from elevation to the episcopal bench by his own bodily infirmities, the other by the *mental infirmity of the monarch*‡ or minister of the day.

Among the glorious ranks, then, of departed Liturgical Reformers, let us ever reckon with pride, in addition to the above, Patrick, Burnet, Tillotson, Beveridge, Lloyd, Compton, Tomline, Prideaux, Yorke, Paley, Watson, Shirley, Coplestone; names held famous in their day, and not likely to be forgotten, when many an anti-revisionist, now equally

---

* Christ's College, Cambridge; where the Porteus medals still commemorate this ornament of the Church of the nineteenth century.

† Virg., Æn. vi., 884. From which passage, by the way, it may be noted that the practice (now so common) of scattering flowers over the grave of the departed is, like that of sprinkling dust three times on the body, of *heathen*, not of Christian origin.

‡ It is commonly said that Paley's memorable remark about the "pigeons" (*Moral Philosophy*, B. iii., Chap. i.) effectually barred his promotion under George III. of pious memory.

high in rank, shall have noiselessly returned to his kindred dust, and sleep undisturbed with his fathers.*

And if in future ages Liturgical Revision—like the Catholic Relief Bill, the Test and Corporation Act, the Jew Bill, and other questions of religious bitterness in their time—after long beating about in open sea, with wind and tide against it, shall at length be seen entering the haven with swelling sails, and the flag of peace waving at its mast-head;—if, in the womb of time, those still retreating, still evanescent Greek kalends shall haply dawn, when bishops on the chair of bishops, bishops in the house of bishops, and bishops on the bench of bishops, shall agree to fulfil the late Bishop of London's truly Christian prayer, and discuss the question of Revision "with calmness and candour:" then is it not impossible that the classic name of Thirlwall will be numbered in the above galaxy of talent and liberality, as arrayed on the side of religious progress and Liturgical Reform.

Be that as it may, certain it is that his lordship's Charge of 1845 must irrevocably stand out among the records of the advocates for revision.

LITTERA SCRIPTA MANET.

And whatever cause the Bishop may have since had to alter his opinion—supposing him to have done so—certain it is that he then stood by that much-calumniated class, the Revisionists; that he admitted, what many are indisposed to do, that they have reason and common sense on their side; and was, at any rate, very far from regarding them as those firebrands and disturbers of the Church's peace which they have been considered and designated by others.

I remain, Sir, yours obediently,

June 18, 1858. " INGOLDSBY."

---

* To this list may now be added the name of the late Bishop of Durham, the Hon. and Right Rev. Henry Montagu Villiers.

J

LETTER XIX.

RIDICULE WILL FREQUENTLY PREVAIL.

"It is one of our indisputable facts, that it is easier to laugh ten follies out of countenance, than it is to coax, reason, or flog a man out of one."
—SALMAGUNDI.

"Ridiculum acri
Fortius et melius magnas plerumque secat res."—HOR. Sat. i. x. 14.

SIR,—One, two, three more apples at my devoted head; and in this hot weather too! Whether they be of gold, silver, or lead, I leave to the discrimination of your readers. But to show that I do not despise them (as your Bideford correspondent* would have me to do), and that I still flatter myself to win the race, I will e'en stop and pick them up, and so pocket the affront. This I can do the more cheerfully, as not one of them has hit me, though aimed not without skill, and with an evident design to divert me from my purpose. And so far indeed they have succeeded (which is about as far as most anti-reformers succeed), as to cause a momentary halting to the object of their aversion, which, nevertheless, comes limping after them, *pede claudo*, in spite of all their devices, and will inevitably one day overtake them.

So "T. G." has serious thoughts of giving up your paper,† if it continues to insert any more of these "Ingoldsby Letters;" which, notwithstanding, he is so civil as to say, "all will agree are exceedingly well-written, and full of spirited remarks?" I wonder whether he would have

---

* This writer, I afterwards learned, was brother to the Earl of Essex.

† Letters to the same effect were received by the Editors of most other papers in which the Letters originally appeared; the course adopted by the opponents of Revision being to spite all who advocate it in every way in their power.—"Tantæne animis cœlestibus iræ?"

been better satisfied had they been exceedingly ill-written, and full of stupid remarks?* It is difficult to please all men, I am aware; but I never expected to be blamed for what in any other case one would have thought a strong title to commendation.† Like the poet of old,—

> "Indignor quicquam reprehendi, non quia crasse
> Compositum, illepideve, putetur, sed quia,"—

my error appears to be that I am too severe, too sarcastic; these Ingoldsby Letters "*plus aloës quam mellis habent.*" But it is the unlucky editor who is chiefly in fault; and so, as we can't get at "Ingoldsby," we must vent our spleen on him.

> "Quicquid delirant reges plectuntur Achivi."

Who would be the editor of a paper? especially one that circulates amongst that "*genus irritabile*" the clergy? I know a score of them, at least, who have withdrawn their names from that old-established and orthodox paper, the *Clerical Journal*, because it writes *against* a revision of the Prayer-book. And here we have "T. G.," "and I venture to say many more of your readers," threatening to cease subscribing to the *Church Chronicle*, because "for eighteen weeks 'Ingoldsby' has had unlimited access to your columns, besides honourable mention in your leaders." Well —*pazienza poi*—this Dame Partington method of arresting the tide of public opinion has been tried before, but I never heard of its succeeding. It is the deaf adder practice, which I am afraid possesses our order more than any other,

---

* Bishop Wilberforce said on a certain occasion that "the most unpardonable offence a clergyman could be guilty of was to be *dull.*" Alas, I fear, it is an offence of no uncommon occurrence in the Church!

† On the other hand, it has been admitted by many that "Ingoldsby" has done execution in a masterly manner;—reminding them of the hangman's wife, who said, "any one could manage an ordinary hanging, but to make a fellow die comfortably was the peculiar prerogative of her husband."

and may partly account for that harsh judgment passed upon us by Lord Clarendon—that "clergymen understand the least, and take the worst measure of human affairs, of all mankind that can read and write." Possibly this may be owing to the declaration we make at the outset of our career of implicit obedience to our spiritual leaders, who certainly in this respect set us but a very indifferent example.

But we are not altogether without encouragement in other quarters; at least I well remember, some twelve years ago, hearing a certain Dorsetshire squire declare he would give up taking the *Times* if it went on any longer giving prominence to the letters and speeches of "that fellow Cobden." The letters and speeches, nevertheless, went on appearing week by week, and found admirers in others, if not in the Dorsetshire squire; who kept his word, however, and, to my knowledge, took the *Morning Herald* for three weeks at least. Whether he takes it still or not I am unable to say; but it is pretty generally known that the corn laws were repealed, and that the Prime Minister said the repeal was chiefly owing to "the unadorned eloquence" of "that fellow" Richard Cobden. It is equally certain that the *Times* has in a measure espoused the cause of the Liturgical Reformers,* and that too in a tone little calculated to recommend its articles to "T. G.," "C. W. T.," "and, I venture to say, many of its clerical readers," who have doubtless in consequence followed the squire's example, and transferred their subscriptions to the *Morning Post*, because it lately insinuated that "Lord Ebury was a fidgety man."

Then there is another heavy complaint against "Ingoldsby"—that he introduces "all sorts of extraneous

---

* This was in 1858. See its article of May 6th in that year. That it did not long continue in that mood is only in accordance with the well-known character of that versatile organ of public opinion.

matter (for example, the Deanery of York) under the head of a reply to the Bishops."

But is it so clear that the Deanery of York *is* altogether extraneous to the business in hand, and that the bishops* had nothing directly or indirectly to do with that matter? May there not be such a thing as "*petimusque damusque vicissim;*" one good turn deserves another;—a kind of give-and-take, claw-me-claw-you system in the Church, as in other professions? Which of the bishops was heard to raise his voice in denunciation of that appointment, which drew down upon the Minister of the day the all but unanimous condemnation of the press, " which is not an unimportant consideration in a question of this sort?" Was it not left to the independent member for a Scotch district to call for an explanation of this mode of filling the high places of the Church in the middle of the nineteenth century?—and did not the lame defence set up by the Chancellor of the Exchequer † rest mainly upon the recommendation of an archbishop? So " Ingoldsby " was not so very far wrong in connecting the Deanery of York with the Premier's support of the bishops in their opposition to Lord Ebury, though he did but hint at the possibility of such a connexion, and was far from assuming what subsequent explanations have since elicited at the bar of public opinion.

But then I am told that all this bantering, quizzing, " carping and cavilling," does not help forward the cause of Liturgical Reform, and that " words of soberness " would

---

* In subsequently *doubling the Dean's salary* the bishops bore certainly a principal part. See Parliamentary Reports for August, 1860.

† Mr. Disraeli. See Letter xvi., p. 110, note. The author is happy to be able to refer to the subsequent appointments to the Deaneries of Ely, Chichester, Ripon, Exeter, Lincoln, Lichfield, and several others, as resting on far more satisfactory grounds, as far as the public are concerned.

do more to promote our object. This depends upon how people look at the matter. There always were, and always will be, two schools of philosophers in the world—disciples respectively of Democritus and Heraclitus; to the former of which I must plead guilty to giving the preference, if it were but for this reason, that it is easier, as well as more agreeable, to laugh than to cry, to smile than to frown, perpetually. Now, I apprehend the bulk of mankind are of the same opinion; and if you can succeed in enlisting the laughing school on your side, you have a better chance of winning the day, than if your cause were in the hands of the frowning philosophers. This is just what I am trying to do, and have been trying for about eighteen weeks. The frowners have had it all their own way ever since 1689, and it cannot be denied that they have made but very small progress. Democritus only entered the lists last February, and has at least accomplished the negative result of stirring up the bile of the *anti*-revisionists, which is one step gained, and certainly so much more than Heraclitus had achieved in nearly two hundred years.* And as it is said that

"Envy will merit, as its shade, pursue,
But, like a shadow, proves the substance true;"

so I think it may be assumed that there is some truth in what "Ingoldsby" has thus jestingly written, or he would hardly have drawn forth the inveterate hostility with which he has been assailed.

I am, as your readers will have probably observed, a great believer in proverbs, especially in classical ones. They speak the wisdom of the ancients, and like the ἔπεα πτερόεντα of the poet, wing their way surely and rapidly to the

---

* Even the *Clerical Journal*, one of our most virulent opponents, was constrained to admit that "The Ingoldsby Letters have done much to call public attention to the question of Liturgical Revision."—*Clerical Journal*, October, 1859; March, 1860; January, 1862.

desired end, and there stick fast in the præcordia with their barbed points.

Now it has not been for nothing that such universal currency has obtained for the proverb I have adopted as my motto for to-day. It is the old story of the Gordian knot, which admits of but one solution. It is beauty's door of glass, impregnable to all but the diamond key. "The *understanding*," says Locke, "is the very last thing people in general have recourse to in regulating their conduct." Engage their feelings, their humour, their interest, and the day is yours. The eye and the ear are more easily captivated than the heart. Amuse, and you will secure attention; which is all that the cause of *truth*, the cause in short of the LITURGICAL REVISORS, requires.

"OMNE TULIT PUNCTUM QUI MISCUIT UTILE DULCI;
LECTOREM DELECTANDO PARITERQUE MONENDO."

One word, in conclusion, on the last paragraph of one of my opponent's letters. He says he "should read my reviews with great pleasure were they on a different subject; but on the Prayer-book or on our bishops he feels they are out of place." For the compliment in the former part of this paragraph I thank him; and when I write for pay, and not from a strong sense of duty, I will let him know, if he will send me his address, and I shall hope for his subscription to the Review in which my articles appear. For the latter part, I wholly deny (to the best of my recollection, and certainly of my intention) having written one syllable that could be directly or indirectly construed into irreverence towards the Prayer-book, as far as it is the legitimate exponent of the Word of God. Where it is the mere compilation or the *invention* of Man,* I see not

---

* For example, Lord Stanhope shortly after this gave notice in the House of Lords for a motion to expunge from the Prayer-book the services

why it should be less open to criticism than any other human production.

Finally, as regards the bishops. Whatever may be your correspondent's views upon the subject, I, not having the pleasure of being a Bishop's Chaplain, an Honorary Canon, or a rural Dean, have yet to learn that their lordships have any title, any *jus, sive divinum sive humanum,* to exempt them from fair remark upon their sayings and doings any more than the humblest Priest or Deacon in the Church.

> "Ut miremur te, non tua, primum aliquid da
> Quod possim titulis inscribere *præter honores.*"

The mere designation of "My Lord" was never intended, in this free country of England, to act as a coat of mail to its lay or clerical possessor, in order to screen him from the swift-winged arrows of wit, or the fisticuff of the ruder literary pugilist. Prime Ministers, Lord Chancellors, Judges, M.P.'s, Magistrates, and other lay dignitaries, have long ago quietly resigned themselves to pay this penalty for their ill-rewarded services; and it would be strange indeed, if the mere possession of £5,000 or £8,000 a year, whether by Bishop or Dean, were to purchase for them immunity from this universal law of humanity.

The bishop who exceeds the bounds of his province, and, not satisfied with ruling his own diocese with a rod of iron,* must needs lay down the law for the Church at

---

for the 30th of January, the 29th of May, and the 5th of November. Who shall say that there was not in those three services much that was open to just criticism; much calculated to excite feelings of irreverence rather than of devotion, as they were then appointed to be read in church? The quiet way in which that reform was carried out might serve to dispel the fears of those who shrink from *all change* as a thing too horrible to contemplate.

* One bishop of the day, for example (Wigram of Rochester), was severe upon beards, whiskers, cricket, and archery; while another (Wilberforce of

large, can hardly expect to escape the critic's pen if he make a false step. The prelate, on the other hand, who bears himself meekly and considerately towards his weaker brethren, as remembering that he also is compassed with infirmity, will seldom require the aid of self-elected champions, like your well-meaning, but somewhat indiscreet, correspondent;* whose exertions, I fear, in their behalf, will give occasion to some of their lordships to exclaim (as others have done before them), " Leave me if you please to protect myself from my enemies; but save me—oh! save me from my FRIENDS."

        I remain, Sir, yours obediently,
June 25, 1858.   " INGOLDSBY."

LETTER XX.

STRIKE WHILE THE IRON IS HOT.

"Perrupit Acheronta Herculeus labor."—HOR., Od. i., iii. 36.

"Persta atque obdura; seu rubra Canicula findet
 Infantes statuas, seu"——   In., Sat. ii., v. 40.

      " Proceed, and persevere
 Should the red dog-star infant statues split,
 Or" . . . .   FRANCIS.

SIR,—It will be easily believed I can have no motive but one for continuing these Letters at this torrid season,

---

Oxford), with equal severity, denounced *post-prandial eucharistic* celebrations. See Letters L., CX.; also see an able Tract entitled "Hints on Common Sense for Clergymen, by One of Themselves." W. J. Johnson, 121, Fleet Street, E.C. 1878.

* Amongst other curious features of the Liturgical Revision movement, not the least remarkable is the fact that the cudgels in behalf of the bishops have been, in every instance that I am aware of, wielded by others than themselves, and unfortunately in the great majority of instances by *anonymous* writers, leaving it to be naturally inferred that such persons wrote not without episcopal connivance, if not at episcopal suggestion.

when even Parliament flags, and it is venial in a Prime Minister to doze. But if it required all the perseverance of a Hercules to force a passage across Acheron, so I am persuaded that neither heat nor cold, frowns nor ridicule, opposition nor neglect, must be regarded by the sincere Liturgical Reformer, if he aspire to carry the object of his hopes to a successful issue.*

One of your late correspondents, who assigns to me a title to which I fear I have small pretension—that of a "Philosophical Reformer"—thinks I am somewhat impatient, and that I ought to be abundantly content if, "after a life of labour," I could die congratulating myself that the sacred cause, in which I have been *only three years*† engaged, had made a perceptible progress towards its completion! He further hints that I have forgotten my history, which tells such wearisome tales of more than Trojan sieges, and interminable crusades against all manner of abuses, civil and ecclesiastical.

Alas, my unknown friend, it is only because my memory is too keen, my mind's eye too wide awake, that I am impatient of any further delay in this matter. "Time and I against two," may be, as you say, an excellent argument. But unfortunately the right reverend prelates, with whom we are at issue on this occasion, are beforehand with us. "Time and the bishops against a thousand," is the watchword they have been using these 200 years, and they have got their hand pretty well in. And unless we can manage, like Hamlet and Laertes in the play, to exchange rapiers in this our life-and-death scuffle, I much fear their turning my friend's proverb to good account against us before we have done with them.

---

* See Letter XLI.
† Now, alas, extended to twenty! (November, 1878).

So at least it was, or something very like it, in 1689; so in 1772; so also, I imagine, in 1834; and so, I have a strong inward conviction, their lordships mean it to be now.* And so it doubtless would be, if they had no other opponents than men of the stamp of your "philosophical" correspondent to deal with. I will remind him meanwhile of another proverb; and as he will allow that

"Good reasons must perforce give way to better,"

I hope he will lay it to heart, and forgive Ingoldsby's "impatience" for the future. "Strike while the iron's hot," says our motto. So up with the hammer, say I, and down on the anvil. Up with the hammer again, and down on the anvil again. We are making an impression. We *have* made an impression. All that is now wanting is to keep fanning the coals, plying the bellows, dealing the blows hard and sharp on the glowing mass till it assumes a shape and a consistency. Once allowed to cool, ay, even to Midsummer heat, all the work will have to be begun again, which would tire out a very Cyclops;†

"Ibi omnis
Effusus labor."——

Any result better than that. It is miserable, and a standing reproach to our order, that this needful reform should have been in agitation off and on for now nearly 200 years, with so little actual advance made. Nor is it altogether easy to account for this. Much, no doubt, is due to the apathy of the one part; more to the *vis inertiæ* of the other; little, I suspect, to the real active

---

* And I was not very far wrong in my calculation, seeing they have got help from High, if not the Highest, quarters.
† This the Bishops reckoned on, and not without reason. It will be long before another "Ingoldsby" will be found to carry on this most thankless struggle for a quarter of a century continuously!

opposition of any party; but most of all do I attribute the stagnation of our cause to the want of some *one* persevering spirit, not so much to lead on the charge, as to keep it constantly alive, against all the *rather seeming than real* obstacles it has and always will have to encounter.

For the encouragement, however, of those who are given, it would seem, as much too quickly to despond as "Ingoldsby" is possibly to be too sanguine, I tell them that the day of deliverance is not so far from dawning as they imagine. Let them take heart, lift up their drooping eyelids,

"And bid the lovely scenes at distance hail."

Ay, and not so very distant either,—

"Aquæ nisi fallit augur
Annosa cornix."

In prospect most assuredly they are, as may be gathered from several unmistakable signs.

Long before land is sighted, the experienced mariner is well advised of his nearing the *optata arena*. The soundings gradually lessen, bits of floating wood or sea-weed are discerned on the wave, land birds hover round the ship, the dark clear green of ocean assumes a muddier tint; all these, and more, are joyous and familiar harbingers of port a-head to the home-sick sailor. And of this nature I take to be a certain signal lately descried from the mast-head of our apparently becalmed vessel.

The character of the *English Churchman* is pretty well known as the organ of a party that has hitherto strenuously resisted all attempts at "touching the Prayer-book." Yet if any of your readers, "J. G." for example, will take the trouble to refer to one or two of its recent leading articles, they will see something like terms of compromise offered to the Reformers, which can hardly be regarded in any other light than as a flag of truce held out from a beleaguered fort. Whether the assailants may be disposed to listen to the terms, is another thing; but the despatch runs as follows:—

"If Lord Ebury, or those who support him in this matter, believe that some abridgment of our present services is required, why do they not come forward with a definite plan? As an illustration is better than any other mode of explanation, suppose they had made some such a proposal as the following:—That an humble address be presented to Her Majesty, that she will be graciously pleased to give her Royal leave and licence to the Convocations of Bishops and Clergy for the Provinces of Canterbury and York,* and to a Synod of the Bishops of Ireland, to consider and decide *synodically* upon the following rubrics, and to make such alterations in them, or additions to them, as may most effectually and beneficially carry out the objects sought to be attained thereby, with a view to the said rubrics being added to the Book of Common Prayer, under the sanction and authority of the ecclesiastical and civil powers of the United Church of England and Ireland."

And then follow the suggested RUBRICS, not less than eight in number, and not remarkable either for brevity or clearness; but still showing a willingness to redress an admitted evil, the too great length of our present Morning Service. Now we hail, I say, this sign, more for the indication it gives of a disposition to listen to an accommodation than from any particular approval of the suggestions them-

---

* "Nothing without the Bishop" used to be a saying of the early Church. We have improved on this now-a-days, and "Nothing without Convocation" is the watchword of the modern Ritualistic Priest.

selves; or any opinion that they are calculated to answer the purpose for which a COMMISSION OF INQUIRY is sought for by Lord Ebury and the bulk of Liturgical Reformers.

Château qui parle, femme qui écoute, l'un et l'autre vont se rendre.* We have here evident symptoms of a beating to parley. The besieged would fain either divide or divert the forces of the enemy. The frail one gives tokens of surrender. This is but a first advance, it is true; but it speaks volumes.

> "Who listens once will listen twice;
> Her heart, be sure, is not of ice,
> And one refusal no rebuff."

And so it is here: for a *second* proposition shortly followed this first attempt at feeling the pulse of the Revisors. The article, indeed, is headed somewhat fiercely, "*Abridged Services* versus *Corrupted Services;*" but much allowance will be made for a half-starved garrison, that has had to stand so long on the defensive; and any suggestion coming from them should be received with the kindest attention. This *second* proposition is a considerable amplification of the previous outline, and goes into minute details as to the required modifications of, or additions to, rubrics, with a view to carry out the idea of abridgment; and the principle is applied, it may be observed, with greater freedom to "working days" than to the "Sundays and Holy Days" throughout the year. So far so good. For the scheme itself I must refer your readers to the paper in which it appeared about a month ago, and which would have been noticed at the time but for the pressure of other matter that could not so well bear postponement. I will only further remark, that the suggestions themselves, while they betray no small pains in endeavouring to provide for an

---

* "Bride of Lammermoor." Vol. ii., Chap. vii.

admitted want, are prefaced by this significant observation:—

"We lay the following paper before our readers for *consideration*, so that they may be SOMEWHAT PREPARED, whenever the PROPER TIME for ACTION shall arrive."

What that "proper time" may be, is among the dark events of the future; but that *some* definite time is contemplated by the writer, and that he is one who speaks from authority, is clear. Our own opinion, meanwhile, is thus far decided:—

First, that nothing short of a ROYAL COMMISSION will effectually meet all the difficulties of the case.*

Secondly, that the time is gone by when *mere* Abridgment will satisfy the demands of those who call for such Commission.

In the early stages of the Reformation, it is well known that a slight concession on the part of the Pope and his adherents—the doing away, for instance, with the sale of Indulgences and relics; the granting the cup to the laity, and permission to marry to the clergy; the performing the service in a language "understanded of the people," and the like—would have been accepted as a boon, and, in all probability, have staved off the greater reform for many a year—possibly to this hour. But when, at length, these reasonable demands were tardily yielded as a *palliative*, and in evident fear of something worse impending, the boon was scornfully rejected; and the stern answer of Luther and his small band of heart-and-soul Reformers was, IT IS TOO LATE.

And such, I suspect, would now be the reply of the great body of those who seek, and have long sought, to revise the Liturgy of our Church, and render it more pliant,

---

* But it must be an honest Commission, not containing a majority of members well known beforehand to object to all Revision.

more various, less faulty, less formal, and therefore more generally acceptable to the people. They would say of such proposals as this of the *English Churchman*, however ingenious and well devised in itself, IT IS TOO LATE. We are willing to include such suggestions, if thought desirable, among others that shall be submitted for approval to a competent Commission; but they cannot now be accepted as a *substitute* for Liturgical Revision in its more comprehensive form. They will no longer serve the purpose they might have done a few years ago, of silencing objectors, or even dividing the ranks of those who call for a thorough and searching Revisal of the Book of Common Prayer.

"As an illustration (to quote the *English Churchman*) is often better than any other mode of explanation," suppose we were to refer to the recently reported case of the CONFESSIONAL in BELGRAVIA?* That matter being, however, *adhuc sub judice*, I shall not enter into the particular accusations brought forward, or the apology set up.† Suffice it to allude briefly to the *fact* that the Bishop of London has found it necessary to withdraw his licence from a certain clergyman of seven years' standing, against whom charges have been made of carrying the confessional in our Church to an extreme hitherto supposed to be confined to the Romish Ritual. Now, that this practice is gaining ground in our country, the affairs of East Grinstead, Boyne Hill, West Lavington, and others, sufficiently declare. Also, that it rests its defence upon the terms used in our Service for the Consecration of Priests, and the Office for the Visitation of the Sick,‡ will, I conceive, be readily granted.

It becomes, therefore, a serious and necessary part of

---

* To what extent this plague-spot in the Church subsequently spread, is too notorious to require further notice in this place.
† This was the well-known case of Poole *versus* the Bishop of London.
‡ See Vol. II., Letter LXXIII.

our argument, whether we shall allow the ranks of the Reformers to be divided by accepting terms, however plausible, for accomplishing *mere* Abridgment, leaving the other question *in statu quo*—that is to say, for still further irritation, and consequent agitation: or whether it would not be more prudent to go into the whole question at once, and endeavour to allay future heats by what the late Bishop of London so wisely called "a calm and candid" examination of the matter.

I commend this portion of my letter to the grave attention of your correspondent "Sobrius," whose extracts from the *Christian Observer* I read with interest. The passage was new to me, and may afford matter for future observation; but at present I must conclude, having already trespassed largely on your columns,

And remain yours, &c.,

July 2, 1858. " INGOLDSBY."

P.S.—Since the above was written, my attention has been called to the letter signed " Cantab." in your last.

I hope it is not necessary for me to assure any of your readers that it was inserted wholly without my knowledge or participation—not that I disagree with Sydney Smith's searching application of the "small-toothed comb" to a particular class, as a general rule. But I should be sorry that "C. W. T.," or any of your correspondents, should think that I reckon them under the designation of the "pompous gentlemen," or the individuals satirised in the concluding epigram.* On the contrary, I am sincerely in-

---

* "On me when dunces are satiric,
  I take it for a panegyric.
  Hated by fools, and fools to hate,
  Be such my motto, and my fate."--SWIFT.

The writer of the letter, as I afterwards learned, was the Rev. W. D. Ryland, of Brackley, near Banbury.

debted to them for their desire to check any apparent, though
not intentional, levity in these Letters when treating of
things serious. And so far from bearing them the slightest
ill-will in consequence, allow me to say, through your means,
Mr. Editor, that I shall at any time be happy to make their
personal acquaintance, as also that of my well-meaning, but
somewhat over-zealous friend, " A CANTAB."

LETTER XXI.

THE DEBATE IN THE HOUSE OF LORDS ON THE STATE SERVICES.

"FESTINA LENTE."
"Slow but Sure."

SIR,—It is not my fault that I cannot get on faster with
my "Reply to the Bishops." I have done my best; and
you will bear me witness that I have lost no time since we
embarked together on this undertaking. But there is always
something or other crossing one's path which must be first
attended to; and so our vessel makes little apparent way,
though I am fain to hope it is not altogether becalmed, much
less driven by contrary winds away from the haven where
we would be. We tack and tack, but we keep the port
still in sight; or at least are steering by a compass which
tells us we are moving forwards *surely*, though according to
our motto it may be *slowly*, and in the right direction.

It is inconceivable in how great a variety of aspects this
well-known adage is regarded by different individuals according to their respective idiosyncracies.

The ambitious Wiltshire farmer, for example, considers
he has made no small progress in bucolic science, if he has
adopted the six-coulter drill in lieu of broad-cast for his

turnip sowing. The Somersetshire agriculturalist boasts that he has overcome the terrors entertained by his Dorsetshire cousin of firing his ricks by the introduction of a portable steam-engine into his stack-yard. The good old-fashioned Church-and-King Worcestershire divine congratulates himself that he has not lived in vain if he has established a Sunday-school in his parish, a cow club and clothing club, and has had "regular double duty ever since *he* came to the living." The Archbishop of Canterbury and "the great majority of the bishops, which is not an unimportant consideration in a question of this sort," think they have made a considerable innovation upon routine, and have largely relieved their brethren the working clergy, by giving them *permission* to drop the Lord's Prayer before the sermon, and to use the Litany apart from the Morning Service, "provided the whole of the Morning and Evening Service be used at some portion of the day."*

And now, behold—such is the rashness of man, such the tendency of all things to hurry down hill when once they are set in motion—

"Sic omnia fatis
In pejus ruere, et retro sublapsa referri;"—

we have the Bishops of London and Cashel confessing that they "see no harm" in Earl Stanhope's motion for expunging the three State Services of November 5, January 30, and May 29, from the Prayer-book: while the Bishop of Oxford himself—*Et tu, Brute*—consents to the proposal, without any fear of such a measure "shocking the simple feelings of the vast mass of the less-educated poor in England, and doing a mischief, the extent of which no man can conceive."

As, however, the debate upon the above motion bears so

---

* This absurd condition simply renders the relief (to those who stand upon it) wholly inoperative in the rural parishes.

closely upon the subject we have in hand, I hope, Mr. Editor, neither you nor any of your readers will think I am wandering far from my text, if I devote this Letter to a few remarks upon it.*

In the first place, we must all, I think, agree with Lord Ebury in accepting the present motion as but an instalment of the larger measure contemplated by his lordship. For though some of the prelates who voted for Lord Stanhope's proposition, did so on the professed principle of the two questions standing on totally different grounds, it was admitted by the Archbishop of Canterbury that one main reason for *his* supporting the motion was, that the services had become "already practically obsolete, and that their exclusion from our Prayer-book would be very generally sanctioned by public opinion,"—two reasons which the Liturgical Reformers have constantly advanced in favour of their contemplated reforms in certain portions of the RUBRIC, if not in the actual services of our Church.

Secondly, one would think there could hardly be two opinions, supposing the State services are to be done away with at all, as to the expediency of repealing the Acts of Parliament upon which they stand, as suggested by Lord Ebury, and supported by the Earl of Malmesbury. Upon what fine-drawn process of reasoning the Bishop of Oxford would retain the shadow, while parting with the substance, I confess myself to be incapable of fathoming.

Thirdly, it was consolatory to hear the following remarks from the Bishop of London (Tait) :—

"As it appeared to be the wish of their lordships that the debate on the 6th of May should not be protracted, many of those who desired to express their sentiments upon that occasion were unable to do so; and a sort of impression

---

* See further on this subject, Letter xxxiv.

seemed to have got abroad that many of them were afraid of the slightest change, as if they felt that they were living in a house that was somewhat tottering, and that to begin to alter it in any way might bring it altogether to the ground. For his own part he was glad to have the opportunity of stating that he opposed that proposition on no such ground."

This is at least consolatory; for there can be no doubt such an opinion has been promulgated, and has even been made the subject of boasting by our neighbours across the Channel, if not by some of our Dissenting brethren at home. The following, from the *Times* of May 24th, has, we know, been extensively circulated; and it is well that an antidote is now supplied to the effects likely to be produced by such a statement:—

" The *Univers* contains the following remarks on the withdrawal of Lord Ebury's motion for a Revisal of the Liturgy:

"'The arguments which decided the fate of the motion may be summed up in a few words. A revisal of the Liturgy would have produced division in the ranks of the clergy, and have proved to the world the little unanimity existing in the legislature on the principal dogmas of Christianity. This confession is precious, since it proceeds from Anglican bishops, or from persons enjoying great authority in their Church. The Liturgy, in a word, remains as it is. The Anglican structure is so dilapidated that it is dangerous to touch it. It is felt that the removal of one stone would lead to a general downfall. It remains, therefore, erect; but the least shock will entail an immense ruin, for its foundations have been laid on shifting sand.' "*

I confess that I am not surprised at such an idea presenting itself to the mind of the enemy, when I have it

---

* Speech of Lord Ebury on the Revision of the Liturgy, p. 31, *Second Edition*. London: Murray, 1858.

myself under the handwriting of a venerable archdeacon of our own Church,* in reference to the contemplated Liturgical reforms, that "it is at all times dangerous to pull stones out of an old building; but to clean the windows, and allow us to see a little more clearly out of them, may not be so much amiss."

What the archdeacon may mean by "cleaning the windows" does not appear; but, for my own part, I would rather attend first to the perishing and crumbling stones, if there be any; removing those that are decayed, and replacing them by such as shall keep the edifice in a decent state of repair.

> "When ancient fabrics nod, and threat to fall,
> To mend their flaws, and buttress up the wall,
> Thus far 'tis duty."

And no further than this do the views of many Liturgical reformers extend. And thus far one would conclude the Bishop of London is prepared to go, if we may be allowed to judge from his lordship's observations on the 28th ult.

" He believed the strength of the Church of England to consist *in its ability to adapt itself to the wants of the age in which we live;* and if he could have been convinced that the noble lord's proposition of May 6th *was required by the wants of the age, he should not have hesitated to give his assent to it.*"†

We feel assured, that the more the Bishop of London gives his mind to the consideration of this question in all its bearings, the more he will feel that "the Prayer-book as it is" is NOT as capable as it might be made of " adapting itself to the wants of the age in which we live," and that

---

* The late Ven. Archdeacon Bonney of Lincoln.
† On these remarks of the Bishop of London, see " A Series of Letters to Lord Ebury, by Aquila de Rupe," Letter ix., p. 63. 1860.

some relaxation of the provisions of the Act of Uniformity is called for, if the Church would extend, or even retain, its hold upon the affections of the people.

The Bishop of Oxford, however, thinks differently; and so far from regarding Earl Stanhope's motion as an instalment in favour of that of Lord Ebury, he thinks its effect will be to make the success of that motion less likely. The Bishop of Oxford "objects ALTOGETHER to ANY alteration of the Book of Common Prayer." He told us so before.* Where the need of repeating himself so often? But we venture to think that the Bishop of Oxford, though a law unto himself and to the clergy of his diocese, is not yet recognised as the dictator of the universal Church; and it may be that the pertinacity with which his lordship thus repeats HIS determination to resist ALL change in the Prayer-book may induce some persons, who might not otherwise have been anxious for such a measure, to think that there may not be so much harm in a COMMISSION of INQUIRY, if it be but to see whether everything is so perfect as the Bishop of Oxford says it is.

"Though it might appear to *some* to be an easy thing to amend that book *at the present time*, he thought *the present time* was far from favourable for such a purpose."

We never expected the Bishop of Oxford, with his numerous avocations, to have found time to read THE INGOLDSBY LETTERS;† but it would be saving his lordship the trouble of again vainly repeating that stereotyped phrase "at this present time," which convinces nobody, if you would refer his lordship, or one of his chaplains, to the passage in which that favourite phrase of his is carefully

---

* And tells us so again in his Charge of November, 1860.
† And yet I suppose he *did* find time to read them, as he told me himself, "You have written many hard things against me, but I FORGIVE YOU." I had rather he had acted upon the advice here honestly given.

analysed.* It is to be regretted that any one, especially a prelate so gifted with the power of speech as the Bishop of Oxford, should waste so much breath, that might be better employed, in repeating an argument whose only effect is to make the hearer conclude it is used to conceal the real ground of opposition.

The following is also a repetition of his lordship's speech in Convocation on February 10th.† Our present Book of Common Prayer, it appears, "contains the prayers that have come down from the earliest times of the Christian Church. In it we have inherited the earliest prayers of the Catholic Church, free from the superstitions and abuses of more modern times; and I should see with the greatest fear any attempt to introduce into it what are called amendments.

"Their lordships must never forget the wisdom of the old canon laid down by Saint Augustine, one of the greatest fathers of the Latin Church,"—a piece of information for which the House of Lords was doubtless under considerable obligation to the Bishop of Oxford, as well as for the exceeding wisdom displayed in the quotation from that father's works which follows :—" *Ipsa mutatio consuetudinis, etiam quæ adjuvat utilitate, novitate perturbat.*" ‡

> "A Daniel come to Judgment!—yea, a Daniel!
> O wise young judge, how do I honour thee!
> 'Tis very true :—O wise and upright judge!
> How much more elder art thou than thy looks!"

What a pity that profound sentiment is not engraven in letters of gold on the doorway of the new Houses of Parliament! What wearisome hours of legislation it would spare!

* See Letters x., xv., pp. 57, 104. "This is not the Time."
† See Letter xi., p. 67. "The Precious Inheritance," &c.
‡ A sentiment made use of by the celebrated Dr. Gauden in 1660, and the late Bishop of Salisbury (Hamilton) in 1855.

What an escape it would authorise from the fœtid effluvia of Father Thames!* What an excuse for legislators in the month of July seeking their peaceful and flowery parterres in the country, taking leave with a clear conscience of the

"Fumum et opes strepitumque Romæ."

But I must not allow the infectious influence of the Bishop of Oxford to carry me beyond the bounds of prudence and discretion. Suffice it to say, that if St. Augustine's "canon" is to become henceforth the law of the land, we have nothing to do for the remainder of our lives but to eat, drink, and be merry—Prime Ministers and Secretaries of State to pocket their salaries, and say nothing about it—bishops and archbishops to stay quietly in their dioceses, and not trouble the House of Lords with their presence or their speeches —and your present correspondent to put up his pen, his occupation being fairly gone, and to sign himself for the last time,

Yours obediently,

July 9, 1858. " INGOLDSBY."

LETTER XXII.

SUGGESTIONS FOR THE CONSIDERATION OF A ROYAL COMMISSION.

"Egregio inspersos corpore nævos."—Hor., Sat. i. vi. 67.

SIR,—Your modest correspondent "Humilis" (who, I am glad to find, is a disciple of Euclid, Bacon, and Newton, which fully accounts for his humility) seems bent on making a further diversion in favour of the bishops, by calling upon

---

* The state of the river was at that time made a serious reason for not attending the two Houses of Parliament; it was also humorously introduced into the epilogue of the Westminster Play, in reference to the proposed (and wise) suggestion to remove the school to a more salubrious atmosphere, existing as it then was "in æternis *fæcibus* et facibus."

me to give in a schedule of my own projected alterations in the Book of Common Prayer. He even invites me to publish an *editio expurgata* of the entire volume,* and promises " to purchase one copy out of his limited income of £88 a year." This offer, I admit, is liberal on his part, but hardly sufficiently tempting to induce me to close with it. I will, however, so far indulge his curiosity as to depart to a certain degree from the safe generalities in which too many are apt to indulge when speaking of a Reform of the Liturgy; and set down for his approval or disapproval, as the case may be, a rude outline of what I, as an individual speaking for myself, think is *principally* WANTING to make our Prayer-book more *practically useful* than it now is, and less open to objection, while the projected reforms may be safely, and without great difficulty, effected :—

I. In the first place, I am of opinion that the present usual Morning Service, consisting of Prayer, Litany, and Communion (even when there is no administration), with Sermon, is too long for the generality of worshippers by fully one-third of the time it occupies.† And I think it would be a great improvement on the present system were these several Services to be ordered in such a manner that they should be read either at different times on the same day, or *differently on different Sundays*‡ according to the circumstances of the congregation ; one rule being practically more desirable for towns, another for villages.§

---

* Specimens of a Revised Liturgy have been published both in England and Ireland, but I am bound to say with no very great success.

† See Letter VII., pp. 40, 41.

‡ For example, the Litany and pre-Communion on alternate Sundays, the "Dearly beloved" abridged, only one Creed at one Service, the Lord's Prayer less frequent, &c. &c.

§ The division of Services in country villages would be very inconvenient in practice; their abridgment, on the contrary, in almost all cases most desirable.

II. I am of opinion that some *latitude should be allowed to the minister* (on occasion) in the selection of Lessons for Sundays; that *parts* of chapters, say twenty or thirty verses, might be often advantageously substituted for whole chapters; and that the Second Lessons should be so arranged as to bring the Gospels and Acts occasionally into the Afternoon or Evening Service, and the Epistles into the Morning.* It would also be desirable that Lessons from the canonical Scriptures should in many cases be substituted for those now taken from the Apocrypha.†

III. That only one Creed should be read at any one Service; and that the Athanasian Creed be at least limited in its use to Trinity Sunday, as being too scholastic for the general class of worshippers, though in some respects a desirable profession of faith on the part of the Church at large as to the doctrine of the Trinity. At the same time I cannot but feel that the efficacy of the Creed for this purpose would not be lessened, but rather increased, were the damnatory clauses omitted.‡

IV. That at the period of Easter shorter portions of Scripture, expressive of the several leading events of the crucifixion, should be read at the Communion, instead of entire and lengthy chapters as at present; also that proper Lessons should be appointed for Monday and Tuesday in

---

* This suggestion was adopted in the Revised Lectionary, which first came into use January 1, 1872; but there is room for improvement even on it, as most people, I believe, will admit.

† The retention of the story of Tobit, Bel and the Dragon, and Susanna and the Elders, *in the public service*, will hardly be defended by any one. This question is fully discussed in an able tract, entitled, "What the Memorialists Want." New York: 1856.

‡ Bishop Marsh, in his Comparative View of the Churches of England and Rome, says, " I do not mean to defend the anathemas in the Athanasian Creed. They are no part of the Creed itself, and might have been consistently rejected from the Creed when adopted by our Reformers." Rivingtons: 1814. See more on this subject, Vol. II., Letters LXXV., LXXXIX.

Passion week, and on a few other occasions, such as Advent, for example.

V. That a few of the Epistles selected for the Communion Office might be advantageously exchanged for others; and in like manner, in two or three instances, the portion of Scripture selected for the Gospel.*

VI. (And this is the only question I approach with diffidence.) That the Occasional Services, including the Catechism, should undergo a careful re-consideration; with a view, if possible, to meet the scruples of those who are offended at certain terms made use of therein, without compromising any vital principle of the Christian faith.†

VII. The form of Absolution in the Visitation of the Sick notoriously gives rise to much painful controversy;‡ and would not be less efficacious for all purposes if conveyed in more general and declaratory terms.§ This service is also, in general, far too cold and formal in its expressions for the present state of religious feeling among the educated poor; and, with the exception of the Scripture portions of it, might be easily better adapted to its intended purpose.

VIII. In the Solemnization of Matrimony the service might be advantageously abridged by the omission of some obvious parts; while the homily at the conclusion

---

* For example, the 1st Sunday after the Epiphany, Epistle. The 4th Sunday in Lent, Gospel; &c.

† This question is largely gone into in an article in the *Edinburgh Review* for January, 1861, No. 229. A paper also has been recently put forth by the Association for Promoting a Revision of the Prayer Book; and another by the Rev. Charles Girdlestone, in a Letter to a Member of Parliament; in both of which documents the doctrinal part of this subject is temperately entertained: April, 1862.

‡ See before, Letter xx., p. 144.

§ See Fisher's "Liturgical Purity," chap. ii., pp. 50, 51.

should be either omitted or abbreviated, or at least made *optional*, as it is in practice.

IX. In the Churching of Women, when used in the course of the regular service, the Lord's Prayer (with the short sentences preceding it) should be omitted.

X. The Psalter might, with considerable advantage, be differently and more equally distributed for Sunday use; so as to bring the most interesting portions before the larger congregations assembled on that day; and not, as at present, to exhibit together Psalms of a totally incongruous significance.*

XI. The Services for the Consecration of Bishops and Ordination of Priests and Deacons should be reduced in length at least one half; both as an inducement to greater numbers of the people to attend on those solemn occasions, and also out of consideration to the age and very possible infirmities of those who have to take a principal part in the performance of these services.†

XII. Generally, there can be no question that the *Rubric* should undergo a careful revision, with a view to adapt it to the present usage, and to alter such parts as are found practically inconvenient; to which may be added the change of a few obsolete terms or words, which are liable to mislead, and which might be better replaced by those now in use.

"Ut silvæ foliis pronos mutantur in annos,
Prima cadunt; ita verborum vetus interit ætas."

As no man in his senses would wish to retain the dead

---

* It is to be regretted that *two versions* of the Psalms are in use; let us hope that a time may come when even this anomaly may be removed; though I should most earnestly deprecate any material deviation from Cranmer's beautiful and harmonious rendering as given in our Prayerbook.

† See the observations of the Bishops of London and Lincoln on this subject, Letter IX., p. 50.

leaves of November amidst the verdant foliage of July, I can conceive no sufficient reason why, in forms of daily use for purposes of devotion, such words as *after* for *according to*,* *let* for *hinder*, *prevent* for *assist*, and (shall we say it?) *Catholic*† for *universal*, should be maintained, when an opportunity offers for replacing them by their equivalents.

I am aware that I am treading on tender ground, and am far from expecting these suggestions to meet with the approval of "Humilis," or many of your other readers. My only object in setting down my views on this matter is, to meet the statement of the Bishop of Oxford,‡ that "the alteration of the Prayer-book is *not so easy a matter as some persons imagine*."

Now, if it were not for the expense of the undertaking, which would not be much reduced by the spirited offer of "Humilis," I see not why the above twelve suggestions (with the exception possibly of No. VI.) might not be carried out with perfect facility by a well-selected commission of as many divines, devoting as many months to the consideration of the subject. And though, doubtless, there would still be a residuum of persons who would not be satisfied with the alterations, either as not going far enough, or as going too far, yet I venture to say the ranks of those who are dissatisfied with *the Prayer-book as it is* would be materially broken by the above suggestions being carried out; while the Prayer-book itself would still retain all its distinctive features, only set forth with greater per-

---

* See a tract entitled "The Liturgy and the Laity," by Edward Shirley Kennedy. Hatchard & Co., 1860; p. 9.

† This word requires perpetual explanation to disabuse the minds of the common people of the notion that it has reference to the Roman Catholic Church.

‡ Letter xxi., p. 151.

spicuity by the removal of some palpable blemishes, and the introduction of some obvious improvements.*

That the bishops should object to such reasonable reforms as these, is to me quite incredible; and I can only account for their conduct on the supposition that their lordships are either fearful of opening the floodgates to much greater changes than any contemplated in the above list, and so conjure up a host of imaginary difficulties which might arise,†

> "Then on the point of their own fancy fall,
> And feel a thousand deaths in fearing one;"

or else (which I should be loth to believe) are, what the *Times* would make them out to be, too fond of their own case to engage willingly in "a troublesome controversy to which they do not feel themselves equal," and so aim how they may best evade it altogether on the weak principle of "Give peace *in our time*, O Lord." In the former case, I would refer their lordships to the opinion passed upon persons of their advanced years by no incompetent judge of character :—

> "It seems it is as proper to our age
> To cast *beyond ourselves* in our opinion,
> As it is common for the younger sort
> To lack discretion."

In the latter, I would warn them that even their own ease and quiet, if that be their object, may be better consulted by a timely concession to the pressure from without, than by a further persistence in attempting to stem a tide that has now set steadily in, and which may be still directed into a comparatively narrow channel; but which, if much

---

* After the above was written several tracts appeared in which other suggested alterations were set forth in detail. See report of the Revision Association for April, 1862.

† Amongst this number were the Bishops of Chester (Graham), Llandaff (Ollivant), Bath and Wells (Lord Auckland), and the late Archbishop of Canterbury (Longley), all, but one, now dead (1878).

longer resisted, threatens to force its way over all interposing barriers, and will not then be so easily controlled.

> "The current that with gentle murmur glides,
> Thou know'st, being stopped, impatiently doth rage;
> But when his fair course is not hindered,
> He makes sweet musick with th' enamel'd stones,
> Giving a gentle kiss to every sedge
> He overtaketh in his pilgrimage;
> And so by many winding nooks he strays,
> With willing sport, to the wild ocean."

Commending the above to the kind interpretation of our spiritual guides,

I remain, Sir, yours obediently,

July 23, 1858. " INGOLDSBY."

P.S. Since the above was written I observe that Lord Ebury has given notice of renewing his motion next session,* if nothing is done by the bishops during the recess in this matter. Surely, if "peace in their time" (as the *Times* insinuates) is their lordships' object in shrinking from the question, they will at length perceive that they are not taking the best way to secure it, by shutting their eyes to the remedy of an evil which many of them have admitted, and which few of their number venture to deny.

LETTER XXIII.

THE MANY-HEADED MONSTER, LITURGICAL REFORM.

> "Eheu fugaces, Posthume, Posthume,
> Labuntur anni." Hor., Od. ii. xiv.
>
> "The years glide away,
> Lost to me, lost to me."
> *Ingoldsby Legends.*

ALAS! as in Horace's days, even so in ours, Mr. Editor, time is ever on the wing. Years roll along; suns rise

---

* This was done; but, as before, without success.

and set; the greater and lesser luminaries of this our earth shine for their appointed hour, and then are seen and heard no more. Meanwhile, various are the issues of human affairs. Progress is made in some things; stagnation occurs to many; retrogression to a few. Certain reforms, real or imaginary, are fiercely agitated for a while; and are at last either floated safely to shore by the breath of public opinion, or are carried down Lethe's darkly-flowing tide to the land of oblivion, never to return again. Others, like Banquo's ghost, will not allow themselves to be thus quietly disposed of; but in spite of all efforts, active or passive, positive or negative, to lay them, will continually re-appear on the world's stage, if not to push us from our stools, yet certainly to allow rest to neither lay nor clerical legislators, sleeping or waking, till they obtain for themselves a hearing, and after hearing, redress.

Of this latter class is LITURGICAL REFORM.

Let not the combative prelate of 1858, who in February last threw his wet blanket of passive resistance over this importunate spectre in "Anne's large chamber;" or who was preparing to silence it for ever with the more active measure of a "decided vote in another place" on the 6th of May,* had not Earl Grey come timely to the rescue, and warned the evil spirit to depart till a more favourable opportunity should offer—let not such a one, or the more retiring bishop, who may even now be meditating in his closet the terms in which to couch his next triennial Charge, denouncing Liturgical Revision as an unclean thing—let him not lay the flattering unction to his soul, that the giant has received his death-blow from any one of these formidable operations, or can ever receive it from all of them combined.†

---

* See Letter XIV., p. 96—7.
† However it may be lulled for a season, the spirit of *enquiry* on this

I tell their lordships fearlessly that the monster is many-headed;

> "Bellua multorum est capitum:"

it is many-tongued, many-lived: witness the signatures to the Derbyshire petition, amounting now to 463 names, different mostly to the 320 who signed the petition of 1857.

> "Non Hydra secto corpore firmior;
> Vinci dolentem crevit in Herculem;
> Monstrumve summisere Colchi
> Majus, Echioniaeve Thebae."

It has a vitality, and reproductive power about it, which argues it to be of no human growth:

> "Merses profundo, pulchrior evenit:
> Luctere, multa proruct integrum
> Cum laude victorem, geretque
> Proelia conjugibus loquenda."

Yes, to be discussed by our wives and daughters over the tea-table. And the time will come surely—I think it will come speedily—which shall proclaim, in accents which he that runneth may read, that "this counsel and work was NOT OF MEN."

The year 1845, with all its incidents great and small, passed insensibly away, and was gathered to its fathers of 1689, 1772, 1834, and the rest. The Charge of the Bishop of St. David's, like that of other bishops, had been delivered, *printed by request*, published at the moderate price of two shillings; and was, I fear, in a fair way of meeting with the inevitable fate which has overtaken less able Charges than this, when it was rescued from the fangs of the grim destroyer by the notice taken of it by Lord Ebury in the House of Peers, in May, 1858.

Not so the question of Liturgical Reform, Liturgical

---

subject is far too deeply grounded on *truth* and *honesty* to be *ever* permanently set to rest, and must ultimately prevail.

Revision, Revision of the Prayer-book, or by whatever other name the chimæra rejoices to be called.

The year 1857 arrives at its stealthy tortoise pace. The New Corn Law has been irreversibly registered in the statute-book. Dorsetshire squires and Lincolnshire farmers have learned to acquiesce in the doctrines of free-trade as an accomplished fact; and tithes are paid, and rents and rates collected, with as good a grace as they ever were, or ever will be. The would-be Popish Bishops of Birmingham, Westminster, Northampton, and Newcastle have been banished the kingdom by universal acclamation; and, thanks to Lord John's celebrated "Durham Letter," my Lords of Lincoln, Oxford, St. David's, and the remainder of their right reverend brethren, reign in undisputed possession of the ecclesiastical territory of Great Britain. The Russian war has been brought somehow or other to a conclusion. Even the Indian rebellion has assumed a shape to relieve our minds from any immediate anxiety. Everything is calm and death-like around,

> "Still as night,
> Or summer's noontide air,"—

when, behold, the ghost of Liturgical Reform again rises to the surface; bloodless its visage, marrowless its bones; regardless of the still small voice which would charitably re-consign it to the sulphurous and tormenting flames whence it has momentarily escaped, whispering blandly in its ear, "Rest, Rest, perturbed Spirit!"—deaf to the mystic, tri-literal spell, which has ere now succeeded in remanding the hateful object to "a more convenient season"—NOT YET; NOT YET; NOT YET;—on hearing which, as at the crowing of some village cock, it has been known, in days gone by, to slink noiselessly away like a guilty thing; and bishops have been seen to smile, and heard to say,

> "Why so, being gone, I am a man again."—

The year 1857, we say, arrived, and brought with it an unusual accession of strength to the cause of Liturgical Reform. Not pamphlets only, but duodecimos, and even one smart crown octavo, bound in scarlet, showered down from Paternoster Row, thick as leaves in Vallombrosa, advocating a Revision of the Prayer-book in a variety of ways; and, what is more to the purpose, met with a rapid and steady sale; were lent and borrowed, read, marked, learned and inwardly digested—everything, in short, but *answered*; were quoted, criticised, canvassed; reviewed in newspapers, magazines, and other periodicals, daily, weekly, monthly, quarterly. High Church organs were on the alert, and loud in their call to Union. The cry of "the Church in danger" resounded, as of yore, from the watch-towers of the *Guardian*, the *English Churchman*, the *Clerical Journal*, and the *Morning Post*. The veteran prelates of Bangor* and Exeter (Philpotts) led the vanguard of the opposing force; warning their respective clergy, and through them the kingdom at large, to beware of the leaven of a certain subtle and dangerous book—"not the less dangerous for being ably and powerfully written"—entitled "Liturgical Purity our Rightful Inheritance." And, finally, towards the autumn of that eventful year, our present right reverend subject, the Bishop of St. David's, thus addressed his assembled clergy from the bishop's chair of his diocese in Wales:—

"My Reverend Brethren,—I cannot address you on this occasion without," &c. &c. &c.

After a passing allusion to the Russian war just concluded, his lordship then proceeds to dilate at some length upon the Papal Bull of December, 1854, on the Immaculate Conception; the Denison controversy; and finally, the

---

* The Right Rev. Christopher Bethell, who died the following year.

difference respecting the Real Presence, still distracting the Scottish Episcopal Church, and aiming to extend its baneful influence to our own.* All these subjects the bishop treats with that clearness of judgment which characterises his lordship's Charges in general, and which makes his hesitation, and apparent vacillation, on the matter of Liturgical Reform the more conspicuous and the more to be deplored.

He then passes from the Eucharistic to the Baptismal Controversy of the day; and, as connected therewith, takes occasion to attack Mr. Fisher's treatise on Liturgical Purity to which his right reverend brethren of Exeter and Bangor had already referred. This book the Bishop of St. David's characterises as "an elaborate work, written with considerable ability, but not so remarkable on this account as because there is reason to believe that it represents the views of an active party, which is bent on accomplishing a radical change in the character of the Church."

"I am not aware," his lordship proceeds, "that these views have been ever in our day so clearly expressed, or so openly avowed. It is, as far as I know, the first time in our memory that a Revision of the Liturgy has been proposed, or rather demanded, for the express purpose of adapting it to a peculiar system of doctrine, for which its partisans had hitherto been satisfied with the shelter which it found in the language of our present formularies. And in this point of view the attempt may be regarded as perhaps the most glaring example that has occurred in our Church of that dogmatical intolerance to which I have been directing your attention. The pretext for this attempt has been furnished by a polemical artifice which is very common, though not

---

* See the *Guardian*, *English Churchman*, and *Clerical Journal* for March, 1860. This question, like the rest, has now passed away; while that of Liturgical Revision remains, and *vires acquirit eundo*.

on that account the more creditable, by which the disputant first affixes his own definition to an ambiguous term, and then charges his opponents with the worst consequences he can deduce from the meaning which he imputes to them."

I leave it to Mr. Fisher, who is abundantly able to defend himself, to reply to this paragraph as he best may.* Meanwhile I have thought it due to the Bishop of St. David's to quote the above passage at length, as being part of the evidence we are bound to produce in order to prove his lordship no Liturgical Reformer, in Mr. Fisher's acceptation of the word.

The bishop concludes as follows :—

"The author's historical review of the various phases through which our Liturgy, and other formularies, have passed before they were brought to their present shape, will, perhaps, so far as it is correct, lead others to a very different conclusion, and will inspire a feeling of gratitude for the result which has been worked out through this long conflict of jarring opinions, prejudices, and passions, together with a resolution not to throw away that which has been thus providentially preserved. Of the consequences that would probably ensue, from the success of this attempt, to the peace and welfare of the Church, I need not speak, as I believe the danger of such an event to be very remote; and I have only adverted to it as an illustration of an evil which is manifesting itself among us in a great variety of forms."

The counsel for the defence were proceeding to show, by quotations from other of the bishop's writings, that though the right reverend prelate might not be prepared

---

* Our own opinion is, that though Mr. Fisher has demolished the status of the non-natural interpretation of the Baptismal Services, he has not been equally successful in establishing his own in its room.

to go Mr. Fisher's length in "purifying" the Prayer-book, yet there was nothing to prove him averse to a more moderate measure of reform. Nay, they were prepared with abundant evidence to place the bishop in the front rank of this latter class of revisionists. The judge, however, observing that it was now dinner-time, and that there seemed small prospect of the case of Thirlwall *versus* the Bishop of St. David's being concluded to-day, said he should adjourn the further hearing to the next opening of the court.

Meanwhile I remain, yours, &c.,
July 30, 1858.   "INGOLDSBY."

LETTER XXIV.

INSUFFICIENCY OF SUPPLEMENTAL RUBRICS.

"Dimidium facti qui *bene* cœpit habet."

SIR,—Your indefatigable correspondent, Mr. C. H. Davis, has not given a satisfactory explanation of his statement that I "*once* disdained the proposals of the *English Churchman* for a set of supplementary Rubrics."* The question is not as to *once* or *lately*, but as to *ever* or *at all*.

I did not, and do not, disdain any proposition, from whatever quarter it may come, for the better arrangement of the Church Services, or for reducing the too great length of the present Morning Service. I simply said, and say still, that the suggestions of the *English Churchman*, however ingenious, come TOO LATE to serve as an escape from the main question of a thorough Revision of the Prayer-book; and cannot now be accepted as a *substitute* for this last; however deserving the recommendations themselves

---

* See Letter xx., p. 141. A more elaborate article *in favour* of structural Revision appeared in the *English Churchman*, April 25th, 1860.

may be of a careful consideration by the Commission to whom the details of Revision must be primarily submitted, and by whom they must be prepared for the public eye.

It is of the utmost importance that when the work is set about at all, it should be *begun well*.* That is to say, that it be taken in hand not lightly, unadvisedly, or timidly, but in an honest intention to face boldly every difficulty, and an earnest desire to remove as many as possible of the blots which now confessedly adhere to and deform the Book of Common Prayer.

That this beginning, and I trust *good beginning*, is not far distant, I have before stated is my firm conviction; and moderation, like that of Mr. C. H. Davis, will not hinder the work from proceeding, any more than will the immense labour and pains that have been bestowed by other workmen in pioneering the way for a temperate reform.

I remain yours, &c.,

August 13, 1858. . "INGOLDSBY."

LETTER XXV.

THE PEOPLE'S CALL FOR A REVISION OF THE LITURGY.
THE BISHOP OF ST. DAVID'S.—NO. III.

"Servetur ad imum
Qualis ab incepto processerit, et sibi constet."—HOR.

"From his first entrance to the closing scene,
Let him one equal character maintain."—FRANCIS.

SIR,—Though it will prolong our examination into the complicated case now before us (and which has been still further complicated by the various interpolations by which

---

* See "Liturgia Recusa," by Aquila de Rupe (the Rev. Richard Bingham), chap. ix., p. 57; on WELL BEGUN, HALF DONE. 1660.

it has been interrupted), I know of no way in which to do full justice to the Bishop of St. David's views on Liturgical Reform except by making a further extract from his Charge of 1857.

Not that I hold any man, much less a bishop, to be bound for ever by what he may have said, written, or published some nine months ago; but when such sentiments are in corroboration of what the same individual had expressed in writing twelve years before, and has never been known to retract; and when their author has reached the mature age of three-score years, it is but fair to presume that the public have not only his lordship's δεύτεραι φροντίδες, which are proverbially the best, but his deliberate judgment on the matter in hand—a matter to which, as bishop, his attention must have been almost daily directed during this long interval.

Three times at least since 1845 had his lordship met his assembled clergy.* Three times had been reciprocated between them the rare privilege—

"Vivas audire et reddere voces."

Three times had each Liturgical Reformer in the diocese of St. David's—and to my own knowledge they are far from being contemptible either for their number or their intelligence†— had the opportunity of stating his grievance, discussing freely the question of Revision, and expressing his hopes as to the probability of the fact being realised. Whether such a degree of familiarity subsists between the Bishop and his clergy in that part of the kingdom as to admit of this inter-

---

* In advocating an increase of the Episcopacy, in the debate of July 4, 1861, Lord Ebury laid stress on "the distance that now subsisted between the *Prince Bishop* and the bulk of his clergy." See Report in the *Daily News* of July 5th, 1861.

† In no part of the kingdom is the desire for an Abridgment of the Services more strongly felt and acknowledged than in Wales.

change of thought and language; or whether, as in some dioceses with which I am acquainted, "the inferior clergy" stand in such awe of their seldom-seen diocesan that all the talking is on one side, all the listening on the other —a kind of one-sided intellectual engagement—

"ubi tu pulsas, ego vapulo tantum"—

I will not pretend to say. But certain it is that the bishop himself, in 1857, did not shrink from enunciating to what extent he might be looked upon as a Liturgical Reformer, and therefore to what extent it may be presumed he was not unwilling his clergy should follow his lead.

I am the more inclined to draw this conclusion, from an incident, trifling indeed, but, like straws thrown up before the wind, not wholly insignificant as indicating from what quarter it blows. It is a personal affair, it is true, but I may be excused introducing it here, as really by no means irrelevant to the matter in hand.

Ten lustrums have well-nigh passed over my head, and grey hairs and sundry other tokens proclaim that I am no longer young. I have, in fact, seen my fair share of life in all its various phases, and was prepared to go to my grave subscribing to the record of the wise man, that there is nothing new under the sun:—when, behold, a new thing did befall me, and that from a quarter whence I least expected it.

In the autumn of 1857 I received by post a Bishop's Charge, with the words "*From the Author*" written on the title-page. That charge was the Bishop of St. David's, upon which we have been for some time engaged.

Now, I have received "from the Author"—as which of us has not—by post, by private hand, by bookseller's parcel, by all the various methods of transmission suggested by this literary and expansive age, books, tracts, essays, pamphlets of every conceivable quality, and well-nigh innumerable in quantity; but never, until November, 1857, was it my fortune to be honoured by a *presentation copy of a Bishop's Charge*. And though I have presumed frequently —too frequently I fear—to intrude upon their lordships with trifling effusions of my own, I had come to the conclusion that I must look for no return, not even a line by way of acknowledgment, from that quarter; in short, that their lordships' motto was surely, like that over the lion's den,

"Omnia me advorsum spectantia, nulla retrorsum"—

which, being interpreted, means, "Cast thy bread upon our waters, if you please, but look not to receive it back again, even after many days." Judge, therefore, of my delight at finding an exception to this universal rule in the instance of so distinguished a prelate as the Bishop of St. David's; and who shall say, the charm once broken, I may not be similarly favoured again?*

To turn over the well-printed pages, and to swallow eagerly the contents, was, of course, my instant and agreeable occupation, till my eye rested at length, at p. 53, upon the following note:—

"See 'The People's Call for a Revision of the Liturgy, in a Letter to Lord Palmerston,' by the Rev. James Hildyard of Ingoldsby, 1857."

Now, if your readers have borne with my egotism thus far, and have not forgotten my remark on notes to Bishops' Charges in a previous letter,† they will enter into my feelings at meeting the above note in this place.

Now is my fortune made, thought I to myself: now is

---

* It is due to their lordships to say that I have since been frequently so favoured; but alas! I find them, in the main, *silent* on the subject of Revision.

† Letter XVIII., p. 126.

my chance of being appointed a Bishop's Chaplain or a Rural Dean at least, in my old age. Now is there some hope of exchanging the "fens and fogs of Lincolnshire"* for the pure air of the mountains in Wales; henceforth will my intellects have fair play, which for thirty years, first at Cambridge, then at Ingoldsby, have been condemned to vegetate in the Bœotian atmosphere of the Bedford level.† So from the margin my eye glanced rapidly to the passage denoted by the asterisk, which ran as follows:—

"The most mischievous effect that there seems room to apprehend from the attempt itself‡ is the prejudice it may raise against ALL *proposals for Liturgical changes*, though conceived in a widely different spirit, and directed to a wholly distinct object. I trust, however, that it will only serve as a salutary warning against the principle which it so boldly avows, *and will not deter the more liberal and enlightened friends of the Church from* PERSEVERING IN THEIR ENDEAVOURS *to bring about such modifications of her Liturgical usages as may adapt them to the altered circumstances and growing needs of our times.*"§ Is it not amazing that this same prelate should, within three short months after delivering the above sentiments, be found speaking in Convocation against the most moderate revision of the Prayer-book;‖ and within three months more, in the House of Lords, be heard as one of the only three prelates who ventured to raise their voices in denunciation of a Royal Commission of Inquiry into that book, as moved for by Lord Ebury?¶

---

* An expression attributed to his late Majesty King George III.
† "Bœotum in crasso jurares aëre natum."—HOR., Ep. ii. i. 244.
‡ Alluding to Fisher's " Liturgical Purity."
§ Bishop of St. David's Charge for 1857, p. 53.
‖ The revision *at that time asked for* was confined to "adaptation to the habits and requirements of the age;" see Letter IV., p. 21.
¶ Lord Ebury's motion, May 8th, 1860, was simply "That a humble address be presented to Her Majesty the Queen, praying that she may be

"Within three months!—
Let me not think on't;—Frailty thy name is Thirlwall!
Three little months; or ere those shoes were old
In which he stepped from the episcopal chair,
Like Palmerston, all smiles; why he, even he;—
O heaven, a beast that wants discourse of reason
Would have stay'd longer!—
It is not, nor it cannot come to, good!"

But we have not yet done with this Charge of 1857. The Bishop in the bishop's chair proceeds as follows :—

"It would, indeed, be surprising if, while all around us has been undergoing such vast and momentous changes, the regulations of public worship continued to be as well suited as ever to their original purposes, and if no inconvenience could now arise from an ACT OF UNIFORMITY, ALWAYS OF QUESTIONABLE EXPEDIENCY, *and passed two centuries ago.*"*

Always of questionable expediency! Why then retain it? Why strengthen the hands of those who insist that this Act shall *not be touched* in their day? Why vote with the Bishops of Salisbury and Oxford against a Royal Commission, as one step at least towards repealing or modifying the provisions of that Act?

" There is a strong conviction," the bishop proceeds, " in many minds, one which has of late been fast gaining ground, and is making itself more and more distinctly audible, that such a supposition would be no less contrary to fact than to antecedent probability, and that *it is highly desirable to*

---

pleased to appoint a Commission to consider whether the Book of Common Prayer and Canons of the Church be not susceptible of alterations calculated to give increased efficiency and stability to the religious institutions of the country."

* See Letter No. III., p. 17. The laws of Solon were enacted to continue in force for *one hundred* years. The Bishop of Durham (Baring) characterises the Act of 1662 as one " disastrous in its consequences as it was cruel in its intention."—*Charge to the Clergy of Gloucester and Bristol,* 1860.

provide a remedy for the inconvenience which has arisen from the existing incongruity between the state of the law and *the wants of the Church."*

And here is inserted the asterisk inviting the reader's attention to "The People's Call for, &c." What his lordship saw then to elicit this approving notice of that particular pamphlet out of many by the author of the "Ingoldsby Letters," or what he has since heard or seen to make him alter his views, I am ignorant; but if ever words proclaimed a bishop as an advocate for Liturgical Revision, as sought for by all moderate reformers, surely the above passage may be considered as doing so. Indeed, had Lord Ebury required evidence for the first two clauses of his three-fold proposition:—

1st. That a revision of the Liturgy is desired;

2nd. That it is desirable;*

he could hardly have put into the box a better witness than the Bishop of St. David's, as cited above. He was deterred, I suppose, from doing so by the saving clause contained in a subsequent passage, which we shall refer to in our next, and which would scarcely bear out the *third* of Lord Ebury's propositions; namely, "That the *method* by which it is proposed to effect a revision is both constitutional and *expedient."*

The bishop, on the contrary, gives it as his opinion, that

---

* For example, Bishop Thirlwall observes, "I protest against *the compulsory use of the Athanasian Creed*, as not only an evil on account of the effect it produces on many of the most intelligent and attached members of our Church, but *a wrong in itself*. . . . It may be possible for theologians to shew by technical arguments that it is a legitimate development of doctrine implicitly contained in Scripture: but this, however fully admitted, would not justify the Church in exacting assent to their conclusions under the penalty of eternal perdition. This is in fact creating a new offence against the Divine Law, and introducing a new term of salvation on merely human authority."—*Commissioner's Report*, p. x.

"the most important among the objects which such friends of the Church* have in view might be accomplished without any change in the language of our formularies, simply by enlarged facilities for a freer use of the contents of the Prayer-book and the Bible. Out of this treasure might be brought 'things new and old,' which, by means of a judicious selection and arrangement, would amply suffice for the ordinary use of the household of faith."

"This therefore would seem to be the object which should take precedence of all others in every plan for the *improvement of the Liturgy*. It would be effected mainly by some slight alterations in the Rubric and the Calendar. But after this had been done, there would *still remain some deficiencies to be supplied, and there might be yet room for a further Revision*, which would contribute, though in an inferior degree, to the usefulness of the materials already at our disposal."

Can anything be more clear than this? Can the Bishops of Lincoln and Oxford gainsay this position of their right reverend brother?

"It might be desirable," for instance, proceeds the Bishop of St. David's, "to provide a greater number of Services for special occasions of regular and frequent occurrence, as well as a greater variety of extraordinary Prayers and Thanksgivings."†

Will the Bishops of Lincoln and Oxford dispute this?—
"It would *then be time to consider*, whether the *language* of the Prayer-book required or *admitted* of *improvement*, for purposes as to which, in principle, all would agree, however they might differ from one another in the details of

---

* The Moderate Reformers.
† This was afterwards attempted by the Special Services Committee of Convocation. It also forms a conspicuous feature in the American scheme for a Revision of the Book of Common Prayer. New York, 1856.

its practical application. For in the abstract none would deny the expediency of removing *all needless occasions of offence* or mistake arising from an obsolete or ambiguous phraseology."*

But I must conclude, having exceeded the limits of a letter, and having still somewhat to say upon our present subject. Would that I could here close the chapter! But, alas! in my next it will be my painful office to trace out the irregular curve by which an escape is effected from what our Transatlantic neighbours would call "the fix" in which we appear to have secured our learned and right reverend authority.

Meanwhile I remain, yours, &c.,
Aug. 20, 1858. " INGOLDSBY."

LETTER XXVI.

THERE IS A LION IN THE PATH.
THE BISHOP OF ST. DAVID'S.—NO. IV.

"Look ye there, now—*but* again! I hate *but;* I know no form of expression in which he can appear that is amiable, excepting as a butt of sack. * * * It is a sneaking, evasive, half-bred, exceptious sort of a conjunction, which comes to pull away the cup just when it is at your lips."—THE ANTIQUARY.

SIR,—Archbishop Whately, in his last Charge, observes that "those persons are surely deserving of blame who are always complaining of some supposed faults, while they strenuously oppose every measure by which it is possible that a remedy can be applied."†

Whether the Archbishop of Dublin had in his eye the

---

* On this part of the subject some original remarks were made in a tract by Edward Shirley Kennedy, B.A. London: Hatchard, 1860.
† Charge by the late Archbishop of Dublin. London: 1858.

conduct or the writings of any particular individual, I cannot say; but I fear our readers will see but too much reason to apply the remark to the right reverend prelate now occupying the see of St. David's.

In our last, methought we had the flag of that learned divine fairly nailed to the mast of the good ship Liturgical Reform, and himself, like a second Nelson, prepared to do or die in the ensuing deadly strife. At least, such I am bold to say is the conclusion ninety-nine men out of every hundred, capable of drawing an inference, would arrive at, on perusing the extracts we produced from the Bishop's Charge of 1857. And no doubt we had his lordship in this position, and should have held him to his guns, had our hero been an admiral, or even a sea captain, accustomed to look a difficulty in the face, or prepared to turn his blind eye towards it.

But unfortunately on the present occasion we have neither of these characters to do with, but, as we ventured before to hint,* a kind of marine divinity; neither fish, flesh, nor fowl. So his godship contrives to give us the slip just as we thought we had him safe. Our modern Proteus was aware of the approach of the enemy; or at least conscious that he had laid himself open to the lynx-eyed observation of the Liturgical Reformers, by the somewhat unguarded admissions he had made; and thus, as we shall presently see, Pastor Aristæus is fairly baulked of his game.

Nothing that I am acquainted with is so difficult to lay hold of as the words of a man who does not mean to be caught napping. By day-light you have no chance with him; and by night he leads you on through bog and mire, a sort of moral *ignis fatuus*, that

"Like the circle bounding earth and skies,
Allures from far, but as you follow flies."

---

* See Letter xv., p. 101.

He sleeps with one eye open, one ear awake. He speaks with but one side of his mouth. He has two tongues, like the ancient Tyrians,—one for the present, the other for the future. The opinions of such a man, however valuable they might be, become utterly worthless when applied to the wear and tear, the rough and ready business of life. With such a one there is an everlasting rock a-head, a difficulty in the way, a lion ithout. He wants that alloy of baser metal which renders far inferior minds so much more useful when you come to hack and hew your way through the thorny entanglements which beset the course of all legislation, whether for Church or State.

With his knowledge of languages, and his skill in seeing, but not solving, a difficulty, the Bishop of St. David's would have made an excellent plenipotentiary to the court of Rome, St. Petersburgh, or Madrid, but is ill adapted to win upon the confidence of plain, blunt, straightforward John Bull, whose aye is aye, and whose no is no, and who likes to have people of a similar cast of mind to deal with.*

His lordship had evidently no wish to be screwed down to the literal application of the passages quoted in our last, which led us, along with many of our too credulous friends, to cry out, rather prematurely,

EUREKAMEN, EUREKAMEN, SUNCHAIROMEN.

Behold, a prelate bold enough to declare himself a Liturgical Reformer in spite of the Bishop of Oxford! one not afraid to set the *Guardian* and *Clerical Journal* at defiance; wrapping himself, like another Chatham, in the folds of his conscious rectitude, and proclaiming aloud,

---

* It was well observed by some one of Lord Palmerston, that "he had the happy knack of always saying exactly what he meant;" hence his popularity with the House of Commons and with the nation at large.

> "There is no terror, Burgess, in your threats,
> For I am armed so strong in honesty,
> That they pass by me as the idle wind,
> Which I respect not!"

So off he goes; not violently indeed; nor at a tangent— as we Cambridge men are apt pedantically to express ourselves; for people in general, especially ladies (unless of the Somerville class, which is scarce), have not the remotest idea of what a tangent is—but at that sidelong, sinuous, meandering gait, which is best illustrated by the wrigglings of a certain amphibious animal, whose name, to avoid vain repetition, I will not again mention, but whose peculiarity of action renders it extremely difficult to apprehend, being altogether exceptional, *sui generis*, at variance with all the laws of motion, as laid down by Newton and others in the books.

I shall not, of course, attempt to follow my subject through this labyrinth, or "maze," as the antiquarians call it: I am not furnished with the needful clue, and my argument will brook no further delay.

Suffice it to say, that the conclusion the bishop arrives at is no conclusion at all. He sees all the impediments in the path of legislation, but finds no way of escape. Convocation *might* do what is needed, but cannot. It has been praised indeed, I think a little more than it deserves,* by Mr. Fisher, "for the readiness which it has shown to address itself to this subject, and the desire it has manifested for a revision of the Prayer-book; but"—oh, these *buts!* If there is one word in the English language more detestable than another, it is the combination of letters which goes

---

* Witness, for example, its reception of the Dean of Norwich's motion for a Revision of the Prayer-book, March, 1861. Mr. Fisher's commendation reminds us of the proverb,

"Praise undeserved is satire in disguise."

to make up the monosyllable BUT.* Give us a downright No, *I won't*, or YES, *I will*, and we understand you. But who can make anything of your BUTS? Their manufacture into anything practical is more difficult than that of a certain curious material into a silken purse—a feat which no amount of artistic skill has yet succeeded in accomplishing.

So it appears that, as in the storming of Cronstadt by a Napier, so in the carrying out of Liturgical Reform by a Thirlwall, there are half a hundred very excellent reasons why the thing should be done, *but*, unfortunately, twice as many why it should not. "It is evident that Convocation, as at present constituted, is UTTERLY INADEQUATE to such a purpose; and it is *more than doubtful*, it is *altogether improbable*, that its constitution *will ever be so modified* as to render it a fit instrument for so great a work."—*(Charge, &c.)*

"Off with his head—so much for Buckingham!"

How the advocates for the further session of the two Houses of "the Church Legislature" may like this sweeping condemnation from one of their most talented and conspicuous members, I know not; but most cordially, I believe, do the Liturgical Reformers reciprocate the sentiment; while at the same time it does not lead them to sit still, like the Turk, acquiescing in their destiny, with arms folded, crossed legs, and pipe in mouth; but they open their jaws wide like Englishmen, and call for a ROYAL

---

* See more of this obnoxious monosyllable at Letter xxxvii. We may indeed say of it with our great dramatist,

"I do not like *but yet;* it does alloy
The good precedent: fie upon *But yet;*
But yet is a jailer to bring forth
Some monstrous malefactor."
Ant. and Cleop., Act ii., Sc. 5.

COMMISSION to displace on the present occasion this incapable remnant of antiquity so graphically depicted by the bishop.

His lordship, however, objects to a Royal Commission, as we shall see when we approach his speech in reply to Lord Ebury, on May 6th; and he sketches out an *ideal* Convocation, or Church Parliament, which exists, and is likely to exist, nowhere but in the prelate's own brain, whence there is small hope of its emerging as a second Minerva, armed *cap-à-pié*, to carry all before it by argument or force.

The bishop thinks that "a mode *might* be devised, in *perfect harmony* with the Church's ancient institutions, for gathering the sense both of the clergy and the laity on questions affecting their common interests and objects as faithful members of her communion."—" *But*,"—here again, of course,—"*many difficulties* will, no doubt, have to be overcome before any such plan can be matured and carried into effect. It will probably be only fashioned by degrees, with the aid of experience, and arrive at whatever success it may attain through many failures and disappointments."

I fear this golden era will prove analogous to those Attic Kalends with which the historian of Greece is doubtless familiar. A sort of ever-flowing river, pleasant to contemplate, especially at this season of the year, but which is sooner swum across by a bold adventurer than forded dryshod by the unlettered rustic.

This chimerical Church Council would not have to contend, it appears, "with difficulties depending on the will of any who are foreign or hostile to the Church, *but* only with such as may arise from a divergency of views and opinions on secondary points, among those who are *perfectly unanimous* on the main object." Where, I wonder, are these happy spirits to be met with?—Supposing them, however, to have an existence anywhere besides in the prelate's fertile imagination, mark what follows as the fruit of this " perfect unanimity : "—

"It is true that such a representation of the Church, *however complete*, would be *even less capable than Convocation now is of any action* that would possess legal force, or exert any other than *a purely moral influence!*"

So, with this conclusion, in which we must admit very little is concluded, the bishop winds up his remarks on the subject of Liturgical Reform, and we shall for the present follow his example. Only let us observe, in passing, that if this homœopathic specimen of legislation, which, on his lordship's own showing, is less than infinitesimal, a degree of frigidity somewhere below zero, an amount of capability inferior only to "utter incapacity," is all that he is prepared to offer in the place of Convocation *as it now is*, and as the only machinery for accomplishing the "desired, desirable, and expedient Church Reform," it might have been as well to retire at once from the field, and allow Lord Ebury's COMMISSION to have at least a trial. It is a sound maxim, in all cases, to make use of such tools as you have, if you cannot get at such as you would like; and I never heard the position of the poet controverted by any wise man,

"Si quid novisti *rectius* istis,
Candidus imperti;—si non, HIS UTERE MECUM."

"Farewell; and if a *better* system's thine,
Impart it freely,—or MAKE USE OF MINE."

I remain, yours, &c.,

August 27, 1858.   "INGOLDSBY."

P.S.—I regret to see that one of your correspondents hints that you "have said enough about Liturgical Revision." You, of course, are the best judge how far the ventilation of this particular subject injures the circulation of your journal. But all well-wishers to the cause you have so steadily advocated must know that nothing but untiring perseverance presents the smallest hope of our succeeding in the object we have in view. And it is as well, therefore, that all cowards should at once leave the ranks, and understand that we have no intention whatever of relaxing in our exertions, and mean to give no quarter to our opponents until the concession of our main point relieves us of all further anxiety. The Fabian policy of the bishops must be met by similar tactics on the part of the reformers; and TIME alone will show on which side TRUTH, the great arbiter of Victory, has all along been ranged.

If this fresh instance of "the Confessional" in the diocese of Oxford,* countenanced, as it would seem, by the bishop, does not open the eyes of the public to the necessity for *some inquiry* into the working of the Book of Common Prayer, nothing I fear will.

LETTER XXVII.
THE BISHOP OF ST. DAVID'S AN ANTI-REFORMER.—NO. V.

"En hæc promissa fides est?"—VIRGIL.

"Pleasures are like poppies spread,
You seize the flower, its bloom is shed;
Or like the snow-fall in the river,
A moment white—then melts for ever;
Or like the Borealis race,
That flit ere you can point their place;
Or like the rainbow's lovely form,
Evanishing amid the storm."—BURNS.

SIR,—Tam O'Shanter did not more effectually realise the truth of this unrivalled simile,

"When he frae Ayr ae night did canter,"

---

* The notorious "battle of the Boyne," followed shortly after by the West Lavington affair, so mysteriously hushed up; the exposure at St. Alban's, Holborn, in February, 1867; with other instances, alas! too numerous to mention; shew what a cancer was eating into the very vitals of the Church for want of a timely remedy being applied.

than did the Liturgical Reformers the vanity of putting their trust in bishops, upon reading the Report of the Bishop of St. David's Speech in Convocation on February 10th, 1858.

In vain did they look for a repetition of those memorable expressions of 1845, "the NEED THAT EXISTS for a *Revision of the Liturgy;*" . . "the very *unenlightened* and *injudicious friends of the Church;*" . . "the LAPSE OF YEARS, and ALTERED CIRCUMSTANCES;" . . "the carrying *into effect* any *measures to supply that want;*"—and the like. In vain did their eyes peer about to discover any trace of those more memorable words of 1857, "proposals for *Liturgical changes,* though conceived in a *widely different spirit;*" . . "I trust it will *not deter* the MORE LIBERAL and ENLIGHTENED FRIENDS OF THE CHURCH from PERSEVERING IN THEIR ENDEAVOURS to bring about such modifications of her Liturgical usages as may adapt them to the *altered circumstances* and growing needs of our times;" . . "It would indeed be surprising if no inconvenience should now arise from an ACT of UNIFORMITY, *always* of QUESTIONABLE EXPEDIENCY, and *passed two centuries ago!*" . . "There would *still remain* SOME DEFICIENCIES *to be supplied,* and there might be YET ROOM for a FARTHER REVISION;" . . "it would *then be time* to consider whether the *language of the Prayer-book* required or admitted of improvement;" . . "for in the abstract *none would deny* the *expediency* of removing all *needless occasions of offence.*"*

Alas! how grievous the disappointment, when instead

---

* See Letter xxv., pp. 172—176, &c. How truly to this Prelate do those well-known lines apply:

"Be these juggling fiends no more believ'd,
  That palter with us in a double sense;
  That keep the word of promise to our ear,
  And break it to our hope."—*Macbeth*, Act v., Sc. 7.

of this golden fruit which the Reformers looked to gather from their boasted tree, they crunched between their teeth dry ashes like the following:—

"I heartily concur with my right reverend brother, the Bishop of Oxford, in deprecating every attempt that has lately been made *so* to alter the Book of Common Prayer as," &c.

"I also entirely concur with what has fallen from my right reverend brother, the Bishop of Lincoln, with regard to the supposed length of the ordinary services."— "I do not think that under proper management the whole time occupied by the service is *ever* found by any attentive member of the congregation to be *wearisome or excessive.*"

Doubtless, had we begun our review of the right reverend Prelate's opinions on the subject of Liturgical Revision at the epoch of Feb. '58, instead of '45 and '57, we might have extracted some drops of consolation, sucking patiently

"Apis Matinæ more modoque,
 Grata carpentis thyma *per laborem*
 Plurimum;"

and, like enough, those youthful Reformers who are not acquainted with the contents of his lordship's Charges of '45 and '57 might have thought there was a good deal to be gleaned from sentences like the following:—

"I must say, that if *either on this or on any occasion* it should *appear desirable to institute an inquiry* whether *any improvements* may be effected in the present order of the services, or any of them, such an inquiry ought to be instituted solely by those who are acquainted with the history," &c. "Whilst I say this, I do not mean to dissent by my opinion that IMPROVEMENTS OF CONSIDERABLE VALUE *might be effected in our services*, simply by a substitution of one variable element for another, and little changes which would *remove a number*, not of very important, but *still well-founded objections;* and I do MOST HEARTILY DESIRE that so far the question *should be kept open*, and should *receive our attentive consideration.*"—(Bishop of St. David's in House of Lords.)

But *cui bono*, may I ask, the keeping this matter from century to century as an OPEN QUESTION?—What the profit of this "attentive consideration," if it is all to evaporate, as it infallibly would do, in *words?**—more especially when supported in the House of Lords, within less than three months, by a point-blank speech against the *only feasible mode* of accomplishing the preliminary steps to the desired result.

Here, again, behold the wisdom of Archbishop Whately's remark, referred to in our last, and which will bear more than one repetition: "Those are surely *deserving of blame* who are always complaining of some supposed faults *while they strenuously oppose every measure* by which it is *possible* that a remedy can be applied."—"POSSIBLE," observe— not "desirable" or "expedient;" but POSSIBLE. That is the question. And that is what every wise man will ask himself, if he is desirous that a thing be done at all. It is of little use building imaginary edifices of *conceivable* methods for carrying out *conceivable* plans, which it is well known beforehand will never be executed, and the machinery of which is of far too delicate a character to stand the test of every-day life. Such castles are, indeed, erected *in nubibus;* such ploughing is verily performed on the sea-shore.

Whereas, let a Commission of earnest men be once set fairly to work, with a *bonâ fide* desire to meet the known sentiments of the majority of English Churchmen; and a

---

* The late Dean of Ripon (McNeile) well designated Convocation as "Vox et praeterea nihil."

willingness, as far as possible, to comprehend the views of moderate Dissenters; it would be strange indeed if they did not produce *some* beneficial result from their labours. They would have the Report of the Commission of 1689 before them, both as a guide and a warning; and would have little difficulty, if they addressed themselves to the task, in separating the chaff from the wheat in that somewhat miscellaneous heap. They would, it is to be hoped, have *more time* given them to digest their materials than was afforded on that occasion; while the present postal system of the country would furnish them with incomparably superior means of ascertaining the sentiments of all classes interested in rendering the Prayer-book as nearly faultless as man can make it. Above all, it is to be trusted, such Commission would be so constructed from the outset, as not (like that of 1689) to contain within itself the elements of spontaneous combustion; but be animated by one simple desire to do all with a single view to the glory of God, and the benefit of His people.

That the construction of such a Commission is *possible* there cannot be a shadow of doubt. Whether it will please God to open the eyes of our rulers to avail themselves of a quiet time like the present for setting this matter at rest; or whether it is destined to remain still "*open*," as the Bishop of St. David's would have it, until some violent excitement again forces it upon the consideration of the public, and causes that to be done in haste which might now be done with caution and judgment, time alone will show.

Meanwhile, Mr. Editor, let it be the consolation of your contributors that the issue does not rest with them; while I trust their apparent feebleness will not lead them to relax in their endeavours; remembering always that this battle is essentially the Lord's, and trusting that in it, as in other engagements, He will increase strength to them that have no might.

I remain, yours, &c.,

Sept. 3, 1858. "INGOLDSBY."

NOTE.—The following letter to the Editor of the *Church Chronicle* appeared in that paper the same day with the above:—

"SIR,—Allow me to call the attention of your untiring correspondent 'Ingoldsby' to the following extract from Dr. Beattie's interview with King George III., at Kew, August 24th, 1773: from which it will appear that even that high Tory monarch was a Liturgical Reformer:—

"'When I told him that the Scotch clergy sometimes prayed a quarter, or even half an hour at a time, he asked whether it did not lead them into repetitions? I said 'it often did.' '*That*,' said he, '*I don't like in prayers;* and, excellent as our Liturgy is, *I think it somewhat faulty in that respect.*' 'Your Majesty knows,' said I, 'that three services are joined in one, in the ordinary Church Service, which is one cause of those repetitions.' 'True,' he replied, 'and *that circumstance also makes the service too long.*' From this he took occasion to speak of the composition of the Church Liturgy; on which he very justly bestowed the highest commendation. 'Observe,' his Majesty said, 'how flat those occasional prayers are that are now composed, in comparison with the old ones.'

"Hoping that the above passage may in any measure tend to strengthen the hands of those who are indefatigable in their endeavours to work out this most desirable reform in our Church,

"I remain, yours truly,

"A BARRISTER.

"*Lincoln's Inn, Sept.* 2, 1858."

LETTER XXVIII.

KING GEORGE III. ON THE LENGTH OF THE CHURCH SERVICE.

"Νήπιοι, οὐδὲ ἴσασιν ὅσῳ πλέον ἥμισυ παντός."—HESIOD.

"Fools blind to truth: nor knows their erring soul
How much the half is better than the whole."—BULWER.

SIR,—There are two valuable contributions to the cause of Liturgical Reform in your last, which call for a passing notice. One, an article from the Rev. C. H. Davis, extending to not less than seven columns of closely-printed matter; the other from A BARRISTER, which, though short, is very much to the point, and calculated to aid materially in promoting the success of one branch of our complicated subject.

By the bye, it is remarkable how much closer the gentlemen of the legal profession (when they are not paid by the line or folio) address themselves to a question than those of my cloth, if I may say so without offence. Is it because the lawyer's business is simply to *prove his case*, and he finds that brevity is more efficacious for that purpose than prolixity; while the clergy are habituated to the notion that their sermon *must* last for half an hour or twenty-five minutes, and consequently (being obliged by the prevailing fashion to preach two of these every Sunday for fifty-two weeks in succession) acquire a lax habit of expression which adheres to them in other matters? Certain it is that in the voluminous correspondence I possess on the subject of Liturgical Reform, amounting to near 3,000 letters, the contrast between the two is most obvious.

To give a couple of specimens of the legal style :—

"Sir, I approve of shortening the Service, because I think that more people will go to church.*
"*Lincoln's Inn, Jan. 5, 1856.*"   "A Lawyer.

"Dear Sir,—I will send at once for the pamphlet to which you call my attention. *I quite concur in its object.*
"*Lincoln's Inn, June 27, 1856.*"   "A Lawyer.

Can one of the Bishop of Oxford's *verbosæ et grandes orationes* produce more conviction on the mind of the reader than letters like these? I have had my misgivings lest "Ingoldsby" should be tedious; and have studied to limit the length of my communications to such a compass as I thought the patience of your readers would tolerate. But, alas! even I—schooled as I am in wading through long treatises and loosely-written MSS. on the subject of Revision—even I shrink from encountering a letter, or, more properly, an essay, like this of Mr. Davis's, extending to a page and a half of your journal, terminated, moreover, by the formidable announcement (*To be continued!*)—How few, therefore, will profit by your laborious correspondent's lucubrations I dread to think: and I regret it the more, as the letter in question, had it been divided into sections of one or two columns at a time, might have been of considerable service to the cause.

Hoping that this hint will be as kindly received as it is intended, I will now proceed to notice the Barrister's extract from the writings of Dr. Beattie.

So, it appears, the exemplary Protestant monarch, George III., found the Liturgy of our Church "*somewhat faulty* in respect of *its repetitions;*" and had reason to complain that owing to the junction of three services in one, the present Morning Service of the Church was *too long.*

---

* See Letter xxxv.

And yet the Bishop of St. David's "entirely agrees" with his right reverend brother of Lincoln in thinking, that "under proper management the whole time occupied by the Service is *never* found by any *attentive* member of the congregation to be *wearisome* or *excessive*."*

What "proper management" may mean, I know not. But I know that few individuals ever more deservedly earned the reputation for unaffected piety, and a reverence for religion, than the honoured grandfather of the illustrious person who now adorns the throne of these realms; and I would add that, in such a matter,

"Errare mehercule malim cum Platone, quam cum istis vera sentire;"

I had rather err with George III. in seeking to abridge the Morning Service, within the bounds where reason and devotion can have fair play, than retain its present dimensions though all the bishops on the Bench should concur in affirming that it is *not* too long, and *never* found "wearisome or oppressive" by any sincere worshipper.

The remark of George III., it must be remembered, was made so far back as 1773; when railroads and steampackets had not reticulated our lands and ploughed our seas; when the electric telegraph was a fact as little dreamed of as the possibility of ascending to the regions of the sun; when the penny postage and the book-post had not added wings to the interchange of thought; when, in short, time was measured by hours and not by seconds, and space by yards instead of by thousands of miles.

What the same monarch would have thought of a Service lasting on an average from one and a half to two hours, at this age of the world's history, it is impossible to say; but sure I am that his practical common sense would not

---

* See Letter v., p. 29, and vi., pp. 32—37.

have been wanting to the occasion; while his well-known moral courage would not have prevented him from giving utterance to his opinions.

And now a word with Mr. Davis, whose exertions in the cause of Revision have been unintermitting.

He divides the various sections of Liturgical Reformers into *six* primary classes, with all the subdivisions which may result from the union of any of them taken two and two, or three and three together, as the case may be.

I shall not attempt to follow him through all the permutations and combinations which might arise from the above classification. But as he has been pleased to hazard a conjecture as to the rank "Ingoldsby" holds in his republic of Reformers, I will set his mind at ease as to my own views, leaving others to do the same or not as they please.

Mr. Davis, then, sums up Ingoldsby's creed, under a combination of the three following heads:—

1st. That of the Rubrical Revisionists; in which class I find myself enlisted in company with Archdeacon Sinclair of Middlesex, Archdeacon Allen of Salop, and the Dean of Norwich (Pellew); to which honourable trio might be added Archdeacon Musgrave of York, Archdeacon Stonehouse of Lincoln, the Dean of Manchester (Bowers), the Dean of Bristol (Elliott), the Dean of Tuam (Plunket), and some others.

2nd. That of the non-doctrinal Revisionists; among whom are numbered Bishop Short of St. Asaph, and the Rev. Ashton Oxenden, Proctor in Convocation for the Diocese of Canterbury, who has of late retired from the battle-field,

"And back recoil'd, he knows not why,
E'en at the sound himself had made."[*]

---

[*] Mr. Oxenden, now Bishop of Montreal, came forward again in March, 1861, as seconder to the Dean of Norwich's proposition before Convocation for a Revision of the Prayer-book.

3rd. That of the "Comprehension Scheme Revisionists." For the Advocates of this "scheme" we are referred to the List of the Liturgical Revision Society of 1854, and the catalogue of subscribers to the "Clerical Petition," printed in the *Record* of the present year, consisting of 463 names; among whom, however, the name of Ingoldsby will *not* be found.

Not that I object to the idea of Comprehension. I hold, on the contrary, with Archbishop Tillotson and Bishop Burnet, that every effort should be made to embrace *the greatest possible number* in the pale of the Church. But I would not have this accomplished at the price of driving as many Churchmen out, as we brought Dissenters in. In all my publications upon this subject (amounting to not less than five, exclusive of these Letters), I believe there is no trace of my willingness to sacrifice any *essential* Church principle, either for the sake of peace, expedience, or comprehension.

But, notwithstanding this, there is vast room for improvement in various portions of the Book of Common Prayer, especially its Calendar, Offices, and Rubric. Much also might be done to meet the views of the more moderate Dissenters, the Wesleyans for example, without affecting the value of the Prayer-book as a manual for the Orthodox Churchman.

Hoping that this exposition of my creed, thus in a manner extorted from me, may be satisfactory to Mr. Davis, and give offence to none,

I remain, Sir, yours, &c.,

Sept. 10, 1858. " INGOLDSBY."

P.S.—There is a letter in your last publication which I am sorry to be obliged to pass over, but which I read with great interest; I mean the one from the Rev. Charles

Girdlestone of Kingswinford, whose character gives weight to whatever he says; and I must say I cordially agree with him in the desire he expresses that your other correspondents would follow the example of Mr. Davis and Mr. Tyndale, in attaching their names to their contributions. We should then know, not only who Excubitor, Humilis, A Subscriber, A Barrister, M.A., Cantab.; M.A., Oxon., Observer, U. G. O., Glaucus, Gulliver, Rusticus, Crito, Pictor, and other powerful *advocates* of our cause are, but (which is more to the point,) who are C. W. T., T. G., and two or three other feeble opponents of it.

By the bye, what a severe satire is that of Mr. Girdlestone's upon the occupants of the Episcopal Bench, that "no *advocate of truth* ought to shrink from incurring some risk of obloquy, or SOME LOSS OF THE PROSPECTS OF PREFERMENT, by the *honest avowal* of independent opinions temperately expressed."*

LETTER XXIX.

THE BISHOP OF ST. DAVID'S IN THE HOUSE OF LORDS, NO. VI.

MAY 6, 1858.

"Utcunque in alto ventu 'st, exin velum vortitur."
                                                                PLAUT. *Epid.*

"As when a ship by skilful steersman wrought,
Nigh river's mouth or foreland, where the wind
Veers oft, as oft so veers, and shifts her sail,
So varied he."   MILTON.

SIR,—It is said in Lardner's Life of Sir William Jones, that it was a fixed principle with him, from which he

---

* See Letter xxx., p. 200. I am happy to say, that the case is now different to what it was in 1858; the "advocates of truth" have since come boldly forward, and *attached their names* to their writings. Let us hope that the time will also come when such advocacy shall no longer be considered a bar to all prospects of preferment.

never voluntarily deviated, not to be deterred by any difficulties that were surmountable from prosecuting to a successful termination what he had once deliberately undertaken. I have also heard it stated by a descendant of the celebrated Lord Teignmouth, that the latter was wont to say that he owed all his success in life to a golden rule early inculcated upon him, and which he repeatedly had occasion to apply, *Never make a difficulty*.

With all his good qualities—his learning, his industry, his eloquence—I fear the above rules have formed no part of the training of the Bishop of St. David's, of whom I purpose taking my leave to-day, more in sorrow than in anger.

Whatever disappointment the Reformers might have felt (and to my knowledge it was not small) at perusing the Bishop's speech, as delivered in Convocation on Feb. 10th of the present year,* it was trifling in comparison of what they sustained on finding the same prelate addressing the House of Lords on the evening of May 6th, and again recording his sentiments as hostile to Revision; at any rate speaking point blank *against* Lord Ebury's motion for a COMMISSION of INQUIRY into the Book of Common Prayer.

The Bishop's speech on that occasion being reported in the papers of the following morning, it is unnecessary for me to go into it in detail, more particularly as we have already devoted an unusual amount of space to an endeavour to arrive at his lordship's views in the matter of Liturgical Reform. Suffice it to say that the impression produced on my own mind, on reading the report of the above speech, was much the same as in days gone by, when I was studying the harangues of one Gorgias of

---

* See Letter XXVII., p. 184.

Leontium, whom Plato introduces in the character of a Sophist—one, that is to say, whose trade it was to argue against his own and everybody's convictions; a special pleader, engaging to prove to the satisfaction of all comers that the worse is the better cause; in other words, to make out that black is white.*

It grieves me to make the comparison; but the honesty of a public critic compels me to say that such is the only conclusion I have been able to arrive at after repeated perusals of the learned Prelate's speech on May 6th. One tries over and over again, but to no purpose, to fix his lordship to some definite expression of opinion. One finds half-a-dozen BUTS, supported here and there by an *if*, or a *whereas*, or an *however;* while one looks in vain for an AYE or a NO, a "To be" or a "Not to be;" and again and again one retires foiled by the unavailing search. The ball flies off from the glazed coat of our pachydermatous opponent, and again and again one cries out in despair,

"Quo teneam vultus mutantem Protea nodo?"

"Say, while he changes thus, what chains can bind
These various forms, this Proteus of the mind?"

I am aware that the Bishop may say there is nothing in this speech to preclude him from being considered an advocate for a Revision of the Liturgy,† provided *he* had the doing it, or the nomination of those to whom the task should be entrusted. But as I apprehend that responsibility is not likely to devolve upon his lordship, or to fall to the lot of any other *individual*, it seems puerile to blow hot and cold in this manner:—

---

* A lengthy correspondence on the Bishop of St. David's inconsistency was published in the *Standard*, by the Rev. J. W. Burgon of Oriel (afterwards Dean of Chichester), Dec. 20, 1869.

† See his lordship's elaborate defence of himself in his Charge of 1860.

"'To hang between, in doubt to act, or rest;'

"And live a coward in one's own esteem,
Letting I dare not, wait upon I would,
Like the poor cat i' the adage."

I had rather be a dog and bay the moon, than such a Reformer. For most assuredly, if the revision of the Prayer-book is to wait till the doing of it shall be *attended with no risk*—till the Bishops of Exeter and Oxford on the one hand, and Mr. Fisher and Mr. Gell on the other, shall be *equally* satisfied with the result—we may make up our minds to abide the dawn of doomsday, and acquiesce with the best grace we can in all the acknowledged "imperfections" of the book as we now have it.

Who ever heard of change unattended with some degree of danger? But what wise man was ever deterred in consequence from attempting the improvement of that which is notoriously faulty? I have read, indeed, of an old woman who went out in the rain because her almanack told her that the weather was to change on the morrow; and "as it never changes (as she sourly observed) except for the wuss," she thought she had better make sure of to-day. We all know the story of the veteran Reformer, Dr. Paley, respecting another old woman, cousin-german to her of the umbrella, who "left off thinking at all for fear of thinking wrong." But I never heard of *men*—Bishops, at least, and other Legislators—arguing thus, if we except a certain conspicuous individual of the former rank, who quoted not long ago, with consummate gravity, and I am told not without effect upon the House of Lords, that truism of St. Augustine's,

"Ipsa mutatio consuetudinis, ETIAM QUÆ ADJUVAT UTILITATE, novitate perturbat;"*

a sentiment worthy, indeed, of being engraven on the portals

---

* See Letter XXI., p. 152. See also Bishop of Oxford's Charge, 1860.

of the Vatican, but ill adapted to the British House of Legislature in the middle of the nineteenth century.

Who expects a Roebuck and a Newdegate to be equally content with the forthcoming Reform Bill? But will that consideration deter the noble Earl (Derby) from embarking upon that sea of troubles? I trow not; or if, by any accident it should, I apprehend the people of England will not be so easily reconciled to the plea that "it is impossible to please all parties, and therefore it is better to please none." For my own part, I am content that it should be so in that particular instance; but it must not be forgotten that the Reform Bill dates from 1832, not 1662, like the Act of Uniformity. It is not *merely* "a precious inheritance of our fathers," but *that*, and something else engrafted upon it by their venturous progeny.

It will be time enough to acquiesce in our Reformed Prayer-book, as having attained all the perfection of which it is capable, when it can date its reconstruction just thirty years back; but not till then. And sure I am that nothing but THE WILL and A VERY SMALL AMOUNT OF MORAL COURAGE on the part of our spiritual rulers is wanting to put us in possession of such a book as shall stand the test of another century before it again calls for amendment.

The conclusion of the Bishop of St. David's speech on May 6th is too remarkable not to be afforded a niche in this attempt to put on record his lordship's sentiments on this matter:—

"He did not recede in the *slightest degree* from *any* opinion which he had *ever* expressed upon this subject."

What those opinions are, your readers have had an opportunity of ascertaining from the extracts already furnished in these Letters.* And it is but in accordance with them that he proceeds to say that—

---
* See Letters XV., XXIII., XXV., XXVI., XXVII. See also Charge of the Bishop of St. David's, Oct., 1860: Rivingtons, London.

"So far as INQUIRY was concerned, he should be QUITE FAVOURABLE to ANY measure which held out a prospect of *really ascertaining the feelings and wishes of the great body both of the clergy and laity.* He DOUBTED very much, however, whether such would be the effect of a Royal Commission."

Whether it was Lord Thurlow or Lord Eldon who "*doubted* of everything but *proposed nothing,*" I at this moment forget, nor is it material to inquire. But one cannot help feeling that when a Commission is earnestly sought for by many for the express purpose of "*ascertaining the feelings and wishes of the great body both of the clergy and laity*" on the matter of Revision, it would have been more consonant with the declared sentiments of one professing to be "*quite favourable* to ANY measure which *held out a prospect* of accomplishing that object," to have voted for the issue of such Commission, unless he were prepared to offer a better alternative;*—to have acquiesced, in short, in what he could get, rather than detain the House with his DOUBTS, leaving the matter exactly where he found it; that is to say, where it has been for the last two hundred years, and where it will be for the next two hundred, as far as rests with the energy and decision of character of such legislators as the right reverend prelate.†

I have the honour to remain, Sir,
Yours very obediently,
Sept. 17, 1858. "INGOLDSBY."

---

* See passage from Horace, quoted in Letter XXVI., p. 182.
† It was hoped that by his absence from the House of Lords on the night of May 8th, 1860, when twenty prelates combined in their opposition to Lord Ebury, the Bishop of St. David's had come to the conclusion that it was time something should be done. This hope was dispelled by the publication of his Charge in the autumn of that year. He did, however, ultimately screw up his courage to vote with his Lordship on May 19, 1863.

LETTER XXX.

THE REV. CHARLES GIRDLESTONE AND CHURCH PATRONAGE.

"Who dares think one thing, and another tell,
My soul detests him as the gates of hell."—POPE.

SIR,—The fourth prelate on our list is the Bishop of Winchester (Sumner), who has been recently charging the clergy of his diocese, and in doing so makes mention of Revision of the Prayer-book among other matters.

But before entering upon his lordship's sentiments on that question, I have a word to say with one of your correspondents, and shall take occasion *en passant* to make a few observations upon bishops in general, and the Bishop of Winchester in particular.

It is with regret that I find Mr. Girdlestone so soon repenting of his advice to your more timid correspondents, to attach their names to their contributions. So long, however, as they do so, they must expect to be taken at their word, and can have no cause for complaint if your readers draw their own conclusions from their remarks, though they may not be exactly in accordance with what the writers themselves might wish.

Accordingly, when I lately read in Mr. Girdlestone's letter, that "no *advocate of truth* ought to shrink from incurring some risk of obloquy, or *some loss* of *the prospects of preferment* by the *honest avowal* of independent opinions temperately expressed,"* it sounded to me, and I must say still sounds, very like a tacit, though severe and not altogether unjust, rebuke upon the present occupants of the episcopal bench.

---

* See Letter XXVIII., p. 194.

Allow me to detain you a few minutes while I endeavour to explain myself to the satisfaction, I hope, of many of your subscribers, if not of Mr. Girdlestone, whom I am far from wishing to bind to my own interpretation of his words, the purport of which, it appears, I have misconceived.

A reference to the Clergy List will show that the archbishops and bishops of the English Church have in their joint patronage *about three thousand pieces of preferment,** including almost all the archdeaconries, some of the deaneries, most of the canonries and prebends, with nearly all the other cathedral appointments, such as chancellorships, precentorships, treasurerships, subdeaneries, and the like. This is about one-fourth part of the entire preferment of the Church, so far as it deserves the name. But more than this—it will be observed, in looking carefully into the episcopal patronage, that not only in numerical amount, but also in pecuniary value, and certainly in dignity or *éclat*, the right reverend bench have their full share of the means of dispensing substantial benefits among those who find favour in their sight.

I am far from objecting to this arrangement of Church patronage;—on the contrary, *in principle* I think it right that it should be so;—I have, moreover, great pleasure in coinciding in the spirit of Mr. Girdlestone's remark, that there are in the number of "the present occupants of the episcopal bench" many individuals to whose judgment and disinterestedness the patronage of the Church may in the main be safely confided.

But still, when we find it widely circulated in the public

---

* Supposing, which it is not unreasonable to do, that there are on the average *three* expectants for each of these preferments, it is not difficult to account for the 9,500 signatures to the celebrated Westminster Manifesto of 1860, popularly called "the Ten Thousand."

papers, and hear it repeated in every one's mouth, that "THE BISHOPS have declared UNANIMOUSLY *against a Revision of the Prayer-book*"—when we hear the Bishop of Oxford, in particular, pronouncing authoritatively that "the Prayer-book *shall not be touched*" in his day—when, further, we read of a prelate, of so diametrically opposite opinions to this last as the Bishop of Winchester, addressing his clergy in the following words (and that, too, in a *reforming* Charge), that "there were *some reforms* he had felt bound *to resist*, such, for instance, as the Revision of the Prayer-book;" that "an attempt to accomplish such revision had been made in the last session of Parliament, but that it met with very little support from any one, and *none from any member of the episcopal bench;*"*—I think I am not greatly misreading human nature if I infer that the above three thousand pieces of preferment (no inconsiderable slice of the ecclesiastical cake) are not likely to find their way into the mouths of those "*advocates of* TRUTH" who have not been deterred by any "risk of obloquy, or *loss of the prospects of preferment*, from the honest avowal of independent opinions temperately expressed."

But Mr. Girdlestone says, "it is only a limited portion of Church patronage that is in the hands of our bishops," and he is "not aware that they are more apt than those who administer the greater part of it to wield their influence with a view to this object in particular."

Is this certain?—I doubt it. At any rate, it is a matter easily admitting of proof;† and I shall be glad to be informed of any instance of a Liturgical Reformer being promoted *by a bishop* within the last five-and-twenty years;

---

* See Letter XIV., p. 97. Note †.
† I regret to say that, after twenty more years of observation, I cannot point to the case of a single Liturgical Reformer of my acquaintance, (and it is far from small,) being *episcopally* promoted.

while I have under my eye some score or more of most excellent and laborious clergymen, worthy of advancement in their profession, who have, notoriously for this single reason, hitherto met with nothing but cold looks from their diocesan. In fact, they have become marked men ever since they hung out the banner, though it were but the small pennant, of Liturgical Reform. What bishop's chaplain, rural dean, or *honorary* canon, is to be found in the ranks of the Revisionists? And though such a phenomenon may arise—and I am far from saying it will not—its appearance on the stage at this moment would astonish the religious world about as much as the comet now blazing in the north, a renascence of the Phœnix of Araby the blest, or a flight of black swans.*

Meanwhile, happy, thrice happy they, who, like the Reverend Charles Girdlestone, can write reforming letters and pamphlets† from the well-furnished library of a benefice *in private patronage*, valued at nine hundred and fifty pounds per annum, or who can repose in their fiftieth year,‡ after a life of no small labour and activity, upon the *otium sine dignitate* of a college living, earned literally by the sweat of their brow, of the annual value of six hundred pounds, like your unepiscopally-promoted servant,

Sept. 30, 1858.   " INGOLDSBY."

---

* These observations were remarkably confirmed by the publication of the 9,500 names attached to the Westminster Manifesto of 1860; among whom may be counted 160 *rural* deans, each of them holding his nomination direct from the Bishop; while of Deans *proper*, who are *independent of Episcopal control*, only *five* are to be met with!

† Mr. Girdlestone published in 1862 an able Tract, entitled "Black Bartholomew's Day." W. J. Johnson, 121, Fleet Street.—Also "A Letter to an M.P. on Revision of the Liturgy." 17, Buckingham Street, Adelphi.

‡ Now in his *seventieth*, still the Rev. James Hildyard, B.D., Rector of Ingoldsby, Lincolnshire; having sat impatiently under the Charges of three successive Bishops for 33 years.

P.S.—I see that Mr. Girdlestone, in his δευτέραι φροντίδες, imputes "UNWORTHY TIMIDITY" to the present occupants of the episcopal bench!—which charge, however, having been made by others in a higher position (who have said in public that their lordships' opposition to Reform might be resolved into the one principle of "Give peace in our time, O Lord!"),* I imagine he considers himself at liberty to repeat, without fear of being quoted as the originator of the imputation.

LETTER XXXI.

THE BISHOP OF WINCHESTER, THE RIGHT REVEREND CHARLES RICHARD SUMNER.

"All viewed with awe the venerable man,
Who thus with mild benevolence began."—POPE.

SIR,—The persons and characters of the two Sumners are well known. Their presence, courtesy, and moderation, command very general respect. It is rare indeed, if not unprecedented, that two brothers should for so long a period† have occupied such distinguished positions in the Church. Still more rare is it that individuals so situated should have given so little offence to any one, so much satisfaction to many.

Whatever may be their other merits, we have a clear proof in this that the qualifications of an English gentleman, as well as of an English Churchman (not always found united), are an important recommendation in one about to be elevated above his brethren into the highest offices of

---

* See before, Letter XXII, p. 159.
† It was at that time thirty-six years since the Bishop of Winchester, and thirty-four since his brother, as Bishop of Chester (afterwards Archbishop of Canterbury), had been consecrated.

the Church. Whatever depends upon a gracious manner, gentle forbearance, courtesy, and consideration towards equals or inferiors, is safe in such keeping. The oil that prevents the jarring of the ecclesiastical machine flows in an unbidden stream from such lips, and we hear of none of those unpleasant collisions which array the clergy against their Bishop in some dioceses, to the injury and distraction of the whole Church.

But, unfortunately, every virtue has a tendency to degenerate into its proximate vice. Thus, bravery will sometimes verge upon rashness, caution upon timidity, seriousness upon Puritanism, cheerfulness upon levity, gravity upon formality, eloquence upon verbosity, and so forth. And as the zeal of a Philpotts or a Wilberforce will occasionally break forth into the fire of unseemly controversy, so the mildness of a Sumner will be apt to betray the cause of truth, from an unwillingness to grate upon the feelings of individuals, or the apprehension of provoking a strife " of which no man can foresee the end."

It is to this amiable weakness that we must attribute the fact that our venerable Primate is found wanting to himself and to the Church at the present crisis.* Pseudo-Romanism stalks unabashed through the land, fostered secretly by those who are solemnly pledged to resist it to the utmost;† while earnest Protestants look in vain to the dignitary, highest in place of power, for the bold hand that should check its pride. Meanwhile, the Bishop of Winchester, whose private sentiments are pretty generally understood, and are not obscurely exhibited in his speech

---

* Read the Speech of His Grace the Archbishop, on the renewal of Lord Ebury's motion, May 8, 1860.

† Some of the Right Rev. Prelates discovered their mistake when it was almost too late to stay the mischief. "Principiis obsta" is a wise maxim, and cannot be too carefully borne in mind. See Letter xxxix.

before Convocation in February last, commences the said speech by an eulogium upon the opinions of his right reverend brethren of Lincoln, Oxford, and St. David's :—

"I rise for the purpose of expressing the extreme satisfaction with which I have listened to, I think I may say, *every word* and *every sentiment*, which my right reverend brethren have addressed to your Grace. Indeed, so *entirely do I concur with them*, that I should have thought it quite unnecessary to make a single remark, if I did not feel the importance *at the present moment* of making it known elsewhere that there is a very strong and *universal* concurrence amongst the Bishops of our Church in the sentiments which have been so ably expressed. As such a concurrence does exist, I feel the importance of making its existence known *at this particular moment.*"

ECCE QUAM JUCUNDUM!—What a pity it is that their lordships cannot inspire the inferior clergy, the priests and deacons of the Church, with this delightful attribute, so peculiar to themselves, of dwelling together in unity.

There is something marvellously cohesive in the texture of the episcopal toga. It is extremely difficult to tear, and has the almost miraculous property of rendering the wearers as coherent one with another as the material of which their robes are constructed. However opposite their sentiments may notoriously have been before donning the magic lawn, the right reverend conclave becomes thenceforth, like the heads of colleges in the university,* all of one

---

* The following lines are worth preserving, as showing the tendency of persons in an exalted position to hang together:—
    "The Master of Jesus does nothing but tease us;
    The Master of Sidney's of the very same kidney;
    The Master of Christ's fits in to a trice;
    The Master of Emmanuel follows him like a spaniel;
    The Master of Pembroke his likeness from them took;
    The Master of Peter's has the very same features;

mind, one colour, one purpose, one creed; and woe betide the hapless individual who ventures to interpose his opinions betwixt the wind and their unanimity.

One who felt keenly in his day the force of this remark (as any one who has a mind may do now if he likes), has compared their lordships somewhat irreverently to a herd of the larger cattle, when offended by the attack or even the bare appearance of a yelping cur. "They butt," says the admirable Sydney Smith, "with an extended front;" —and if the leaders fail in tossing the delinquent clerk with their horns, the rank and file in the rear, the chaplains, secretaries, archdeacons, and rural deans, will instinctively trample him to death with their feet. Or should he haply escape this fiery ordeal, he will carry with him to his kennel inglorious bruises, and a plentiful bespattering of mud, to make him rue for ever the day that he ventured to intrude on such hallowed ground.

The Master of Bene't (C.C.C.) holds just the same tenet;
The Master of Cath'rine's of the very same pattern;
The President of Queen's is as like as two beans;
The Master of Caius (Keys) is as like as two peas;
The Provost of Kings says the very same things;
The Master of Clare fits in to a hair;
The Master of Trinity with them has affinity;
He of Trinity Hall differs nothing at all;
The Master of John's 's like the rest of the dons;
The Master of Magdalene (Maudlin) comes after them twaddling;
The Master of Downing (Dr. Frere) comes last of all frowning."

A select number from this body, consisting of five with the Vice-chancellor, under the name of the CAPUT formerly governed the University, and no new statute could be even submitted for the consideration of the Senate at large, until it had received the *unanimous* consent of this petty conclave,—a single *veto* being sufficient to stop all further proceedings.

The consequence was, as may be easily imagined, that no real reform was introduced into the University till the CAPUT itself was knocked on the HEAD, as it now is.

Mutatis mutandis—such is exactly the present position of THE CHURCH. Let us hope that here (as elsewhere) it may shortly be said (1879),
"Tempora mutantur—nos et mutamur in illis."

Who would have anticipated, *à priori*, a Sumner agreeing in "*every word* and *every sentiment*" uttered by a Wilberforce?—Yet so it is; at least so his lordship says; and "he is an honourable man. So are they all; all honourable men."

And they all agree in this one point, that the Prayer-book SHALL NOT BE TOUCHED in their day. Why is this? What can be the reason—except that they have all imbibed a strong tincture of that "unworthy timidity" which Mr. Girdlestone attributes to their lordships?*

"One touch of nature makes the whole world kin."

And so this alloy of UNWORTHY TIMIDITY acts as an amalgam of surpassing force upon Oxford and Winchester, St. Asaph and St. David's, Lincoln and London, Chichester and Hereford, Bath and Wells and Llandaff.†

The Bishop of Winchester says in his late Charge (which I quote in preference to his speech before Convocation, as being of more recent date) that we may "depend upon it that no alteration of *any kind* would be suggested in a revision of the Prayer-book which would not meet with *violent opposition*, and which would not lead to many heart-burnings."

It may be so; and I am sorry for it. But does his lordship think that the Church will thus escape these heart-burnings? Have the Confessional in Belgravia and the Battle of the Boyne (resting, as they profess to do, upon the *unaltered letter* of the Prayer-book) been attended with no "heart-burnings?" Have Messrs. West, Poole, Bennett, Denison, Gresley, Randall, and Liddell, met with no "violent opposition?"‡

---

* Letter xxx., p. 204. Postscript.

† The names of these were respectively, Wilberforce and Sumner, Vowler Short and Connop Thirlwall, Jackson and Tait, Gilbert and Hampden, Lord Auckland and Ollivant; of whom only three now survive (1878).

‡ The disturbances at St. George's-in-the-East and many other churches had not then broken out; but they owe their origin to the same cause, "the unaltered letter of the Prayer-book." More of this hereafter.

Metaphor apart, far-seeing men anticipate a coming struggle between the advocates for the *letter* and the advocates for the *spirit* of the Prayer-book; and, taking counsel from all history, they think it more prudent to meet the danger half-way, than to shut their eyes to its approach, and allow the enemy to gain strength by delay.*

But as I observe your space, Mr. Editor, is more than usually occupied at this time with "the Boyne Commission," I will not longer detain you, but remain always,

Yours, &c.,

October 8*th*, 1858. "INGOLDSBY."

LETTER XXXII.

THE REV. CHARLES GIRDLESTONE AND THE BISHOPS.

"Of all my writings, all my midnight pains,
A life of labours,—lo! what fruit remains?"
POPE (*Travestie*).

SIR,—" Praise undeserved is satire in disguise." At least so sings the poet. And so I cannot but think must Mr. Girdlestone have felt, when he penned that short letter in your last.

Let me, however, before proceeding further, return my acknowledgments to this gentleman, for his kind consideration in not wishing, by throwing any additional burden in my way, to divert me from prosecuting to a successful issue the object we both of us have at heart :—

"For here forlorn and lost I tread,
With fainting steps and slow;
Where wilds immeasurably spread
Seem lengthening as I go."

---

* The subsequent legal proceedings, culminating in the Public Worship Act, fully justify the vaticinations in the text; 1878.

Three whole years* of agitation on this subject, above 3,000 letters from my own pen, the same or a larger number received and filed, with newspaper articles, reviews, and pamphlets beyond calculation, still leave me building upon but a little more solid foundation than Hope, the "fool's paradise," as it has been called by some; the "indestructible instinct of the soul," as it has been more courteously styled by others. Any one, therefore, who, like Mr. Girdlestone, so far shows sympathy with a fellow-workman as to spare him, though it be but the feather-weight of a letter (if irrelevant to the cause we have in hand), so far proves himself a friend, and so far has, as he deserves, our sincere thanks.

Nevertheless, I cannot allow the good feeling evinced by this gentleman towards myself to lead any of your other readers to suppose that I acquiesce in the acquittal which Mr. Girdlestone would pass upon their lordships, the bishops, with regard to the non-promotion of Liturgical Reformers.

I lay great stress upon this matter; for in my judgment herein lies no small portion of the want of success which has hitherto attended every attempt to reform the Liturgy, even to the extent, as the Bishop of Winchester says, of introducing "an alteration of *any kind* into the Prayer-book." The grand obstacle has ever been the wet blanket that has been invariably cast by the bishops upon the head of the solitary Reformer, whenever or wherever he happened to show his face. No wonder others have been deterred; no wonder the cause gains few proselytes. It is not every one that has a fancy to be sent to Coventry, even though it be the ancient capital of Mr. Girdlestone's diocese.

---

* The above is a very insufficient representation of the toil bestowed by myself and others on this matter. I gave in at last in 1863 from sheer despair, and disgust at the thankless nature of the task I had undertaken; but my views on the subject remain unshaken to this day, for the best of reasons, that not one of my arguments has been answered, or can be.

But we must hear this reverend gentleman plead in his own words.

"Our bishops," says he, "*might* have done *much for* Liturgical Revision. They have done all they could to *hinder* it. I am sorry for them; for on their heads lies the chief responsibility of that violent revolution which is sure to follow on the protracted denial of temperate reform. But I do not believe that our bishops, as a body, are more actuated in the disposal of their patronage by abhorrence of church-reforming clergy than most lay patrons, or than those who act for the Crown. My own 'slice of the ecclesiastical cake,' to which your correspondent so amusingly refers, is a case in point.—My third letter on Church Reform was published in 1834. In 1837, I was presented to the Rectory of Alderly by the Crown; and in 1847 to my present benefice by a lay patron; and in the same year I was appointed *Rural Dean* by my diocesan, by whom also I was offered, within this twelvemonth, an *honorary* Stall at Lichfield,* although I did not accept it."

If this be, as I conclude it is, the case for the defence, again I say, "Save me from my friends!" You, perhaps, have not access to that most useful publication, the *Clerical Directory*. In this manual we have an account of the Rev. Charles Girdlestone's university and other performances, which, as I am an entire stranger to that gentleman, and cannot, therefore, be supposed to be influenced by personal considerations in enumerating, I will here extract :—

He was, it appears, originally of Wadham College, Oxford, where he took his B.A. degree forty years ago, and is consequently now not less than sixty years of age. He was a first-class man in classics; second-class in mathematics

---

* The Ecclesiastical Commission, if it has effected nothing else, has at least succeeded in bringing the honorary Canonries into contempt.

and physics; elected Fellow of Balliol by *examination* (no small honour to any man); university examiner; select preacher in two several years, 1825 and 1829; appointed to a Crown living in 1834; and to the Rectory of Kingswinford by *a lay patron*, Lord Ward (to his credit be it spoken), in 1847.

And now, in his *sixty-first or second year*, comes the *Episcopal* patronage showered on the head of this distinguished member of the University of Oxford. He is appointed *Rural Dean* by his diocesan, and *offered* an HONORARY STALL in Lichfield Cathedral; which post, seeing that the acceptance costs more than the preferment is worth, Mr. Girdlestone very prudently "declined!"

And this is the case set up in defence of the bishops as *not dis*countenancing, nay rather as *occasionally promoting* Liturgical Reformers!—the Bishop of Lichfield (Lonsdale) is, I believe (nay, I know, for I was proctor when he took his doctor's degree at Cambridge upon his elevation to the Bench), an honourable and worthy man; a gentleman; a scholar; a man of letters; and moderate in his theological views; and I can well understand the pleasure with which his lordship would see a clergyman of Mr. Girdlestone's attainments installed in his cathedral. But an *honorary* stall—a *rural* deanery!—Our too sensitive flesh and blood revolts from the idea. Many a curate would turn away in disgust at the offer of either.

"Far, far aloof the expecting Chaplain hides,
The famished Vicar scowls, and passes by."

The aforesaid Directory gives a long list of Mr. Girdlestone's literary productions up to the present year. But, alas! among these thirty or more publications, there is ONE bearing the ill-omened title of "Three Letters on Church Reform," 1832-4. A little leaven leavens the whole lump. Here is the character of the man proclaimed at once. *Hinc illæ lacrymæ.* Hence the questionable compliment of a rural deanery and *honorary* canonry *offered in his sixtieth year* to one of the most talented clergymen in the diocese to which he belongs.

Compare these antecedents with those of Bishop Wilberforce, in the aforesaid Directory (as referred to by your caustic correspondent "Glaucus," not long ago), and then say, "Look on this picture and on that." Why, the rector is a Hercules compared to the bishop, when tested by this standard. Yet notice the comparative fortunes of one who sails still glibly with the tide,* and one who breasts it manfully,

"With lusty sinews throwing it aside,
And stemming it with heart of controversy;"—

of one who points out with no sparing hand the defects in our Liturgy, and one who lays down the law, as born to command and to be obeyed, that the Prayer-book SHALL NOT BE ALTERED, AND NOT BE TOUCHED IN HIS DAY.

And is there nothing in all this to depress the cause of the Reformers?—Remove this obstacle, and many a pen and many a tongue that is now silent will tell a tale very different to that which has hitherto reached ears polite. The public will not then be any longer abused by the oft-repeated but never established assertion that "the majority of the clergy are against revision;"† that it is "a poor, weak, miserable agitation;"‡ that it is only "here and there a

---

* "As Sherlock at Temple was taking a boat,
The waterman asked him which way he would float?
'Which way!' quoth the doctor, 'why, fool, *with the stream.*'
To St. Paul's, or to Lambeth, was all one to him."
"Mutato nomine, de, &c."

† After enormous pains taken to collect signatures from the clergy of every class to this effect, *not nearly half* of the body responded to the call. See Lord Ebury's Speech, May 8th, 1860; p. 9; Hatchard.

‡ Archdeacon Denison in Convocation, March 14th, 1861.

solitary disaffected individual who asks for it;" that the rest are quite satisfied with "the precious inheritance of their fathers as it has come down to them," and only wish to transmit it "UNALTERED and UNTOUCHED" to their children.

I could instance many other cases besides the one selected above in proof of my position;—

"Pudet haec opprobria nobis
Et dici potuisse, et non potuisse refelli:"—

but time and space compel me to conclude. Before doing so, however, I would beg your insertion of the following, from the *Times* of October 9th, 1858, which may serve as a contrast of patronage episcopal with that of the once-despised town-council of a provincial borough:—

"A LAUDABLE EXERCISE OF PATRONAGE.—The town-council of Newcastle-on-Tyne have appointed the Rev. R. Anchor Thompson, author of 'Christian Theism,' to the vacant Mastership of the Virgin Mary Hospital in that town—a situation worth from £500 to £600 per annum. Mr. Thompson's Essay carried off the first of the Burnett prizes (value £1,800) at the adjudication in 1855; but while the Scottish Kirk, which has but few good things at its disposal, lost no time in seeing to the adequate promotion of the second prize-taker, Mr. Tulloch, who is now Principal of St. Mary's, the English Church, with a Burnett prizeman at its head, left Mr. Anchor Thompson to *toil away in the humble curacy of Binbrooke,* Market Rasen, just as the palm of honour*

---

* We fear this is no solitary case, and that to the clerical profession, *above all others*, may be applied the lines,

"Full many a gem of purest ray serene,
The dark unfathomed caves of ocean bear;
Full many a flower is born to blush unseen,
And waste its sweetness on the desert air."

The Town Council of Newcastle-on-Tyne may boast of having removed this blot from the Church, *as far as rested with them*.

found him some three years ago, allowing the recognition of his merits to come from the corporation of a town with which he *had no connexion.*"

Surely these examples are a sufficient refutation of the malignant remark of the *Quarterly Review* for January, 1834, which we have frequently heard repeated in a variety of ways for the last five years, without being able within our own experience to produce a *single illustration* in proof of its truth :—

" We ourselves cannot imagine a better *recipe* for changing a curate into a rector, an archdeacon into a dean, a prebendary into a bishop, than a smart pamphlet in favour of Church Reform. If, in addition, it should deny the authority of the *Ten Commandments*, it might make its author an *archbishop*."

The last paragraph speaks volumes for the taste and wit of the author of the article.

I remain, Sir, yours, &c.,

October 15, 1858. " INGOLDSBY."

LETTER XXXIII.

THE BISHOP OF OXFORD ONCE MORE. (THIRD BUT NOT LAST TIME OF APPEARING.)

"A man full of words shall not prosper upon the earth."
PSALM cxl. 11.

SIR,—Having with much patience and diligence arrived at the second page of the *Guardian* newspaper of Feb. 17th, 1858, which has furnished us thus far with our text in the matter of the Bishops *versus* the Liturgical Reformers; and having disposed of four out of the ten prelates who delivered themselves of their sentiments in "Anne's large chamber," at the meeting of Convocation, I was in hopes of being permitted to commence upon the fifth, whoever he might be, and thus at length to attain the "key-stone of the bridge" over which it is my destiny to carry my readers in this our toilsome march. Conceive, then, my dismay when, instead of the Right Rev. Archibald Campbell Tait, who stands next on the list, and whose opinions would be listened to with interest (not only by reason of his rank in the Church, but more for his conduct in the matter of the Confessional and other practices of the Romanising party) I found myself confronted with a second edition of the Bishop of Oxford.

Unfortunately, the laws of Convocation do not include in their code that salutary check imposed upon loquacity by the regulations of the two Houses of Parliament, whereby an orator, however eloquent, is prevented from intruding more than once on his audience in the course of the same debate.* Had this rule been in force in "Anne's chamber" as well as at St. Stephen's, the wholesome warning of "*Spoke, spoke,*" would have prevented the Bishop of Oxford from rising *thirty-five times*, as he is represented to have done on the occasion to which we are referring;—and the course of our letters would have run smoother than it is likely to do, if I am to attempt keeping pace with all the windings and turnings, the checks and the interruptions, caused by the frequent interlocutions of this Prelate, as exhibited in the next two pages of the *Guardian*.

I have no intention, however, of doing anything of the kind. To follow the Bishop of Oxford through the meanderings of his first address I found no easy matter; and here

---

* This rule, however, seems to have been set at defiance by the "Home Rulers" of 1877-8, to the disgrace of the Parliament that allowed such scenes to run to such an extent as they did unchecked.

is a second of equal length, with 3, 4, 5, up to 35 speeches, looming in the distance! Alas! who is sufficient for these things?

> "Non mihi si linguæ centum sint, oraque centum,
> Ferrea vox, omnes ritu percurrere possim."
> "So here my muse her wing maun cow'r;
> Sic flights are far beyond her pow'r."

I shall therefore take the liberty of skipping (as one does the dull pages of a novel) the Bishop of Oxford's further observations; and proceed at once with those of the Bishop of London (Tait), very much to my own relief, and, I have little doubt, that of the generality of my readers.

One word, however, at parting with our present right reverend subject, though I am aware that I lay myself open to the charge of uttering " nasty " sentiments " from a nasty mouth."*

It is pretty clear from these 35 appearances of the right reverend prelate, in the short debate to which we are referring, who it is that is all this while pulling the strings of that resuscitated *corpus mortuum* ycleped CONVOCATION;† just as it is pretty apparent who it is that has been at the bottom of all this ferment in the Church, all this " troubling Israel " about auricular Confession, Credence tables, offertory, crosses, bowings, genuflexions, candles, altars, incense, Eastern posi-

---

* An expression said to have been made use of by Bishop Wilberforce when assailed by unpleasant sounds at Bradford, in the autumn of 1858. The same "nasty noises" were repeated at a London Confirmation, and in the Senate House of Cambridge, in the presence of his Royal Highness the Prince of Wales (January, 1861). The subject of these unfriendly salutations will say, "Populus me sibilat—at mihi plaudo Ipse domi." It may be so, but they are nevertheless significant of something not exactly as it should be.

† Whichever of the prelates may be absent at any time from Convocation, it cannot have escaped notice that the Bishop of Oxford is always present—*Et quorum pars magna fuit*, may, I believe, be added without fear of contradiction from any quarter.

tion, and the like, albeit he proclaims himself to the "hard-headed" but "nasty-mouthed" Yorkshiremen, "a back-bone son of the Reformed Church of England!"

It is not usual for an English prelate to ticket himself "THIS IS A BISHOP!" nor did I ever before hear of its being needful for one of their lordships to advertise himself "a back-bone son of the Reformed Church." *Qui s'excuse, s'accuse.* Good wine needs no bush. A bishop's creed is pretty well known without the necessity of his crying it in the market-place. The "hard-headed Yorkshiremen" (of whom your present correspondent prides himself in being one) have been used from their childhood to think for themselves; and no Jacob's voice with oily accents will ever induce them to grasp with cordiality the hairy hand of an Esau, until all their senses are convinced that there is no mistake about it. A son of Anti-slave-trade Wilberforce knows well the importance attached by public opinion to the verdict of that independent community, the great county of York. And as the return of Brougham to the House of Commons, in 1830, by that then undivided constituency, did much towards sealing the fortunes of the first Reform Bill, so we are inclined to think that the "nasty noises" from the "nasty mouths" of the men of Bradford will convince the Bishop of Oxford that he must hark back in the path he has been treading for the last six or eight years, and that the question of "No Popery" in the English Church is already pretty well decided by the popular voice.

The text of the Bishop's *second* speech before Convocation, and the last we shall notice, was "MUCH ADO ABOUT NOTHING." It was an attempt—a lengthy one, of course, but by no means, therefore, conclusive—to explain how far the Act of Uniformity* does or does not allow of the *smallest deviation*

---

* The Rev. D. Mountfield, in his able work, entitled "Two Hundred

from the *exactly prescribed* form of ritual " to be used in all churches and chapels daily throughout the year."

Now, I am no lawyer, and I have not taken counsel from " dear Phill,"* or any other gentleman learned in ecclesiastical jurisprudence. But, inasmuch as I believe there is scarcely a clergyman in the land (including all the prelates) who has not more or less broken, and does not continually break, the rigid letter of the Rubric,† it appears to me very like beating the air to occupy so much time in discussing an Act which all parties, with one consent, have agreed can no longer be literally maintained.

How many priests and deacons, for example, say *daily* the Morning and Evening Prayer, either privately or openly, " not being let by sickness, or some other urgent cause ? "

How many " curates ministering in every parish church, being at home, and not otherwise hindered, say the same in the church or chapel where they minister, and cause a bell to be tolled thereunto a convenient time before they begin, that the people may come to hear God's Word, and to pray with them ? "

How many observe all the saints'-days in the calendar; reading the collect, epistle, and gospel for the day, with sermon, and offertory sentences following?

How many use the offertory on the Sunday, except when the Holy Communion is administered ; and how often is that ?

How many read the Athanasian Creed thirteen times

Years Ago" (pp. 65, 66), gives a concise report of the different views taken of the *spirit* of this Act, at the time of its promulgation. Whatever views may be now taken of it by some of the clergy, certain it is that *in practice* not one individual in a thousand observes it *literally*.

* Chancellor Phillimore, so styled by Bishop Wilberforce in his correspondence with that gentleman, learned in ecclesiastical law or lore.

† See Lord Ebury's Speech of May 6th, 1858; also May 8, 1860; also Dr. Muhlenberg's Tract, entitled " What the Memorialists Want," where this branch of the subject is fully discussed : New York, 1856.

a year,—to wit, "on these feasts, Saint Matthias, Saint John Baptist, Saint James, Saint Bartholomew, Saint Matthew, Saint Simon and Saint Jude, and Saint Andrew"?—How many read it oftener than three times a year?—How many only once?—How many not at all?—How many "mutilate" the Baptismal, Burial, or Marriage Services?—How many of the bishops adhere strictly to the order for Confirmation? —How many of the clergy deviate from the Church's rule in administering the Holy Communion?—By how many is the Commination Service read, whole or in part?—How many use the precise form of Absolution as given in the "Visitation of the Sick," &c. &c.?

Let the Bishop of Oxford answer these questions, and many more that might be asked of a similar nature, à la mode of his protégé, Mr. West, "putting" his victims "through the Ten Commandments;"* and then it may be time enough to inquire whether the Act of Uniformity allows of a Clerk in Orders using "any portion of the Prayers taken exclusively from the Book of Common Prayer," when celebrating a third service in his church on Sunday, with sermon following.

To my mind the whole discussion savours of littleness, and a desire to bind the souls and bodies of the clergy of the nineteenth century with such fetters as the Church of Rome alone knows how to forge. From this bondage, by the blessing of God and the nerve of the Reformers of the sixteenth century, we have been delivered; and we should be degenerate "sons," indeed, "of the Reformed Church of England," if we tamely suffered them to be again fastened round our limbs.†

---

* The story of the "Boyne-hill Confession," like that of the 5th of November, should "never be forgot," until a revision of the Prayer-book makes the recurrence of such transactions impossible.

† To the Protestants of this age may be applied (with the variation

The Bishop of Oxford may continue to make converts in the vicinity of Cuddesdon and Boyne-hill—

"Illâ se jactet in aulâ:"—

there let him reign supreme, lord over willing slaves.* He has made few proselytes in this neighbourhood, or generally in the Northern parts of the kingdom. Let us trust that the example set by the hard-headed citizens of Bradford may act as an encouragement to the more easily-led sons of the South of England. And let us hope, for the sake of peace and quietness within the Church, that its *really* Protestant members will no longer allow themselves to be led astray through the idea of a "pure ritual," which has seduced its votaries by hundreds into the bosom of the Church of Rome.†

I remain, Sir, yours, &c.,
November 4, 1858. "INGOLDSBY."

LETTER XXXIV.

THE STATE SERVICES EXPUNGED FROM THE PRAYER-BOOK.

" Remember, remember the Fifth of November,
Gunpowder Treason and plot;
I see no reason why Gunpowder Treason
Ever should be forgot."

SIR,—One is more than ordinarily reminded of this quaint rhyme of our forefathers by the fact that Friday, the 5th

---

of a single word) the advice of St. Paul to the Galatians (v. 1), "Stand fast in the liberty wherewith Christ has made you free, and be not entangled again with the yoke of bondage."

* "Jove justly placed him on a stormy throne,
His people's temper is so like his own."

† A check has been put of late to this Romeward migration, through the force of public opinion, and the decisions of the Law Courts as far as they have been obeyed; but that it was *then* alarming, ample proof is given in the following letters.

inst., was the first occasion, for the space of 250 years, on which the churches and chapels of the land were not ordered by Act of Parliament to ring to solemn service in commemoration of the double event of the day. The Rubric, as it still stands in our Prayer-book, is as follows :—" A Form of Prayer with Thanksgiving, to be used yearly upon the Fifth day of November, for the happy deliverance of King James 1. and the Three Estates of England from the most traitorous and bloody-intended massacre by gunpowder (1605); and also for the happy Arrival of his Majesty King William on this day (1688), for the deliverance of our Church and nation."

Now, it is impossible to deny that these are two most memorable epochs in the history of this kingdom; and, as connected with our providential deliverance " from the Bishop of Rome and all his detestable enormities," deserving of perpetual thanksgiving to the Almighty Protector of these realms.

But it has seemed good to the wisdom of Parliament to do away with this annual commemoration. Lord Stanhope has moved, Lord Derby has consented, and the Bishop of Oxford has signified his approval,* that this State form of prayer and thanksgiving shall no longer appear as a portion of the Liturgy of the Church of England. So away it goes, " bag and baggage," root and branch, no more to cumber the ground, and no one found to say a word in its defence, or to rescue a single limb from the ruthless hatchet of its destroyers.

Now, is it not worth while to pause and see whether this was not a piece of somewhat hasty legislation, which might have been done better had more time been taken for consideration?

---

* See Letter XXI., p. 147.

In the first place, the Bill passed the Houses of Parliament in the month of July, when the combined influences of the elements, fire and water, the comet in the heavens, and the Thames upon earth,* had marvellously thinned the attendance of the Opposition, and when Government itself was fain to get over the remaining business of the session as quickly as it could, leaving to amateurs, like Lord Stanhope, to hurry through measures like this, unlet and unquestioned in their course of destruction.

It is a pity Lord Ebury did not choose the 6th of July, instead of the 6th of May, for introducing his truly philanthropic motion to the notice of the Legislature. He would not have seen such a formidable array of lawn sleeves set over against him; and we should not in that event have heard from the Premier's mouth of "almost the whole of the Episcopal Bench differing from his lordship."

But it is a very different thing to ask modestly for a Commission of Inquiry into the short-comings of the Liturgy (which is what Lord Ebury sought), and to sweep away three entire services of 200 years' standing after ten minutes' discussion in the middle of the dog-days, leaving posterity to inquire with amazement what has become of them.

What good reason was there why they should thus die the death in 1858, rather than in 1758 or 1958? and why was Excision and not Revision the order of the day? The fact is, if the truth must be told, it was attended with *less trouble* to expunge the three services altogether from the Book of Common Prayer than to submit them to a patient and judicious *Review*—a review which might have retained the memory of the events, and have still expressed a nation's gratitude for such a signal deliverance as that of November the 5th, 1605;

---

* This was before the gigantic drainage of the metropolis was commenced. See before, Letter XXI., p. 153.

while it would have got rid of the fulsome expressions justly objected to, which, though appropriate perhaps at the time they were composed, were quite out of place in the present stage of our history.* Proper psalms, lessons, and one appropriate collect, could have never come amiss, or grated upon the ears of the religiously disposed hearer—unless a disguised Romanist—while we question whether the total obliteration of such services does not imply a decline in the vital piety of the country, if not a secret hankering after those Popish practices from which the providence of God and the zeal of our forefathers have delivered us and our children.

It may be late to make these observations now. A spasmodic attempt was indeed made by Lord Dungannon, the Duke of Marlborough, and the Bishops of Bangor (Bethell) and Chichester (Gilbert), to rescue some portion of the services from the hand of the innovator; but in vain.† The work of demolition had begun; the hatchet and hammer were in the hand of the iconoclast and his allies:—

> "Mahon seized a flambeau with zeal to destroy;
> Oxford led the way,
> To light him to his prey,
> And, like another Helen, fired another Troy."

" Down with them! down with them! even to the ground," was the cry; and there they are, prostrate before the triumphant foe, never to rise again.‡

---

* See Letter xix., p. 135, *Note*.
† See remarks of Lord Ebury on this subject, May 8, 1860.
‡ The warrant under which these services were done away with was as follows, subsequently confirmed by Act of Parliament:—

" Victoria R.—Whereas by our Royal Warrant of the 21st day of June, 1837, in the first year of our reign, we commanded that certain forms of prayer and service made for the 5th of November, the 30th of January, and the 29th of May, should be forthwith printed and published, and annexed to the Book of Common Prayer and Liturgy of the United Church of England and Ireland, to be used yearly on the said days in all cathedral and collegiate churches and chapels, in all chapels of colleges and halls within our

But the warning may not come amiss to those who are now advocating a *general Revision of the entire Liturgy*. To Reform, is one thing; to Destroy, another. Let them beware how they press their object too eagerly under a Conservative Government. Let them be well advised who it is that directs the movements of the ecclesiastical portion of the State machine. Twelve Irish bishoprics were once sacrificed by an eminent statesman (Lord Derby) by way of improving the Church in Ireland. Three parts of the prizes in the English Church were swept away (not without the consent of the bishops), as the readiest mode of quickening the clerical profession.* The sponge is a convenient implement

---

Universities of Oxford, Cambridge, and Dublin, and of our Colleges of Eton and Winchester, and in all parish churches and chapels within those parts of our United Kingdom called England and Ireland:

"And whereas in the last session of Parliament addresses were presented to us by both Houses of Parliament, praying us to take into our consideration our proclamation in relation to the said forms of prayer and service made for the 5th day of November, the 30th day of January, and the 29th day of May, with a view to their discontinuance:

"And whereas we have taken into our due consideration the subject of the said addresses, and, after due deliberation, we have resolved that the use of the said forms of prayer and service shall be discontinued:

"Now, therefore, our will and pleasure is, that so much of our said Royal Warrant of the 21st day of June, 1837, in the first year of our reign, as is hereinbefore recited, be revoked, and that the use of the said forms of prayer and service made for the 5th of November, the 30th of January, and the 29th of May, be henceforth discontinued in all cathedrals and collegiate churches and chapels, in all chapels of colleges and halls within our Universities of Oxford, Cambridge, and Dublin, and of our colleges of Eton and Winchester, and in all parish churches and chapels within the parts of our United Kingdom called England and Ireland, and that the said forms of prayer and service be not henceforth printed and published with, or annexed to, the Book of Common Prayer and Liturgy of the United Church of England and Ireland.

"Given at our Court, at St. James's, the 17th day of January, 1859, in the 22nd year of our reign.

"By Her Majesty's command. "S. H. WALPOLE."

* "Mr. Alderman Copeland called the attention of the House to a return made to the House (No. 317 of this session) by the Ecclesiastical Commis-

in certain hands.* There are plenty of things in the Prayer-book which admit of, nay, which imperatively call for, amendment. But let the Liturgical Reformers bide their time, and look before they leap; or they may chance to awake some fine morning in July, and discover, to their astonishment, that they have got for their pains a very different article to that pure and reformed Prayer-book which, under an *honest* Commission, they will, we trust, one day secure.

I remain, Sir, yours, &c.,

November 11, 1858. "INGOLDSBY."

LETTER XXXV.

THE BISHOP OF LONDON, THE RIGHT HON. AND RIGHT REV. ARCHIBALD CAMPBELL TAIT.†

"Hæc cedo ut admoveam templis, et farre litabo."—PERSIUS.

"When with such offerings to the gods I come,
A cake thus given is worth a hecatomb."—DRYDEN.

SIR,—The antecedents, as they are called, of the Bishop of London are rather remarkable; and, as they in some degree probably affect his lordship's sentiments on the matter of

---

sioners, of the very large sums paid by them to solicitors, surveyors, and other officers, and to the manner in which the affairs of the Ecclesiastical Commission were carried on. The hon. member complained that an enormous sum of the money received by the Commissioners, and *intended for the augmentation of poor livings*, was swallowed up by the extravagant expenditure on their establishment, and by the charges of lawyers, surveyors, and architects. For the year ending August 31, 1860, no less than £47,000 was spent in distributing £96,500. He hoped that the Government would either, during the recess, issue a commission, or early next session appoint a committee, to inquire into the affairs of the Ecclesiastical Commission." *Parliamentary Proceedings, August* 5, 1861.—Mr. Henry Seymour in the session of 1862 obtained a Committee of Inquiry into the doings of the said Commission.

* As proved pretty decidedly when afterwards made use of by Mr. Gladstone to abolish the Irish Church altogether!

† The present Archbishop of Canterbury (1878).

Liturgical Revision, it may not be amiss to pass them in review before our readers.

His lordship, as is well known, is a native of North Britain, being born in Edinburgh in 1811; and having received his early education in the High School of that capital, so justly celebrated for the distinguished men it has produced. In 1827 he went to the University of Glasgow; and thence, in 1830, to Balliol College, Oxford, where he graduated with distinction in 1833, and was elected Fellow the following year. Here he remained, filling the office of College Tutor and University Examiner, until 1842, when, upon the death of Dr. Arnold, he was selected as the future Head Master of Rugby School from amongst about thirty candidates, several of them of the very highest academical distinction.* We next find Dr. Tait appointed to the Deanery of Carlisle, and acting as one of the Oxford University Commissioners, in which capacity he is said to have exhibited very liberal views; and, finally, in 1856—being then in his 46th year—he was elevated by Lord Palmerston to his present conspicuous post.

Now, although this rapid career of advancement is highly creditable to the individual, and although his lordship's conduct in all the stages through which he has passed redounds greatly to his credit, and reflects no small degree of praise upon those by whom he has been promoted—yet, it is but just to add that there appears little in it to make his lordship practically acquainted with the details of Liturgical Reform.

---

* The competition for this post has always been severe. On the occasion of Dr. Arnold's election, a humorous poetical effusion recorded the "names and colours" of the competitors, ending with the following description of the late head-master of Shrewsbury School, afterwards Greek Professor at Cambridge, and Canon Residentiary of Ely :—

"Spangled all with medals o'er—I think he won some ten a day
Proudly charges on the foe the thrice illustrious Kennedy."

It is true that, as Dean of Carlisle, Dr. Tait was in every sense of the word a working clergyman ; and there are many who remember with gratitude the earnestness with which, during the short period of his residence amongst them, he applied himself to the supervision of the local charities, educational establishments, &c.

But still there is nothing in all this to have brought his lordship into practical contact with the machinery of the Book of Common Prayer, as it works in the vast proportion of churches throughout the country. A cathedral, with its dean, archdeacon, canons, precentor, organist and choristers, is no measure of the ordinary run of parochial churches; and a prelate who has acquired his experience of these last through the medium of the head-mastership of a school, a deanery, or the rectorship of one of the large London parishes, with the assistance of three or four curates, is in no condition to sympathise with the feelings of the ten or twelve thousand parochial clergy who have the whole management of their village or district devolved upon their hands for the fifty-two weeks in the year. Hence the remarks attributed to one of the right reverend prelates*—" the clergy should do their own work ;"—" what can *you* want with a curate ?"—" there would be nothing for him to do." And hence, probably, the sympathy of the Bishop of London with his " right reverend brother" in this matter, rather than with " the inferior clergy," the priests and deacons of his extensive diocese.

Not that I mean to say the bishop does *not* sympathise with these last. He is, on the contrary, reported to be extremely considerate towards them, and desirous in every reasonable way to meet their wishes.† But I see in the

---

* Bishop Jackson, of Lincoln, in 1856. The remarks quoted in the text were made to the rector of a small country parish seeking a curate.

† In a speech in the House of Lords, July, 1861, his lordship observed that " the less bishops interfered with the independent and well-disposed clergy in

above remarks an explanation of his otherwise unintelligible statement before Convocation, that "the clergy are more inclined to shorten the services than the laity." Let the laity speak for themselves. I have heard them do so in somewhat decisive terms.* But, as one of the clergy, I am of opinion that had his lordship had the benefit of some twelve years' experience as a country parson, working single-handed in a parish of 2,000 souls (and the case is not very different, if we limit the number to 1,000, or even 500, or less, as far as the Sunday duties are concerned), he would have seen a satisfactory reason for the complaints of so many of his humbler brethren of the cloth.

"In *towns*," the bishop admits, "the case is *different*." Now it is precisely in towns, where there are usually one or two curates to assist the rector or vicar, and a supply of unattached clergy at command, that it seldom happens that one individual is called upon to perform the *whole* "double duty," including two sermons. It is precisely in *towns*, therefore, that the objection of the lengthy morning service should weigh *least* heavily upon the clergyman, whatever it may do on his congregation. Yet here it is that the bishop admits the existence of the evil; whence it is fair to conclude that had his lordship had similar experience of country parishes, he would not have refused relief to the incumbents of the ten or twelve thousand villages scattered throughout the land.

As for the "country people not liking to be dismissed with a service of a quarter of an hour or twenty minutes of the Litany," who ever asked for that? What the advocates for abridgment ask for is, that the *average* length of

---

their dioceses the better:" a sentiment in which the author of the "Ingoldsby Letters," after upwards of thirty years' experience, cordially concurs.

* See, for example, the letters of two gentlemen of the Law, quoted in Letter XXVIII., p. 190.

the morning service be as nearly as possible assimilated to those of the afternoon or evening, (occupying about an hour, or an hour and a quarter,) and which, according to all my experience, extending to nearly every county in England and Wales, are for the most part (except in the dairy districts) attended by the common people with much greater frequency than that of the morning.

What harm would ensue to the spirit of piety, about which so much has been said, if the morning congregation were dismissed at a quarter or half-past twelve o'clock, instead of at one, or even at two, as is often the case when there is a large number of communicants? Is there no other way of honouring God on the Sabbath morn than by a two hours' attendance at church? May we not also be permitted to honour Him "whose Temple is all space," by the quiet study of His Word at home, or the peaceful contemplation of His glorious works abroad, the opportunity for appreciating which at other times is denied to the hardy sons of toil? Is it so inconsistent with the genius of Christianity to wander occasionally into the fields on that sacred day, with mind and body attuned to holy thoughts, and in such mood to—

> "Find tongues in trees, books in the running brooks,
> Sermons in stones, and God in everything?"

I care not who judges my words, as I have no doubt they will be judged by the "rigid righteous" and the Puritan,—

> "Who hold the notion
> That sullen gloom is sterling true devotion;"—

but, as a plain country parson of a quarter of a century's experience,* and having officiated in a great number of parishes during the whole of that time, I do not hesitate to express my conviction that we are in the habit of much over-

---

* Now rapidly approaching half a century, and with views in this respect only confirmed by everything I have since seen and heard.

rating the importance of the *mere time* spent in the offices of religion within the walls of a church,

> "Where men display to congregations wide
> Devotion's every grace, except the heart."

Did not our Saviour harangue the multitudes from the mountain and upon the sea-shore, as well as in the synagogue? Did not John the Baptist preach repentance in the wilderness? Did not Philip the Deacon expound the Scripture while driving in a chariot? Did not St. Paul proclaim the Gospel to the polished Athenians from Mars' Hill? It is as possible to overdo as to underdo the formality of public worship. And it is not unreasonable to attribute much of the present craving for the innocent relaxation of body and mind on the Sabbath-day,* to the fact that an overstrained attempt has been made to represent a twice-a-day attendance at church as "the one thing needful."

This, indeed, ought we to have done, and not to leave the other undone. The mere formal act of going through the two or three Sunday Services, though enforced by episcopal authority, is not likely to be more acceptable to the Almighty now than it was in the days of the Pharisees, who, "sitting in Moses' seat, bound heavy burdens and grievous to be borne, and laid them on men's shoulders, while they themselves touched them not with one of their fingers; who did all their works to be *seen of men*, made broad their phylacteries, and enlarged the borders of their garments, and *for a pretence made long prayers.*"

Let us beware lest, while we exact this discipline with such strictness as some would do, we lose the inward grace and retiring piety, *the life of faith* exhibited in works of love —the open hand, the pure heart—the man, in short, of God.

---

* Great efforts [were being made at that time to throw open to the public on the Sunday, the Crystal Palace at Sydenham, the British Museum, and other places adapted to intellectual improvement.

"Quin damus id Superis de magnâ quod dare lance
Non possit magni Messalæ lippa propago,
Compositum jus fasque animo, sanctosque recessus
Mentis, et incoctum generoso pectus honesto ;
Hæc cedo ut admoveam templis, et *farre* litabo."

It is not the length, or number of services that constitutes true devotion; any more than it is the costliness of the gift cast into the treasury which marks the sincerity of the donor. The widow's mite may outweigh the merchant's thousands in the all-seeing eye; and the *willing* worship of *half an hour* overbalance the studied genuflexions and lip-service of half a day.

I have confined myself on the present occasion to this branch of my subject, because it is that to which the Bishop of London's attention seems to have been particularly directed; and his remarks upon it before Convocation and in the House of Lords would imply a willingness to give his mind to its further consideration. The more his lordship talks over the subject with the experienced clergy and enlightened laity of his diocese, the more he will probably feel inclined to carry out his own observation on Lord Ebury's motion of May 6th—that "if he could have been convinced that the noble lord's proposition was required by the wants of the age, he should not have hesitated to give his assent to it."*

Feeling persuaded that Bishop Tait will, sooner or later, arrive at this conviction,

I remain, Sir, yours, &c.,
Nov. 16, 1858. "INGOLDSBY."

---

* I would here strongly recommend to my reverend brethren the perusal of a Tract recently published by W. J. Johnson, 121, Fleet Street, entitled, "Hints on Common Sense for Clergymen, by One of Themselves;" the author being generally understood to be the Hon. and Rev. E. V. Bligh.

LETTER XXXVI.

THE BISHOP OF LONDON'S PRIMARY CHARGE.

"Ac veluti magno in populo quum sæpe coorta est
Seditio, sævitque animis ignobile vulgus;
Jamque faces et saxa volant, furor arma ministrat:
Tum, pietate gravem ac meritis si forte virum quem
Conspexere, silent, arrectisque auribus adstant;
Iste regit dictis animos, et pectora mulcet." VIRGIL.

SIR,—In his Primary Charge to the clergy of his important diocese the Bishop of London (Tait) makes allusion to his comparative youth, while speaking with the authority which his high position warrants, in the presence of many who are his seniors in age, and consequently more experienced than himself.

The Charge, however, speaks all the wisdom of grey hairs, blended with the energy of one not yet passed the meridian of his days. It displays a due appreciation of the responsibilities, as well as difficulties, of the post occupied by its author. At the same time it evinces a decision of purpose upon matters of present controversy, calculated to act with much power in steadying the vessel of the Church as she moves along over the waves of the unquiet sea on which she is now tossing.

No one can rise from a perusal of this document with any doubt as to the direction to which the compass points, in that which the bishop justly calls "the greatest diocese in England."

That the trumpet should in this case utter no uncertain sound is of great value at the present moment; and thousands of faithful men will rally at the blast, and gather round a standard thus boldly unfurled, and hoisted aloft in the midst of a city more conspicuous than that of the Seven

Hills in the palmiest days of her glory; how much more so now that the latter has fallen from her high estate, and is sunk into the depths of superstition and spiritual debasement!

It would be presumption in me to attempt to add a lustre to that which has received its ample meed of praise in a responsive echo from the heart of every true-born son of the Church. But I may be allowed, as bearing on the object of these Letters, to notice two features in the Charge which particularly arrested my attention.

The presence of many distinguished ministers of our Church, whom it were long to mention, not unnaturally suggested to the bishop the remark, that "it would be an ill day indeed for the Church of England if all her ministers were tied down, as some would have them, to the onerous duties of a cure of 2,000 or 3,000 souls."

The effects of the Ecclesiastical Commission of 1836 are already but too apparent in lowering the general stamp of our clergy in point of literary attainment. As we have before had occasion to observe, to reform is one thing, to destroy another.* The sponge that wiped away summarily three-fourths of the prizes of the Church unquestionably did much to divert into other channels the highest class of intellect and energy among the rising generation of students.† And it is to be feared these results will become more and

---

* See Letter xxxiv., p. 225.

† Dr. Vaughan and Professor Stanley, as cited by Lord Ebury, bear testimony to this *fact*, let it be explained as it may. See Lord Ebury's second Speech, p. 26. Hatchard & Co.; 1860. See also Charge by the Bishop of Oxford, Nov., 1860. This result of the Ecclesiastical Commission was anticipated by Archdeacon (afterwards Bishop) Butler, in a pamphlet, entitled "Thoughts on Church Dignitaries;" and the experience of the last forty years bears conclusive evidence that the highest class of academical graduates shrink from holy orders as a profession, while the vacuum is supplied by shoals of *Literates* whom bishops dare not reject.

more evident as the operation of the Commission is more and more extended. The root of the evil lay in the *disposal*, not the *existence*, of such patronage as was then connected with our cathedrals. The blame is altogether due to those of bygone generations whose selfish nepotism or political favouritism provoked the application of the hatchet, and caused that noble tree to be hewn down and cast into the fire which merely required a dexterous use of the pruning-knife to enable it to have borne much fruit for future service in the Church; fruit which posterity will in vain look for from this quarter.

How, for instance, can a bishop, with his overwhelming weight of correspondence, his personal interviews with those of his clergy who seek his aid, the never ending, still beginning, routine of official calls on his time, his expected hospitality, his occasional preaching, and the like;—how can the dean, with the constant interruption to which his position exposes him, with the possible responsibility of a cure of souls;—how can the four canons residentiary, with their coming and going, their annexed archidiaconal, parochial, or professorial charge;—how can this handful of men, whose time is already disposed of, find that "learned leisure" which is essential to the production of works of genius? And yet who can deny that, *without* the occasional production of such works, the whole clerical profession must languish, and incur by insensible degrees the contempt of the literati in our own and other lands,* however efficiently one branch of it may be meanwhile discharging its duties in the sight of God and man.

He was no bad judge of human nature who said,

---

* In the debate on Mr. Bouverie's motion, for the Relief of the Clergy from the perpetual obligation of the Clerical Oath, it was stated that "there was at this time a great dearth of men of talent in the profession;" April, 1862; and no man can deny that such is the case in 1878.

"Magnæ mentis opus, nec de lodice parandâ
Attonitæ, currus et equos, faciesque Deorum
Aspicere, et qualis Rutulum confundat Erinnys:"—

a sentiment as applicable to want of leisure as to want of cash; nay, more applicable in fact to the former than to the latter. And he would be but a sorry friend to the Church, as Bishop Tait observes, who would reduce all her ministers to one dead level of mediocrity, by compelling them to tread throughout their lives the same monotonous routine of parochial work.

I pass with pleasure to his lordship's remarks on the Diocesan Home Mission; especially that passage where he commends the efforts now made to bring the masses within reach of the Gospel through the teaching of the Church, disentrammelled from that stiffness and formality which has been one cause of its comparative want of success.

"The days," says his lordship, "when there was great fear of the Church of England *dying of her dignity* are, thank God, past." That such days are *on the wane* there can be no doubt, especially in towns, to which the bishop more immediately refers. But we can hardly admit such days are *past*, when we find Bishop Wilberforce contending in Convocation for the rigid maintenance of the Act of Uniformity;* and deprecating "going to Parliament for any alteration in the existing state of things," though there is not one clergyman in a thousand who now-a-days observes that Act to the letter.

He must be blind indeed, or wilfully perverted in his "views of *truth*," who has not discovered that there are millions of our fellow-Christians, even in this country— (how much more, then, in our Colonies?)—who are utterly incapable, and ever will be, of entering into the lengthy

---

* See Letter xxxiii., p. 220.

and highly spiritual services of our usual public worship, even if they could be induced to frequent our churches, and room could be found for them at our customary gatherings within the sacred walls.* Why, then, not grapple with the difficulty; and fling aside the "coils of red tape," which compress the capabilities of our Church; and which, but for the hindrance of those in authority, would long ago have been relaxed, if not cut through by the sharp sabre of public opinion?

It may seem strange to some that in a Charge occupying between four and five hours in the reading, no mention should have been made of a Revision of the Book of Common Prayer; especially in a diocese where that subject had been brought under the notice of the Legislature during the year in which the Charge was delivered.

I see, however, in this an additional proof of the discretion, or rather caution, which characterises this document throughout. The bishop cannot but have observed in how different a light that matter is now viewed to what it was when he made his remarks before Convocation, and delivered his opinion in the House of Lords on the motion for doing away with the State Services of the Church.

Dr. Tait, therefore, may be considered as at present *uncommitted* in his judgment as to the expediency of issuing a Commission of Inquiry into the Liturgy; and as his lordship has shown himself in this Charge to be no halter between two opinions, we hope that we shall one day hear that he has given in his adhesion to the cause—nay, possibly, that the name of the Right Reverend Prelate stands at the head of a list of Commissioners, appointed for the purpose of receiving

---

* The very questionable proceeding of preaching in theatres and in the open air was adopted to meet this difficulty, the Bishop of London setting the example by preaching in Covent Garden Market, on Sunday, June 30, 1861. I am not aware, however, of a repetition of this (1878).

evidence, and reporting upon the possibility of improving the
BOOK OF COMMON PRAYER.*

I remain, Sir, yours, &c.,

November 25, 1858.   "INGOLDSBY."

LETTER XXXVII.

THE BISHOP OF LINCOLN'S CHARGE, OCTOBER, 1858.

"Talk of disruption!—why, my Lords, was ever disruption more complete?"—LORD EBURY, *May*, 1858.

"Barbaras ædes aditure mecum,
Quas Eris semper fovet inquieta,
Lis ubi late sonat, et togatum
Æstuat agmen."
THE SAME (from GRAY), *May*, 1860.

SIR,—While on the subject of Charges, it may be as well to take this opportunity of noticing two that have been recently published, wherein the subject of Liturgical Revision is handled—the one by the Bishop of Lincoln (Jackson), the other by an author hitherto unknown to fame—as far as this matter is concerned—the Venerable Richard Charles Coxe, Archdeacon of Lindisfarne.

One would have thought the Bishop of Lincoln had sufficiently delivered himself of his sentiments upon Revision, on presenting the memorable petition of one-fifth part of his Clergy to Convocation in February, 1858.† But it seems his lordship is determined to show that his opinions have

---

* On the Bishop of London's silence respecting the subject of Revision, see the remarks of the Rev. R. Bingham ("Aquila de Rupe"), p. 63—whose concluding words we most heartily echo, that " while we wait for the fulfilment of our hopes, our watchword must still be Patience, Perseverance, and Prayer; thanking God for the past, and taking courage for the future." London: 17, Buckingham Street, Adelphi, W.C.

† Letter II., p. 11.

undergone no change from anything he may have subsequently heard or read. So, in his Charge to the assembled Clergy in October last, his lordship thus expresses himself:—

"No doubt the Prayer-book is susceptible of improvement. Rubrics might be advantageously altered, the Table of Lessons might be amended and supplemented, shorter services supplied for the week-day and for children, and additional prayers and thanksgivings provided for different occasions. But such alterations would not satisfy those who desired revision. The controversies of the last three centuries would have to be fought over again, and questions would be raised which it would be equally perilous to decide either way, or to leave without decision. The result would be to cause universal disappointment, or to overthrow that wise toleration which the Church has always allowed within certain limits to different interpretations of Scripture and of her own formularies. It is, moreover, doubtful whether the revised Prayer-book would be accepted by all the thirty-three colonial dioceses, many of which have their own Synods; and thus an important link would be destroyed between the Church of England and her daughter Churches.

"As for the length of the services, he did not think the complaints that had been made were well founded, so far as adults were concerned, provided that they diligently and devoutly joined in the responses. When the Lord's Supper was administered, the service was, perhaps, over-long for the communicants, and he should suggest that in country parishes the singing should be diminished and the sermon shortened —which would be much better than omitting it altogether. In towns where there were three services he should willingly give his consent to omit the Litany, if it were said with either of the latter services. *He should also recommend early celebrations, as well as those at noon.* This mode of meeting the difficulty would be far better than agreeing to any scheme which would dislocate the deep meaning of our services, dissolve the connexion between the Prayer-book and its ancestral Liturgies, and shock the feelings of the most earnest and devoted sons of the Church—far better than submitting the Prayer-book to the indifferent and even hostile criticism of a Parliament, of whom many were not of our communion, or even of our religion."

The above is from the *Clerical Journal* of November 7th, 1858, while the Charge was in course of delivery; and though I have no means of knowing how that journal came by the report, yet, having been present at one of the rehearsals, I am able to say, as the Bishop of Oxford did of the *Times* report of the proceedings in the House of Bishops, last February, that "somehow or other it has contrived to be marvellously correct."*

To analyse, piecemeal, this portion of the bishop's address, would be to go over again the "Ingoldsby Letters" of last Spring, to which I must, therefore, beg to refer your readers. But I shall not think it time misplaced to notice such parts of it as differ in any material degree from his lordship's observations before Convocation.

In the first place, we have in this passage a distinct admission on the side of the Liturgical Reformers, that—

1st, The Prayer-book *is* susceptible of improvement.

2nd, That Rubrics might be advantageously altered.

3rd, That the Table of Lessons might be amended.

4th, That shorter services might be supplied for the week-day and for children.

(Why not for Sundays and adults?)

5th, That additional Prayers and Thanksgivings might be provided for different occasions.

Is not this conceding everything that has been asked for

---

* Letter II., p. 12.

by one class of Revisionists for the last five or six years? It is, as I have before said, a plain *concessio principii*, a yielding of the whole matter in dispute.

But here, alas! comes in the "BUT;"—those horrid *buts*, of which we have had so much reason to complain.* What a pity there is no antiquated Canon of the Church forbidding the use of BUTS to all Bishops and Curates, till the question of Liturgical Reform is fairly settled! Were there no BUTS in 1549, 1552, 1559, 1604, 1662?—and yet the Prayer-book, by the providence of God, contrived to weather the adverse storm; while here the book is, in 1859, bending like a reed before the wind, and unable to raise its head against the united BUTS of Lincoln, Oxford, and St. David's.

Let us see, however, what the present impediments amount to. They appear to be *four* in number, while the bishop admits that there are *five* reasons why the Prayer-book *should* be reformed.

BUT the 1st—" Such alterations would not satisfy those who desire revision."

The opinion, on the contrary, of others who have given their mind to the consideration of this subject is, that such alterations *would* satisfy a *very large number* of those who call for a Revision of the Prayer-book. And what if there remain, as doubtless there ever will do, a small *residuum* of dissatisfied? Are we to wait till *every one* admits that he is satisfied, and cries out, " Hold, enough!" This would, indeed, be to wait "till the consummation of all things;" till bishops, at least, and Prayer-books had alike become the prey of all-devouring time.

" The controversies," proceeds the bishop, " of the last three centuries would have to be fought over again, and questions

---

* Letter xxvi., pp. 179, 180, 181.

would be raised which it would be equally perilous to decide either way, or to leave without decision."

Why, is not this the very echo of the state of the Church at this moment, whether we encounter the ordeal of Revising the Prayer-book or no? Do not the columns of the daily and weekly press,* reviews, magazines, Bishops' and Archdeacons' Charges, teem with a "revival of the controversies of the last three centuries?" And are not questions raised every day on Baptismal Regeneration, Priestly Absolution,† Auricular Confession, the Real Presence, and the like, as between the Articles and the Prayer-book, which call for some authoritative decision, or some such modification of the expressions used as shall allow of individuals taking their own view without impugning the honesty of their brethren? ‡

I would here refer my readers to a pamphlet entitled "Clerical Oaths a Hindrance to Unity."§ The *original* title, the author tells us, was, "The English Clergy, High Low, and Dry, Weighed in the Balance and Found Wanting?" Why found wanting? Why, but for lack of this very revision, *the withholding, not the granting*, of which "causes universal disappointment, and tends to overthrow that wise toleration which the Church" by her Articles, if not by her Prayer-book, clearly *intended* to "allow within certain limits to different interpretations of Scripture and of her own formularies."

We must now proceed to BUT No. 2—a novel and certainly most curious specimen of the genus. It appears "doubtful whether the revised Prayer-book would be accepted by all

---
* See the *Guardian, Record, English Churchman, Clerical Journal*, &c.

† See a singularly inconclusive argument on these questions in "Five Discourses on the Revision of the Liturgy," by the Rev. Charles John Vaughan, late Head Master of Harrow. Macmillan, Cambridge; 1860.

‡ On this point Mr. Fisher is very severe upon the Evangelical Clergy.

§ By the Rev. Robert Matthew Milne, of Hildenborough, near Tunbridge. London: Partridge & Co., 34, Paternoster Row; 1858.

the thirty-three Colonial dioceses, many of which have their own Synods; and thus an important link would be destroyed between the Church of England and her daughter Churches."

As if that which is decent and in order here, were sure to be alike suitable at the poles or the equator. As if, for instance, that which best served to edify a congregation in England some three centuries ago, must be surely best not only for England now, but also for Hottentots and Zulus, Chinese and New Zealanders, Patagonians and Esquimaux, and that to the very end of time.*

The Colonial dioceses, according to the bishop's statement in October last, amounted at that time to thirty-three. Some five or six have been created since, making the total in round numbers about forty; and, judging by the rate at which these new dioceses have been created of late, there is every reason to believe that there may be fifty of them in the course of a few years, possibly a hundred before the end of this century.† So, by the bishop's argument, we are to go on perpetuating what he admits to be *defects* in the Prayer-book, and what others maintain are *errors*, and what the Bishop of Oxford calls "all its imperfections,"‡ lest by possibility our "revised" (and we would hope *improved*) Prayer-book should not commend itself to the various "Synods" of these blooming daughters whom we have dotted about over the face of the earth!§ What would the Bishop of Lincoln say if some of these scions

---

* See "Questions of the Day," by the Rev. Charles Girdlestone, p. 36; also, Robert Hall, on "Terms of Communion." Works, vol. ii., p. 9.

† Is it not high time to question the expediency of creating so many "my lords," who have no *civil* status, and never will have, to justify the title, and whose rapid return to the home country, there to absorb the scanty remains of prizes in the Church, gives just offence to many?

‡ Letter xiv., p. 92.

§ Thirty bishoprics have been founded in our colonies since 1841. This was in 1862. How many have been added since I am unable to say.

were to re-enact the part of Goneril and Regan in the play, (as the American Church has done,) and carve out a Prayer-book of their own, in the "Synod," say, of Tinnevelly or Hong Kong?—an event by no means improbable, especially as far as relates to the Abridgment portion of our subject?* Who knows but that some of them may be at this very moment plotting emancipation from the leading-strings in which the too tender care of their Anglican mamma would retain them? I can fancy hearing across the wide Pacific murmurs borne along the breeze, not loud but deep, in accents similar to these:—

"'Tis the infirmity of age: she hath ever but slenderly known herself."

"The best and soundest of her time hath been but rash; then must we look to receive from her age not alone the imperfections of long-engrafted condition, but therewithal the unruly waywardness that infirm and cholerick years bring with them."

"Pray you, let us hit together; we must do something, and i' the heat."

I wish I may be mistaken; but it is my misfortune to take a different view of human nature from that entertained by the Bishop of Lincoln; and I cannot persuade myself that the growing Church of our vast Colonial Empire will long submit to be bound by the effete Canons and worn-out Rubrics of the Anglican Church, without an attempt being made to improve upon them where they are defective, or manifestly ill-adapted to the circumstances in which the

---

* The author has seen letters from Australia and New Zealand, written in admiration of Lord Ebury's speech in the House of Lords, May, 1860. More than one American Prelate has also expressed his sympathy with the movement, and, I believe, has *acted on it.*

several dioceses find themselves placed.* And then what becomes of the bishop's argument? What will such logic be worth, except so far as it goes to prove, (in addition to other illustrations which might be adduced,) that the child has shown itself wiser than the parent, the scholar outstripped his teacher in the march of education?

The celebrated Pope Gregory showed more wisdom twelve hundred years ago, when appealed to by St. Augustine as to how he should treat his new diocese, our progenitors of the sixth century. Being consulted on the question of the diversities of Customs and Liturgies of different churches, the answer of Gregory was such as might have been anticipated from a prelate of his enlightened mind, ere yet the *pia et religiosa calliditas* of Popery had conceived the idea of embracing the whole universe in one Procrustean framework of its own construction. It was—that "the English Bishop was NOT BOUND TO FOLLOW THE PRECEDENT OF ROME, but that he might *select whatever rules or parts* appeared the *most eligible*, and best adapted to promote the piety of the infant CHURCH OF ENGLAND, and dispose them into a system *for its use.*"†

"Go thou and do likewise," would have been the advice of that profound statesman to the Bishops of Tasmania and Sierra Leone, were he living in the middle of the nineteenth century instead of at the end of the sixth;—at any rate, it may be taken for granted that he would not have been found recommending the Church to *retain* "all her imperfections," *in order* that she might the more effectually propagate them throughout all parts of the world.

---

* See some sensible remarks by General Alexander, at the "Conference on Missions." Nisbet and Co., Berners Street; 1860; p. 16.

† Such there is every reason to believe, from internal evidence, and the omission of *particular direction* in things comparatively indifferent, was the expansive scheme for Church government and membership originally intended by the Great Founder of our Faith.

I must reserve the remaining two BUTS of the Bishop of Lincoln's Charge for my next; and am, meanwhile, yours, &c.,

January 3, 1859. "INGOLDSBY."

LETTER XXXVIII.

CHARGE BY THE ARCHDEACON OF LINDISFARNE, MAY, 1858.

"Nunquam animam talem dextrâ hâc, absiste moveri,
Amittes; habitet tecum, et sit pectore in isto."—VIRGIL.

SIR,—In days of old we read that *Bos est locutus;* but what the ox said, history does not inform us. In these days Archdeacons are sometimes requested to print their Charges; and we owe it to this fact that the world is put in possession of the thoughts of the Ven. Richard Charles Coxe, Archdeacon of Lindisfarne, on the "vital question of a Revision of the Liturgy."*

We know nothing whatever of the Venerable R. C. Coxe, and should have been innocent of the offence of reading the twenty pages to which his Charge extends, but for the circumstance of its having been noticed, soon after its delivery, by a Mr. Prideaux Selby, in a Newcastle paper which was sent us. Mr. Selby's letter having demolished the outworks of the Archdeacon, there is nothing for us to do but to storm the citadel, which the builder has thought fit, injudiciously as it appears to us, to erect on a sandbank instead of on a rock.

The Archdeacon says that "Lord Ebury's declaration in

---

* Precisely similar sentiments to those expressed in the above Charge were shortly afterwards published, "at the request of the clergy," by the Venerable Charles Dodgson, Archdeacon of Richmond. Rivingtons: 1860.

the House of Lords on the Revision of the Liturgy has made it clear that *repose on that vital question will not be allowed us;*"*—in other words, Lord Ebury's persisting in bringing forward his motion *compels the Archdeacon to speak out,* however reluctantly, lest his silence should be construed into assent. " *Tacent, satis laudant,* our foes will say."

This is a valuable admission, and shows the penetration and judgment of the writer. We hope Lord Ebury will make due use of it when he next appears before the public.

"*Septimus, octavo propior, jam fugerit*"—*mensis,*—that is to say, it is now seven, or nearer eight months since Lord Ebury's speech of last May was delivered in the House of Lords, published next morning in the *Times* and the other daily papers, repeated in every journal, Lay and Clerical, London and Provincial;—since revised and edited by his lordship himself, and now circulating in its third edition;—and yet the only *attempt* at a REPLY to it are the three addresses to the House, on the occasion of its delivery, from *one* English Archbishop, *one* Irish, and *one* Welsh Bishop! So that, according to the Venerable Richard Charles Coxe's theory, we must " entail the discredit of *acquiescence or approval* upon all the others." Shame on the Right Reverend Prelates! Shame on the chaplains and rural deans! Shame on the remainder of the Archdeacons!† What, not one found to support the hero of Lindisfarne in his solitary protest, and to echo the quotation from his Bishop's Charge, that our Liturgy is " a precious inheritance bequeathed to us by our forefathers, which

---

* Preface to the Charge of the Archdeacon of Lindisfarne, 1858. See also Charge by the Bishop of Ripon (Bickersteth), October, 1861.

† Seven other Archdeacons have since expressed themselves on the subject of Revision; of whom Archdeacon Stonehouse of Lincoln, Archdeacon Musgrave of Halifax, Archdeacon Law of Wells, and Archdeacon Allen of Salop, have more or less signified their *approval;* while Archdeacon Denison (of course), Archdeacon Churton of Cleveland, and Archdeacon Dodgson of Richmond, have pronounced against it.

we wish—may I not add, and are resolved—to transmit unmutilated and unimpaired to those who come after us!"

We thought this sentence had been a rescript of the Bishop of Oxford's peroration in Anne's large chamber last February;* but on looking more closely to the Archdeacon's pamphlet, we find it distinctly attributed to his own diocesan; at whose palace the public have been since apprised the Bishop of Oxford was staying when he indited his late celebrated letter on the Reading or Lavington case.

"Like will to like," they say; so, with every respect for the Bishop of Durham,† we cannot help fearing there must be with his lordship a slight leaning Oxfordwise, when he thus adopts the *ipsissima verba* of the Patron Saint of the Tractarians.

The Archdeacon is next surprised that there should be so great a similarity between the demands of the present Reformers and those of the Millenary Petitioners in the reign of James I.; and he argues that, if the thousand Petitioners were wrong in 1603, *à fortiori*, Lord Ebury's 320 Petitioners must be wrong in 1857.

Archdeacon Paley, we are inclined to think, would have gone a different way to work; and would first have *proved* that the Millenary Petitioners *were* wrong, before he drew Lindisfarne's rash conclusion from his premises. For instance, Paley would have shown, or attempted to show, that—

1. Interrogatories administered to infants in baptism *is* a desirable custom of the Church, and sanctioned by Holy

---

* Letter xiv., p. 91.
† Dr. Longley, afterwards Archbishop of York, and Canterbury; in which latter capacity he presided over the "Royal Commission for inquiry into the Rubrics and other matters in the Book of Common Prayer," 1867-8, from which, however, nothing has hitherto resulted but an empty REPORT, a sort of *brutum fulmen—Vox et præterea nihil*. (1878.)

Scripture or Apostolic usage, or by the practice of the earliest ages of Christianity.

2. That Baptism *may* be conveniently administered by *women*, according to the views of the English Church.

3. That the term *priest* and the form of *absolution*, as given in our Prayer-books in the Ordination Service and Visitation of the Sick, are never abused, or open to abuse.

4. That the Canonical Scriptures are *not* generally preferable to the story of Tobit and his Dog, Bel and the Dragon, Susanna and the Elders, and some other Apocryphal chapters,* now read publicly in the Church.

5. That non-residence was *not* then (as till very lately in the English Church) a great and crying evil.

6. That Episcopal *commendams* and clerical *pluralities* are *not* greatly to be deprecated.

7. That excommunications by laymen *are* expedient.

8. That the Ecclesiastical Courts did not, and do *not still*, require to be reformed, &c., &c.

Such, as is known to many of my readers, is a brief summary of the principal grievances presented to King James, at the Hampton Court Conference. Whether the Archdeacon of Lindisfarne presumed upon the ignorance of his audience, who requested the publication of this Charge, or whether he simply exposed his own, we presume not to say. But we are bold to affirm that he will find few people south of Roseberry Toppin who will agree with him in thinking that the petitioners of 1603 *were* altogether mistaken in their " views of truth," or of the desirableness of Church Reform at that day. And if 250 years have since elapsed, and, though *some* of the grievances are happily now redressed, several of them yet remain—it by no means, in our judgment, argues either want

---

* This was one of the points upon which stress was laid by Lord Ebury in his Address to the House of Lords, May, 1860. See his Speech, p. 24.

of wisdom or want of piety in Lord Ebury's petitioners, or his lordship himself, that they still press to be heard, and refuse to be silenced by either Archdeacons in the North or Bishops in the South, "resolving" that "the precious inheritance of their fathers shall be transmitted unmutilated and unimpaired to those who come after them."

I had a few more words to say on this head; but as you request your correspondents to be brief, I will here take leave of the Archdeacon, and remain yours, &c.,

January 10, 1859. "INGOLDSBY."

LETTER XXXIX.

THE BISHOP OF LINCOLN'S CHARGE (*continued*).

"As was to be expected, the Bishop of Lincoln is totally opposed to a Revision of the Book of Common Prayer. We agree with his lordship that the proposed changes would interrupt the current of their true meaning (*videlicet*, of the services), deface their likeness to the ancestral Liturgies of the holy Church, shock the feelings and dislocate the association of multitudes of the most attached and devout members of our own Church, which could only be admitted and authorised by submitting our Prayer-book to the legislation of indifferent, in some cases, and even hostile hands."—*Clerical Journal*, Jan. 8th, 1859.

SIR,—I have not forgotten my promise to continue my Review of the Bishop of Lincoln's Charge.* It occurred to me, however, while thinking what I should say on the remaining two BUTS, that a passing notice of the Archdeacon of Lindisfarne's pamphlet might not come amiss to some of your readers, served up sandwich-fashion, with a very little salt and mustard, between the two slices from the loaf of the higher and drier dignitary.

My dread above all things is lest "Ingoldsby" should be voted a bore, and your journal suffer from the countenance it

---

* Letter xxxvii., p. 246.

has afforded to his hebdomadal infliction.* Not having, therefore, the skill of the accomplished Mons. Wieniawski,† or modern Paganini, to fiddle for half an hour together on one string, I am driven to all manner of shifts, this among others, to vary the entertainment in order to stave off ennui from my readers.

The bishop's *third* objection, or BUT No. 3, is that he "does not think the complaints that have been made as to the length of the Services are well-founded, so far as adults are concerned, provided they diligently and devoutly join in the responses."

Now it is clear that the former part of this proposition must still be a matter of opinion, in which people will differ according to their feelings, which vary much with the various temperaments and habits of individuals. The Bishop of Lincoln, it would seem, likes "long prayers;" Ingoldsby does not. And such I suspect to be the case with any indefinite number of persons taken two and two together at random, from that enormous mass constituting the PUBLIC, for whose convenience as well as edification it should be our business to cater in the matter of public worship. Meanwhile it must be remembered that it is always in the power of those who are partial to repetitions in prayer to have any amount they may choose of them in their *domestic* devotions, and to hire their servants with that understanding; whereas it is *not* competent to those who hold, with Solomon, that seeing God is in heaven and we upon earth, *therefore* our words should be few, to flee from "the wordy torrent" in *Church*, without an unseemly interruption to the Service. And it is to be feared that thousands for this simple reason habitually absent themselves from the Morning Service (a

---

* See Letter XIX., p. 130.
† A violinist at that time performing with great applause in London.

fact which the bishop does not deny in the case of the *daily prayers*),* while it by no means follows that they make a point in consequence of attending in the afternoon or evening.

As for "diligently and devoutly joining in the responses," however lovely in theory, I appeal to the experience of your readers, whether such a beatific vision is not rather exceptional than otherwise in the general run of congregations, and one therefore, which can hardly be accepted as an argument for or against an universal rule.

"When the Lord's Supper is administered," the bishop hesitatingly admits, "the Service is *perhaps* over-long for the communicants;"† and the *Union*‡ considers that "when the Holy Communion is administered, it is sufficient, *with the sermon and singing*, to form one entire service." We cannot, however, agree with the bishop as to his mode of meeting the difficulty, namely, "that in country parishes the singing should be diminished,"—being that part of the service in which the country people take the greatest delight—"and the sermon shortened, which would be much better than omitting it altogether."

As to the inexpedience of "omitting the Sermon altogether," most people will agree with his lordship. But as for *shortening* it, the expression is so entirely a *relative* one, that it is difficult to give an opinion on the subject without more data than the bishop has supplied. Some people would call half an hour's sermon a long one. Some find from

---

* "I believe there are hundreds and thousands of the laity who would willingly attend the Daily Service, if, instead of half or three-quarters of an hour, it were to last not more than ten minutes or a quarter of an hour."—*Bishop of Lincoln in Convocation.* Letter IX., p. 52. See also the Bishop's Letter to Rev. F. C. Massingberd, *Lincoln Chronicle,* Jan. 27, 1860.

† Such is also the opinion of the Bishop of Llandaff. See Letter XLIX.

‡ A High Church organ of the day; now, I believe, superseded by the *Church Times.*

twenty to twenty-five minutes sufficient for all ordinary purposes. If, therefore, the bishop would have his clergy reduce even this last short measure, on what are commonly called " Sacrament Sundays," where would he fix the limit?—would a quarter of an hour, would ten minutes, would five suffice?* "*Depunge ubi sistam.*"—Where are we to stop?" An intelligent writer in one of your numbers, under the signature of "T. T.,† Holton," furnished us lately with an admirable letter, headed " Short Sermons and Long Services," being a communication to a friend who (acting on the Bishop of Lincoln's theory) had been preaching on Communion Sundays a series of short quarter-of-an-hour sermons on the Offertory Sentences. The writer being, as he states, a minister of fifty years' experience, observes " that the whole matter in dispute has grown out of the irresistible fact of *the repetitions and length of our Liturgy;* and that, rather than abridge this last, our bishops, by their unwise opposition, lead numbers of our clergy to shorten or omit the sermon, which *nineteen out of twenty of the people come to hear;* not considering that 'faith cometh by hearing,' and that where one person is converted by the prayers, a thousand are regenerated by the faithful preaching of the Word of God, carried home to the heart in answer to prayer by the Holy Ghost."‡

---

* It may be observed that it is not the quantity but the quality of the sermon, and *the mode of its delivery*, which makes it long—a point not sufficiently considered. We have known the same person fall asleep over a sermon of a quarter of an hour's length—*read*, not preached—who would have listened gladly to one of double the length if delivered extempore with animation and effect.

† The veteran and respected Reformer, T. Tyndale, of Holton near Oxford, long since gone to the " Rest which remaineth for the people of God."

‡ This excellent clergyman was a lineal descendant of the great translator of the Bible, and knew too well the value of that book to wish its exposition curtailed in order to make room for " vain repetitions," many of them of human invention.

To the tacit rebuke of this octogenarian I would commend the advocates for a lengthy " Form of Prayer ;" only further remarking that *another* Master in Israel has well observed, that " it is one of the surest signs of a degenerate age of the Church when preaching is made *secondary* to praying,"* as it infallibly would be were the Bishop of Lincoln's doctrine to be carried out; the more so, as his lordship intimates in another portion of his Charge that even six administrations of the Holy Communion is but a scanty allowance in the year ;† and the Reviewer of the Charge (in the article quoted at the head of this Letter) insists that *monthly*, if not *weekly*, Communion *ought* to be the rule.‡

The removal of the Litany to the afternoon or evening, suggested as another make-shift, and acted on by the bishop-resisting Rector of St. George's-in-the-East,§ would be no relief to those parishes (by far the majority in the country) where there are only two services; as it comes clogged with the self-defeating provision, that " it be read at *one* of the *two* subsequent services !"

---

* Milner's " Church History," vol. iii., p. 131.

† In his Charge of October, 1861, the Bishop of Lincoln (Jackson) would seem to recommend Monthly Communion and Weekly Offertory in all Churches in his diocese, a piece of advice subsequently acted upon by several of his clergy.

‡ The Bishop of Lincoln appears here to be in accord with his right reverend brother of Oxford:—

" Three years ago the whole number of parishes in which there were monthly or *more numerous* celebrations, were returned to me as 180; this year they are returned as 435. I trust that this increase may spread through the whole diocese."—*Bishop of Oxford's Charge*, Nov., 1860; p. 11.

In February, 1862, it was officially announced in the *English Churchman*, that at a certain church in Oxford there would be *twice a-week* early celebrations at 7 a.m., *besides the weekly Communion on Sunday*. I believe it is now not uncommon to meet with *daily* " early celebrations " in several of the so-called High Churches both in town and country.

§ The Rev. Bryan King, of whom more hereafter.

Lastly, the bishop recommends " early celebrations, *as well as* those at noon;"—and concludes that "this mode of meeting the difficulty would be far better than agreeing to any scheme which would dislocate the deep meaning of our services, dissolve the connexion between the Prayer-book and its ancestral Liturgies, and shock the feelings of the most earnest and devoted sons of the Church."

Methought I was here reading one of the Bishop of Oxford's neatly-rounded periods, and I had a dreamy recollection about "shocking feelings" in one of his lordship's lengthy harangues. But upon referring to the passage I find that it was only the " simple feelings of the *less educated poor*" that were in danger of being "shocked," by our " altering this or that," or "one thing being left out and another put in," and our thus "doing a mischief the extent of which no man can conceive."* Whereas the Bishop of Lincoln apprehends the danger on behalf of " the most earnest and devoted sons of the Church." They say, however, that extremes meet. Hence, I imagine, the sympathy between the country bumpkin, lolling over the Psalms and Te Deum, and dozing through the Litany, and the uncompromising High Churchman, who so adores our " beautiful and incomparable Liturgy " that he can detect in it no flaw, and wishes not a syllable to be altered.

But surely the Bishop of Lincoln ought to know that an abridgment of the services, so far from "dissolving the connexion between the Prayer-book and its ancestral Liturgies," is the very thing most calculated to restore it to the ancient pattern. Look at the first Prayer-book of King Edward VI.,† and compare it with the accumulated compilation of 1662. Not that we object to the additions *per se;* but we object to them *quoad* they *are* ADDITIONS, and

---

* See Letter xiv., p. 94. † Letter vi., pp. 36, 37.

not simple *variations*. Had one form been appointed for the first Sunday in the month, another for the second,* another for the third and fourth;—one portion when the Holy Communion is administered, another when it is not; one when the Litany is read, another when it is not, and so forth;—there would have been little reason to complain. And no one can deny that the further we go back to " ancestral Liturgies," the more we find *brevity*, not *prolixity*, to be the type, till we come to the Fountain Head of all prayer, Whose word was, " *After this manner pray ye;* "—I need not add what *that manner* was.

As for " early celebrations," so prevalent in Roman Catholic Churches, and now attempted to be revived in our own; if the Bishop of Lincoln really wishes such to become the practice in his diocese, let us hope, for the sake of quietness in this portion of the kingdom, that the recommendation may be accompanied with a severe caution against such pranks as those exposed in your journal under the head of " Tractarian Progress at St. George's-in-the-East." Not that there is any *present* danger of the fen divines† following

---

* This plan is approved of by Mr. Palmer, author of "Origines Liturgicæ," and has been now for years practised with success by the author of these Letters. "Go thou and do likewise," he would say to any of his clerical brethren whose eye may chance to light on this passage.

† Even the Lincolnshire fens, however, were at that time not *wholly* exempt from a taint of this malaria. See *Stamford Mercury*, March, 1860, with the following comments, taken from *The Downshire Protestant:*—

" A PUSEYITE FUNERAL.

"The *Union* of last Friday publishes an account of the obsequies of a lady who, in her lifetime, doubtlessly belonged to the Church of England, and lived in communion with our Reformed Church, but who, being dead, was consigned to the grave with all the pseudo-solemnities of Popery or Paganism, by priests of the Church of Rome, *professing to be clergymen of the Protestant Church of England.* This was, no doubt, according to her own desire; but what then? Who taught her to desire that the 'Holy Sacrifice' should be offered, in two parishes, after her decease? Who taught

the example of the clergyman of that parish, who, dating his letter on "the eve of St. Nicholas," invited his friend

her to request that her coffin should be 'duly incensed by a priest,' and that *prayers should be offered up for her departed soul?*

"Such teaching belongs essentially to Rome, let the teachers assume what name they please. The *Union* gloats over the account of this burial ceremony, with the unction and enthusiasm of a ghoul. We quote the particulars:—

"'We have received the following *interesting* account of the funeral of Mrs. Bills, of Linwood House, near Market Rasen, Lincolnshire, which took place on Monday, the 30th ult. *Subsequent to her decease* and previous to the day of her funeral, the Holy Sacrifice had been *specially* offered at two different parishes, the *proper vestments* being used; and each evening *the Litany for the Faithful Departed* was said in the room where the body was laid in a coffin covered with violet cloth, having on the lid a long pink *Latin* cross, a plain shield with an interception, and a wreath of fresh immortelles, red and green. On the morning of the funeral, before leaving the house, the choir were requested to sing the "De Profundis," during which *the coffin was duly incensed by a priest*, who afterwards *offered up prayer for the soul of the departed*, the mourners and friends holding the usual lighted tapers. At the time appointed the procession was formed, the body being borne upon a bier and covered with a violet-coloured pall, having on it a cross similar to the one upon the coffin, with the words "Regnavit a ligno Deus" running round the upper portion of it. The *processional cross* was carried by *a novice belonging to a brotherhood* lately commenced in the neighbourhood under the Confraternity of the Holy Cross, of which the nephew of the deceased is Secretary. As the procession came in sight of the church, the tolling of the bell ceased, and a peal was struck up. The body was met at the churchyard gate by *four priests and the choir*, who, as they proceeded to the church, *chanted* the soothing and cheering sentences at the commencement of the Burial Service. The bier having been placed before the entrance to the chancel, the choir sung the appointed Psalms, and the curate of the parish, the Rev. Walter Stockdale,* read the lesson; after which the "Dies Irae" having been sung as the Introit, the *holy sacrifice* was *specially* offered, the Rev. J. T. White being the celebrant. The altar was vested in black. After the Benediction the procession again formed and moved to the grave, which was lined with evergreens, and *the office* was *concluded* by the Rev. W. Stockdale, the choir singing all the parts which are appointed to be sung. The relations and friends of the deceased, as well as the choristers, were furnished with bouquets, which were thrown on the coffin into the grave.' (See note at p. 128.)

"We are informed, by the *Union*, that the deceased took great interest.

* Now vicar of Morton with Haconby, Lincolnshire, by appointment, in 1862, of the Bishop of Lincoln (Jackson), *in whose patronage the living is.*

R

to a "seven o'clock celebration of the blessed Sacrament of Christ's dear body and blood *for the repose of poor Henry's*

for some time previous to her death, in the arrangements for her funeral. Her burial was to be quite a gorgeous affair. There was to be no 'gloom' about it. On the contrary, *her friends were furnished with bouquets for the occasion*, and as soon as the funeral train drew up to the church-gates the bells rang out a merry peal.

"It would seem that this poor misguided lady, instead of preparing for her latter end in a Christian manner, had been concerned about many other things—about 'memorial cards,' and the '*proper eucharistic vestments.*' She left a paper, addressed to her nephew, containing her final directions in reference to her obsequies. From this most melancholy document we quote the following:—

"'I have to request that my nephew will see to the arrangements respecting my funeral: that I am buried after *a Catholic manner*; that I am carried to the church on a bier, covered with a purple pall, with the proper cross upon it; also that, if possible, he will procure the assistance of *the cathedral choir* (which attended accordingly from Lincoln Minster), and avoid gloominess in all the arrangements; also that the coffin be surmounted by the Christian emblem, the cross. In all other respects I leave the matter in his hands, only requesting that he will bury me *as a Catholic*, in which faith I hope to die and rise again. I further request him for memorial cards to *send out a picture, like one which I have seen in his possession, of a priest offering the holy eucharist in commemoration of the dead,* and upon which is the *glorious* text from Maccabees—"It is a holy and wholesome thought to pray for the dead."'

"'The whole of the funeral arrangements,' says the *Union* triumphantly, 'were carried out by the Confraternity of the Holy Cross; the bier, pall, and processional cross being furnished by them.'

"What comment is needed on proceedings such as these? Here is a picture of a weak-minded woman, born of Protestant parents, and educated as a Protestant, *dying a Papist*, owing to the teaching of so-called Protestant clergymen, and being buried by them, not in accordance with the grand and solemn ritual of our Protestant Church, but with the flimsy *and pagan gauds* of Popery. Would that these enemies of the Church and of Protestantism were fairly handed over to the tender mercies of the Church to which they really belong!"

The following is from the *Rock* newspaper of Sept. 13th, 1878.

"THE 'PRINCESS ALICE' AND ST. PAUL'S, LORRIMORE SQUARE.

"SIR,—The unhappy *Princess Alice*, and Ritualistic folly in juxtaposition! Yet so it is. In the *Standard* of the 11th inst., under the heading 'Funeral Services in London,' is an account of a special funeral service held on the 10th at St. Paul's, Lorrimore Square—a church which the late vicar, Mr.

soul;"* but it is well known to all who are conversant with the secret workings of the human heart, through how slow and imperceptible degrees an advance is made from the lowest to the highest pitch of extravagance.† So much so, that it is remarked by a great observer, that, had we lived in the age of Caligula, we should have become so insensibly familiarised to all kinds of enormities, that even the elevation of the Emperor's horse to the rank of Consul would have hardly astonished us.

"*Principiis obsta*" is a good maxim; and with our fearful experience of the past, we can scarcely be too careful

---

Going, has made notorious for Romanising practices—over the body of a former chorister (Mr. W. Lambert) drowned in the awful catastrophe to the *Princess Alice*. This is how the *Standard* describes the ceremonial adopted on the mournful occasion:—'The coffins'—the wife and daughter also perished—'were placed in front of the communion-table, that of the little girl in the centre, covered with a white pall, with violet cross; those of the parents at either side, covered with violet palls, bearing white crosses. The tops of the palls were literally hidden by flowers. Close to the coffins were three tall lighted candles. The Rev. Mr. Powell chanted the Burial Service of the Church of England, then the Communion Service was celebrated by the vicar, the Rev. W. P. Cay Adams, who was clothed in purple (!) vestments. The coffins were incensed during the service, and amongst the hymns was "Grant them, Lord, eternal rest," &c.' Not till two o'clock were the coffins placed in the funeral car. The service began at seven a.m., so that the whole of the proceedings were made to resemble as much as possible the Roman office for the dead. I have forwarded to the Bishop of London the *Standard's* account of the service, but I shall probably only receive an acknowledgment of the extract, no notice being taken of the unlawful acts of the vicar. When will the Church of England be emancipated from the thraldom of the Romanising and traitorous party? Not, I fear, until the bishops realise their tremendous responsibilities, *or the revision of the Liturgy in a Protestant direction is an accomplished fact.*—I am, &c.,

"Bedford Park, Chiswick." "W. MARTIN BROWN.

* Incredible as it may now seem, such was one of the small beginnings of the practices which led to the "Riots at St. George's-in-the-East."

† " Sic omnia fatis
In pejus ruere, et retro sublapsa referri."
VIRGIL, *Georg.*

for the future. With the warning example of Newman, Ward, Manning, Maskell, Oakeley, and Wilberforce (Archdeacon of Holderness) before us, with not less than *one hundred and twenty-five* of their dupes, as we are assured by a clergyman of the diocese of Oxford,* who shall say that we raise a false alarm? The fascinations of the basilisk are not easily resisted by those who are silly enough to play with the beast. A "processional cross," borne aloft at a consecration before one bishop,† though calling himself "a backbone son of the Reformed Church;"‡ a crozier carried ostentatiously before another,§ who advocates "early cele-

---

* A long list of members of the University of Oxford who have seceded to the Church of Rome may be seen in a pamphlet published by Messrs. Wertheim and Macintosh, entitled *Facts and Documents, showing the Alarming State of the Diocese of Oxford;* to which list might unfortunately be added the names of several more who have *since* joined the Romish Church, though the tendency Romeward is happily *now* somewhat on the decline.

† The following is the report of this transaction, as addressed to the *Record,* by the Rev. W. E. Fremantle, Rector of Claydon, and Rural Dean, who was present on the occasion (January 21, 1859):—

"It is quite true that the Rev. Mr. Perry, Curate of Addington, met the Bishop, the Archdeacon, and the Rural Dean, at the Lich-gate, holding a long bright blue staff in his hand, surmounted by a cross about eighteen inches in length, inlaid with what I supposed to be mother-of-pearl. That he wore a surplice and a black stole with *an embroidered cross at the back of the neck,* and *a cross similarly embroidered on both sides.* That the churchwardens carried shorter staves with small crosses on them, and the clergy in surplices formed the procession. Mr. Perry then led the procession round the boundary of the new churchyard, and the clergy sung the Psalm to a Gregorian chant. I do not know whether processional crosses are legal or not, but in the presence of the Bishop, the Archdeacon, and the Rector of the parish, I felt that whatever my private opinion might be, the responsibility of sanctioning the proceeding did not rest with me."

How far the above is, or is not, a close approximation to the practice in the Roman Church, let those determine who have witnessed similar scenes on the Continent.

See on this subject a well-known tract, entitled "QUOUSQUE? HOW FAR? AND HOW LONG?" suggested by a late Funeral at Oxford. Longmans, 1873.

‡ See Letter XXXIII., p. 218.

§ This was at the re-opening of Newark Church by the Bishop of Lincoln (Jackson), in the autumn of 1859, and continued by his successor.

brations," and weekly or monthly communions in purely agricultural districts, may seem harmless matters in the sight of some, but they can hardly be considered so when viewed in connexion with passing events.

"Hæ nugæ seria ducunt
In mala."

The story of any *honest* pervert to Popery reveals the fact that these apparently trifling beginnings lead imperceptibly to fearful endings. Read their history, and say whether it is not aptly portrayed in the following lines, slightly parodied from those of our sweetest bard:—

"Presumptuous men! with looks intent
Again they stretch'd, again they bent,
Nor knew the gulf between.
The wily Pope sat by, and smil'd:
The slippery verge their feet beguil'd,
They tumbled headlong in."

Beware, ye "most earnest and devoted sons of the Church," beware of stone altars, stone pulpits, lecterns, piscinæ, reredoses, credence tables, steps, images, prie-dieus, super-altars, crosses, banners, flowers, vestments, chasubles dalmatics, tunics, copes, candles, bells, lace, fringes, paintings, illuminated Prayer-books, incense, early celebrations, midnight processions, bowings, genuflexions, processional crosses,*

---

* Winchelsey, Popish Archbishop of Canterbury, in the early part of the fourteenth century, enjoins his parishioners in all parish churches to provide, among other articles, a vestment, with chasuble (marked with a cross, Dr. Hook, *Ch. Dict.*), dalmatic, tunic, and cope, and *processional cross.*—See Baxter's *Church History*, pp. 716—30.

"In delivering his triennial charge to the clergy of his diocese on Tuesday, the Bishop of Chichester (Durnford) referred to the recent perversions to Rome of several of his Brighton clergy, and said distress and grief at such unfaithfulness had bowed down many hearts, but none more than his own. *From one church alone five clergymen had lately passed over to Rome,* and they had to the utmost of their power leavened all they could influence with Romish doctrine. *Craft, subtlety,* and *secrecy* were the characteristics of the Roman propaganda, and in this instance they had

et id genus omne, the toys of your dangerous and subtle foe. Remember the adage,—as applicable to Popery as it is to vice, of which, indeed, the former is all but the synonym—

> "It is a monster of such hideous mien,
> That to be hated needs but to be seen.
> But seen *too oft*, familiar with its face,
> We first *endure*, then pity, then—*embrace*."

With this timely warning to my brethren of the long stole and green scarfs,—I remain, Sir, yours, &c.,

January 22, 1859.   "INGOLDSBY."

TENDIMUS IN LATIUM.

P.S.—The statements in the above Letter are fully borne out by what has subsequently occurred at St. George's-in-the-East.

The following causes of complaint at St. Barnabas, Pimlico, were also made public by one of the churchwardens :—

" 1. That *texts of Scripture in the Latin tongue* have been put up over the arches and doors *all through the interior of the church.*

" 2. That the *cross* that was ordered to be removed by the judgment of the Privy Council has been replaced over the Communion-table.

" 3. That the Commandments have not been set up in the chancel, as ordered by the judgment of Sir S.

---

been unsparingly employed. No man could say how far the poison had extended. Such defections betrayed inward unsoundness and unsettlement, and they asked with fear who shall be the next to forsake our communion ? The path towards Rome had been smoothed for their converts by *excessive and illegal ritual*, and he strongly counselled his clergy to abstain from ceremonials which the English Church had rejected."—*The Rock*, Oct. 11, 1878, p. 819.

It is against these things we *protest*, as did our forefathers of honoured memory. What is all this but an attempt to revive that against which they stoutly fought, and in which cause they died ?

Lushington, but pasted against the wall in the nave of the church.

"4. That the *super-altar* remains on the Communion-table.

"5. That the massive brass candlesticks still remain, and *the candles are lighted with much ceremony in the daytime.*

"6. That the rood-screen, surmounted by a huge *jewelled cross, before which the congregation prostrate themselves,* still remains.

"7. That a small portable kneeling-desk is placed in the body of the church, where the curates chant the Litany, with *their backs turned to the congregation,* instead of from the reading-desk.

"8. That a brass tablet has been set up in the nave of the church to the memory of a late curate, *who is still living,* by the nuns of St. Barnabas, on account of 'the loving words that he spoke to them while curate of that church.'

"9. That *the vestry is fitted up and used as a confessional, with altars, crosses, candlesticks, and service-books for confession, translated from the Papal Breviary.*

"10. That the *whole of the services* are performed with choral music, instead of being read, as ordered by the Rubric, and the Sunday-morning service is subdivided into five separate services, *with the tinkling of the clergy bell between each, to imitate so many masses of the Romish Church.*

"11. That the clergy and officials perform certain ceremonies, *bowings and genuflexions in the performance of divine worship* that are very offensive to the parishioners.

"12. That the parishioners have subscribed about £50,000 for providing themselves with suitable church accommodation, but *owing to the Romish practices of the clergy* they are morally excluded from the use of the churches they have built.

"The result of these practices is—that the Protestant principles of many of the parishioners are being undermined.

Scarcely a week passes but we hear not only of individual and clerical perversion, but of *whole families being handed over to the insatiable maw of the Papacy.* The parishioners have appealed to the Bishop of London, the Consistory Court, the Court of Arches, and the Privy Council, in all of which we had a favourable judgment; but the clergy have stultified those judgments by *replacing all the crosses and ornaments* that were prohibited by those judgments; not only so, but the *church, college, and schools of St. Barnabas are entirely in the hands of Jesuit priests, and used solely for the perverting of our people to the Church of Rome.* I look upon this movement in our Church as likely to bring about the most disastrous results—similar to those of the reigns of Charles the First and James the Second—if not checked in time. For *I am as certain as I am of my existence that the clergy of this parish are bent on perverting the people committed to their charge to the Church of Rome,* and that they let no opportunity slip to accomplish that object.—

"RICHARD HALL,
"Churchwarden, St. Paul's, Knightsbridge.
"*April* 11, 1860."

LETTER XL.

THE BISHOP OF LINCOLN'S CHARGE (*concluded*).

"It has always been the business of the Tractarian party to teach the clergy to suspect and distrust Parliament; but nothing can be more mischievous than to treat the Legislature with anything but confidence and respect. The Church has no real ground of complaint to urge against Parliament. For ourselves—we say it with sincerity, though with sorrow—there are many of the Bishops to whom we should be much less willing to entrust the welfare of the Church than to the House of Commons."—*National Standard,* Vol. ii., No. 13, p. 309.

SIR,—That there should be sufficient grounds for such a sentiment as the above finding admittance into a leading article of your independent journal, is, as you justly observe, more a matter for sorrow than anger, on the part of the best friends of the Church. To repeat ourselves,

> "Pudet hæc opprobria nobis
> Et dici potuisse, et non potuisse refelli." *

The Bishop of Lincoln's *fourth* and *last* reason for objecting to a Revision of the Prayer-book is, that it must be "submitted to the indifferent, and even hostile criticism of a PARLIAMENT, of whom many are not of our communion, nor even of our religion."

Such at least is the report of his lordship's remarks as given by the *Clerical Journal* of Nov. 7th, 1858, before the Charge was published by authority, and on this report our previous observations on the Bishop's Charge have been made. Considering, however, this last clause a somewhat graver business than the former, as involving the reflections of a member of the Upper House upon the general constitution of Parliament, I thought it my duty, before commenting upon it, to satisfy myself that justice had been done to his lordship by the reporters.

Having accordingly purchased the Charge, at the cost of two shillings—not having in this instance† had the honour of receiving a presentation copy—I find, at p. 33, the passage as follows:—

"Finally, such questions must be debated and decided by a Parliament, many of whose members are not of our communion, and some not even of our religion."

This is certainly a milder way of putting the objection than the *Clerical Journal's* "indifferent and *hostile* criticism;" but there is still sufficient of the Tractarian element to justify our application of the passage quoted at the head

---

* Ovid, *Met.* i., 578. See Letter No. xxxii., p. 214.
† See Letter xxv., p. 171.

of this article. No one can deny that the paragraph, even in its qualified form, is calculated to teach the clergy (in the parts of Holland and Kesteven at least) to distrust Parliament, and treat the Legislature with anything but confidence and respect:—a lesson which it appears to me highly impolitic to inculcate; especially as emanating from one of the spiritual Peers, who, though holding their seats from long prescription, and on constitutional grounds, do so, nevertheless, not without occasional demur on the part of independent members of the Lower House.

We will say nothing about the proverb of the bird and its nest; but is it at *any* time expedient for Churchmen to dispute "the *decisions* of Parliament?" What do we not owe to the labours of that miscellaneous body? How incalculable the blessings it has conferred, within the last 200 years, not only upon these realms, but on the vast Colonial Empire under our control; nay, *indirectly*, upon the entire civilised world! How trivial in comparison, how utterly unappreciable, the amount of mischief that may have resulted from any "hasty" piece of legislation! Why, then, regard it with suspicion? Why insinuate that it has the wish or the power to hurt the Church?*

I am not here to panegyrise, much less to defend, the Parliament. It needs no defence or apology from me. To its own master, Public Opinion, it is doubtless prepared to make answer now, as at all times. I only wish, as a humble unit among those Lincolnshire clergy who were taught in October last, in solemn conclave and in the House of God, to distrust the Supreme Legislature—I only wish to enter my protest against any participation in such a sentiment;

---

* "The difficulty," says Dr. Arnold, "will always be, Who is to reform the Church? The Clergy (*some* of them at least) have a horror of the House of Commons, and Parliament and the country will never trust the matter to the Clergy."

and in doing so, to express, I believe, the feelings of a very large portion of my brethren. WE have no ground of complaint against Parliament. It has protected us before now from the arbitrary power of bishops; and we believe it would do so again, were the occasion, which is not impossible, to arise. WE shrink not, therefore, from encountering —nay, we *invite* the attention of the two Houses of Parliament to what some of us believe to be defects, and what many thousands believe to be possible improvements,* in our Book of Common Prayer—the only chapter of the statutes at large which has escaped revision or repeal within the last 200 years.†

The Bishop of Lincoln may have his private reasons for differing from ourselves in this matter. He may have taken umbrage at some " hasty " expressions, not strictly in accordance with the rules of courtesy, let drop by a certain prominent member of the Peace Association, in reference to two or three of the right reverend Prelates. No doubt Mr. Bright did treat their lordships somewhat disrespectfully on a late occasion at Birmingham. But the clergy in general do not smart under the honourable member's lash.

"Let the gall'd jade wince; our withers are unwrung."

Besides, as Sydney Smith very truly observes, "Those who mean to be just should ask, *Who began?*—The real *onus* of a squabble lies on those who *attack*, not on those who retaliate. And men are to be honoured, not degraded, who come forth, *contrary to their usual habits*, to oppose those whom in ordinary cases they would willingly obey."‡ Who

---

* The Bishop of Edinburgh, Dr. Terrot, wrote to the author, Oct., 1861, "I fully admit your fundamental proposition, that the Prayer-book might be improved."

† This statement is made on the authority of the late Earl Russell, and I believe cannot be denied.

‡ See the *Church of England Monthly Review* for May, 1859.

was it that in February last flung stones at the Lower House of Legislature ?* The Quaker speaks in the autumn, the Prelate had spoken in the spring. If the Dissenter has the last word, the Churchman had the first. The bishop opens, the layman replies. The "hasty and ill-informed" Commoner bides his time before retorting on the Peer ; and at length, having gathered up all his strength for the long-suspended blow,

> "Bids him defiance stern and high,
> And gives him in the throat the lie."

But, after all, the House of Commons is not Mr. Bright, nor Mr. Bright the House of Commons, any more than the Bishops of Oxford and Lincoln are the entire Bench of Bishops; or the Bench of Bishops, much less the Church at large, fairly represented by these outspoken members of the body. We have not heard that the Venerable the Primate of England or Ireland, or the Archbishop of York,† or indeed, *any other* prelate, has made it a serious objection to a Revision of the Book of Common Prayer (whose imperfections they *almost universally* admit), that "such a question must be *debated* and *decided* by a Parliament, many of whose members are not of our communion, and some not even of our religion."‡

There is reason to believe, on the contrary, that if the matter *must* be debated at all in Parliament—which is by no means a *sequitur*—there are several of the prelates who

---

* Letter x., p. 62.

† Archbishop Musgrave, who died May, 1860.

‡ The Bishop of Oxford (Wilberforce) has since expressed himself on this subject as follows:—

"An altered Liturgy would have to struggle clause by clause through the two Houses of Parliament; where, whatever might be the vigilance of many true and wise friends, it would have to run the gauntlet between *ignorant and injudicious patrons*, the most dangerous of all, *and crafty and spiteful foes.*"—*Charge*, November, 1860; p. 66.

would have more confidence in the united Houses of Legislature than they have in the discordant Houses of Convocation,* to which last the Bishops of Oxford and Lincoln appear to yield unquestioning allegiance. Convocation, "composed as it is at present," is, in the Bishop of St. David's judgment, "utterly inadequate" to the purpose of Revising the Liturgy; and it is "*more than doubtful*—it is *altogether improbable*—that its constitution will *ever be so modified* as to render it a fit instrument for so great a work." †

Where, then, *are* we to look for redress? What a dead lock we are in; what a *reductio ad absurdum;* or rather, what a fighting with a shadow; what a wrestling with a pasteboard lion! Does not all this tend to show that the only practicable expedient is that of a ROYAL COMMISSION, as asked for by Lord Ebury—a Commission of wise, moderate, and pains-taking men, with sufficient leisure for the work; men of principle and moral courage, having the fear of God rather than of men before their eyes; unswayed by interest; untrammelled by party; unfettered by prejudice; uncommitted by "hasty" expressions of opinion; without partiality; slow to speak, quick to hear, slow to wrath?

Such a Commission of *thirteen* or *fifteen* honest men—and we trust such *are* to be found ‡—as that under Edward VI., of

---

* In a statistical paper, published about that time, *ten* prelates of the Province of Canterbury were represented as being *for* the revival of Convocation, while *ten* were *against* it, neutral, or doubtful. But supposing all the prelates united in their desire to uphold the authority of Convocation, it is certain that body has no power whatever to bind the Church. See opinion of Sir Fitzroy Kelly, Sir Hugh Cairns, and Messrs. Stephens and Jebb, as taken by the Archbishop of Armagh on the attempted repeal of the 29th Canon, Jan., 1861.

† Charge of the Bishop of St. David's, quoted in Letter xxvi., p. 180.

‡ A Commission indeed was issued in 1866, but, consisting as it did of twenty-nine members, was far too bulky to be practical, and the *result* of their labours (or rather *talking*) was NIL. See the Report of the Commission in the *Guardian* of September 8th, 1869. But in vain do we look for *fruit* from even that meagre document.

which Cranmer and Ridley were members—inquiring diligently for two years, *seeking counsel from all quarters*, and digesting their materials into a careful report, according to the best of their judgment, could hardly, under Providence, fail of success. The public would acquiesce in their decision as the best thing that could, under the circumstances, be had. Convocation, if well advised, would accept the verdict of the public with little alteration. Parliament would lastly, and almost as a matter of course, give *legal* sanction to what had thus been anticipated by the voice of the Church and nation;* and all our alarms and differences would vanish into thin air.

To compare great things with small,—

> "Hi motus animorum atque hæc certamina tanta,
> Pulveris exigui jactu compressa quiesc(er)ent."

The working-bees would return to their hives; the hum of controversy would cease; or—if not of controversy—at least the irritating sense of inquiry stifled, and redress refused.

I am, Sir, yours, &c.,
January 18, 1859.   "INGOLDSBY."

LETTER XLI.

THE RE-ASSEMBLING OF CONVOCATION, FEBRUARY 4, 1859.

> "Sive Aquilo radit terras, seu bruma nivalem
> Interiore diem gyro trahit, ire necesse est."—HORACE.

> "Though rapid Boreas sweep the ground,
>   Or Winter in a narrower round
>   Contract the day; through storm and snow,
>   At all adventures—on we go."—FRANCIS.

SIR,—Those of your readers who have kept up with these Letters since last July, may remember how we then

---

* Such was the case with the State Services in 1858; why not with the rest of the Prayer-book in 1862; or, say, in 1879?

said that "neither heat nor cold, frowns or ridicule, opposition or neglect, must be regarded by the Liturgical Reformer, if sincere in his desire to see his heart's wish accomplished."* Since that time we have exchanged the burning influence of Sirius for the vapoury rimes and chilling blasts of Aquarius and Capricorn, while "STILL MUST I ON" is our eternal motto; our cuckoo note, unrelieved by a single variation; our lonely starling, taught to cry nothing but Revision, Revision, as if for the sole purpose of keeping "the anger of our opponents still in motion," or at least, as says the Venerable Archdeacon of Lindisfarne,† to prove "that *repose* on that vital question will not be allowed them."

Has, then, all this screeching and crying, this chattering and scribbling, this chirping of "the stridulous grasshopper,"‡ for the last twelve months, been altogether thrown away? Have we been scouring a brick, washing an Ethiopian, filling a perforated urn, rolling a Sisyphian stone, or labouring at any other of those delightful tasks which the vivid mind of the ancients suggested as typical of attempting impossibilities? Or have we made some sensible progress during this alternation of the seasons? In short, does the month of February, 1859, find us where we were in February, 1858, when No. 1. of these Letters first saw the light? Have we progressed, retrograded, or stood still the while?

In answer to this question, I shall take the opportunity of the re-assembling of the Convocation of the province of Canterbury to compare the present position of the Liturgical Reformers with what it was a twelvemonth ago, and thence to draw such conclusions for the future as the retrospect of a single year of their *active* existence seems to warrant:—

---

* Letter xx., p. 138.
† Letter xxxviii., p. 247.
‡ See this impertinent and insolent observation of the Bishop of Oxford in his Speech in House of Lords, May 8, 1860. Letter xcvi., vol. ii.

active, we say, for up to this time the conduct of the Revisionists has been rather that of passive discontent, than of activity in taking measures to secure attention or obtain relief.*

The 10th of February of last year saw assembled in Queen Anne's Bounty Office a dozen Prelates of the province of Canterbury, including the Primate, prepared to do battle against a Revision of the Prayer-book.† Of this number of "potent, grave, and reverend signiors," some spoke decidedly, others more mildly, against the very idea of the Prayer-book being touched, altered, mutilated, or "purified" in any way whatever in their day.

The chief speakers were the Bishops of Oxford, Lincoln, and St. David's; while the Primate, the Bishop of Winchester, the Bishop of London, and the Bishops of Llandaff, St. Asaph, Hereford, Bath and Wells, and Chichester gave a qualified assent to the observations of their right reverend brethren.

Shortly after the breaking up of this synod, the organs of the press rung the changes upon the notes of the eleven speakers, and gave out that "the bishops had declared unanimously against a Revision of the Prayer-book." The *Morning Post* crowed, the *Guardian* chuckled, the *Clerical Journal* sang a song of triumph, the *English Churchman* bellowed, the *Union* brayed,—in short, there was such a hubbub in the regions of High Church Journalism, as has not been witnessed from the days of Queen Anne herself to the hour on which

---

* The Association for Promoting a Revision of the Prayer-book was not formally organised till October, 1859. It now reckons from four to five hundred members, and has circulated an immense amount of information on the subject throughout the country; but, alas! having to contend against a powerful hierarchy and an indifferent Legislature, it has not produced the impression it ought to have done from the justice of its cause.

† See Letter II., p. 7.

these " mitred fathers in long order " issued from her venerable chamber in Westminster.

But when matters have reached their worst they are apt to mend. The jade Fortune is notoriously a coquette—

> "Ludum insolentem ludere pertinax,
> Transmutat incertos honores,
> Nunc mihi nunc alii benigna."

The holder of a blank in her lottery will be cheered by the turning up of a prize at the next revolution of her wheel; just as, on the other hand, the prelate who lately triumphed at the discomfiture of the Liturgical Reformers, will find himself cast in the mire by the " nasty " hands of the " nasty " citizens of the North.*

But we must not anticipate events. The next remarkable occurrence in the history of Revision was the notice given by Lord Ebury of his intention, notwithstanding all this blowing of trumpets, to persevere in his motion for a Royal Commission of Inquiry—followed in due course, on the 6th of May, by that motion itself, and his lordship's unanswerable speech, supported by the voices of two or three lay lords, and but feebly resisted by his Episcopal opponents.

Now mark the turn of the tide in favour of the Reformers. Here was an opportunity, not only for the remaining prelates of the province of Canterbury who were not present at the synod at Westminster, but for those of York who by the laws of Convocation *could* not be there, to deliver their sentiments on this *vexata quæstio* before the arena of the House of Peers, and the country at large; and thus to signify their acquiescence, or the reverse, in the *alleged* unanimity of their right reverend brethren.

"What silent all?"—*Not one*—neither the Archbishop

---

* See Letter XXXIII., p. 217.

of York,* nor the Bishop of Durham (Longley), nor Chester (Graham), nor Carlisle (Villiers),† nor Ripon (Bickersteth), nor Manchester (Prince Lee), nor Peterborough (Davys), nor Norwich (Pelham), nor Lichfield (Lonsdale), nor Bangor,‡ nor Salisbury (Hamilton), nor Worcester,§ nor Ely (Turton), nor Rochester,|| nor if there be any other northern or southern prelate—*not one* found to echo the voices of Oxford and of Lincoln ! while but three in all—Canterbury and St. David's repeating themselves, and Cashel (Daly) *admitting more than he denied* the need for revision—are found to brave public opinion, when once the subject is brought by its undaunted champion before that decisive ordeal.¶

Is this, then, the vaunted *unanimity* of the bishops? Surely there is much here to encourage the Reformers. Surely this is proof, amounting to demonstration, that their opponents shun inquiry, and shrink from the light of day; thereby tacitly convicting themselves of having weakness or error on their side, while the Reformers claim on theirs the alliance of TRUTH and common sense.

This first brush with the enemy was followed by Earl Stanhope's attack on the State Services, where it is to be regretted that Revision rather than Excision was not the guiding star. Events have since occurred, and are still occurring, to make it not altogether expedient that the memory of the 5th of November should be obliterated from the minds of the British public.** *Diis aliter visum*, however; and the *Gazette* of Jan. 17th of the present year has finally, it appears,

---

* Archbishop Musgrave died May 4th, 1860, almost immediately before Lord Ebury renewed his motion in the House of Lords in that year.
† The Hon. and Right Rev. Henry Montagu Villiers, died Aug. 9, 1861.
‡ The Right Rev. Christopher Bethell, D.D., died April, 1859.
§ The Right Rev. Henry Pepys, D.D., died Nov. 13, 1860.
|| The Right Rev. George Murray, D.D., died Feb. 15, 1860.
¶ A very similar result was observable on the 8th of May, 1860.
** See Letter XXXIV., p. 223.

disposed of that question; though we would still hope that no faithful Protestant will fail in his *private* prayers to bless God for the miraculous frustration of the Popish Plot of 1605.

Parliament breaking up shortly after this *coup d'état*, nothing more was done in the matter of inquiry into the Prayer-book; beyond a notice from Lord Ebury that he should again bring the subject before their lordships in the ensuing Session.

From that time to the present the Reformers have had it all their own way. Their progress may not have been very apparent to the public eye; but it has been, like the efforts of nature during the same interval, advancing slowly and surely, though out of sight to the vulgar, towards an end to be acknowledged of all men in due time.

Petitions have been signed,* meetings held in London, Liverpool, Derby, Plymouth, Bristol, Cheltenham, Southampton, Portsmouth, Brighton, Reading, Chatham, Shrewsbury, Ashbourne, Bishops Waltham, and other towns, on the subject of Revision; memorials have been adopted to her Most Gracious Majesty, as the acknowledged Head of the Church; articles, letters, and reviews innumerable have appeared in the London and Provincial press;—with one unvarying note, "*Volumus Liturgiam emendari.*"

We do not say that all parties hold precisely the same opinions on this matter, or ask for the same amount of change in the Liturgy. It never was so in *any* reform, and never will be. Witness Mr. Bright, and his efforts at reforming the National Legislature, compared with the views entertained on the same matter by Lords Derby, Palmerston, and Russell. It is childish, therefore, to argue against a Reform

---

* See Report of Association for Promoting a Revision of the Prayer-book, Nov., 1860, 1861.

of the Prayer-book, on the ground that "the Revisionists are not agreed amongst themselves."*

They are united in their *dissatisfaction* with the existing state of things; they are united in their desire for Inquiry; they are united in their determination not to rest until such INQUIRY shall be granted :—and Lord Ebury's motion, in some shape or other, will become an *annual* one, if his lordship and his supporters be not effectually silenced by the concession of their reasonable demands.

"*Vox populi, vox Dei,*" is the cry here, as in other matters, and it is not wise to affect not to hear it. Let the Reformers stand firm and be moderate, and the day is theirs. It is simple justice that they seek, and they will have it ere long,—if not under the present, certainly under some, and that not a very distant, Government.†

I am, Sir, yours, &c.,
February 4, 1859.   " INGOLDSBY."

LETTER XLII.

THE BISHOPS OF LONDON, LINCOLN, AND ST. ASAPH ON THE BURIAL SERVICE OF THE CHURCH.

JACKE O' BOTH SIDES.—"Sure I think when once they come to be Lords they cleane forget . . . for I have heard there was some good things in him before he was a Bishop . . . for he wrote a book wherein he saith . . ."
—*A Pleasant Dialogue, by the Worthy Gentleman Dr. Martin Marprelate*, 1640, p. 10.

SIR,—Returning from our digression, we have a few remarks to make on the concluding paragraph of the Bishop

---

* This stale argument may be seen, by those who are curious in such matters, made the most of by the *Quarterly Review* for January, 1834. Strange that men of sense are found to repeat it, and listen to it, even to this day!

† Unfortunately, the cry for Disestablishment has now taken the place of the cry for Reform. Let the Church look to it. They refused the latter when it might have been timely granted; let them beware lest the former, like the cry for Revision, *vires acquirat eundo!* p. 165.

of London's Speech before Convocation in February of last year, wherein reference is made to the "Burial Service" of the Church.

Dr. Tait, it will be noticed, suggests the expediency of keeping *separate* the two classes of Reformers,—the *doctrinal* and *structural*,—" whose combination," he observes, " may be fraught with danger." *Divide et impera*, the ex-master of Rugby is scholar enough to know, was a standing rule in the Roman policy; and it has not lost its influence among those who have to deal with the rebels of a school, or the recalcitrant clergy of a diocese. The Reformers, meanwhile, have scholars too in their ranks; and have moreover (as one of the Reviewers of these Letters has observed)[*] armed themselves " with shafts from old Greek and Latin quivers," wherewith to annoy, if not to repel the enemy. They are fully awake to the importance of union amongst themselves;[†] and they make no secret of their intention to cohere and pull together till they have succeeded in securing a COMMISSION:—after the granting of which it is not impossible they may take diverse courses in laying their *individual gravamina* before that constitutional tribunal, and so pressing their respective claims for redress.

Let not, therefore, the Bishop of London lay this flattering unction to his soul, that the Reformers have any *present* intention of re-enacting the farce associated with the name of " Diana of the Ephesians." Their cry is one and the same—*Vox omnibus una*; which they will neither allow to be put down by the used-up platitudes of a century's date, nor stifled by the more ancient policy of wearisome and

---

[*] See *Illustrated News of the World*, Jan. 8, 1859, p. 3.

[†] Such was the unanimous feeling at a meeting of the Association for Promoting a Revision of the Prayer-book, held in London, July 24th, 1860 and repeated at their annual meeting, November, 1861.

Fabian delay.* If the defendants of the fortress have on their side the advantage of passive resistance, the assailants have, on the other hand, the privilege of choosing their own time and method of attack; and they will not draw off their forces till a surrender or a compromise takes place. They have allies, too, within the walls, as well as without; and though they do not anticipate the perfidy of a Tarpeia, they are not without hope from the dissensions in the garrison itself, and the friendly interposition of the outlying Tribunes of the people, among whom they reckon not a few dignitaries of the Church.†

The Bishop of London's final observation has reference to the subject under consideration. His words are "few and short," it is true; but (as was once remarked, by a bishop, of even *silence*‡) "they speak volumes."

"In what has been said no allusion has been made to the *Burial Service*. That is a separate matter. We are now considering the general services of the Church."

But WHY was no allusion made to the Burial Service? We can tell his lordship. The Bishop of Lincoln, who brought the question of Revision before Convocation last year, by presenting a petition signed by 215 of his clergy, happens to be one of the 4,000 who in 1851 put their hands to a memorial to the Archbishop of Canterbury, "against the indiscriminate use of the Burial Service."§ No wonder his

---

* "Unus qui nobis *cunctando* restituit rem."—*Æn.* vi. 847.

† These are notoriously the very last persons to join in such a movement; it was therefore a significant fact when any of them were found publicly advocating Revision; *e.g.*, the late Archbishop of Dublin (Dr. Whately), and the present Bishop of Durham (late of Gloucester and Bristol), Dr. Baring.

‡ The late Bishop of Lichfield, Dr. Butler, of Shrewsbury.

§ The petition ran as follows:—

" *To the Most Reverend the Archbishops and the Right Reverend the Bishops of the Provinces of Canterbury and York.*

"We, the undersigned Clergymen of the Church of England, desire to

lordship shrinks from any allusion to the Burial Service, now that he has taken his stand in the ranks of the anti-Reformers. And no wonder his evil genius the Bishop of Oxford is equally silent on the occasion. It is an awkward thing at all times to have to swallow one's leek, even though one be not a Welsh bishop; and I fear we shall find, as we proceed, that one at least of these last is in a similar predicament. It is true Dr. Jackson, when he gave his signature to that unlucky document, was not a bishop; perhaps had little expectation of such an honour being ever thrust upon him. The present Bishop of Natal,* too, it appears, is in the same situation as his lordship—and very likely half-a-dozen other

approach your Lordships with the feelings of respect and reverence which are due to your sacred office.

"We beg to express our conviction that the almost indiscriminate use of 'the Order for the Burial of the Dead,' as practically enforced by the existing state of the law, imposes a heavy burden upon the consciences of the Clergy, and is the occasion of a grievous scandal to many Christian people.

"We therefore most humbly pray that your Lordships will be pleased to give to the subject now brought under your consideration such attention as the magnitude of these evils appears to require, with a view to the devising of some effectual remedy."

The following answer was returned by the Archbishop of Canterbury, addressed to Mr. Witts, Secretary of the Committee:—

"*Lambeth, February* 13*th*, 1852.

"REV. SIR,—

"I have recently had the opportunity, which I expected, of communicating to a large assembly of Bishops the memorial respecting the Burial Service which you transmitted to me, signed by 4,000 Clergy.

"The Bishops, generally, sympathize with the Memorialists in the difficulties to which they sometimes find themselves exposed with reference to the terms of that Service.

"But I am sorry to report that the obstacles in the way of remedying those evils appear to them, *as at present advised*, to be insuperable.

"I remain, Rev. Sir, your faithful servant,
"Rev. W. F. Witts." "J. B. CANTUAR.

It is hardly necessary here to record to what heartburnings and death struggles the *unreformed* Burial Service of our Church has since led, and *will lead* if nothing is done to remove the scandal.

* The Right Rev. John William Colenso, D.D.

Colonial bishops—but as these last have expressed no opinion, that we are aware of, *hostile* to a Revision of the Prayer-book, they may be still, for anything known to the contrary, (and probably are,) favourable to such a measure.

But were it otherwise, I cannot say it would surprise me. It is no new thing, (as Canon Wodehouse observes,)* for "eminent persons to be reformers before they are bishops." The same remark seems to have been made 200 years ago by the quaint writer quoted at the head of this article;† whose words, though they may sound saucy to the ears of this generation, are too valuable to be lost, as furnishing a salutary warning to clerical reformers not to be too "hasty" in committing themselves to an opinion upon Church matters between the ages of twenty-five and fifty, if they have any idea of aspiring hereafter to the dignity and formality of the lawn.

Jacke o' Both Sides appears to have been a kind of prelate's jester; a lineal descendant of Wamba the Witless; a creature of the Episcopal Palace, privileged to speak unpleasant truths in a pleasant manner; a modern Horace, who, like his prototype of old,—

> "Omne vafer vitium ridenti . . . amico
> Tangit; et admissus circum præcordia ludit,
> Callidus excusso *Clerum* suspendere naso."

The office, however, owing to its being unsalaried, has been vacant ever since the decease of the renowned Canon of St. Paul's: a fact much to be regretted, as there can be no doubt such a fly-flapper, however scouted in high quarters, is

---

* See his Tract on the Commission of 1689, p. 38. Longmans: 1834.

† "Our Bishops are the cause of all . . . . The truth is, he wrote for no other end but to get a Bishopricke, for he *never wrote since he hath caught one, I warrant you.*"—*Martin Marprelate*, 1640. A Bishop in these days has not much leisure for *writing books;* but he may at least *read them*, and so learn to maintain consistently the sentiments he put on record before his consecration.

extremely useful, not to say indispensable, to the welfare of the clerical body.

Mais revenons à nos moutons, as our neighbours say. Another Right Reverend Prelate, besides the three already mentioned, formerly expressed himself as not satisfied with the language of the Burial Service. In this case we have the author's recorded sentiments to refer to. He has "written" and published "a book;"—oh, that all our enemies had done the same!—"wherein he saith," .... speaking of the last revision of the Prayer-book,—

"Three of these *promised alterations* were never introduced; viz., the insertion of the whole of the preface to the Ten Commandments in the Communion Service, 'I am the Lord thy God who brought thee out,' &c.; in the Marriage Service, the change of the word, 'with my body I thee *worship*,' into 'I thee *honour*;' and in the *Burial Service*, the omission of the epithets, 'sure and certain' hope, the two last of which *seem to be desirable*, nor am I acquainted with any reason why they were not effected."*

Such were the sentiments of the Bishop of St. Asaph (not being then a bishop) in 1832.† But he goes further, and "saith" a great many more things in this "book," which we must reserve for a future occasion. Meanwhile, perhaps, some reader of the *Quarterly Review* will resolve for us this question,—whether the writer of a certain article on "Liturgical Reform" in January, 1834,‡ had *any one else* in his eye besides the ill-fated Prebendary of Norwich, when he penned the following paragraph :—

---

* History of the Church of England to the Revolution in 1688, by Thomas Vowler Short, Student of Christ Church, and Rector of King's Worthy, Hants, 1832. Vol. ii., p. 245. See also remarks of the Bishop of London on the Burial Service in his reply to Lord Ebury, May 8, 1860.
† Died April 13, 1872.
‡ See Letter xxxii., p. 215.

"We cannot imagine a better *recipe* for changing a curate into a rector, an archdeacon into a dean, a prebendary into a bishop, than a *smart* pamphlet in favour of Church Reform: if in addition it should deny the authority of the *Ten Commandments*, it might make its author an *Archbishop!*"

With this "smart" argument we will take our leave of the reforming rector of 1832, and anti-reforming bishop of 1858 : to whom I fear we must apply the stale proverb :—

"*Tempora mutantur:*—Nos et mutamur in illis."

I remain, Sir, yours, &c.,
February 19, 1859. "INGOLDSBY."

LETTER XLIII.

ADJOURNMENT OF CONVOCATION FROM FEBRUARY 11TH TO AUGUST 25TH, 1859.

"The King of France, with fifty thousand men,
March'd up the hill, and then—march'd down again."
Nursery Rhymes.

SIR,—Without wishing to be sarcastic, one is irresistibly reminded of the above achievement of the French Monarch by the somewhat analogous proceeding of the two Houses of Convocation for the Province of Canterbury,—or, as that assembly is styled by one of your contemporaries, "THE PARSONS' BURLESQUE OF PARLIAMENT."[*]

The points of resemblance are striking ; while the most remarkable difference between the two transactions is this —that whereas the Gallic hero was satisfied with once exhibiting himself and his army to the world in this ridiculous

---

[*] The Bishop of London (Tait) designates it "the Rival Parliament over the way." See his speech in reply to Lord Ebury, May 8, 1860.

position, our friends at Westminster seem to take delight in re-enacting their farce so frequently that it has ceased to excite laughter, and has well-nigh arrived at giving birth to feelings of contempt. Surely those reverend and right reverend gentlemen have much to answer for, who, arrogating to themselves the title of "THE CHURCH,"* thus provoke the indignation of one portion of the community and the scorn or pity of another. And surely there must be something more than human in the composition of the Bishop of Oxford, who can thus go on from year to year hoping against hope that it will ever be permitted him to restore "Convocation as it is" to the active powers it once possessed.

Viewing the bishop as he stands thus all but alone in his glory, the picture rises vividly to one's mind's eye of—

"Cuncta terrarum subacta
Præter atrocem animum Catonis."

Not that there is anything atrocious either in the mind or the countenance of the "smiling" prelate;† but there is undoubtedly something extraordinary in his desperate efforts to conquer in this losing battle; something unaccountable in his character that makes him blind to the painful position into which he is bringing the few devoted followers who adhere to his banner. Warwick at the battle of Barnet, after slaughtering his black destrier with his own hand, did not fight in a more hopeless cause than does our stout Priest in

---

* *Vide* Speech of the Rev. H. Mackenzie, Proctor for the diocese of Lincoln: "It must be remembered that *a debate took place in Convocation* upon the subject of those services in a previous Session, and then the *mind of the Church* in reference to it *had become known.*"—*Guardian*, Feb. 16, 1859; p. 158. This reverend gentleman afterwards became Bishop Suffragan of Nottingham, but soon tired of that very anomalous position, and died 1878.

† A title stamped upon his lordship ever after the late Lord Derby applied to him the well-known line,

"A man may smile, and smile, and smile—and be a villain!"

expecting to put back the wheels of time, and make the men of the nineteenth century submit patiently to the thraldom of the fifteenth.*

The flowing tide of three hundred years has swept over "Convocation as it was;" and it needs no Solomon to tell us how different, how totally different, an affair is "Convocation as it is." Could the advocates for its revival point to any *real progress* made by this resuscitated body during the seven or eight years† of its renewed existence, there might be something to be said for it. The utmost that can be alleged in its behalf is, that it has succeeded in unsettling everything and settling nothing. If this consummation is satisfactory to its admirers, so be it. But I suspect that such a conclusion is anything *but* satisfactory to the nation at large.

Or will the advocates for the periodical assembly of this packed ‡ body of so-called representatives of the Clergy, " *not* of the Church,"§ point to the late achievements of Convocation as something *done*, something *settled?* A House divided against itself : the lower part saying one thing, the upper part saying another. The Commons " unanimous ! "

---

* The *Union* is dissatisfied with the present condition of Convocation, and yearns for the age when monastic dignitaries ruled supreme. "The enormous preponderance of the capitular bodies in the Lower House, and the absence of any such balance to the secular element in the Upper as was once afforded by the presence of the Abbots of the greater monasteries, are evils which, though unlike in aspect, are identical in result."

† Now about thirty ; November, 1878.

‡ How far this expression is applicable is shown in the *Edinburgh Review* for January, 1857, vol. cv. See also before, Letter I., p. 5, Note.

§ For using this expression, the Dean of Ely, Dr. Harvey Goodwin (now Bishop of Carlisle), was called to order by Dr. Wordsworth (now Bishop of Lincoln), at a certain Session of Convocation: "The Canon stated that if any one said that the Convocation was only a representation of the *Clergy*, and not of the *whole Church*, 'let him be excommunicated, and not restored until he repent, and publicly revoke that his wicked error;' he hoped the new Dean of Ely would not find himself in that position!"

The Peers dividing half-and-half, the archbishop giving his vote *in the negative* against the *unanimity* of one House, and the expressed will of half the other. One man's voice overruling a couple of hundred; and those calling themselves " the Church!" Is this seemly? Is is profitable for the body which these two Houses are by courtesy supposed to represent? I trow not. I say nothing of the expediency or inexpediency of the particular measure proposed in one House by the Bishop of Oxford, in the other by that tried champion of orthodoxy, the Archdeacon of Taunton;* but I simply assert, as a matter not likely to be contradicted by men of sense, that such scenes are anything but calculated to add strength or credit to the Establishment. And if such is the only offspring produced after seven years' incubation by this Ecclesiastical Synod, I imagine there are few who will care how soon it is consigned to the tomb of all the Capulets, there to lie till another century has decided whether the Church is to stand or fall,—that is to say, *whether it is to adapt itself to the times,* or to persevere in the preposterous idea of adapting the times to what itself was three hundred years ago.

I am not declaiming against Convocation as possibly *it might be* constructed; or as the Bishop of Oxford, could he have everything his own way (which happily for the Church he cannot), would have it constructed. I am a plain country clergyman, and accustomed to look at most things in a common-sense kind of way; and I confess that I cannot see any good gained in thus, year by year, dragging some 200 divines, bishops, deans, archdeacons, and rectors, to the great

---

* Archdeacon Denison was at that time to the Lower House of Convocation what the Bishop of Oxford was to the Upper, the presiding *genius loci;* but he has since lived long enough to repent of "that his wicked error;" to *revoke* all his sayings and doings was out of his power:—
" delere licebat
Quod non ediderit;—nescit vox missa reverti."

metropolis, from their dioceses, deaneries, archdeaconries, and parishes (where it is presumed they *are* usefully employed), to spend time, money, and breath in contradicting one another; professing to be that which they are not; attempting what is not permitted them; and which, if permitted, they have clearly proved themselves incompetent to perform.*

On some future occasion I may revert to the sayings (not the doings, for they have done nothing) of the body just remanded by Her Majesty to their homes. But having not yet finished with the "sayings" of the Convocation of 1858, it is better to conclude with that before opening a fresh campaign. Meanwhile let us hope Lord Ebury will renew his motion for a *real working Commission* in his place in the great council of the nation; where, if the Church is not represented *as it should be*, it is at least not *mis*represented as it is in the so-called "Church Parliament" at Westminster.

I am, Sir, yours, &c.,

February 26, 1859. "INGOLDSBY."

LETTER XLIV.

THE BISHOPS OF ST. DAVID'S, LLANDAFF, AND ST. ASAPH.

"When shall we three meet again?"—*Macbeth.*

SIR,—Recurring to the Report of the Convocation of February, 1858, we find the names of the three above-mentioned prelates standing in conjunction immediately after that of the Bishop of London.

---

* Take for example the abortive attempt to alter the 29th Canon, on parents standing sponsors for their own children!

Now bearing in mind the smallness of the Principality in area and population, as contrasted with the English dioceses, it is surely not insignificant to observe that *one-fourth part* of the prelates, who have hitherto spoken publicly against a Revision of the Prayer-book, is furnished from that distant and comparatively obscure quarter. But when we take further into consideration the state of " the Church in Wales," as supplied by a pamphlet under that title, written by one who appears conversant with the facts he adduces, it is indeed most extraordinary that so considerable a portion of the opposition to inquiry into the working of the Church system, as exhibited in its Book of Common Prayer, should emanate from that section of the kingdom where its operation is notoriously most defective.

In proof of this I will make a single extract from the pamphlet above referred to, which ought to be in the hands of every one interested in the welfare of the Principality; and I will leave my readers to judge whether *some* inquiry is not needed as to the working of the Church in those parts.

" Here is our present condition in Wales, as between the so-called Conformity and so-called Nonconformity:—

Churches and Chapels of the Establishment—		Number of Church Sittings—	
North Wales, A.D. 1851	364	North Wales, A.D. 1851	115,830
South Wales, A.D. 1851	615	South Wales, A.D. 1851	148,718
	979		264,548

Number of Nonconformist Chapels—		Number of Nonconformist Sittings—	
North Wales, A.D. 1851	1,250	North Wales, A.D. 1851	250,592
South Wales, A.D. 1851	1,248	South Wales, A.D. 1851	352,953
	2,498		603,545

Excess of Nonconformist Chapels over Churches and Chapels of
the Establishment 1,519
Excess of Nonconformist over Church Sittings 338,997
Total Increase of Sittings, 1801 to 1851, in North Wales—
  Church of England ... 16,614 ... 7.1 per cent.
  Nonconformist ... ... 217,928 ... 92.9 ,,
  —————   ———
  100

In South Wales—
  Church of England ... 15,204 ... 5.3 per cent.
  Nonconformist ... ... 270,510 ... 94.7 ,,
  —————   ———
  100

Population of North Wales, A.D. 1851 412,114
       ,, South Wales, A.D. 1851 593,607
                                    Total ... 1,005,721*

I have no means of knowing how far the above statistics are correct,—but, assuming them to be so, (as I am not aware that they have been called in question by any one,)† it must be apparent to every unprejudiced reader that *something* is amiss in the Church system as exhibited to the population of Wales. And though Mr. Morgan gives his own solution of the problem, it is equally reasonable to conclude, from the premises, that the manner in which the Services of the Church are conducted, has a share in producing the disaffection.‡

---

* *Letter on the Church in Wales*, by the Rev. R. W. Morgan, Perpetual Curate of Tregynon, Montgomery. Hardwicke, Piccadilly. 1855.

† Mr. Morgan's statement is corroborated by the following from a Charge of Bishop Bethell, September, 1843; p. 11. Rivingtons.

"Of the present state of the Church in my diocese, or of any strong signs of a returning attachment to it, I cannot speak with satisfaction. *There has been a considerable increase of Meeting-houses belonging to sectaries* of different denominations.

"As population advances, and collections of houses are built, *Meeting-houses almost invariably spring up.*"

Why is this? Echo answers, Why? Would it not be well to *try* what Revision might do to stop the growing evil? for that *evil* it is, I think no one will be disposed to deny.

‡ Mr. Morgan lays great stress on a knowledge of the Welsh tongue as

Under such circumstances, one would have expected to find the Bishops of St. David's, Llandaff, and St. Asaph (Thirlwall, Ollivant, and Vowler Short,) to say nothing of the octogenarian Bishop of Bangor (Bethell), among the very foremost to hail any proposition for submitting the Service-book of the Church to a careful scrutiny, in the hope that something might arise to improve their own position and influence in the West.

Not so, however. " Let ill alone " is clearly, for some reason or other, the principle with these right reverend leaders of the Church. Whether the old proverb—

" Μὴ κινεῖν Καμάριναν—ἀκίνητος γὰρ ἀμείνων,"

occurs to the classic mind of a Thirlwall and an Ollivant;—or whether a painful recollection of his passage of arms with the Perpetual Curate of Tregynon makes a Vowler Short reluctant to re-open the question of Church Reform in any shape, lest the tongue of some other hot-headed Welshman should wag irreverently against him,—it is impossible to say. But for myself, an indifferent spectator of a scene which has attracted the attention of the Church for the last three or four years, I must confess there is no feature in the whole controversy so utterly incomprehensible, as that the Welsh Prelates of all people should be found *unanimous* in their desire to retain matters *in statu quo !**

It has been said that when things are at their worst *any* change must be for the better.

---

a qualification for the Episcopacy in Wales. This may be so; (though for my own part I think it would be to the interest of the Principality if their old language were allowed gradually to die out, as is the case with Gaelic in Scotland and Celtic in Ireland;) but surely something besides a mere want of knowledge of *Welsh* must be at the bottom, to account for such a state of things as is described above.

* All the Bishops of the Principality were *silent* when the subject was a second time brought before the House of Lords on May 8th, 1860.

"Qui jacet in terrâ non habet unde cadat."
"He that is down need not to fear a fall."

And thus a Church, whose proportion to Dissent is as stated in the above table, is in a predicament so near the ground, that it need hardly dread the effects of the hurricane, even should it shake to the centre, (as is the terror of a few, both High and Low Churchmen,)* the stout fabric of its Anglican neighbour.

Possibly the well-exercised mind of the Bishop of St. David's has already arrived at this conclusion. At least, for some reason or other, we missed his accustomed presence at the periodical re-assembling of his right reverend brethren in the Jerusalem Chamber, on the 9th and two following days of last month. It is true, indeed, that his lordship holds no very high opinion of the capacity of Convocation to accomplish any matter of real service to the Church.† But we hardly expected to see him so entirely desert the guns to which he stood so manfully during the past year, both in Convocation and in the House of Lords. If, however, he has since seen reason to prefer staying quietly in his diocese, to performing a bootless and expensive pilgrimage to Queen Anne's shrine at Westminster, we cannot quarrel with him for that; and we shall not be surprised if, at the next session of the Church Parliament, the Venerable Bishop of St. Asaph should be left alone, a standing illustration of the truth of the text that "it is impossible for those who were *once* enlightened, *if they fall away*, to renew them again."

We have no wish to be severe; and would fain judge charitably of all men, especially of bishops. We respect worth and talent of all kinds, whether in high or low degree.

---

* See the speeches of the Archbishop of Canterbury and the Bishop of Oxford in reply to Lord Ebury, May 8th, 1860.
† See Charge of the Bishop of St. David's, Letter xxvi., p. 180.

But we must confess our utter inability to understand how a prelate—who five-and-twenty years ago, as a plain country Rector, was looked upon as one of the leading advocates for several important changes in the Liturgy—can reconcile it to his conscience to be *silent* when a slight expression of opinion on his part would have materially strengthened the hands of Lord Ebury, asking for the means of carrying into effect the very changes once approved of, and partly advocated by the bishop.

I am, Sir, yours, &c.,

March 11, 1859.   "INGOLDSBY."

LETTER XLV.

THE BISHOP OF ST. DAVID'S AND THE OCCASIONAL SERVICES.

"Out upon these jugglers, that keep the word of promise to the ear, and break it to the hope."—*Macbeth.*

SIR,—Much has occurred since I last addressed you, but I was unwilling to trespass on your space while occupied with matters of more pressing, though hardly of more vital, interest than that of Liturgical Revision. It is well, however, with a view to our retrospect for the year 1859, to put on record two facts connected with our subject.

First, That before resigning his office of Home Secretary, Mr. Walpole had the honour of laying before Her Majesty a petition, signed by upwards of 10,000 of the laity of Liverpool and its neighbourhood, praying for such a revision of the Prayer-book as should effectually expunge those portions of it which " seem to sanction the doctrines and practices of auricular confession, priestly absolution, and the easy doctrine of baptismal regeneration."*

---

* See Letter XLVI., p. 303. Something akin to this was Mr. Edward Jenkins's motion for "a Royal Commission of Inquiry, &c.," July 5th, 1878. See his speech, published by Strahan & Co., 34, Paternoster Row. 1878.

Secondly, That on Thursday, the 17th inst., Lord Ebury gave notice of his intention after Easter to renew his motion of last May for "a ROYAL COMMISSION to inquire into the Liturgy of the Church of England, with a view to considering how far it is capable of such alterations as may render it more profitable than it now is for the religious instruction and edification of the people."

The importance of this motion it is hardly possible to exaggerate. But as we shall have occasion to refer to it hereafter, it is sufficient for the present, that in the name of all who are interested in this question I take upon myself to express our obligation to his lordship, not only for not deserting the cause he has espoused, but for boldly daring to appear again before the public as the advocate of a reform which has hitherto been opposed by almost the entire Episcopal Bench.*

Among these stands prominent the learned Bishop of St. David's—a prelate from whom better things might have been expected, and whom we do not despair to find one day arrayed on the side of rational progress in the Church.† Such at least is the legitimate inference to be drawn from his lordship's final remarks in the Convocation of 1858, with a few comments on which we shall take our leave of the right rev. prelate:—

"I do not mean to say that I am not *very strongly of opinion* that there is room for *very great* and *important improvements in the Occasional Services*, particularly in the occasional prayers of the Church."‡

---

* Bishop Baring, of Durham, and Archbishop Whately, of Dublin, were, I believe, the solitary exceptions. Such was Luther's position when inaugurating his grand Reformation. "The Bishops," says Froude, "were hostile to a man."—*Times of Luther and Erasmus*, Lect. ii.

† This hope was subsequently dispelled by the publication of his lordship's Charge of 1860.

‡ The Bishop of St. David's in Convocation, Feb., 1858.

Was there no one present to encourage his lordship to proceed in the enunciation of his views? But no sign is given by the *Guardian*, so we assume the sentiment passed unheeded and uncheered by the audience.

"I do not think that they at present meet all the variety of cases which are *continually occurring*. At the same time I am compelled to say that I agree with my right rev. brother (Bishop Sumner of Winchester), that while there is *room for considerable improvements*, which, if we had the power, we should be glad to make, nevertheless, under *present circumstances*, I think with him that such improvements would be dearly purchased by placing the whole subject in the hands of persons on whom we can never depend."

As the bishop does not enter into particulars, or state *what* are the "very great and important improvements" which he is "*very strongly of opinion* there is room for in the Occasional Services," we are at liberty to make our own conjectures on the subject; and if we do him injustice in putting evil imaginations into his heart, which have no place there in reality, we shall be glad to be enlightened by his lordship supplying that gloss on his own words which our powers of criticism have failed to elicit with sufficient accuracy.

By "Occasional Services," then, we understand the various offices,—for the Solemnization of Matrimony, the Public and Private Baptism of Infants and Adults, the Churching of Women, the Visitation and Communion of the Sick, the Burial of the Dead, the Commination, the Services for Confirmation, Ordering of Priests and Deacons, and the Consecrating Archbishops or Bishops, the Consecration of Churches and Burial-grounds, to which may be added the Restoration and Re-opening of Churches, &c.

Possibly the bishop may allude only to these last, or he may refer to the whole. But, in the absence of his own interpretation of his words, we will assume that his lordship refers to the whole of those forms which occasionally (and *only occasionally*) arise in the ordinary working of the Church system.

See, then, what a wide admission is here, if we are right in making the larger application of the bishop's words, " I am very strongly of opinion that there is room for very great and important improvements in the Occasional Services, particularly in the *Occasional Prayers* of the Church." Under this last head there can hardly be a doubt that reference is made to the " Prayers and Thanksgivings upon Several Occasions" as appointed in our Book of Common Prayer to be used immediately " before the two final prayers of the Litany, or of Morning and Evening Prayer;" such as the Prayers and Thanksgivings for rain, fair weather, or plenty; times of dearth and famine, war and tumult, plague or sickness, and the like.*

We entirely agree here with his lordship, and have repeatedly found in practice how meagre and insufficient is this portion of our Liturgy to meet the various demands that are continually arising in this changeful scene through which it is our lot to pass. But are we to go on for another two hundred years submitting to this palpable defect in our forms of public worship, because the " improvements " which we might desire to make " would be dearly purchased by placing the whole subject in the hands of persons on whom we can never depend ? "

Where and when does the bishop expect to meet with a tribunal so exactly to his mind that he would repose entire

---

* Every one's experience must have shown him how lamentably unfit most of these are for cases of ordinary occurrence. Many clergymen, to our own knowledge, were deterred from reading the much-needed Prayer for fair weather during the wet summer of 1860, on account of the clause which speaks of "drowning all the world;" rain may be excessive, and highly injurious, without approaching the measure indicated by reference to the universal deluge.

confidence in its wisdom? By parity of reasoning, the Catholic Emancipation of 1829, the Reform Bill of 1832, the Corn Laws of 1846, and all other measures that ever were attended with risk or difficulty, would to this day have been in abeyance. "Nothing," in short, as is allowed by even the great Tory Dr. Johnson,—"nothing will ever be attempted if all possible objections must be first overcome."* It is puerile, it is utterly unworthy a mind like Dr. Thirlwall's, to argue thus. Better join chorus at once with the Bishops of Salisbury and Oxford, and say "*he wants no change;*" "he is content with the Prayer-book as it is;" "it shall not be *touched* in his day;" than thus to delude his followers with the prospect of a visionary Elysium, which they can never reach by any effort of their own; but will infallibly one by one drop into their graves, with their hopes unfulfilled,† dying in faith, not having received the promise, but having seen it afar off through the imperfect organs of their spiritual guides.

Had the Bishop of St. David's gone so far as to attend the Convocation of this year, and there added his voice to that of the five prelates who were silenced by the casting vote of the president, it would have been something to build upon more solid than *words*.‡ The Bishop of Oxford would then have been able to exhibit to the world what could be achieved by a *Church* Commission, though he objects to a Parliamentary or Royal one; and a *beginning* would have been made, which, as the Bishop of London observed, would have made it difficult to resist Lord Ebury's demand in the ensuing session.

---

* "Rasselas."

† The Venerable Archdeacon Berens, of Shrivenham, Berks, who died about this time, in his eighty-third year, was a case in point. Chancellor Martin, of Exeter, who died Sept., 1860, was another; and there are hundreds more even within the knowledge of the present writer. (1878.)

‡ It was not without reason that *Verba dare* became with the ancients a synonym for *to deceive*.

Not that we altogether approve of the proposition mooted by the Bishop of Oxford* on the occasion to which we are referring, as it can only be regarded as a makeshift or stop-gap, in the vain hope of arresting further progress. What the Church wants is not so much an increase of services, as greater liberty in the use or combination of the materials she has.† But as we shall have occasion to enlarge on this part of our subject hereafter, we will for the present take our leave of the Bishop of St. David's, for whom we entertain a high regard, but in whom we have no confidence whatever as a practical Liturgical Reformer.‡ Meanwhile let us hope that no one will apply to his lordship the following lines, which we remember to have met with in a ballad entitled " The Political Chameleon :"—

> " Waiting to act whichever way
> Is pointed out by Fortune's ray ;
> Void of consistency, he seems
> To take his colour from the beams
> Of interest's bright sun alone,
> Having no colour of his own."

I am, Sir, yours, &c.,

March 29, 1859.   " INGOLDSBY."

LETTER XLVI.

DISSOLUTION OF PARLIAMENT, APRIL, 1859.

" Turne, quod optanti divûm promittere nemo
Auderet, volvenda dies en attulit ultro."—VIRGIL.

SIR,—There are few things which Time cannot accomplish ; but it is hard work contending against time and bishops

---

* See Letter XLIII., p. 285.
† This important point was forcibly insisted on in a Charge of the late Bishop of Gloucester and Bristol (Baring), Sept., 1860.
‡ See Letter XXIX., pp. 195—199.

together. Even Mr. Poole and his ill-advised supporters have had to succumb to the united forces of a bishop and an archbishop; and one only wonders at the simplicity of a curate, who could persuade himself that he had the slightest chance of bettering his position by appealing from Cæsar to Augustus.* Not that we mean to impugn the decision of the venerable Primate : on the contrary, we hail it with heartfelt satisfaction, as giving the death-blow to all attempts to undo what was done at the Reformation.† Our only object in alluding to the case at this moment is, to illustrate the extreme difficulty of striving with the higher powers in the Church; so much so, that, if it were true that the hierarchy *as a whole* are utterly opposed to any Revision of the Prayer-book,‡ we should be disposed to give up the cause in despair, and leave it to the next generation to move in the matter, *melioribus auspiciis*, as may possibly be the case.§

But besides the bishops—whether unanimous or not in their opposition—the advocates for Revision have unfortunately *Time*, with " all the changes and chances " it brings along with it in its sweeping course, to contend with. No sooner have they made the smallest advance towards esta-

---

* The result of Mr. Poole's appeal from the Bishop of London to the Archbishop of Canterbury is well known; and, though we entirely accord with both the former and the latter judgment, the issue of the double trial may well act as a warning to all who may be similarly situated in future.

† Alas, that similar firmness was not exhibited in other cases! There is no denying that Ritualism owed much of its early progress to the encouragement or connivance of several of the bishops.

‡ That there was at that time a division in the Episcopal camp is sufficiently proved by the Charges of the late and present Bishops of Durham (Villiers and Baring), the Archbishop of Dublin (Whately), &c.

§ As of other Reformers, so it will in all likelihood prove of the Liturgical Reformers of this date; " serunt arbores alteri sæculo profuturas,"—one man soweth, another reapeth.

blishing a firm footing on the ever-shifting sands of public opinion, than

"The strong rebuff of some tumultuous cloud,"

coming athwart their path,

"Instinct with fire and nitre, hurries them
Ten thousand miles aloft;"

and lands them helplessly in that limbo of vanities, where "Appropriation Clauses" and other good intentions are floundering to this hour, and will be till doomsday, unless they possess some principle of intrinsic weight to bring them down again to this our matter-of-fact little world.

Thus has it ever been with Liturgical Reformers for the last 200 years. We will say nothing of what happened in 1689, in 1749, in 1762, '72, and '89, to prevent the question of a Revision of the Prayer-book being grappled with by the authorities of the day; or what again so lately as 1834, in the present *reforming* century;—but we will confine ourselves to what has befallen the subject within the last two or three years, during which it has made unusual efforts to attract attention, and has hitherto met with the same fate as before.

In the session of 1857, Lord Robert Grosvenor (now Lord Ebury), as member for the most important constituency in Great Britain (Middlesex), was armed with a petition, signed by 320 individuals, asking for a moderate Revision of the Prayer-book; upon which petition, according to notice given, he was prepared to found a motion for the issue of a ROYAL COMMISSION for the purpose of receiving evidence on the matter, and reporting accordingly.

The member for Maidstone, Alexander Beresford Hope, Esq., who, however, I am happy to see disavows[*] any con-

---

[*] In a letter published during his canvass for the representation of the University of Cambridge, April, 1859. It may be questioned, however,

nexion with " Ultra-Ritualism and Romanist practices," against which we contend, was provided with sundry counter-petitions against the motion; and there was every appearance of a pitched battle being on the eve of coming off on the floor of St. Stephen's, wherein the question of progress or retrogression in the Church would have been canvassed, and probably decided in favour of the former.

Why, then, were the public disappointed, and the issue removed from the forcing air of the Commons to the retarding atmosphere of the Lords?—where

"ut perhibent, aut intempesta silet nox
Semper, et obtentâ densantur nocte tenebræ;—
Aut——"

(we leave the describing the alternative to Mr. Bright's more graphic touch). The fact is, just as Lord Robert Grosvenor's motion was on the point of being made in the House of Commons, the first intelligence of the great Indian Rebellion* reached this country, and, like Aaron's rod, absorbed all lesser objects of interest. His lordship accordingly abstained from pressing the subject of Liturgical Reform at so unpropitious a moment, and contented himself with laying his petition on the table, with an understanding that he would recur to the matter on some future occasion.

Being raised to the Peerage during the recess,† the cause he had espoused was transplanted with himself to a fresh soil; and though in the session of 1858 the now Lord Ebury redeemed his pledge by introducing to the Peers the motion originally designed for the Commons, no one who is

---

how far this gentleman's subsequent conduct bore out his electioneering professions. Witness the part he took on the Royal Commission of 1867.

* See Letter IV., p. 22.

† We do not say that his lordship owed his elevation to this cause; but we can well understand how Lord Palmerston was glad to remove the onus from his own shoulders on to those of the Bench of Bishops.

acquainted with the respective characters of the two Houses will be surprised to find that, on its first appearance in the higher latitude, so startling a subject was listened to with less interest than a similar proposition was calculated to create in the People's House. The bishops, of course, were to a man against it;* and, unfortunately, the right reverend bench is supposed by courtesy to represent, in that House at least, the general feeling of the Church; and so the motion was for the second time allowed to drop without a division being taken, or the real sense of Parliament and the country ascertained.

This happened in May of last year. But how stood matters about a month ago?—Lord Ebury (nothing daunted by his want of success up to this stage, and supported not less by an inward consciousness of the rectitude of his intentions than by encouragement from those who have been manly enough to say *what they think, uninfluenced by either fear or favour*) for *the third time* renewed the notice of his motion for the appointment of a ROYAL COMMISSION OF INQUIRY, to be brought before Parliament after Easter.†

Now mark what follows. The debate may yet come off, or it may not. But if the latter, let no one attribute the failure to any inherent weakness in the cause, or any want of determination on the part of its supporters. There is no contending with the Fates. Just as the Bishops were beginning to waver, and to see that their position was untenable; just as the *Guardian, Clerical Journal*, and *English Churchman* were decidedly modifying their tone,‡ and there was a fair prospect of the subject being discussed with

---

* Letter xlv., p. 292.
† This notice was given on Thursday, March 17th, 1859.
‡ There can be no question that the tone of those three organs of the High Church party was less decided at that time against all Revision than it had been before.

candour and temper;—a *deus ex machinâ* again descends upon the scene, in the shape of a Reform debate of a fortnight's duration, a defeat of Ministers, a dissolution of Parliament, and a change of Government looming in the distance;—the "dogs of war let slip" in every borough and county of the United Kingdom;—well if the Continent of Europe be not also set in a blaze, for the entertainment of those who, having little or nothing to lose, may possibly profit by the confusion.

"I nunc, et versus tecum meditare canoros!"—

Go now, and move that a Royal Commission issue for the Revision of the Liturgy!—You might as well select this opportunity for advocating the instantaneous clearance of the Goodwin Sands, or the levelling of Highgate Hill by Act of Parliament, for the benefit of the public! What chance of the subject's receiving a moment's consideration? Not one man in a thousand would listen to you. No daily or weekly newspaper would find space for a letter on the subject. Who can be surprised, therefore, if Revision should be hung up for another twelvemonth, and all have to be begun again, as if *de novo*, in the session of 1860?* Let Oxford and Salisbury rejoice; let the rural deans of Cuddesdon and the licensed curates of Belgravia triumph; how are the enemy fallen, and the weapons of Protestantism perished!

I have thought thus much necessary, in order to put upon record, while the facts are patent to all, the *real reason* of the slow progress hitherto made with the cause we advocate —the cause, indeed, of JUSTICE and COMMON SENSE, but unfortunately one in which no *party* triumph is concerned, no *class* interest sought to be promoted. It was not so with the Jew Bill; it is not so with the Church-rate question,

---

* Again, in 1860, as in 1858-9, the disturbed state of the political atmosphere militated against the question of Revision being calmly entertained.

or even with the prolonged struggle for marriage with a deceased wife's sister. The cause of Revision is just one of those which, being *every one's* business, is proverbially *no one's* business, and consequently is, of all others, most liable to be set aside by these momentary gusts blowing one time from the N. by N.E., at another from the S. by S.W.* Nor will anything, humanly speaking, ever bring the subject to a final issue, except the indomitable perseverance of a handful of men willing to make it (as it is deserving of being made) the business of their lives, who will be content then, and then only, to sing "Nunc dimittis," when they have witnessed the consummation of their hopes, and can handle such a Book of Common Prayer as is worthy of the advanced intelligence of the age, and of a Church co-extensive with the world.

Trusting that some of our readers, if not ourselves, may live to see that day,

I have the honour to be, yours, &c.,

April 18, 1859. " INGOLDSBY."

LETTER XLVII.

THE LITURGICAL REFORMERS AND THE ELECTIONS.

1st *Cit.*—" We have power in ourselves to do it.
2nd *Cit.*—Are you all resolved to give your voices?
3rd *Cit.*—We may, sir, if we will."—*Coriolanus.*

SIR,—In our last we remarked on the unlooked-for godsend which the excitement of a dissolution had proved to those *statu quoists* who are opposed to any Revision of the Prayer-

---

* Now it is the Russian war, at another time the Chinese, at another the International Exhibition, &c. &c.; all calculated to divert "men's minds" from a subject of permanent interest like the Revision of the Prayer-book, which they think (if they think at all about it) may be taken up at *any* time, and therefore may be put aside from day to day, from year to year, as not immediately pressing for consideration.

book.* And there can be no doubt that such an event will for the moment create a powerful diversion, by necessitating the postponement of Lord Ebury's motion to next year, instead of its coming off after Easter, according to his lordship's notice of March 17th; and who can predict what other cause of interruption may occur between now and Easter, 1860?

I am not so sure, however, that a dissolution "at this present time" is so much in favour of the *anti*-Revisionists as at first sight it appears to be. There is no denying that the question, in one shape or other, has taken its place among the standing topics of the day; and though men differ as to the principles upon which Revision should be carried out, there is a large portion of the community who are of opinion that an *inquiry of some kind* should be instituted, and that the feelings of those who are favourable to Revision should not be ignored, as a few would have them to be; and it is by no means improbable that the influence of these persons will be brought to bear on the elections now taking place, whereby much good may result to the cause by the temporary postponement of Lord Ebury's motion.

Take Liverpool, for example, from whose neighbourhood there lately issued a petition, signed by 10,000 persons, in favour of Revision.† How many of these are probably

---

* If times are quiet, these worthies cry out, "Why disturb them?" If excited, their watchword is, "*This*, at any rate, *is not the time.*" The fact is, indolence, or love of ease (which is the same thing), is at the bottom of all their feigned excuses. The thing is too much trouble: "le jeu ne vaut pas la chandelle."

† See Letter XLV., p. 291. The Petition, which was signed, amongst others, by three Members of Parliament, and a great number of the leading merchants of Liverpool, was as follows:—

"TO THE QUEEN'S MOST EXCELLENT MAJESTY.

"*The Memorial of the Undersigned Inhabitants of Liverpool.*

"May it please your Majesty.

"Your Memorialists being devoutly attached to the Church of England, and to the principles of the Reformation, view with the deepest

electors for the borough or county, and likely to ask a candidate how he would vote upon the question of a Revision of the Prayer-book, in the event of such a measure being brought before the next Parliament?

Take Dublin, again, where an active society has for some time existed, under the title of the " Liturgical Amendment Association," the members of which, it is not too much to say, feel more keenly on this subject than any other.* Those persons, indeed, who have not given their minds to the question can form no conception of the intensity of the feelings of those that have, to whom it may be said to form the " be-all and the end-all " of their existence. So true is this, that it is notorious that at the general election in 1857 several recorded their votes in favour of the Palmerstonian candidate in preference to the Derbyite, for no other reason than that the former was thought more likely than the latter to forward their views in this matter. If, therefore, the same individuals, and those thinking with them, should infer from Lord Derby's reply to Lord Ebury in May last that he and his Government

---

concern and alarm the various attempts recently made to introduce into the National Church of England Romish doctrines and practices, especially those of Baptismal Regeneration, Auricular Confession, and Priestly Absolution.

" Being anxious that the principles upon which your throne is established should be perpetuated, and that the pure Gospel of Christ, for which many of our Reformers were martyred, should be handed down to future generations unimpaired:

" Your Memorialists humbly and earnestly implore your Majesty to cause such a Revision of our Prayer-book to be immediately made, as will destroy for ever the least shadow of a basis for the afore-mentioned doctrines and practices.

" And your Memorialists for your present and future welfare will ever pray.

" *February* 20, 1859."

* The opinion of the Laity in Ireland, and a great mass of the Clergy, has been conclusively proved by the result of the Synodical elections that have taken place there since the Irish Church was disestablished.

are *opposed* to the issue of a Commission of Inquiry into the Liturgy, I can conceive such an opinion largely influencing their votes at the present or some future election.

What is a Reform of Parliament to *them* compared with a Reform of that Manual, which in their eyes is as far superior to the Statutes at Large as is the Bible to every other book that ever was written? And if they are persuaded that the Prayer-book still retains latent seeds of Romanism, or falls short of that perfection of which it is capable,* whether we regard its arrangement, matter, or rubrical directions,—is it surprising that such persons should resent, at the elections, the dulness or perverseness of those candidates for their suffrages who tell them that they are quite satisfied with the "Book as it is," and don't see that it requires improvement? Is it not natural that they should turn in disgust from those Gallios among our public men (and their name, I fear, is Legion) who treat the whole thing with indifference or contempt,† as a Parson's crotchet, a matter in which Laymen have no concern? Whichever of these two classes of Liturgical Reformers we look at, it is impossible to deny that they have the Englishman's *right* to be heard. At any rate, right or wrong, they will make themselves heard if they can. And no Minister of State, or candidate at the hustings, will be able to escape their pertinacity where they act together, as they undoubtedly will do in many cases.

Not to mention other places of less moment, where the question is taken up warmly by both laity and clergy—as the diocese of Oxford, the towns of Reading, Bristol, Plymouth,

---

* See Charge of Archdeacon Musgrave, May 28, 1859 (p. 320). Also Charge of the late Bishop of Gloucester and Bristol (Baring), Sept., 1860.

† Sir G. C. Lewis's remarks on the disgraceful Riots at St. George's-in-the-East, Jan. 30, 1860, were met with "a laugh" in the House of Commons ; and Mr. Edward Jenkins's Motion for a "Royal Commission of Inquiry," on July 5, 1878, was coldly entertained by a more than half-empty House.

Portsmouth, Southampton, Derby, and a few more—look to the University of Cambridge, where a sharp contest is at this moment being carried on,* and see the bitter articles and letters written in the *Record*, *Morning Advertiser*, and *National Standard*, against the late member for Maidstone, as candidate to represent the University in the next Parliament. Can a more worthy member of the late House of Commons be pointed out—if worth may be estimated by singleness of purpose, freedom from party spirit, zeal in the cause of religion, and the bountiful devotion of his worldly substance to every good work—than Mr. Alexander Beresford Hope? Is a gentleman (if the writer may be permitted to speak from a knowledge extending over a quarter of a century) of a noble disposition, kind-hearted towards all, of truly Christian principles, of considerable talents as an author, and no mean abilities as a speaker, to be reviled in language which cannot but recoil on the heads of those who use it, simply because he is suspected of a leaning towards Rome?† Now, that we are no friends to Romanism, is sufficiently proved by the whole tenour of these letters;—but it is one thing to *suspect*, another to *prove*. It is one thing to spend thousands in the building of a gorgeous temple to the glory of God, and to contribute munificently, as Mr. Hope has done, to the establishment of the College of St. Augustine's, Canterbury—another to be an advocate for private confession, genuflexions, crossings, bowings, processions, and other mummeries of the Romanising party. And if Mr. Hope, as a man of honour, has publicly disavowed all approbation of such practices as the above,‡ is he not to be believed? Are we to go on repeating a state-

---

* Between Mr. Hope and Mr. Selwyn, April, 1859.

† The feeling against Mr. Hope on these grounds may be judged by the fact that this Letter was refused insertion in the newspapers in which the greater part of the previous Letters had appeared with approval.

‡ See Letter XLVI., pp. 298–9.

ment, which becomes a libel when no longer founded on fact?

But why bring forward Mr. Hope as connected with our present subject? Why, for this reason;—because, however unjustly he be charged with holding high Tractarian views, the fact remains incapable of contradiction, that when Lord Robert Grosvenor (now Lord Ebury) first brought the subject of Revision before the House of Commons, the individual selected to represent the sentiments of those who are opposed to it was the late member for Maidstone;* and it is well known that on that occasion he presented a certain number of petitions—not of much weight, to be sure—but still such as they were—*against* the issue of a Royal Commission of Inquiry into the Prayer-book.

This stubborn fact, no doubt, gives a colour of reality to the statements of the *Record* and *National Standard*. And unless Mr. Hope is able to satisfy the members of the Senate of Cambridge, that after two years' consideration of the question (then comparatively a new one) he has seen reason to modify his opinions, and to admit that the Reformers have some show of reason on their side—I should fear that the honourable gentleman, with all his other recommendations, will find in the University constituency a good many holding the views entertained by Lord Robert Grosvenor's petitioners (not a few of whom are active members of that body,) and very likely to express their feelings in the shape of an adverse vote at the election.†

But I must not detain you at a time when your space is required for matters of more pressing interest. I was

---

* See Letter xii., p. 79. Mr. Hope was again the chief speaker n opposition to Mr. Jenkins in July last (1878).

† Mr. Hope on that occasion withdrew from the contest, but was subsequently returned, though not without a severe struggle, chiefly on this very ground.

unwilling, however, to let the opportunity of a general election pass, without urging the advocates for a Revision of the Liturgy to put forth their strength, and make themselves heard and felt at this moment. Several of them have already brought the subject before the candidates for their suffrage, and have received somewhat evasive answers. Let them persevere. Let them be strong and of a good courage; let them be neither wearied nor dismayed. All that the candidates care to know is how far the *general opinion* is in favour of such a measure,* and their present indifference will be quickly turned into real or professed approval.

The course of the electors is a simple one—far simpler than going through the tedious and *profitless* process of getting up petitions, only to be laid under the table of the House and forgotten as soon as they are presented. A vote is a vote; and none can say but that the casting vote† may rest with some one Liturgical Reformer, while a score of them combining might decide the day in *many* instances. This secret others know well how to avail themselves of, and why should not we?

"Fas est et ab hoste doceri."

This is our best way of strengthening Lord Ebury's hands when he next comes forward. We can thus show that we are men of deeds as well as words; and cannot fail in thus *forcing* attention to the cause upon those who are insensible to every other species of argument.

I remain, Sir, yours, &c.,

April 25, 1859.   "INGOLDSBY."

---

* It is to be regretted that the Laity in general have not pronounced themselves more distinctly than they have hitherto done upon a question where their interests are involved fully as much as those of the Clergy.

† The value of a single vote may be judged by the fact that the important question of Church Rates was decided in the House of Commons by the casting vote of the Speaker in the Session of 1861, and by a majority of *but one* in a still larger House in May, 1862.

LETTER XLVIII.

ELECTION OF PROCTORS FOR THE DIOCESE OF LINCOLN.

"Ab uno
Disce omnes."—VIRGIL.

SIR,—The general election of members of Parliament is by custom* closely followed by the election of members to the " Church Parliament," or Convocation.

As we have more than once had occasion to speak of this body, we should not further interrupt the course of our " reply to the bishops" by a reference to this extraneous subject, but for the prominence that has been given to it in counexion with the proposed Revision of the Book of Common Prayer, more particularly in the diocese of Lincoln.

Some of your readers may have seen it stated that at the election of Proctors for the said diocese the Rev. Mr. Massingberd† gave it as his opinion, that " if a revised Prayer-book were to be put forth on the sole authority of the State, without reference to Convocation, a very large part of the clergy would *refuse to read it!*"—" They would refuse to recognise the new book as having the *authority of the Church,* and would continue to use the present book until they were ejected from their churches."—" It matters not," he added, " to settle whether they would be right or not; though I myself *am clearly of opinion that they would be right,* and that their bounden duty to *the Church* would require it of them."‡

---

* This custom was interrupted at the Great Rebellion, and a question was raised as to its being revived at the Restoration ; and it may well be doubted whether the Church at large does not suffer rather than gain in public opinion by the further continuance of this anomalous and effete body.

† Ycleped by certain profane persons the " Lincoln Humming-bird."

‡ Speech of the Rev. F. C. Massingberd, Vicar of Ormsby, near Alford, at the so-called Election of Proctors for the Diocese of Lincoln. May, 1859.

Be it so. We are not disposed to argue the question with this reverend gentleman, who doubtless is as well aware as ourselves of the duty of upholding the authority of the powers that be, and submitting to every ordinance of man for the Lord's sake.* But seeing that he lays so much stress on the supremacy of the *Church,* or "Convocation,"—(a very different thing,)—it is a matter of moment to ascertain how this body is constructed, and how far it may be fairly said to represent the National Church.

Of the constitution of the Upper House we have spoken before.† Of the Lower House there are two parts,—*ex officio* members, and proctors (or so-called *elected* members); and it is to these last that we purpose confining our observations to-day, inasmuch as it is through this channel alone that the voice of the clergy at large has any chance of being heard; while the opinions of the laity, forming as they do the vast bulk and backbone of the Church, are altogether ignored.

We have no means of knowing how the Proctors are elected in other dioceses; but as Lincoln is the largest in the kingdom, but one, it may be fairly taken as a sample of the rest; and if the so-called "election" is conducted elsewhere as it is here, a more complete burlesque of the word can hardly be conceived.‡

To be brief, we have shown in a former letter§ that the

---

* "The Church and the Law" were not then openly at issue as they have since notoriously become (1878).

† See Letter I., p. 5.

‡ The writer of these pages put this matter to a very decisive test by standing a contest, at the desire of many friends, in 1867; and a greater farce by way of an *election,* he does not hesitate to say, cannot be conceived. The whole thing is planned and arranged beforehand in secret conclave, and an independent candidate has as much chance of being returned as his own footman: and this is called a *representation* of the clergy, and their voice the "voice of the Church." See Vol. ii., Letter cxxx.

§ Letter III., p. 16.

clergy of the diocese of Lincoln cannot be much less than 1,000—probably they are more. Now, we are told that at the late election of Proctors for these parts " rather more than 100 of the parochial clergy of the three Archdeaconries of Lincoln, Notts, and Stowe assembled in the Consistory Court at Lincoln. The Registrar read the Royal and Archiepiscopal mandates, called over the names of the archdeacons and their clergy, and pronounced *sentence of contumacy* on those not present;" that is to say, on nine-tenths of the clergy of the diocese.*

The names and addresses of 64 of the *un*contumacious are then recorded for the benefit of the public, and to the shame and confusion of the absentees. Whether these 64 express the whole of the assumed 100, or whether 36 of the individuals assembled were too insignificant to be deemed worthy a place in the report, I do not pretend to say; but certain it is that only 64 clerks, and one solitary layman (Sir Charles Anderson, Bart.), appear on the face of a document purporting to give a full, true, and correct account of all that took place on this occasion.

This list, however, scanty as it is, is not without its value, as indicating the stamp of clergy thus condensed into a personification of the constituency of the diocese, the electors of the Church's delegates to their proper house.

Seeing amongst them the names of three individuals, well known in this corner of the diocese as holding *High Church* views, and only observing the name of *one other* beneficed clergyman from the same parts (formerly curate of Dr. Hook at Leeds), I took the trouble to ascertain the proportion borne by the clergy of this section of the county (represented by these four electors), to those of the whole diocese; and I found that, placing one leg of my compass on a centre thirty

---

* See report as published at the time in the Lincolnshire papers.

miles south of Lincoln, and describing a circle round it, with a radius of about nine miles, I embraced just sixty-four parishes, the clergy of which are all more or less known to myself, including the above four individuals, who would be acknowledged by the neighbourhood to belong to the above section of the Church, and, what is more, to be, perhaps, the *only clergy* hereabouts having so strong a bias in that direction.

Now, supposing similar figures to be described over the remainder of the three Archdeaconries of Lincoln, Notts, and Stowe, it is by no means improbable that a similar result would ensue; and thus the whole 64 (or it may be 100) electors are accounted for. And then these Divines thus organised, and agreed in theological views, proceed to *elect* the two delegates for the entire diocese. Sundry speeches are made, in a high tone of eulogy, upon the importance of "the Church"—the Bishop sets to his seal confirming "the election"—and, hey presto, these two gentlemen go forth in the full-blown dignity of " Proctors for the diocese of Lincoln," to meet presently in solemn conclave with the similarly-chosen " Proctors for the diocese of Oxford," " Salisbury," &c., &c.,—and it is these three-score nominees, thus calling themselves " the Church," who lay it down that no alteration of the Prayer-book, however rational, however needed, however " desirable and desired," shall be adopted by the nation, until it has been stamped with *their* approval as the embodiment of the Church of England, Wales, and Ireland, and the vast Colonial Empire of Great Britain.

I need not detain you by arguing upon the absurdity of this position. The thing speaks for itself. Either we must radically alter the system of election to the Lower House of Convocation—whether by substituting *voting papers* and the ballot for *personal* attendance, or otherwise, I pretend not to say—so as to make it a *real* and not a *sham* representa-

tion of the *clergy of England at any rate*, if not of the
Church at large—or we must emancipate ourselves from the
thraldom of its assumed government; and not allow the
question of Revision to be kept any longer in abeyance,
because a clique of one-tenth part of the *English Clergy* meet
once in every three or four years in the county town* to
elect a handful of delegates holding their own views; which
views, through their hired organs of the press, they proclaim
to the world as the VOICE OF THE CHURCH.†

I remain, Sir, yours, &c.,

May 21, 1859. " INGOLDSBY."

LETTER XLIX.

THE BISHOP OF LLANDAFF ON THE LENGTH OF THE
MORNING SERVICE.

" We are of opinion that the length of the Morning Service on Sundays
and Holidays, especially when the Holy Communion is administered to a
large body of communicants, renders it desirable to allow of its being divided
into different services, and used at various hours."—*Report of Committee on
Church Services*, 1854.

SIR,—The sixth Prelate on the list of those to whom our
"Reply" is most respectfully addressed, is the Right Reverend
Dr. Ollivant, Bishop of Llandaff. His lordship's observations
are few, and will not detain us long. He commences by
saying that he has " no wish to protract the discussion ;"—
neither have we. But unfortunately we have no option—
and until our point is carried we must still persevere, or be

---

* The only place where the votes are taken, and that for two or three
hours in one day, making it *simply impossible* for the great bulk of the clergy
in the diocese to *appear* and vote *personally*, however so disposed.

† See Letter XLIII., p. 284. Bishop Baring, in Convocation, May 14th,
1861, observed, " I do not regard the voice of Convocation as   e voice of
the Church. I do not believe that the Church of England looks upon it in
that light."—*Guardian*, No. 798, p. 283.

content to transmit the subject as an heir-loom to the next generation.

The Bishop of Llandaff is deservedly esteemed by all who know him. It is difficult to say whether zeal in the discharge of his duties, or judgment in the fulfilment of them, predominate in his character; and it would argue ill for any cause that found in him an uncompromising opponent. It is with pleasure, therefore, that we trace in the few observations which fell from his lordship, in the Convocation of 1858, a desire to meet at least *one* of the gravamina of the Liturgical Reformers. His remarks are as follows:—

"With regard to the *length of the services*, I conscientiously think that it would be an advantage if, when the Lord's Supper is administered, the service were not so long as it is at present. We have not only the morning service, which takes an hour and ten minutes, but we have the administration of the Lord's Supper, which is a considerable addition to the service; and, in point of fact, where the number of communicants is very great—a state of things which we all earnestly desire—the service does frequently in the large parishes in London occupy from eleven till two o'clock; and that length of service is inconveniently felt by infirm and aged persons, and those who desire frequently to partake of the Lord's Supper."

As the same remark has been made by others, and never been seriously disputed by any one, I shall assume that *this* position is granted; and only inquire why steps are not taken to put legally in force that which all seem to desire, but no one feels at liberty to avail himself of.*

The consequence is that Sunday after Sunday we witness

---

* The writer of these Letters has long made it his practice to "help himself" in this matter, to the satisfaction of all parties concerned, especially on what used to be called, in his younger days, "Sacrament Sundays."

such scenes as are described by Lord Ebury in words which I take the liberty to reproduce on the present occasion :—

"How stands the case with us?"—observes his lordship :—"By these ancient arrangements we have four or five services crammed into one; the result of which is, everlasting repetitions, wearied congregations, jaded attention, compulsory absence : a state of things which, instead of proving a help to devotion, is the means of producing a great amount of that formality, which is the danger of all forms of prayer, and against which our blessed Lord Himself directed some of His sternest rebukes."*

Lord Ebury proceeded to quote a letter from an hon. baronet (Sir Benjamin Hall), containing but too accurate a picture of the services of our Church, as I have myself witnessed on repeated occasions :—of which, indeed, I may say,

"Quæque ipse miserrima vidi,"—

and with regret must add,

"Et quorum pars magna fui."

Might I not pursue the quotation—when we consider the lamentable consequences that have resulted from the obstinate persistence in so inconvenient a practice for the long space of 200 years,†—and exclaim—

"Quis talia fando . . . .
Temperet a lacrymis?"———

But it is best to allow the Baronet (who, being a layman, has

---

* Speech by Lord Ebury in the House of Lords, May 6th, 1858.

† "That the attention of the greater part of an audience can be kept up, through many repetitions, in a service that lasts an hour and a half, or an hour and three-quarters, is as much to be wished as it is little to be expected. Piety stretched beyond a certain point is the parent of impiety. By attempting to keep up the fervour of devotion for so long a time, *we have thinned our churches*, and driven away those fluctuating lukewarm Christians who will always outnumber the zealous and devout, and whom it should be our first object to animate, allure, and fix."—*Memoir of Rev. Sydney Smith*, vol. i., p 81.

at least not the sin to *answer* for) to speak for himself in corroboration of the Bishop.

"I have just returned from our church,—the services lasted from eleven to twenty minutes past two, and consisted of :—1. The Morning Service ; 2. The Litany ; 3. The Ante-Communion Service ; 4. The Sermon ; 5. The Communion ; besides giving out hymns to the congregation. This is enough to kill even a strong man.* And *cui bono?* The people are wearied to death by the repetitions ; and I can conceive no party whatever gaining by it except Dissenters, whose shorter services commend themselves to many persons."†

We shall be told, in answer to this, that *permission* has been given by the bishops to transfer the Litany to the afternoon or evening when the Holy Communion is administered, or when three services occur in the same church in the course of the day.‡ But in the first place I would ask, to *whom* are we indebted for this concession, slight as it is? Was it a *volunteer* on the part of "the authorities," sympathising with the labours of the overtasked clergyman, and the dissatisfaction of his alienated flock? Or was it extorted by the *pressure from without,* and a conviction that the privilege could be no longer withheld ; and that the inevitable result of further resistance to so reasonable a demand would be that every high-minded clergyman would "help himself ;" not choosing to allow his energies to be exhausted and his congregation disgusted, by a servile adherence to the usages of an age different to the present in most respects, but in nothing more

---

* "Strong men" are apt, however, to avoid the danger, by absenting themselves altogether from this lengthy sevice, leaving the benches to be occupied by women, or to betray by their emptiness that there is something wrong somewhere.

† Speech of Lord Ebury, *Third Edition,* p. 11. London : 1859.

‡ See Letter xxxvii., p. 239.

so than its verbosity and tediousness in the matter and manner both of preaching and prayer?

But secondly, is this concession sufficient to meet the necessities of the case? Does it get rid of the monotony and repetitions of other parts of the services? Its simple effect, according to *the letter* of the extorted *permission*, is to transfer the Litany from the morning to the afternoon or evening, *in addition* to the ordinary prayers;—or in other words (to use a homely but apposite proverb), to rob Peter to pay Paul. A writer in the *Church of England Monthly Review* for the present month observes that—

"It is not the *time* only, but the recurrence, again and again, of the same spiritual acts—and those of a nature that, once with reality performed, and having passed away into higher functions, cannot be with reality again immediately recalled—on which the argument rests. Many a man could spend a large portion of the seventy minutes allotted by the Bishop of Lincoln to our Sunday morning service in psalmody and praise, who finds it uncongenial indeed—not to say impossible—to make three hearty confessions of sin in one service. . . . . Surely when complaints are made that our services are inordinately long, it is *scarcely Christian*, as it *is certainly impolitic*, to retort on the objector that the fault lies in himself, and his own unspiritual state!* The complaint itself shows an *awakened interest in the Church's services*, and indicates a spirit and a tendency which should be cherished and encouraged rather than rebuked!"

But though the Bishop of Lincoln appears to have small sympathy with this class of religionists, the Bishop of Llandaff (as we have seen) is not without feeling for that portion of his clerical brethren who venture to sigh out a complaint that "this thing is too hard for them;—they are

---

* See Letters VI., VII., pp. 32—43.

not able to perform it themselves alone;"—"they will surely wear away, both they and the people that are with them," unless some relief be afforded them in this matter.

And here, too, the Bishop of St. Asaph (Vowler Short)—though now safe within the magic circle of formalism and prescription—has a word to say in behalf of a reform of the Liturgy.

"The time, of all others," observes his lordship, speaking as he feels, "when the length of the service is most inconvenient, is that of Ordination."*

"Expertus disces quam gravis iste labor."

I can well believe it—though neither a bishop nor his chaplain—for I have to this day a vivid recollection of the length of this service as conducted at Buckden, on the occasion of my own ordination to Deacon and Priest's Orders, by the excellent Bishop Kaye in 1833-4.

"I had one Ordination service which lasted three hours," observes Bishop Jackson.

"I am sorry to say"—chimes in the energetic Bishop Tait (with somewhat of the *naïveté* of a novice)—"I am sorry to say that one of mine occupied *four hours!!*"

Sydney Smith laid it down that first-class passengers would continue to be locked in upon the Great Western Railway until a Bishop of London or an Archbishop of Canterbury should be roasted alive; and I think we may now venture to predict that the time is not distant when *the Ordination Service* at any rate will be reduced to proportions adapted to the convictions of the hierarchy of the nineteenth century. And when their lordships have realised the benefit conferred upon themselves by such an application of the pruning-hook to the practice of the Church, they will,

---

* See Letter XXII., p. 157.

perhaps, be less severe in judging of their humbler brethren in this respect; and be willing to give them such a measure of relief as befits their inferior position, and of course their more limited capacity of enjoyment.

I must not further trespass upon your space; but in the hope of seeing Hesiod's grand principle of "Half better than the Whole"* recognised even in things spiritual,

I remain, Sir, yours, &c.,
May 20, 1859.   " INGOLDSBY."

LETTER L.

ARCHDEACON MUSGRAVE'S CHARGE TO THE CLERGY OF CRAVEN,
YORKSHIRE, MAY, 1859.

"To set two Bishops together by the ears is neither a thing creditable to the parties concerned, nor can it but be injurious both to the Established Church and to the cause of religion."—*Life of Bathurst, Bishop of Norwich,* p. 319.

SIR,—Though the remark in our motto may be perfectly true as applied to the highest grade in the Church, by reason of its dignity, I hope there is no impropriety in pitting one Archdeacon against another, when, within the short space of a year, their trumpets emit various and discordant sounds in all but contiguous dioceses.†

It is not six months since we had occasion to pass certain strictures on the Charge of the Archdeacon of Lindisfarne (Coxe), as creating an unnecessary alarm in the minds of his brethren, by sounding a note of resistance to Lord Ebury's motion for a Royal Commission, as if it were fraught with

---

* See Letter VI., p. 36.
† The observation is equally applicable to the published sentiments of the Archdeacons of York, Richmond, and Cleveland (Creyke, Dodson, and Churton), 1860-62.

extreme peril to the Church.* Happily, to the eye of the phrenologist, the heads of all Arch-deacons are not cast in the same mould as their hats;† and we have accordingly before us to-day, in the person of the highly-respected Vicar of Halifax, a mind capable of grasping a difficulty, and seeing his way through a problem, which staggers one who, by his misfortune, not his fault, appears to have missed the advantage of a Cambridge education. Hear the Archdeacon of Craven addressing the clergy of the North in the language of sound reason and common sense:—

"As to the Book of Common Prayer, properly so called, *notwithstanding the increasing desire for its revision*, there has hitherto been no authorised change beyond that embodied in the two resolutions of the Bishops and Archbishops issued in May, 1856, sanctioning a slight departure from established usage in the division of the service—principally the Morning Service. It is no part of my duty to canvass the legality of such variation. They, in the exercise of the supposed powers vested in them 'for the resolution of certain doubts' submitted to them, have seen good to approve and sanction it. Their decision, however, not being very clearly or exactly defined, has been diversely interpreted, and has given rise to some diversity of practice, some of the brethren receiving it as allowing a greater latitude than others. *Under the freest interpretation, it is not much that is herein abated of the stiffness of our ritual. But even this slender concession has not been without its use in abridging, in some churches,*

---

* See Letter xxxviii., p. 246.

† Archdeacon Stonehouse (of Stowe), in his recent Charge at Gainsborough, "announced himself in favour of a Revision of the Liturgy, and expressed a hope that some measure might be recommended which would receive the sanction of the Legislature, and ameliorate that of which there was much complaint."—*Lincoln Paper, June* 4, 1859. The Archdeacon of Leicester (Bonney) was also of opinion that "the matter might be safely entrusted to a Royal Commission with powers well defined."

the wearying length of the Morning Service, to the relief alike of the clergy and the laity—in bringing the Litany (assuredly the most solemn and touching of all uninspired compilations of prayer and intercession) before distinct congregations of worshippers—and in placing within the reach of numbers, previously debarred from it, access to the Holy Communion in the evening,* the only time in the day when, through no fault of their own, they could be present at its administration.

"It may perhaps be doubted how far this last result was within the scope of the resolutions to which I have adverted. It was never improbable but that, under the seeming sanction of these resolutions, this and other changes might insensibly steal in. *There is too general a feeling as to the necessity of a greater flexibility in our services not to have led to a belief that, with or without authority, other changes might follow. They were sure to be desired. The exigencies of modern times seemed to require them;* and the question for the future, as it actually stands, is only how they may be effected with least violence to that reverential, that *almost superstitious*, respect for our Book of Common Prayer, which looks upon it as something too hallowed for human hands to touch : too sacred, too inviolable, to admit of possible improvement through any scheme of reconstruction."

We have here the admission of Lord Ebury's two main propositions † :—

1st. That a Revision of the Liturgy is desired.

2nd. That it is desirable.

Into the *third* question, as to the *means* of carrying out the proposed amendments, the Archdeacon does not enter :

---

* The Bishop of Oxford, on the other hand, peremptorily forbids "postprandial celebrations" in his diocese. Charge, November, 1860. See before Letter XIX., p. 137. Hence the now prevalent custom of " early celebrations." in order to *anticipate breaking fast* for the day.

† Lord Ebury's First Speech in the House of Lords, May 6, 1858.

V

but that he sees no objection to a ROYAL COMMISSION, as a channel " both constitutional and expedient," may be gathered from what follows :—

" It appears to me that more might be done—safely and beneficially done, without exposing to controversy any doctrinal truth, or involving the slightest alteration of its distinctive teaching. The *task might be advantageously confided to a Royal Commission*, with duties accurately defined : and those restricted to the re-distributing of the existing services : retrenching vain repetitions : constructing new and shorter offices for occasional or daily use : *revising the selection of the Sunday lessons*, and supplementing known and admitted deficiencies, so as to give a greater completeness to our Liturgy. Surely a Commission, confined to the working out of these or the like specific objects of practical utility, *might accomplish an untold good*, which must commend itself to every dispassionate, and need not alarm even the most sensitive, mind."

The Archdeacon, it will be observed, distinguishes between a doctrinal and a non-doctrinal revision. Nor do we see any reason why the two should be necessarily mixed up. It is greatly to be deplored that a dread of the former, which is demanded by *comparatively* few persons, should be a permanent impediment to entertaining the latter proposition, in which *both* parties are agreed, and against which not one person in a thousand has a word to allege. I trust to be excused quoting at large this portion of the charge, as being at present confined to the columns of a provincial paper; from the obscurity of which let us hope the venerable author will rescue it, and allow his sentiments to be widely disseminated among the clergy and laity of the kingdom.*

" I am not ignorant," the Archdeacon proceeds, " that

---

* The Charge was afterwards printed for private distribution.

more, much more, than this is within the aim of many revisionists, whose desires are not to be satisfied by any mere structural re-arrangement or abbreviation of our services. They would, without fear or scruple, modify or suppress words and sentences involving questions the most delicate and debatable of doctrinal controversy: questions, which, once opened, would be the signal of a strife not to be composed within one generation; setting in more determined array, the one against the other, whatever differences unhappily divide us; not as now to be meekly allowed, with mutual consideration and forbearance, but to be argued with stubborn pertinacity; and that, not only in the Church at home, but in the Christian congregations multiplying with such unexampled success in every quarter of the world.

"The revision, however, most largely desired—the only revision in the contemplation or desire of reasonable minds—has in it no element of doctrinal contention: nothing to affect any one article of Christian belief, or necessarily to awaken any, the faintest, apprehension for the maintenance, in its entirety, of all saving truth. And so long as this is the admitted condition of the proposed revision, it would be well that it should not be refused. It would meet a sensible want; it would relieve a pressure painfully felt; and by the happier adaptation of our offices to the requirements of these times,—so remote, so altered from the times of their construction, two centuries ago,—it would largely add to the excellency of our Liturgy, and endear it the more to the loving and grateful affection, at home and abroad, of all who have at heart the honour of our spiritual Sion; desiring to see its worship moulded to the highest perfectibility attainable, before that day when we hope to mingle in the yet purer and loftier and nobler worship of glorified spirits in heaven."*

---

* The high estimation in which the Vicar of Halifax (brother to the late

This is the language of true conservatism; this it is to be wise in time; nor can I conceive what principle of human nature can set itself to resist such a conclusion, except it be that of *indolence* in some, which creates imaginary difficulties as an excuse for inaction—or that more culpable *indifference* in others, which cares not whether a thing be done well or ill, or done at all, provided it nowise affect either their person or their purse.

I am, Sir, yours, &c.,
June 8, 1859.   " INGOLDSBY."

LETTER LI.

THE BISHOP OF ST. ASAPH ON THE PRAYER-BOOK.

"What! will the line stretch out to the crack of doom?
Another yet? A seventh?"—*Macbeth.*

PURITAN.—" Indeed he wrote such a book, and the words that you repeat I have read in the same."—MARTIN MARPRELATE (1640), p. 10.

SIR,—The Bishop of St. Asaph (Vowler Short) is the seventh prelate on the roll; and one for whom, as a Church Reformer, we entertain an unfeigned respect. It is some time since we promised to extract certain passages from his well-known work on the Church, wherein the cause of Liturgical Reform is advocated in terms plainer than any that have issued of late from the right reverend prelate. Circumstances, however, over which I had no control, have arisen to compel a temporary suspension of our subject; and it is late now to resume where we left off. I must, nevertheless, so far redeem my pledge as to produce two or three passages from the work in question, and I shall then leave your readers to draw their own conclusions.

Archbishop of York) was held by *all classes* in his large parish, is the best practical comment on the above remarks.

Dr. Vowler Short's book on the Church appeared originally in 1832. It is true he was not then a bishop.* It is also certain that Tom Moore, or some other wag, has said that—

"As bees on flowers alighting cease to hum,
So Whigs on places settle—and grow dumb."

Whether the Anti-Reforming Bishop of 1858 was a Whig Rector in 1832, I presume not to say; but "beyond all doubt and controversy" the hive of the latter date had a sting and busy hum about it which we look and listen for in vain in 1858-9. Take, for example, the following from vol. ii., p. 157, of the learned prelate's work :—

" The kingdom has, for the last 200 years, been making rapid strides in *every species of improvement ;* and a corresponding alteration in the laws on *every subject* has taken place. During this period *nothing has been remedied in the Church*. A few Acts of Parliament have regulated some of its *temporal* concerns, and obviated some evils, but the clergy have never been allowed officially to state the disadvantages under which, as a body politic, we labour; or to suggest the methods by which those evils might probably be cured. And if the temper of the mass of Churchmen be little suited to enter on such discussions, as is sometimes asserted ; if there be greater risk in *discussing the question of alterations* than in continuing the abuses under which we labour, the fault is attributable chiefly to those who have long closed our national assembly."

This observation points to the *active* powers of Convocation, as a panacea for all the ills under which we labour—or did labour twenty-seven years ago. But what has the Convocation of 1850-59, during which period its doors have been

---

* On this principle Bishop Thirlwall repudiates the sentiments thrown in his teeth by the authors of "Essays and Reviews" from his introduction to Schleiermacher. See *Spectator*, April, 1861.

opened, and the Bishop of St. Asaph has had the right of ingress and egress, accomplished? What, but to produce an immense amount of words, with few or no deeds? "Much cry," as the saying is, "but no wool"*—reminding one of our great poet's

> "Universal hubbub wild,
> Of stunning sounds, and voices all confus'd,
> Borne through the dark with loudest vehemence."

Not so exactly. We stand corrected by the Rev. Mr. Massingberd, Proctor for the diocese of Lincoln. Convocation *has done* one thing. "It has *prevented* a Revision of the Prayer-book!"

"It may be too much to say that Convocation has *saved* the Prayer-book; but I am of opinion that if Convocation had *not sat*, it is highly probable we might now have been undergoing all the anxiety, danger, and bitterness which must be the inevitable result of an attempt to *revise* or *amend* the Book of Common Prayer."†

So much for the agreement of doctors. Doctor Short considers the abeyance of Convocation the cause of the *continuance of all the evils* under which the Church labours; while Doctor Massingberd raises his hands in pious ejaculation, giving thanks that we *have* a Convocation, as a safeguard *against every attempt at removing those evils!*

These views, I leave it to the Bishop of St. Asaph,

> "pugnantia secum
> Frontibus adversis, componere."

For my own part, never having had the smallest faith in a plurality of cooks, I am not surprised or disappointed at the

---

* See remark of Gregory Nazianzen, quoted at Letter I., p. 2.

† Speech of the Rev. F. C. Massingberd, of Ormsby, Lincolnshire, at the election of Proctors for that diocese, May, 1859.—The resistance offered by Convocation to Dean Pellew's motion, March, 1861, is certainly a practical illustration of that body's *obstructive* capabilities.

result of their consultations, nor have I any brighter anticipations from their future conferences, be they few or be they many.* My only regret is that the solitary production of their culinary skill, " The Report on Church Services," should have hitherto miscarried under their too assiduous care.†

But to proceed with our Bishop. At p. 251 of the same vol., speaking of the suggested amendments of the Puritans at the Savoy Conference, his lordship remarks:—

" When we view the whole question at this distance of time, it is *impossible not to wish that several concessions had been made* on points which, while they affect not the doctrine or discipline of the Church, *have been and are offensive* to many who conscientiously adhere to what is ordered; and which, had they been granted at the period of which we are speaking, might probably have tended to conciliation."

And is it too late to " concede and to conciliate" even now? " Have we parted company for ever?" "Are Euodias and Syntyche," as Lord Ebury observes,‡ " never to be reconciled? Are no attempts again to be made in that direction?" Is a closer union with our Dissenting brethren a thing *even now* not worth contending for, especially in an age when they are building stately churches§ after the model of our own, and when one of their most able writers is propounding the question whether they are, or are not, to have a Liturgy? ||

---

* Up to this date (November, 1878) the vaticinations in the text have been amply verified.
† See Speech of Dean Pellew, 1861. Hatchard, Piccadilly.
‡ See Lord Ebury's First Speech, p. 20, *Third Edition*. 1859.
§ In London, Manchester, Southampton, Halifax, Birmingham, Cambridge, St. Leonard's, and most other large towns, may be seen chapels belonging to the so-called Dissenters, which would do credit to the purest ages of Ecclesiastical architecture.
|| See " A Chapter on Liturgies," by the Rev. Charles Baird, edited by the Rev. Thomas Binney. London: Knight and Son. 1856.

What the particular changes are which the Bishop, as a simple Rector, thought not undesirable in 1832, I must reserve for my next,—being too important for the close of a letter, especially in the dog-days. It is not by any choice of mine, you will easily believe, that I find myself working double tides after a whole twelvemonth's agitation,* but so long as a Revision of the Book of Common Prayer, on the principles of its Preface, remains unattempted—hot or cold, wet or dry, seed-time or harvest, winter or summer—

"Dum memor ipse mei, dum spiritus hos regit artus,"

so long do I hope to be found, with pen in hand, ready to do battle with all comers in this sacred cause.†

Meanwhile I have the honour to remain, yours, &c.,

June 15, 1859.   "INGOLDSBY."

LETTER LII.

REV. VOWLER SHORT, B.D., STUDENT OF CHRIST CHURCH, ON THE BOOK OF COMMON PRAYER.

"The sharpest strictures on his own acts are to be found in Dr. Vowler Short's own writings. Never was there culprit more condemned than he by the evidence of his own mouth."—*Letter on the Church in Wales*, by the Rev. R. W. MORGAN, p. 32.

SIR,—I am told that I ought to show more respect to the dignity of the lawn, and not to hold every bishop bound by what he may have preached, spoken, or published some twenty years ago:—that such a tenacious memory, according

---

* Alas, that twenty years should have elapsed, and still little or nothing done in this matter! November, 1878.

† The republication of these Letters in his seventieth year, and at the distance of twenty years from their first issue, is at least an unanswerable proof of the writer's convictions on this head, not having been made a bishop in the interval, like the Rector of Kingsworthy, Hants! (1878.)

to the poet, makes a man an unwelcome guest at a symposium, and is equally ill-calculated to recommend a humble clerk to the favour of his spiritual superiors:—that such a mode of warfare may be all very well in the House of Commons, "composed as it is at present," with many of "its members ill-informed and hasty;"* and venial enough amongst the gentlemen of the Press, when they are minded to expose the inconsistencies of the *Times*, as it eats its own words at intervals of five or six years, or months, or it may be days: but that for a Country Parson to proclaim to the world that "the now anti-Revisionist Bishop of St. Asaph was known as a Liturgical Reformer when simply Rector of Kingsworthy, Hants," is flat treason, highly impolitic, and, according to the best authorities, altogether uncanonical.

The past no man can recall; but I will endeavour for the future to abstain from these unpleasant reminiscences; and will content myself to-day with setting before your readers, without note or comment, a few passages from a work happening to lie at this moment on my table, entitled, "A Sketch of the History of the Church of England to the Revolution of 1688, by Thomas Vowler Short, B.D., Student of Christ Church, and Rector of Kingsworthy, Hants."†

I shall confine myself to the second volume; and as the subject is one adapted for students in theology, and not unlikely to be a text-book for ordination (especially in the diocese of St. Asaph), I recommend it to the consideration of the rising generation of clergymen.

At § 512 the learned author observes of the CANONS:—

"They are in number 141, and at the present day form the basis of ecclesiastical law as far as the clergy are concerned. Many of them have been superseded by subsequent

---

* See Letter x., p. 62.
† J. H. Parker, Oxford. Rivingtons, London. 1832.

Acts of Parliament; and the *hand of time*, together with the *change in customs*, has rendered them *so generally neglected as a code*, that it is *much to be wished* they were *remodelled*, and sanctioned by legal enactment."

At § 540, speaking of the authorised translation of THE BIBLE, the writer proceeds :—

"Above two hundred years have now elapsed since this review; and the Church has subsequently contented itself with *discovering inaccuracies*, without attempting to correct them. The whole question of a new translation is one of considerable delicacy,* but the opinion of Archbishop Newcome, supported as it is by the concurrent testimony of nearly *thirty divines of considerable weight*, ought not to have remained without due and public attention. . . . . These amendments might be sanctioned by authority, so that they might be used at the discretion of the minister; a step which would at least prepare the way for their ultimate introduction into the text, and show a *wish to make use of the growing knowledge of the country for the improvement of the services of the Church.*"

The above extract, on a subject collateral to our present one, is of an importance that can hardly be exaggerated.† But we pass on to quote the following "note," as not without its value at "this present time" :—

"If at the Savoy Conference the *whole services had been shortened*, the MORNING SERVICE so arranged that there might have been more unity in the various parts of which it is composed, and *repetitions had been thus avoided*, particularly

---

* See Dean Trench on the Authorised Version, &c.: London, J. W. Parker, 1858. The whole of the concluding chapter, on "The Best Means of Carrying out a Revision," might be applied, *mutatis mutandis*, to a Revision of the Prayer-book.

† Two groups of translators of the Bible have been at work for many years; with what result remains still to be proved. (1878.)

with regard to the Lord's Prayer; .... had the method of distributing the elements at the Lord's Supper been altered, in case of a large number of communicants, a custom which many clergymen have from necessity been *forced to introduce* ; had the godfathers in baptism answered *in their own names;* ... had the words, 'with my body I thee worship;' 'in sure and certain hope;' and 'it is certain from God's word,' in the respective services (of marriage, burial, and baptism) been changed; had the *reading the Apocrypha* been discontinued; and the *table* of LESSONS *new framed;**—the Prayer-book would probably have been equally edifying, and less liable to objections."†

Tolerably bold this for a bishop—we beg pardon, *a rector*—who, continuing his remarks on the said Conference, observes very justly in reference to its failure :—

" When men entertaining opinions *at total variance with each other*, meet for the purpose of discussing them, unless they are possessed of extraordinary forbearance, the distance

---

* On a revision of the Calendar with a view to a fuller selection of Sunday lessons, the Dean of Norwich observes that "the more any serious Churchman reflects on this desirable object, the deeper does its importance become impressed on his judgment. Some of the lessons now in use are confessedly better adapted to private than to public perusal; and the whole present table of proper lessons comprises only a limited portion of God's Word; the great bulk of which is thus kept out of reach of the poor untaught man who cannot read it himself, and whose chief means of obtaining any knowledge whatever respecting it, consists in hearing it read in the church on the Lord's day. A new and enlarged table of lessons, therefore, for Sundays, would prove the occasion of much additional usefulness, by placing a wider range of chapters at the option of the officiating minister, and thus open fresh treasures of Scripture to the humbler members of the Church."—*Convocation, &c.*, by the Hon. George Pellew, D.D. London, Rivingtons: 1857. See also Speech by the same in Convocation, March, 1861. Hatchard; pp. 13-16. Also Rev. C. Girdlestone, "Black Bartholomew's Day," p. 10; 1862.

† A "New Lectionary," as it is called, came into operation January 1, 1872, and was probably the result of the observations in the text; but even here there is room for improvement, as is pretty generally allowed, even by those who are thankful for this first small concession to public opinion.

between them is likely to be increased rather than diminished. The only method, under such circumstances, from which any favourable result could rationally be expected, would be, if the *more moderate persons* belonging to the ruling party were selected; and who, having by private communication gained an insight into the points in which alteration was chiefly demanded, were *directed by their commission* and were *themselves disposed* to concede everything which might be given up with safety to the constitution of the Church." (§ 701.)

Let us hope that such principle of selection will guide those who may have the appointment of the next Commission; no good will ever come from one composed of persons *of notoriously opposite opinions* to start with.*

Speaking in just commendation of our Liturgy after its final review in 1662, the author adds (§ 749)—

"The only question which admits of any doubt is, whether some *reasonable objections* to it may not still be obviated—whether some verbal alterations may not be made with advantage, and a further amalgamation take place in the *three services* which are now generally *used together* in the morning, by which an *unnecessary repetition* of the same or similar petitions might be avoided."

Speaking of the Commission of 1689 (§ 806), we find the author designating its members as "divines, many of whose names form the brightest ornaments of our Church;" and after enlarging on the points recommended by that Commission,† and expressing an opinion that "*shortening the time occupied by the prayers* is an object most, perhaps,

---

* And yet this was precisely (and it would seem studiously) the character of the Commission on the Rubrics which sat from 1867 to 1869 with no appreciable results.

† Its great defect was that it meddled too much with the existing Prayer-book, often where no change was needed.

required," and observing that the American Prayer-book (formed in great measure upon the recommendations of the said Commission) contains " changes which, upon the whole, appear to be judiciously made," the author concludes as follows (§ 810) :—

"It would surely be desirable, if *every objection* which a sober and reasonable member of the Church might make to these formularies were *as far as possible obviated*. There were many things which did then, there are some things which do now, *offend the true friends of the Church* of England, who willingly comply with the Liturgy and Services as established by law, because they esteem the Common Prayer-book, *as a whole*, to be a most excellent composition ; but who, nevertheless, regard it as a *human production, and therefore capable of improvement*, as well as requiring from time to time verbal alterations, as the language of the country gradually varies. And the *quiet friend of reform* cannot but feel sorry that this attempt was then dropped, and has *never since been carried into effect*."

Exactly so. What a pity that no Lord John Russell, or other Prime Minister, had the penetration—

> "This flower unheeded to descry ;
> And bid him round earth's altars shed
> The fragrance of his blushing head."

What an addition he would have proved to the bench of bishops ; what a support to Lord Ebury in his annual motion; what a thorn in the side of his mitred brethren in Anne's large chamber! But alas,—(as Paley long ago observed,[*]

---

[*] On the Propriety of Requiring a Subscription to Articles of Faith, p. 45. London, 1774. See also Letter of Sydney Smith to Lord John Russell, April 3, 1837; "Pretended heterodoxy is the plea with which the bishops endeavour to keep off the Bench every man of spirit and independence, and to terrify you into the appointment of *feeble men*."—*Memoirs*, vol. ii., p. 399. Is it not so to this very day ? 1878.

himself a victim to the stereotyped system of Church patronage from time immemorial to the hour at which we write, which shuts the door of preferment against all independence of thought or action,)—" the man who attacks a flourishing establishment writes with a halter round his neck." The Rector of Kingsworthy, however, (unlike the Rector of Kingswinford),* saw the expediency of altering his tack in time, and so was safely landed at last in the See of St. Asaph, there to live and die, an unreforming member of the Bench of Bishops.

Meanwhile I have the honour to remain,
The still reforming, and therefore unpromoted,
June 21, 1859.   Rector of INGOLDSBY.

LETTER LIII.

THE BISHOPS OF HEREFORD, BATH AND WELLS, AND CHICHESTER.

> "And yet the *eighth* appears, who bears a glass
> Which shows me many more."—*Macbeth.*

> "Another mizzling, drizzling day;
>   Of clearing up there's no appearance;
> So I'll sit down without delay,
>   And here at least, I'll make a clearance.'
> *Ingoldsby Legends.*

SIR,—So writes my popular namesake;—and, under similar atmospheric influences, I will follow his example.

With much patience and perseverance we have disposed of seven out of the ten Bishops who are reported to have taken part in the debate on the Prayer-book in the Convocation of February, 1858. There remain yet three,—Hereford, Bath and Wells, and Chichester. But as these last (like the Bristol candidate following Mr. Burke) appear to have con-

---

* See Letter xxx., p. 203; of the Rev. C. Girdlestone.

tented themselves with "saying ditto" to the preceding speakers, we see no reason why we should not imitate them, and refer our readers to our past letters for a "reply" to their remarks.

We must be excused, however, making an exception in favour of the first-mentioned prelate, the Bishop of Hereford, whom one is surprised to find bowing so meekly to the Bishop of Oxford, when we bear in mind all that passed on the occasion of the former's elevation to the Bench. But as it is in all cases commendable to forgive and forget, so especially must it be with the hierarchy, having so many eyes fixed upon them. We must remember, too, that the Rev. Renn Dickson Hampden, D.D., Regius Professor of Divinity, and the Right Rev. R. D. Hereford, are, according to our rule, no longer one and the same person. Bishops are no more bound by the sermons they preached when at the University, than by the Church Histories they published when plain country Rectors.* *Nous avons changé tout cela.* The rochet has displaced the gown, the apron superseded the cassock; and hocus pocus, at the word,—

"Qui color albus erat, nunc est contrarius albo."

White becomes black; black white. The old are boiled young again; the young old. Liberals are metamorphosed into Conservatives; Tories into Liberals. Latitudinarians are good High Churchmen; Evangelicals† can see no harm in a little mild Tractarianism. All former blemishes in the Prayer-book vanish.‡ The Bible is incapable of improvement.

---

* See Letter LI., p. 325.

† A well-known Northern Dean, formerly of this school, shortly after his elevation, wrote to a friend:—" I don't know how it is, but somehow or other, I find myself becoming more and more of a High Churchman every day I live."

‡ A remarkable illustration of the observation in the text came under the knowledge of the author in the case of the late Bishop Jeune, who as Master of Pembroke College, Oxford, about this time gave it as his opinion

What, touch our beautiful and incomparable Liturgy! What a fuss about nothing!—*Le jeu ne vaut pas la chandelle.** What do they want, these restless Liturgical Reformers?— They only want to be bishops themselves. But they are greatly mistaken. They will find, when they are a little older, that the top of the Church pyramid is only reached by creeping or flying,† not by agitating an unpopular cause. So the Bishop's Chaplain or Secretary must not be seen speaking with them. The Rural Deans do not take wine with them at the Visitation dinner. Licensed curates are ill-advised if they sit next to them during the delivery of the triennial charge.

And is this to be wondered at, when the celebrated Divinity Professor of 1847, (the personal friend of Whately ‡ and of

---

that "the Athanasian Creed would be far better removed from the English Prayer-book, as is done in the American." The same gentleman when subsequently challenged (by the author) as Bishop of Peterborough to assist the Revisionists in this matter, replied, "Oh, all that has been satisfactorily answered by Waterland long ago!"

Comment is superfluous.

* The Archbishop of Canterbury (Sumner), in reply to Lord Ebury in the House of Lords, May 8th, 1860, observed, "We think a verbal revision *would not be worth its cost;* a doctrinal revision would throw the Church into confusion."

† "What (says Sydney Smith) can you expect of a whole profession where there is no more connexion between merit and reward, than between merit and beauty, or merit and strength?" *Works,* vol. i., p. 84.— This scandal, though somewhat mitigated since the time at which the worthy Canon wrote, still remains, and will continue to do so, while by far the largest portion of Church patronage is dispensed upon personal or political considerations.

‡ His Grace the Archbishop of Dublin (Whately) is reported to have said in the House of Lords in 1840, that—

"He was for remedying those changes of that great innovator, Time, who (as was said by Lord Bacon) was insinuating imperceptibly many alterations, and was changing things for the worse if they were not changed for the better; and he would ask whether, in the alterations made by the first Reformers, they intended that their amendments should never be changed; whether they were like the laws of the Medes and Persians, unalterable; and whether it were their intention that the door should be locked, and the key buried and lost for ever."—*Lord Ebury's Speech,* Third Edition, p. 15, 1859.

Arnold,*) thus expresses himself in the "House of Bishops," on Wednesday, February 10th, 1858?—

"I *perfectly agree in all that has been said* respecting the Revision of the Liturgy. . . . I am happy to find that this discussion has been raised; and I think it most desirable that on this matter the public should understand that THE BISHOPS ARE PERFECTLY UNANIMOUS!"

We ten, we happy ten, we band of brothers!—

> " Old men forget; yet all shall be forgot,
> But they'll remember with advantages,
> What feats we did that day. Then shall our names,
> Familiar in their mouths as household words,—
> Sumner the Primate, Lincoln and Winchester,
> Oxon and Hereford, Asaph and St. David's,
> Be in their flowing cups freshly remembered.
> This story shall our chaplains teach their sons,
> And——"

But it is time we proceeded with the second of the three Prelates on our list to-day, the esteemed Bishop of Bath and Wells (Lord Auckland), who confined his observations to the following sentence:—

"The subject is so exhausted that I will content myself with expressing my concurrence in the opinions of my right reverend brethren—that no alteration should take place in our services." †

---

* See Life by Stanley, vol. i., p. 325–330. Fellowes, London, 1858.

† The Bishop was rather more diffuse in his Charge of April, 1861:—" I am far from thinking that any work of man is so perfect as to be incapable of improvement, or that any form of Divine worship adapted to the age in which it was imposed might not require alteration in order to be made suitable to another generation; but when this revision is sought for with a view to change some essential doctrine, it is impossible to accede to any such demand without imperilling the faith which the reformers of the Church of England advocated and which the Church has held ever since the Reformation. And this constitutes in my mind an invincible objection to *any revision at the present moment.* Our Liturgy and Articles are constructed upon a broad basis, which includes in one communion pious men who profess opinions widely different from each other. The relation the Church now bears to the State

After what had just fallen from his right reverend brother, common politeness required nothing less from this last speaker, who is too well bred to give the lie direct to any one, *à fortiori* to a brother of the apron. But inasmuch as Lord Auckland's name is returned as a Liberal in Dod's Parliamentary Companion, we do not anticipate a very strenuous opposition on his part to any Commission of Inquiry it may please Her Majesty to issue either in this or any future Session of Parliament.

Passing, therefore, *per saltum*, to our last remaining Prelate, the Bishop of Chichester (Gilbert), we find him adopting the brevity of the preceding speaker, and observing:—

"I do not wish it to be supposed that any difference of opinion exists; and I beg to say that the sentiments which have been expressed meet my entire approval."

What a pity this "unanimity" of the Bishops cannot influence the subordinate clergy of the dioceses thus peacefully represented! How smoothly would the stream run in the neighbourhood of West Lavington and Boyne-hill! What a sinecure to preside in the Court of Arches, or even the Queen's Bench, so far as "Mandamuses" on Bishops and Archbishops are concerned.*—But, alas!

"Nihil est ab omni
Parte beatum."

The good easy prelate must submit, as he best may, to

---

causes an additional difficulty in determining the authority to whom this work of revision should be entrusted; but as the objects are still *in limine*, it is unnecessary to enter into a discussion of them; but I think they are such as to justify me in expressing an opinion that it would involve great danger to the peace and unity of the Church to make any attempt *at the present time* to alter our plain, our full, and our devotional Liturgy."

* The case of "Poole *versus* the Bishop of London" was then before the Court. How many have since followed, it is needless to say. Their name is Legion—and all arising from an unrevised (and misinterpreted *because* unrevised) Book of Common Prayer.

his Golightly or his Westerton at home, though he can, with comparative impunity, ignore the existence of the Liturgical Reformers "in another place." And we can only express a hope that worse may not be behind; and that an extensive schism* be not the result of this determination of those in power to do nothing towards improving or amending "the incomparable Liturgy of the Church of England."

I remain, Sir, yours, &c.,

June 29, 1859. "INGOLDSBY."

LETTER LIV.

"THAT VERY ECCENTRIC AND NEBULOUS AFFAIR CALLED THE CONVOCATION OF THE PROVINCE OF CANTERBURY."

Times Newspaper, June 24th, 1859.

" Ubi Sisyphu' versat
Saxum sudans nitendo, neque proficit hilum."
CIC. *Tusc. Quæst. I.*

SIR,—The journal from which the above definition of CONVOCATION is taken is so extensively read, that according to the Latin proverb, it would be *actum agere*, or, according to the English one, "killing a dead cat," to throw another stone at a body that has been so fearfully mauled by your powerful contemporary.

But still, as our self-tormenting ecclesiastical Tantalus *will* persevere in calling itself "the Church," and in that character *will* persist in issuing its decrees, not only upon the subject of Church Rates, the Divorce Act, and the Jew Bill,†

---

* Serious thoughts were at that time entertained of establishing a Free Church of England in the heart of the Metropolis; an idea which has been since carried into practice, and seems likely to spread. Small blame to them!

† See the speeches of Archdeacon Denison, Mr. Jebb, and Canon Wordsworth (now Bishop of Lincoln), as reported in the *Guardian* for June 29, 1859.

but also upon the proposed Revision of the Book of Common Prayer, in which millions, not having the smallest voice in Convocation, are deeply interested—it becomes our duty to notice their proceedings in this last matter, lest (agreeably to the Archdeacon of Lindisfarne's theory) we should, by our silence, be assumed to give consent. *"Tacent, satis laudant,"* our foes will say.*

On Wednesday, then, June 22nd, the two Houses of Convocation for the Province of Canterbury assembled, as usual after the meeting of Parliament, " for the despatch of business!"—the members of the Upper House in Queen Anne's Bounty Office, under the presidency of his Grace the Primate; the members of the Lower House in the Jerusalem Chamber, under the presidency of the " Prolocutor," the Dean of Bristol (Elliot).

The Upper House consisted of his Grace the Archbishop, and eight other Prelates; a remarkable falling off from the gathering of February, 1858.† Among those conspicuous by their absence, were the Bishops of St. Asaph and St. David's, whilst amongst those equally conspicuous by their presence was the Bishop of Oxford (Wilberforce), *hic et ubique*, as a matter of course,—

> " Cui sese parvus Iulus
> Dat comitem, sequiturque virum non passibus æquis."

To pass *in medias res*,—the Bishop of Oxford moves and carries the following resolution:—

" That his Grace the President be requested to direct the Lower House to appoint three members of that House to act with certain members of this House as a joint committee, to prepare the draft of such occasional services as may seem needful to carry out the report of a committee on the services of the Church received by Convocation on the 20th of June,

---

* Letter xxxviii., p. 247.   † See Letter ii., p. 7.

1854; and to report these drafts to Convocation, that Convocation may consider whether it is expedient to address Her Majesty thereon."

The motion is lengthy. The Bishop of Oxford is not "a man of few words," and the debate upon it extends to five columns of the *Guardian*. We shall only at present notice the inconsistency of the proposition with the general professions of the mover; who, while he confesses that it would be "a *great boon* to give the Church *greater elasticity* in her services," yet proposes to accomplish this object without "*touching* the Prayer-book *in any way!*"

In the article referred to in our motto, the *Times* observes of Convocation, that it "willingly anticipates the worst pains of the damned," by straining after delicious fruit seemingly within its reach, but no sooner does the hand approach the prize, than an envious wind bears all away. The Bishop of Oxford out-herods this involuntary martyr of the heathen mythology, by imposing on *himself* the task of an eternal game of bob-apple, in undertaking to supplement the Prayer-book from itself *without so much as touching* the volume!

The idea irresistibly occurs to us of a juggler at a village feast, astounding the gaping rustics by offering to remove a hen from underneath a hat without touching the latter. For seriously (as the matter is too grave a one to treat thus lightly)—

"Spectatum admissi risum teneatis, amici?"—

is it not carrying reverence for the *statu quo* of the Prayer-book a little too far, to fence about in this manner to preserve all its admitted "imperfections," lest by *touching it* we should "loose from its settings one gem of that precious inheritance of our fathers?"*

No wonder "the leading journal" pronounces of a con-

---

* See Bishop of Oxford's Speech in Convocation, Letter XI., p. 72.

clave where such scenes are exhibited, that "by its actions it betrays the rottenness of its condition, and its almost farcical character as a representative of the clergy of England."* No wonder the same organ of public opinion feels entitled to assert, that "any dozen of working and reasonable clergymen you meet with repudiate it:"—to which might be added, with equal truth, that ninety-nine out of every hundred sensible laymen regard its proceedings with a smile; while with some, we fear, the smile borders closely upon a sneer.

The Bishop of Gloucester (Baring), speaking of this assembly, appears to have expressed an opinion, that "the Lower House of Convocation—already in a mist—could not sit more than three days without getting into a storm." But even that were better than to make itself ridiculous. Nothing so fatal to efficiency as this last. Poverty has notoriously many evils connected with it; but the poet has reckoned it as chief, that "it makes men ridiculous."† Why *poverty* should do this I don't exactly know, and am sorry if it does, for it is certainly by no fault of its own: but sure I am that Convocation could not take a more effectual way to bring itself and the Church it professes to represent into contempt, than thus to excite periodically the risible organs of the only animal gifted with the power of smiling.

However, as the Committee moved for by the Bishop of Oxford has been appointed by this self-constituted legislative body, notwithstanding some opposition from three of the assembled Prelates, we will wait the presentation of its Report; from which, doubtless, it will appear to the satisfaction of all beholders, ourselves amongst the rest, how it is

---

* The solemn farce enacted on the attempt to repeal the twenty-ninth Canon almost justifies the above severe censure of the *Times*.
† "Nil habet infelix paupertas durius in se,
Quam quod *ridiculos* homines facit."—Juv., *Sat.* iii., 152.

possible to give the Church *greater elasticity* in her services, without *touching* that jewel, the Prayer-book.

Meanwhile we congratulate our readers on this *premier pas*, although a somewhat crooked one, taken outside the pale of antiquated routine; more especially when we bear in mind the observation of the Bishop of London (Tait) when this matter of "the Special Services" was first brought before Convocation,*—to the effect, that "the granting of such a Committee *would render further resistance to Lord Ebury's petitioners more difficult than ever.*" Trusting, therefore, to see a second and a third step speedily taken, and feeling assured that any movement in the direction pointed out by Lord Ebury will prove, upon experiment, a far simpler thing than the self-contradicting proposal of the Bishop of Oxford,

I remain, Sir, yours, &c.,
July 6, 1859.   " INGOLDSBY."

LETTER LV.

POSTPONEMENT OF LORD EBURY'S MOTION.

" Vitæ summa brevis spem nos vetat inchoare longam."—Hor.

SIR,—As we anticipated,† the distracted character of the now-expiring session of Parliament has necessitated the postponement of Lord Ebury's motion to the spring of 1860, when his lordship pledges himself to renew it.

We cannot say that we are otherwise than pleased at this determination on his part. To "be with caution bold," is a combination of qualities not always forthcoming; and we

---

* See his Speech in Convocation, reported in the *Guardian*, Feb. 16, 1859.
† Letter XLVI., p. 301.

think Lord Ebury entitled to praise for having resisted the importunity of his followers to urge the question of Revision to a *present* decision at all hazards.

That he would have met with a fair amount of support, might reasonably be calculated on by those who have watched this matter through its various stages from the spring of '57 up to the present moment. At the same time it is equally certain, that, if it be true, as he stated in the House last Friday, that "he had four-fifths of the right reverend prelates against him," there would have been a formidable number of lay Peers who, whatever might be their private convictions, would have felt a scruple in giving a vote on such a matter in opposition to a proximate unanimity amongst the Lords spiritual. We trust Lord Ebury may be mistaken in his estimate of the right reverend bench. We have too high a regard for the order to believe that four-fifths of them would, upon a poll, be found arrayed on the side adverse to PROGRESS in the Church, while everything else is progressing around it.

The real fact we believe to be, that the bishops, as a body, are more liberal than the clergy they are assumed to represent; but being many of them far gone in years,* it is hardly to be expected that they should take the initiative in moving in advance of their brethren. It is well known as a rule that useful reforms rise from beneath rather than from above; and when the junior portion of the Bench discover, as they will do upon inquiry, that a large number of the younger clergy are not afraid of innovation,† we believe they will no longer

---

* It is an objection to the hierarchy that, like the Pope, they are rarely promoted from the ranks till they are past the meridian of their days, and are naturally averse to incurring more trouble than the routine of their official duties entails upon them. This is, no doubt, one enormous difficulty the Revision question has to contend with.

† A careful examination of the list of the celebrated 10,000 shows that the great proportion of the signatures consisted of the *elderly* clergy. Full

set themselves in array against a proposition founded on the principles of justice and common sense.

Lord Ebury has allowed the Prelates a twelvemonth's breathing time; at the expiration of which, his Grace the Archbishop of Canterbury undertakes to show cause why the bishops should further resist* his lordship's motion. In the meantime we have no fears for the result; or if we have any, they are founded entirely on the spirit of the motto we have adopted for our letter of this day. The uncertainty of life at the best warns us against laying schemes for the future.

"Man is like a thing of nought, his time passeth away like a shadow."

And bearing in mind the rocks and the shoals, the Scyllas and Charybdises of Parliament, through which Lord Ebury has hitherto had to navigate his frail vessel, with but a handful of determined men labouring at the oar, we cannot but regret these repeated postponements, however unavoidable they may be on his lordship's part—

"To-morrow, and to-morrow, and to-morrow!"—

But we will not anticipate evil. The work, we believe firmly, is of God; and, according to Luther's well-known distich,—

"Ist's Gottes werk, so wird's bestehen;
Ist's Menschen's, so wird's untergehen." †

That it has hitherto advanced, and rapidly of late, no one can deny: it remains to be seen whether it is to receive a check at this stage of its history, or to proceed with accumulative force to a successful issue. Meanwhile it is for all who are interested in its success to exert themselves

---

half of the number are now gone to their rest, let us charitably hope to their reward. (1878.)

* See on this matter the next Letter, No. LVI., p. 347.
† See Letter XXIII., p. 162.

in support of Lord Ebury, who stands as it were single-handed, a modern Decius, in front of the enemy. That the opponents of Revision are on the alert we have certain information.* Let us not be wanting on our part. We have no great faith in petitions; but we have very great faith in *the Press*, which, to the best of our belief and knowledge, is mainly with us.† If any one thinks otherwise, we invite, nay, we challenge, contradiction. Let the opponents of Revision come forward and produce the *Guardian, Clerical Journal, English Churchman, John Bull, Standard,* and *Morning Post,* in defence of their position; and we pledge ourselves in return to overwhelm them with such a body of counter-evidence from newspapers and magazines, both London and provincial, as they are little prepared to expect.‡

We give them nine months from this date for the accomplishment of their share of their task; and, life and health permitting, we bind ourselves to produce No. 1 of our REPLY at the expiration of three weeks from the appearance of their highly interesting manifesto: to be continued in regular succession from week to week, till they, or you, Mr. Editor, shall cry out,

"Ohe! jam satis est."—"Hold—enough."

I remain, Sir, yours, &c.,
August 3, 1859.   "INGOLDSBY."

---

* More than one of the Right Reverend Prelates, to our own knowledge, issued instructions to his "Rural Deans," to invite the clergy of their respective "deaneries" to "petition both Houses of the Legislature" *against* the proposed Revision of the Liturgy.

† Almost the whole of the Newspaper Press, with the exception of the High Church organs, in some form or other advocated Revision; while of the Magazines we may mention the *Edinburgh, Dublin, Church of England Monthly, Christian Observer, British, &c.*

‡ This challenge has never been accepted, though "THE LETTERS" have gone through three editions, and been extensively circulated in all quarters.

LETTER LVI.

HIS GRACE THE ARCHBISHOP OF CANTERBURY (SUMNER).

"Sic vita erat: facile omnes perferre ac pati,
Cum quibus erat cunque una; iis sese dedere;
Eorum obsequi studiis; adversus nemini;
Nunquam præponens se illis; ita facillime
Sine invidia laudem invenias, et amicos pares."

TERENCE.

SIR,—I hasten to correct an error into which I was led in my last, through the imperfect report which had reached me of the proceedings in the House of Lords on the 29th ult.

So far from having stated, that on Lord Ebury's re-introducing the subject of Liturgical Reform next session the Bishops would "further resist the motion," it appears that the expression made use of by the Archbishop was, that "whenever his Lordship should again bring forward his motion, the Bench would give it their best attention and consideration."[*]

This last, it cannot be denied, is a somewhat different representation of the case to what has doubtless met the eyes of many of your readers, as well as my own, in the public papers, and far more in accordance with the character of the individual now occupying the chief seat in the English Church next to the Sovereign; a character not inaptly portrayed in the lines of the dramatist prefixed to our present article.

His Grace has probably discovered that the LOVE OF PEACE

---

[*] That these two expressions partook, in the event, of the nature of a distinction without a difference (as is very apt to be the case when a Bishop or a Prime Minister wishes to shelve a troublesome question), will be judged by all who read the report of the debate in the House of Lords, May 8th, 1860, or receive Episcopal or Ministerial letters on business.

which, as commendable in all men, is particularly so in one situated in his position, will be better promoted by a timely concession to public opinion in this matter than by further resistance. It is nearly six years* since the Archbishop gave expression to the sentiment, that "he lamented the divisions of the Church on no account more than this— that they tended to place at a greater distance than ever *the improvements which every one acknowledged* might be made in some parts of our excellent Liturgy;" and it is not surprising if increased experience has led him to consider whether he might not have adopted a mistaken policy in LETTING ILL ALONE; whether, in short, a church divided against itself were not more likely to be healed by the application of remedial measures (albeit not unattended with risk), than by being left to prey upon itself till the fire should die out of its own accord, or earnest men cease in despair to look for aid from those in place of authority and power.†

Whatever peril may be involved in making a change, certain it is that the plan of leaving matters as they are has had a tolerably long trial, without leading to any beneficial result. It is exactly a century since one of the predecessors of the most Reverend Primate thus expressed himself :—

"*Ornatior*, quidem, *accuratior*, plenior, *brevior*, et potest ea fieri, et *debet:* sed tranquillis hominum animis; non temerariis qualia vidimus et videmus, ausis; non inter *media dissidia* mutuasque suspiciones."‡

---

* Report of Convocation, Feb. 1st, 1854.

† The alternative, we are sorry to say, is, that many have joined the ranks of the Liberation Society, or the Free Church movement, in simple despair of seeing a Reform of the Liturgy in their time. (1878.)

‡ See Lord Ebury's Speech of May 8, 1860, Third Edition, p. 9. Hatchard, Piccadilly; also Answer to Paley's Considerations on the Propriety of Requiring a Subscription to Articles of Faith. . . . . . "There are some things in our Articles and Liturgy which we should be

Alas, for poor human nature; alas for the Church:—

> "Such is the moral of all human tales,
> 'Tis but the same rehearsal of the past;
> And History, with all her volumes vast,
> Hath but one page." *

The same obstacle which occurred to the mind of a Secker in 1761, rises before the eye of a Sumner in 1859;† and there the barrier will still remain, until some bold Alexander arises who will scorn to dally childishly before this everlasting knot, and earn for himself an immortality of fame by proving that though it be the part of a wise man to foresee difficulties, a higher praise is his who dexterously and fearlessly accomplishes their solution.

In addressing the Upper House of Convocation in February, 1858, the present Primate was fain to admit that if we were constructing a Prayer-book for the first time, "some of its services might be framed with some slight difference," and that there are too many repetitions of the Lord's Prayer, which "might be omitted before the sermon" without any violation of the Rubric, requiring only the "toleration" of the bishops!—Is this the limit of the "improvements which *every one acknowledged* might be made in our Liturgy?" Is it because such amendments as these cannot be carried out, that his Grace "laments the *divisions* in the Church?"

The fact is, your Grace is arguing in a circle. It is the Prayer-book that *creates the divisions;* and then the divisions, according to your Grace's theory, must *retain the Prayer-*

---

glad to see amended, many which we should be willing to give up to the scruples of others; but the heat and violence with which redress has been pursued preclude all hope of accommodation and tranquillity; we had better *wait, therefore, for more peaceable times,* and be contented with our present constitution as it is, until a fairer prospect shall appear of changing it for the better."—PALEY, *Works,* vol. iii., p. 331 (Edit. 1825).

* BYRON, *Childe Harold.* † See Letter xxxi., p. 205.

book as it is. And unless, like your predecessors extending now over two centuries, you would have these divisions transmitted to your successor with increasing aggravation, you will submit to the stern necessity of the age, and grapple with the difficulty while it is comparatively under your control.

"Timely concession" (to quote the words of a Right Reverend legislator) "may still disarm the impending innovation of its violence—may counteract its ill effects, and guide the stream of public opinion;"* while, believe me, the hour is gone by for the united Bench of Bishops, supposing them to be united (which they are not), wholly to arrest it.

To offer it further resistance will be interpreted into a wish to conceal something unsound at the bottom, something that will not bear the searching light of day; such a light as it is the purpose of Lord Ebury's Commission to bring to bear upon the Service-book of the Church.

Why wait for worse times? Why incur the danger of the matter falling into less friendly hands?† Why run the risk of having that extorted from you by force which you might now concede with a tolerable grace? Why be compelled to yield on terms of capitulation, what you might offer as a boon, and be thanked for your pains? They are the most dangerous of all counsellors who know not when the time for concession has arrived. The untenable fortress will only invite by its obstinate resistance a stronger force for the necessary work of effecting an entrance; and the temper of

---

* History of the Church, by Thomas Vowler Short, vol. ii., § 596.

† Even the Bishop of Salisbury (Hamilton), averse as he is to a Royal Commission of Inquiry into "the inestimable inheritance of our forefathers," is constrained to speak of the noble Lord, the promoter of the present Inquiry, as "an attached member of the Church of England."—*Charge by the Bishop of Salisbury*, 1858; p. 53. (Rivingtons.) And the Bishop of Oxford (Wilberforce) commenced his reply to Lord Ebury on May 8th, 1860, by admitting, that "the noble Lord had no other object in view than the benefit of the Church of which he was a member."

the assailants is not likely to be improved by the vexatious process of an expensive and protracted siege.

Trusting that I speak to ears not unwilling to hear the words of soberness and truth, albeit too frequently pre-occupied by flattery and toadyism,

I remain, Sir, yours, &c.,

August 17, 1859. "INGOLDSBY."

LETTER LVII.

THE DEAN OF NORWICH ON REVISION.

"Caution does not mean doing nothing; nothing is so incautious as that. It only means not attempting to do everything at once."—*Times*, August 1st, 1859.

SIR,—The following notice of a Motion on the Revision of the Prayer-book has been laid before Convocation by the Hon. and Very Rev. George Pellew, Dean of Norwich :—

"That the Upper House of Convocation be invited to concur with this House in a humble petition to Her Majesty, that she will be pleased to appoint a Commission to consider whether the Book of Common Prayer may not be better adapted than it now is to the circumstances of the Church, *without the omission of the smallest portion of its present contents*,* namely—

"1st.—By some modification of the Rubric, so as to dispense with certain repetitions which occur in the public services as at present used.

"2nd.—By enlarging, and in some instances altering, the Table of appointed Lessons.

"3rd.—By a re-arrangement of the Psalter, *and substitution of the Bible version for that of Cranmer*.*

---

* The words printed in *italics* were omitted when the motion was actually submitted to the House, March 14, 1861. See the Dean's Speech, Hatchard, 1861.

"4th.—By the use of but one creed at each public service—the Apostles' or Nicene Creed—except on Trinity Sunday, when that of St. Athanasius may be read.

"5th.—By allowing the officiating minister, at his discretion, to transfer the Litany or Communion Service from the morning to the afternoon or evening; and by the addition of certain prayers or services—for humiliation, thanksgiving, home and foreign missions, and other special occasions.

"The Commission to be strictly required to confine itself to the above and such other points as may be specially submitted to it by Her Majesty; and on no account whatever to interfere with the doctrines of the Church as contained in her Articles, Canons, and Liturgy."

This is an important document, and we are glad to have the opportunity of inserting it in these Letters, which profess *inter alia* to give an historical record of the present movement in the Church. The Dean is a man of mark, and has the merit of being one of the earliest and most consistent advocates of Liturgical Reform, *within certain prescribed limits*. His discourse upon Convocation, delivered before the Archbishop of Canterbury a year or two ago, was a very able production; and we entirely agree with the author that in order to command the respect of the country, it is expedient that that "nebulous and eccentric body" (as the *Times*, not the Dean, calls it) should address itself to the real practical evils of our system, instead of occupying itself in discussing recent acts of the Legislature.

We are sorry we cannot go quite so far with the Dean on the present occasion. We think he has unnecessarily hampered his Commission by conditions, which would to a great extent defeat the ends for which it is required.

In the words of our motto of to-day, "nothing is so incautious as doing nothing." The principle upon which the Dean would proceed is that of *festina lente;* a very good one, provided you move at all. Whereas, under the restriction of insisting on "the omission of not even the smallest portion of the contents of the Prayer-book," it is easy to see how little could be done towards removing those defects which are, after all, the real grievance, and which, with many, constitute the main ground for inquiry.

Again, by stipulating that the Commission should confine itself to certain prescribed limits, and "on no account interfere with the doctrines of the Church of England as contained in her Articles, Canons, and Liturgy,"—we should be leaving all that portion of the public who are calling for investigation into certain Romanising practices of the day as dissatisfied as ever. They will say that they have not had a hearing; and that until they *are* heard, they will make their voices echo with a louder and yet a louder strain.*

We are convinced, therefore, that the proposition of the Dean, though designed with the best intentions, would fail in securing the desired end. While therefore, accepting the first, second, and fourth clauses as far as they go, we cannot but rejoice that the motion, in its present state,† did not come before Convocation at its late session.

With regard to clause No. 3—while we think the present *arrangement* of the Psalter might be materially improved, especially on the Sunday,—we are not prepared to substitute the balder version of the Bible for the more harmonious and popular one of Cranmer. We should prefer to see some passages in this last better rendered than they now are, and keep the remainder intact, out of tenderness to the public taste, which we are persuaded would cling tenaciously to the familiar version of the Prayer-book.

Clause No. 5 is one about which there cannot be much

---

* The Irish Church Synods have taken the matter boldly in hand for themselves, and have reformed their Prayer-book accordingly.

† The form of the motion was subsequently altered. See note, p. 351.

difference of opinion; but we wish even greater latitude were given, with permission to *alternate* the three several portions of the morning service; thus avoiding repetitions, relieving the clergyman as well as his flock, and affording that variety which is a law of all nature around us, and gives an ever-new character to the daily scenes and occupations of life.*

I remain, Sir, yours, &c.,

September 12, 1859. " INGOLDSBY."

LETTER LVIII.

THE RECTOR OF ST. GEORGE'S-IN-THE-EAST.

" Hæ nugæ seria ducunt
In mala."—HOR., *Ars Poet.* 451.
" Trifles such as these
At length to serious mischiefs lead."—FRANCIS.

SIR,—I question whether any single matter connected with the present controversy has done more to open the eyes of the public to the necessity of revising the rules and rubrics by which the Church is ordered than the absurd vestment squabble now raging in the parish of St. George's-in-the-East.†

Public opinion, the advice of his Bishop, and all the principles of decency and common sense seem set at defiance by an Oxford clergyman of about fifty years of age,—not a young inexperienced curate, but a rector of seventeen years' standing and twenty-three years in holy orders,—upon what

---

* We have reason to know that this view of the services is entertained by not a few of the most eminent of the High Church party, and has in many instances been acted on, whether with or without the *permission* of the Bishop, it is bootless to inquire.

† These disturbances, which commenced with the matter of the peculiar *dress* used by the officiating minister, in 1859, continued with more or less violence for above a year, and were only terminated at length by the Rector being compelled to quit his parish. See Letters LXIV.—LXVI.

grounds?—Let the readers of the *Clerical Journal, English Churchman,* and *Guardian,* if those three papers any longer resist a Revision of the Liturgy, take note, and be wise in time.* The ground upon which the Rev. Bryan King persists in maintaining, *aut per se aut per alios,* certain obsolete usages and grotesque vestments in the church of St. George's-in-the-East, is the *letter* of THE PRAYER-BOOK.

It is a matter with him (at least, so say his friends), not of arrogance and pride, not of a desire for notoriety, not of independence as against Episcopal authority, but—of Conscience. He has given his "unfeigned assent and consent" to every tittle of "that jewel, the Prayer-book," and by it, *coûte qu'il coûte,* he is resolved to abide. Nay, he defies,—after the example of his Master in Logic, Dr. Pusey,—bishops, churchwardens, the law and the Gospel, powers human, and powers divine, to shake his position so long as *that jewel* remains untouched.

Now this is a very serious matter if Mr. Bryan King is right; and we may conclude he is so, or he would surely not have been allowed to proceed thus long, single-handed, ignoring the public opinion, which, by unprecedented demonstration in his church, has been brought to bear against him.

I do not profess to be deeply learned in the details of ecclesiastical architecture, sedilia, altars, super-altars, reredoses, crosses, piscinæ, ambreys, and the like: still less do I enter with any degree of interest into the millinery department† of chasubles, albs, stoles, maniples, dalmatics, anti-

---

* From whatever cause, it is certain that the tone of these three papers became much modified soon after this date. The *Clerical Journal,* indeed, veered ultimately round to the side of the Revisionists.

† The following, from a tract entitled "How Popery is Brought In," is worth preserving:—

"The Pope's Church hath all things pleasant in it to delight the people withal: as for the eyes, images gilded, painted, carved most finely, copes, chalices, crosses of gold and silver, banners, &c., with relics and altars; for the ears, singing, ringing, and organs piping; for the nose, frankincense

pendiums, fringe, lace, red, white, green, black, or blue; or the other paraphernalia of a mediæval altar—pede cloths, corporals, candlesticks, and so forth.

But there are, unfortunately for the peace of the Church, those within her pale who think more, it would seem, of such trifles than they do of the weightier matters of the law,—judgment, mercy, and truth. So when a certain rector, or rector's deputy, appears during divine service, in a London parish, habited not in an ordinary linen surplice, with the graceful appendages of scarf and University hood, but "in a *yellowish white cloak, fastened close round his neck*, with trimmings consisting of *broad gold lace* embroidery, and a cross woven in the back;" and when, upon a tumult being raised in consequence, the conduct of the said *priest* is defended upon the ground that he "*was vested as every clergyman of the Church of England is statutably bound to be*, in the 'ornaments of the minister,' *as directed in the Book of Common Prayer;*"* I think a case is made out at least for INQUIRY, if not for alteration or better definition of the law in question.

The Rubric upon which all this "miserable controversy" (as Bishop Tait calls it) turns, is this :—

---

sweet; holy water of their own hallowing and making; priests, an infinite sort; masses, trentals, dirges and pardons. BUT WHERE THE GOSPEL IS PREACHED, THEY KNOWING THAT GOD IS NOT PLEASED BUT WITH A PURE HEART, THEY ARE CONTENT WITH AN HONEST PLACE APPOINTED TO RESORT TOGETHER IN, A PREACHER TO THE PEOPLE, A DEACON FOR THE POOR, A TABLE FOR THE COMMUNION, WITH BARE WALLS OR ELSE WRITTEN WITH SCRIPTURES—HAVING GOD'S ETERNAL WORD SOUNDING ALWAYS AMONGST THEM IN THEIR SIGHTS AND EARS."—*Pilkington, Bishop of Durham; died* 1575. W. T. Gibson, 12, Haymarket, London, S.W., 1878.

* See Letter of the Reverend John Purchas (author of the "Directorium Anglicanum") to the *Times*, August 31, 1859, defending the dress worn at St. George's-in-the-East by the officiating clergyman in the early stage of the riots. On the death of this gentleman, Oct. 18, 1872, a requiem mass was celebrated at his church in Brighton *for the repose of his soul*. See on this last subject, " QUOUSQUE," p. 8. Longmans, 1873.

"And here is to be noted, that such Ornaments of the Church, and of the Ministers thereof, at all times of their Ministration, shall be retained, and be in use, as were in this Church of England, by the authority of Parliament, in the second year of the reign of King Edward the Sixth."

It might be very well to lay down such a law, and possibly to enforce it, two or three hundred years ago, when some definite rule was needful to distinguish between the contempt of all ecclesiastical apparel on the part of the Genevan school on the one hand,* and the attempt to retain all the practices of the Romish priesthood on the other. It might also have been a matter of indifference some twenty years ago to let this Rubric rest in peace like many of its brethren, when there was no appearance of Romanism, as an active principle, amongst us. The Laity and the great body of the Clergy might have been well content to regard as *obsolete* and *harmless* what they would have long ago eradicated, had it been found productive of serious inconvenience.†

---

* Bishop Hooper's objection to the canonical habits in 1550 is well known. See Short's *History of the Church*, vol. i., § 321.

† As one specimen out of many of the excesses to which this matter of the *Vestment Rubric* ran about that time, the following is perhaps worth putting upon record :—

A MIDNIGHT SERVICE AT ST. MICHAEL'S, BRIGHTON.

"A Constant Reader" sends to the *Sussex Daily News* the following account of Christmas-eve proceedings in the above-named church:—

When I entered, twelve candles in two rows were being lighted by a robed figure ; two high tapers were already alight, one on each side of the reredos. The organist passed, surpliced, bowing to the altar, to his seat. Then issued from the vestry door sounds of chanting,—"O come, all ye faithful," then a *priest*, in scarlet cassock, amber and white satin vestments, bearing high a gilt cross and crucifix. As this passed down one aisle and up the nave, some of the congregation bowed their bodies in its direction, lowly. After it followed ten or twelve boys in scarlet cassock and surplice, then men choristers in surplices, then a priest in cowl and cope, then the Rev. C. Beanlands with brown velvet cowl (or what looked like a monk's hood thrown

But that the case is different now, I imagine few will deny. And I shall be surprised if we do not find the Bishop of London admitting, when next the question of Liturgical Reform is brought forward, that, on the matter of "the vestments" at any rate, he has become a convert to the necessity for some modification of the *litera scripta* of the Prayer-book. And as we are told that one change, even the minutest, in the sealed Book, involves an appeal to Parliament, we trust his lordship will no longer stand in the doubtful position he at present occupies, but at once give his voice and vote in favour of a Royal Commission of Inquiry. I remain, Sir, yours, &c.,

September 27, 1859. "INGOLDSBY."

LETTER LIX.

CORRESPONDENCE BETWEEN LORDS LYTTELTON AND EBURY.[*]

"Mobilitate viget, viresque acquirit eundo."—VIRGIL.

SIR,—The above motto, which I adopted three or four years ago on the title-page of one of my early pamphlets on

---

back), white and amber satin robe with embroidered cross reaching to the extremities of the dress. On this broad cross was embroidered the nude figure of the crucified Saviour. After the procession had passed into the chancel, *the three priests knelt, one behind the other*, on the altar steps, from time to time with their backs to the people, and in front of the altar, chanting what I found was the Communion Service, though it was unintelligible, except in the Gospel, when, at the words, "The Word was made flesh," low bowing took place, as also at several other parts of the service. Although very little of the reading or chanting was to be understood, there was evidently much not to be found in the Prayer-book. Very many English Church people have an idea that Ritualism is simply an excess of music and decoration. Most desirable would it seem that those who think thus should see for themselves its development, as in this case. *Image worship, mummery, priestcraft, hollowness*, are, *must be*, evident to every one who will once undertake the painful task of attending such a service. (1874.)

[*] The correspondence was published in the *Guardian*, Sept. 7th, 1859.

the Revision question, is again brought to mind by finding that I have to make my selection week by week from half-a-dozen publications connected with this matter, and all more or less deserving attention.*

Lord Lyttelton's is a new name as connected with this controversy; and it is bare justice to add that no Layman has a fairer claim to be heard in the matter. His Academical distinction was of the first order, and his classical attainments are known to be very considerable. Since leaving the University he has distinguished himself in the ranks of theological literature by an edition of the Gospels and Acts with explanatory notes, calculated for the edification of the general reader, and evincing in his Lordship sincere piety and reverence for things holy.†

When, therefore, such a one steps forward as an opponent of Lord Ebury, it is important to distinguish how far he agrees, and how far he disagrees, with the last-mentioned nobleman, whose piety is disputed by none; and whose regard for things holy is best appreciated by those who are most intimate with his private life.

To confine this letter to the shortest compass, consistently with the nature of the case, I shall exhibit Lord Lyttelton in the first place as agreeing, in the second as wholly or partially disagreeing, with Lord Ebury.

1. Lord Lyttelton admits that "abstractedly he does not object *to any amount of alteration* in the Liturgy."

This admission at once severs him from the *finality* men, represented by the Bishops of Oxford, Salisbury, and Exeter (Wilberforce, Hamilton, and Philpotts).

2. Lord Lyttelton does not approve of Convocation as it

---

* The number of these, advertised from time to time by the Revision Association, amounted at that period to above a hundred.

† This unfortunate nobleman committed suicide, April 18th, 1876.

is; but observes, that "If the Church had a *reformed* Convocation—a *real* representation of clergy and laity—he would allow it perfect freedom, in full and fair discussion, to propound changes for the consideration of the *Crown and of Parliament.*"

This would, no doubt, satisfy most of the reasonable advocates for Revision; but his Lordship does not, I fear, establish a greater probability of obtaining this " real representation " than Lord Ebury does of obtaining his Royal Commission, which surely is a matter far *easier* of accomplishment than the former.

3. Lord Lyttelton thinks " there is much to be said in favour of Lord Ebury's intended motion for a ROYAL COMMISSION, to be confined to matters of convenience and order, and avoiding doctrinal points."*

For the practical difficulty involved in this view of the Commission, which has been urged by others—(I may instance Dean Pellew, and Archdeacon Musgrave)—I must refer my readers to a former letter.† Far better grant full powers *while you are about it*, and so cut off occasion for future agitation from those who would infallibly continue the outcry, and justly so, on the plea that they had not had so much as a hearing.

4. In his second letter, Lord Lyttelton admits that "*other results*" (though he denies that *peace* would be one) would be obtained by granting the Commission. By these " other results " I conceive are meant the removal of repetitions, shortening the present service, and some of the offices; improvement of the Calendar, reconciling conflicting rubrics, adaptation of others to the habits of the age, settlement of

---

* See on this view of the subject an able article in the *Church of England Monthly Review*, May, 1859.
† See Letter LVII., p. 353.

the vestment question, and several minor points, well known to those who have given their minds to the subject:—and, I ask, are not these things worth contending for, even though they should not result in *perfect peace* to the Church, which it seems hopeless to obtain, whether we belong to the movement party, or to those who cry out somewhat strangely, " Let *well* alone" ?

5. With regard to the *scope* of a Royal Commission, Lord Lyttelton is "disposed to admit that on general principles there is *no reason* at all why it should be *confined in any way*, if it be clearly understood that no liturgical changes are to be made except by proper Church authority."

What this means is rather ambiguous. Is Convocation understood by the term " proper Church authority," when we have just been told that it is *not* a " real representation of the Church"?—Or are the BISHOPS to be necessarily a consenting party before anything is done?—If so, what would have become of the Act of Uniformity under Elizabeth (the parent of our present one), which, we read, was "enacted by the Queen, with the assent of the LORDS (under that name, the spiritual Lords then in the House having *all of them opposed the enactment*), and of the Commons?"* Are the bishops in the nineteenth century to claim for their order a negative power in Church matters which was not conceded to them in the sixteenth ?

6. Finally, Lord Lyttelton sums up thus :—" If this point were duly settled, if it were fixed that the Commission were only to inquire, and that no enactment of any kind were to be made without Church authority, and if the Commission were fairly constituted, I, for one, will at least say this, that I

---

* See "Occasional Papers on Church Matters," by William Winstanley Hull, Barrister-at-Law, p. 5. London: Seeleys. Too much praise cannot be awarded to this gentleman, now called to his rest, for his exertions to remove the blemishes attaching to our generally excellent Book of Common Prayer.

think a *proposition for a general inquiry ought not to be lightly rejected*. A Commission appointed, and acting with no foregone conclusion, and *without restraint*, would be, as I conceive, unobjectionable in principle."*

This is the right view to take of the subject, and, but for the unlucky hitch about this undefined, undefinable, "Church authority," would be unexceptionable.

But we must now exhibit Lord Lyttelton as *differing* from Lord Ebury. And we believe we shall be doing the former full justice in saying that the main points of *difference* between the two may be summed up under the following heads:—

1. That the proposed measure will not tend to the *Peace* of the Church.

2. That the aim of the 463 "Clerical Petitioners" is *one-sided*.

To enter into this matter at length is neither my intention, nor my province, that I am aware of. I was not one of the 463, who, as Lord Ebury observes, are perfectly able to defend their own position;† and as Lord Ebury does not profess to identify himself with all their views, it is premature to pronounce how far his lordship may go with the Petitioners on the three points selected by Lord Lyttelton as distinguishing the readers of the *Record* from the readers of the *Guardian*.‡

But as for *Peace*, I am sure Lord Lyttelton must be as

---

* Mr. Disraeli once observed, in reference to the state of the Church:— "I am myself in favour of *free inquiry* on all subjects, civil and religious, with *no condition* but that it be pursued with learning, argument, and conscience."—Speech at Aylesbury, Nov. 15, 1861.

† The leader of these, the Rev. Philip Gell, has done so in a pamphlet entitled "Thoughts on the Liturgy," Wertheim, 1860. See also Fisher's "Liturgical Purity," p. 162, &c. Second Edition.

‡ This was written twenty years ago; it is due to the Petitioners to say that we believe Lord Ebury has since become a convert to their opinions.

well aware as any other man of common observation, how far remote from *that* is the present state of the Church. Why, therefore, dread an inquiry which offers even the smallest *hope* of removing the existing irritation, and can scarcely make things worse than they now are? Let Laymen, like Lord Ebury and Lord Lyttelton, meet with clergy of "no foregone conclusions" as elements of a Royal Commission of thirteen or fifteen members, and all experience would fail us if they did not do something to allay the present ferment in the Church. At any rate, so long as the controversy is conducted in the tone exhibited by the two noble Lords, upon whose views we have taken the liberty to comment thus freely, the example cannot but be of inestimable value, as showing that Churchmen can "agree to differ," and give each other credit for the best of motives, while possibly they may arrive at diverse conclusions.

I remain, Sir, yours, &c.,

Sept. 30, 1859. "INGOLDSBY."

LETTER LX.

LORD EBURY AND THE "MORNING POST."

"Diram qui contudit Hydram,
Notaque fatali portenta labore subegit,
Comperit invidiam supremo fine domari."—HOR. *Ep.* ii., i. 12.

SIR,—Amongst other anecdotes of the Bar, I have heard of a certain junior, who, being at a loss to reply upon a weak case, applied to his leader for instructions, and received for answer—" Oh, abuse the plaintiff's attorney!" It is upon this principle, I suppose, that your High Church contemporary, the *Morning Post*, has indulged its readers with an article in disparagement of Lord Ebury, as the acknowledged leader of a party seeking a Revision of the Prayer-book.

Lord Ebury is simply meeting the fate of all Reformers,* from the good old days of

"Romulus, et Liber pater, et cum Castore Pollux,"

down to the more recent era of Cobden, Bright, Roebuck, and Lord John Russell. Luther, Oliver Cromwell, and a few more in their generation, passed through the same fiery ordeal, the only effect of which was to prove that they were made of genuine metal, and of sterner stuff than to be turned aside from their fixed purpose by anile fears and the malignant tongues of envious inferiors.†

Observe, I hold no brief to defend his lordship against his caluminators, who have now, for the second time, let fly their envenomed arrows at his head in the dark columns of your courtly contemporary. But as I know a little of his lordship's domestic habits, and the high esteem in which he is held for piety, charity, and true nobleness of mind, I think it but fair, in his temporary absence on the Continent, to say a word in reply to the unfounded representations of his anonymous traducer.

Can that man, then, be an enemy to religion, (as he is assumed by the writer in question to be,) who, principally at his own cost, has granted the land for, and built and endowed a church and parsonage, of approved ecclesiastical character, within two miles of a populous village near his residence, where the spiritual accommodation of the neighbourhood was previously insufficient; who himself daily performs the office of chaplain to his household, using for the

---

* Whether in Physic, Law, or Divinity, "every true belief has had its martyrs, and the attack has naturally been first directed against those who have been eminent in position, and remarkable for zeal and ability."—*History of Homœopathy* (to which the present writer has twice owed his life).

† "Urit enim fulgore suo, qui prægravat artes
Infra se positas; extinctus amabitur idem."—Hor., *Ep.* ii., i. 13.

"He knew that for *envy* they had delivered Him," was the shrewd conclusion of one whom experience had taught something of human nature.

purpose the Liturgy of the Church of England, though not perhaps according to the strict rule of some of our modern theologians, who judge it high treason to "the Church" to deviate one iota from its prescribed schedule of "Matins and Evensong"? Is that man a dangerous counsellor in things pertaining to the edification of the people, who voluntarily undertakes the task (which we are told Lord Lyttelton also does) of teaching the adult youth of his tenantry in an evening school? Are such the signs of a traitor to the Gospel, and the pure doctrines of the Apostles? —We may look long and in vain for tokens like these in many who are loudest in their denunciations of his lordship, and open-mouthed in their laudations of that immaculate "jewel, the Prayer-book."

The fact is, Lord Ebury is half a century before his age. In another fifty years the reformation he is now inaugurating will be in full operation; and men will wonder as much at the retrospect of our present system, as we now do at the adoption by the Romanists of a tongue "not understanded of the people" for the purpose of conveying the blessed knowledge of the revealed Word of God.

Lord Ebury has allowed himself to be put at the head of a faithful band, who will not be deterred from their object by the sneers of the *Morning Post*. And the opponents of Liturgical Reform may rely upon it that they are mistaken if they think to succeed in their efforts to stay the present movement. They *may* possibly, by further resistance, give greater impetus to the impending changes;* but they have no more power to arrest them, than they have to stem the insetting tide of the Atlantic, or to forbid the sun running his appointed course in the heavens.

The men who have shown themselves for years proof

---

* This they have unquestionably succeeded in doing. The Revision sought for in 1878 is far more sweeping than that demanded in 1858.

against calumny, neglect, misrepresentation, and ridicule, when they stood almost alone, are not likely to shrink now that they are enrolled in an organised Association,* and are receiving encouragement from all parts of the Kingdom. We bid them go on and prosper: only warning them against divided counsels and internal dissensions. Success is certain to crown their efforts ere long; and the delay which has occurred will prove to have been not without its use, in giving consistency to their operations, and teaching them the value, not only of co-operation and combination, but, much more, of forbearance and Christian charity one towards another.   I remain, Sir, yours, &c.,

October 19, 1859.   "INGOLDSBY."

LETTER LXI.

THE BISHOP OF SALISBURY ON REVISION.

"It was a most refreshing event to my heart, that when Lord Ebury moved for a Commission, the Bishops were present in great numbers, and were unanimous in opposition to his motion."—*Charge by the Right Rev. Walter Kerr Hamilton, D.D.*, August, 1858, p. 53.

SIR,—The charge from which the above extract is taken is the second delivered by the present Bishop of Salisbury. The primary one was published in 1855; and amongst other matters contains, at p. 26, the following quotation from the writings of one of his lordship's predecessors (Bishop Burgess, we believe):—

"Parliament being a mixed assembly of all who profess and call themselves Christians, it is perhaps better to tolerate *almost any amount of abuse in the Church*, than to seek

---

* Association for Promoting a Revision of the Book of Common Prayer and a Review of the Acts of Uniformity.   President, Lord Ebury. 17, Buckingham Street, Adelphi, W.C.

the removal of it through legislation which *may be exercised in a spirit not derived from the Church."*

It will occur to some of our readers, how the same sentiment was conveyed by the Bishop of Lincoln to his clergy last autumn,* when we took the liberty of questioning the policy of thus distrusting the National Legislature in matters affecting the Church.

At p. 37, we recognise the celebrated apophthegm of the Bishop of Oxford, quoted from St. Augustine, on Lord Stanhope's motion for removal of the State Services from the Prayer-book† :—

"Ipsa mutatio consuetudinis, etiam quæ adjuvat utilitate, novitate perturbat."

Are these two prelates aware that they have been anticipated in the adoption of this sentiment by the notorious Dr. Gauden, so far back as 1660; that divine having made use of the authority of this "greatest Father of the Latin Church" to stem the Revision contemplated in his day? In spite, however, of his opposition, and that of most of the Bishops of the period, 600 changes were introduced into the volume; *which very changes* the present Bishops of Oxford and Salisbury are so much enamoured of, that they will not hear of the book being again *touched!*

The same Ancient Father has elsewhere said, *Inculcanda repetenda,*—to which principle we presume we are indebted for this repetition of the extreme danger of meddling. To what extent the Bishop of Salisbury adopts the sentiment, may be inferred from the following extract from his charge, worthy of being engrossed as a rider to the words of St. Augustine.

After warning his clergy on no account to deviate from the established rules of the Church, his lordship proceeds :—

"Such conduct would place me in a position of having

---

* Letter XL., p. 265. † Letter XXI., p. 152.

to *undo* things *which have been acceptable to the parishioners*, and may in themselves *be working for good!*"

If the southern clergy are such "willing bondsmen" as to bow to this dictum of their superior, we should be wasting both oil and labour in seeking amongst them for support in favour of Lord Ebury's movement.* We have the satisfaction, however, of knowing that in other parts of the king-

---

* The following appeared in the *Ecclesiastical Gazette* for Sept. 1860:—

"*Diocese of Salisbury.*—The first united meeting of clergy and lay consultees for the deanery of Bridport was held on Tuesday, 21st August. The question *submitted to the meeting by the Bishop* was—'Whether it would be desirable at the present time to make any alterations in the Book of Common Prayer? the following alterations having been suggested in various quarters:—

"'1. Alterations in the Rubrics.
"'2. Alterations in the Calendar of Lessons.
"'3. Division of the present Morning Service.
"'4. Shorter Services for Week Days.
"'5. A distinct Sunday Evening Service.
"'6. Occasional Services, as for Harvest Thanksgiving, Missions, &c.'

"A resolution was proposed and seconded, 'That whilst deprecating any interference with the doctrine of the Prayer-book it is the opinion of this meeting that a revision of the calendar and rubrics by Convocation, if the license of the Crown can be obtained for that purpose, is now desirable.' This was negatived by a majority of 16 to 12 clergy, and 13 to 2 laity."

The form in which the Synod was convoked is here subjoined:—

"Dear Sir,   "Bridport, July 31st, 1860.

"A meeting of the Clergy and Lay Consultees for the Deanery of Bridport is proposed to be held at the National School-room, Gundry Lane, Bridport, on Tuesday, August 21st, at half-past one o'clock, which it is hoped you will be able to attend.

" Divine Service at eleven o'clock, with Holy Communion.

"We remain, Dear Sir, your obedient Servants,

"L. Foot,
"Alex. Broadley,
"Thomas Sanctuary,
"R. S. Hutchings, } Rural Deans.

"The subject *proposed by the Bishop* for consideration will be found on the other side" (as above).

"Luncheon at one o'clock."

dom the bishops have rather encouraged than otherwise the attempts that have been made of late by some of the clergy to adapt the services to the feelings and accommodation of their parishioners; and it will only require a few more years of toleration on their lordships' part, to make those usages general, which are now exceptional and experimental.*

We cannot, however, be surprised at the stern conduct of this Draco of the nineteenth century, when we meet with the following passage in his Charge of 1855 (pp. 50-51):—

"I feel that the blood of the Apostles (so to speak) is in my veins, and that by it I have been ennobled. . . . . I fear not to say that I have received, by the putting on of Apostolic hands, the spirit of power, and of love, and of a sound mind."

No wonder that under such a persuasion he should, in his Charge of last autumn, thus address his reverend brethren (p. 31):—

"I do again, my brethren, as I did in my first charge, most seriously advise you (indeed, I dare not be silent) to have *daily service* in your churches."

There is plenty here, no doubt, of the "spirit of power;" but how far that of "*love*, and of *a sound mind*," is also exhibited, we leave those to judge who have seen the *working of all attempts to revive the daily service* (as advocated by a few other bishops) *in country villages!* And as for its utility even in towns, let any one who would see the fruits of thus striving to revive an antiquated custom, take the trouble of walking any morning, about half-past eight, into a church not a hundred yards from the National Gallery, and witness (as we have repeatedly done) some five or six persons, besides the curate and a *boy clerk*, forming

---

* The author has acted on his own responsibility in this respect, with the entire approval of his congregation, for the last twenty years. (1878.)

the congregation at "*matins*," out of a population of nearly 20,000 souls, besides the casual passers-by, and then let him say if this be not to make darkness visible; to expose the nakedness of the land; to prove, in fact, either that the daily service had better be discontinued altogether, or that the Book of Common Prayer should be so altered as to adapt the service to the circumstances and habits of the age.*

Not so, however, thinks the Bishop of Salisbury. On the contrary, he proceeds, shortly after the above paragraph, to give utterance, in the exuberance of his joy, to the words with which we have prefaced these remarks, and with which we shall conclude:—

"It was a most refreshing event to my heart, that when Lord Ebury moved for a Commission, the Bishops were present in great numbers, and were *unanimous in opposition to his motion.*† . . . . We possess such a treasure in that book, and in it, amidst all our differences, such a bond of *union*, ... such lively affection is felt by rich and poor, young and old, learned and unlearned, for that inestimable inheritance which we have received from our forefathers, that they dread lest we should, in attempting to improve it, run risks very disproportionate to any advantage we could gain by a change."

If this be so—if rich and *poor*, learned and *unlearned*, *young* and old, are so attached to this "inestimable treasure," —how comes it that his lordship is compelled to make the following admission in the course of the same Charge?—

---

* Even in Cathedrals the daily service is practically a failure, which has led to its having been called by Coleridge the "Petrifaction of religion."

† In his Charge of 1861 the Bishop of Salisbury thus expressed himself: "The resolution of the House of Peers in the matter was most encouraging. Not one noble lord who was present when the subject was brought forward could be found to second Lord Ebury's proposition." On May 27th, 1862, the number of Bishops present at the debate on Lord Ebury's renewed motion was reduced to seventeen.

"Why is it that our children, after leaving our teaching, go in so many instances, without any scruple, to the Meeting-house instead of to the Church?"

Why, indeed?—We pause for a reply—which we think it will puzzle the united wisdom of Lord Ebury's opponents to furnish, in any other intelligible form than *that the Common Prayer-book and services of the Church are not what they might be,* and what they ought to be, in order to *retain* the affections of the "young, poor, and unlearned," when at liberty to think and act for themselves.

I remain, Sir, yours, &c.,

Nov. 3, 1859. "INGOLDSBY."

LETTER LXII.

THE TIMES NEWSPAPER AND THE BISHOP OF CHESTER.

"Gratiano speaks an infinite deal of nothing—more than any man in all Venice. His reasons are as two grains of wheat hid in two bushels of chaff; you shall seek all day ere you find them, and when you have them, they are not worth the search."—*Merchant of Venice.*

SIR,—Milton, it is clear, is quite wrong. It is a mistake to suppose that the day of oracles is gone by.* So long as the English public allows itself to be represented by the *Times* newspaper, so long will the Apollo of that mighty shrine continue to utter his vaticinations in "words deceiving." Not that the oracle is itself deceived; it is too clever for that. But it knows the weak side of its worshipper, the indolent Demus, and acts accordingly. "*Populus vult decipi,*" says the organ of Printing-house Square,—"*et decipiatur.*"

---

* "The oracles," says Milton, "are dumb;—
  No voice or hideous hum
Runs through the archèd roof in words deceiving:
  Apollo from his shrine
  Can no more divine,
With hollow shriek the steep of Delphi leaving."

Whether the Bishop of Chester (Graham), sometime Master of Christ's College, Cambridge, and in those days notorious as a Church or Chapel Reformer, is in league or not with the occupants of the Temple, I will not pretend to say. We all know that in the olden time the priestess, sitting on her boiling tripod, was aided by a prompter behind the scenes; and so it may be now. At any rate the coincidence is curious, that on the 27th of October we have in the *Times* the somewhat unusual sacrifice of a whole column to the Bishop's opinions on Church Questions as set forth in a recent charge to his clergy, followed up, *within four days, by a leading article* of more than a column's length, in laudation and adoption of the same.

We have read carefully both the extract and the leader, and have come to the conclusion, that a greater amount of " nothing " was never, probably, since the days of Gratiano, delivered in so many words.

Some people have this happy art in a remarkable degree, and the Bishop of Chester may be one of them. An art, valuable indeed, and allowable enough in the *Times*, having in its vocation to cater day by day for millions of people incapable of thinking for themselves, and equally incapable of digesting the strong meat of original thought or depth of argument. But for a bishop,—who visits his clergy *but once in three years*,[*] and has then the privilege of addressing a highly-educated audience, many of them of powers of mind equal, if not superior, to those of the speaker,—we hold it to be unpardonable to occupy the time of his victims for a full hour[†] in telling them what they all knew perfectly well

---

[*] In the diocese of Norwich the episcopal visitation is happily held only once in seven years, a custom apparently continued since the days of Parker. See Hook's *Life of Archbishop Parker*, Chap. xiii.

[†] Some Bishops' Charges have been known to occupy three hours in the delivery. Their lordships now, wisely, *divide* their Charges.

before; bidding them to be good boys, "preach shorter sermons,"* read the service slowly and distinctly, and *let the Prayer-book alone.*

This might be all very well, "*sub rege Medo;*" when bishops *lauded* it with impunity over Christ's inheritance; and when it was as much as a poor clerk's place was worth to speak or think for himself.† But do the Bishop of Chester and the *Times* seriously believe that the clergy of the nineteenth century are to be thus gagged, and led captive at the apron-string of their triennial monitor? We have a different opinion of some of them; and though we believe them ready, for the most part, and desirous to aid the bishop in every good work, we also believe they have far too much self-respect to be put down by a stream of words, blandly delivered, full of oil and honey, "signifying nothing."‡

And now for the *Times.* We rejoice to have that popular organ so far on our side as to hear it proclaiming that it has "*strongly advocated at various times* the expediency of certain alterations in the order of the Church Service, and the allowance of some shorter form of Sunday service than the one we at present have; and that it continues, and *will continue,* to press this point."

So far, so good. Indeed, some three years ago such an admission from "the leading journal" would have been hailed

---

* The Bishop's words were, "If, in the ordinary Sunday morning service, there is any real cause for shortening its duration, I should myself, if engaged in parochial duties, seek to *meet the exigency by confining my sermon within narrower limits,* particularly on Sundays when the Sacrament of the Lord's Supper is administered."—*Charge of John Graham, Bishop of Chester,* Oct., 1859.

† Doctor Balguy, we are told in Hoadly's Memoirs, was repeatedly warned by the Bishop against publishing anything which "might prejudice his chance of preferment." We are not sure that the times are much improved in this respect as far as the clerical profession is concerned.

‡ The bishop, as Master of Christ's College, Cambridge, was conspicuous for this art beyond any individual known to the author.

with delight. But, as is usual with those who resist a reasonable reform until it can be resisted no longer, the good word of the *Times* in this matter is now coldly received; and its readers rather question the expediency of closing the door against further concession, than thank the tardy donor for what has been extorted by sturdy and obstreperous knocking. Is this, they ask, to be all?—Why may not *some other* of the demands of the Revisionists be attended to, and accepted or rejected "upon the merits," not upon the *ipse dixit* of the *Times* or the Bishop of Chester?—We do not profess to endorse *the whole* of those demands. We do not believe that Lord Ebury, whose "objects" even the *Times* recognises* as "practical," professes to endorse the whole of them. But we are sure that neither the noble lord, nor the British public, whether at home or in the colonies, will rest satisfied with merely "abbreviated services," though they may be encouraged to persevere in their thankless task by having extorted so much from their spiritual rulers.

If it be true that "there are expressions in the Liturgy which *cannot* be accepted by *anybody* in their strictly literal sense—which *nobody*, High Church or Low Church, *does* understand in their literal sense—and which *nobody accepts as obligatory*,"—then does the *Times* itself make out an argument, stronger than all its professed assertions to the contrary, for the expediency of Revision, notwithstanding the dangers which, according to the Bishop of Chester, *might* attend the operation.

I have the honour to be, Sir, yours, &c.,
Nov. 9, 1859. " INGOLDSBY."

---

* In a letter to Edward Webster, Esq., August 16, 1861, Lord Ebury observes, " Without entering into the merits of the advanced views you have put forward, of this I am sure, that the statement of them by a member of our Council will prejudicially affect the gaining of those *smaller Reforms of which alone we* have now some slight hope."

LETTER LXIII.

LITURGICAL REVISION AND CHURCH REFORM.[*]

"Embryos and idiots, eremites and friars,
White, black, and grey, with all their trumpery."
MILTON.

SIR,—It is stated by Macaulay, that, prior to the issue of the Royal Commission of 1689, the booksellers' stalls groaned under the weight of tracts written on *both sides* of the question of a Revision of the Prayer-book.

The main difference between the circumstances of those times and the present, is, that whereas the Press has teemed of late with able treatises in *favour* of Revision, there has not appeared as yet so much as a single pamphlet deserving the name of a Reply to any of these.[†] Is it because they are unanswerable? If so, why are not the remonstrances of so many independent witnesses attended to? If capable of an answer, why does not some champion step forth from the ranks of the statu-quoists, and expose the unreasonableness of these repeated demands? Certain it is that, up to the present period, it has been, as it were, a revived "Battle of the Books," in which, however, the combatants are in respect of numbers most unequally matched.

The pamphlet now lying before us consists of thirty pages, in the form of a letter addressed to the Prime Minister as adviser of Her Majesty the Queen in all matters affecting the welfare of her subjects, amongst which the conditions of public worship may be justly reckoned. It is dedicated to

---

[*] A Letter to Lord Palmerston, by the Hon. and Rev. Atherton Legh Powys, M.A. Hatchard, 1859.

[†] Since the above was written, some half-dozen publications have appeared feebly defending the *statu quo* of the Prayer-book, while at least five times that number have issued on the other side.

Lord Ebury, as the champion of Liturgical Reform, "to whose honesty of purpose, zeal, perseverance, and discretion, the advocates of that measure look, under Providence, for ultimate success in that all-important work."

It would be difficult to do justice to this able little tract by any attempt at abbreviation. One of its greatest merits is the terseness and point with which it is written,—qualities which would be lost in any epitome.

Suffice it to say, that the author (who is brother to Lord Lilford and the Bishop of Sodor and Man) enters upon his task with spirit, and the independence of one who has nothing to gain or lose from the productions of his pen. He goes straight to his object, the face of his enemy, like Cæsar's soldiers at the battle of Pharsalia; he hits hard, and leaves the scars deep and lasting. The weapons he uses are partly argument, partly ridicule, according to the spirit of his motto,

"Ridiculum acri
Fortius et melius magnas plerumque secat res."

"For Ridicule will frequently prevail,
And cut the knot when graver Reasons fail." *

This art Mr. Powys thoroughly understands, and we can imagine the smile which would curl the lip of our ever-blooming Premier (Palmerston), if he found time to glance at the following graphic illustration of an historical event of the last ten years:—

. . . . "So have I seen, my lord, on the surface of the extensive warren near my rustic home, swarms of grey and black conies disporting themselves of an evening at the lord of the manor's cost—(more frequently, I fear, at the tenants')—*on the first report of a distant fowling-piece* give each other one hasty glance, and then in an instant turn their guilty

---

* Letter XIX., p. 130.

tails, pop into their burrowed homes, and vanish as if they had never been. Even thus of these curious fowl, bred under other skies, and hatching their eggs on English ground, the flight below was as instantaneous, ludicrous, and magical. But their dusky plumage is only *folded and laid by* for sunnier days in the Church of England's future; while their temper is not sweetened by the hearty kick that warned them off the pavement, and told them to 'move on.'"

"They are gone below to concoct another plot, and that is, to *poison the sources of education and religion*, by tampering with the press, the pulpit, the universities,* and the schools, till the time arrives when a *practicable breach can be made*, and the besieging force can again advance with greater probability of success."

But what connexion, it may be asked, have these insignificant little creatures, "white, black, and grey," with the object of these Letters, and the pamphlet under review? He must be simple indeed, who, after the scenes now being enacted at St. George's-in-the-East, (and of which we have but as yet seen the beginning,)† does not recognise in the above that undermining spirit of ever-restless Rome,‡ *semper*

---

* This has been effectually done for the last twenty years.

† The riots, to which the mummeries at that Church led, are now happily terminated; but we regret to say that similar practices have been elsewhere adopted with comparative impunity.

‡ The following lines appeared in the *Lincolnshire Chronicle* of August 17th, 1878, and are well worth the space they will occupy in this volume:—

"'No peace with Rome!' was once the shout
Of bravest hearts in times of yore;
'No peace with Rome!' the words rang out,
And echoed round from shore to shore.

'No peace with Rome!' our statesmen vowed,
As tyrant Popes they held in check;
'No peace with Rome!' men sang aloud,
When men were men, on land, on deck.

eadem, which, like the sly inhabitants of the woodlands, works in the dark places of the earth, in the still of moonlight, and at early dawn; and only ventures to show itself to the garish eye of day, when it can do so with safety, and with means to retire rapidly to its fastnesses on the first symptom of approaching danger. The black spirit or the white spirit, the red spirit or the grey, may, indeed, like the many-coloured denizen of the warren, have *seemingly* disappeared; but it is not clean gone. *Evasit, excessit, erupit;*—but it is still hard at hand, all ears, and all eyes, ready for the next favourable opportunity to reappear on the scene of its late devastation. And reappear it will, and resort again and again to its former mischief, unless, like Carthage of old, its strongholds are levelled with the dust, its foundations laid bare by the ploughshare, harrowed in, and "sowed with salt."*

We thank the honourable and reverend author for his lively contribution to the good cause, and in conclusion (to use his own most daring challenge), we confidently "defy his statements to be met, or his position to be turned."

    I remain, Sir, yours obediently,
Nov. 17*th*, 1859.   "INGOLDSBY."

  'No peace with Rome!' our Fathers said,
   Counting their lives not dear to them;
  'No peace with Rome!' though Bishops bled,
   And Clergy did the fire contemn.

  'No peace with Rome!' let's shout it still,
   Though craven hearts are in our land;
  'No peace with Rome,' till God fulfil
   The last dread doom with his own hand."
           WM. PARKER,
      Hanthorpe House, near Bourn, Lincolnshire.

* Judges ix. 45.

LETTER LXIV.

RELIGIOUS DISTURBANCES AT ST. GEORGE'S-IN-THE-EAST.

[The following letters are reprinted verbatim from the pamphlet in which they appeared at an early stage of the disturbances, which rose subsequently to such an alarming height as to require, at one time, the presence of not less than 400 policemen to keep the peace.]

"Pro re pauca loquar."—VIRGIL.
"A word spoken in due season, how good is it."—PROV. xv. 23.

SIR,—Understanding from my publishers that inquiry has been made after the two following letters, written at the commencement of the religious riots at St. George's-in-the-East, I am not unwilling that they should reappear in a more permanent form, if by any means their circulation may tend to set in its true light the origin of, and foundation for, the unhappy strife which has, alas! too long prevailed in those parts.

It has been the fashion very much to misrepresent the real character of this unprecedented struggle between a minister and his flock, carried on now with more or less of acrimony for well-nigh eighteen years.* On the one hand, it has been treated as the act of a "lawless and irreligious mob,"† setting all decency and order at defiance, scrupling not to desecrate the House of God, and aiming ultimately at the destruction of the Established Church. On the other hand, we have had the clerical actors in the scene represented as Papists, or Jesuits in disguise, seeking,

---

* The Rev. Bryan King was presented to the living of St. George's-in-the-East in 1842, from which time to the present (1859), more or less of dissatisfaction existed in the parish as to the mode in which the service of the Church was conducted.

† So called in an address to the Rev. Bryan King, published in the *Union* newspaper, December 24, 1859.

under the garb of the Anglican priesthood, to introduce into our Church all the abuses and chicanery of the Romish system; in fact, to undo the work of the Reformation, and bring back again that state of ecclesiastical affairs which existed under the Marian dynasty, with haply the single exception of fire and fagot.*

Now, as usual in most cases of bitter and prolonged controversy, the truth lies somewhere midway between these two exaggerated extremes. Both parties have been driven, in the course of the conflict, further than they probably either of them contemplated at the commencement. A great principle is now felt to be at stake; and each party considers himself to be the representative of that side which is diversely espoused and advocated in this matter through the length and breadth of the land. Men and angels are the spectators; the issue has become one of life or death to the respective combatants.

It was with a view to judge impartially, to the best of my ability, of the real merits of this question, freed from all the colouring of party representation, that I made it my business to be an eye and ear-witness of the mode in which the service was conducted at the above church in November last; when the riots were still comparatively in their infancy, and men and boys had not, as yet, been haled before the courts of law to answer for the part they had taken in the proceedings. The plain unvarnished tale I then delivered is nothing more than the evidence I should have been prepared to give at the time before a Committee of Inquiry, had I been examined as a disinterested witness in the case. The facts are uncoloured, the statements un-

---

* The obstinacy and pertinacity with which the chief actors in the scene persisted in carrying out their views, leads one almost to think that the fires of Smithfield are not yet altogether extinct in the *spirit* of the age, if they be so in the letter.

distorted; and at the interval of twelve months* I see no reason to alter or to recall a single word then written.

The question, therefore, resolves itself into a matter of dispassionate judgment as to which party is right and which is wrong; and it is with regret that I feel bound to give my deliberate verdict against my reverend brethren, the officiating clergy, on this occasion.

Are, then, the other party—the so-called "mob"—free from blame on their part? I think they were, in the first instance, under the very peculiar and, happily, isolated circumstances of the case. But as I am aware that my opinion here is at variance with that of many estimable people, both lay and clerical, I feel bound to explain myself more at large than would otherwise be necessary.†

In the first place, what I saw in November, 1859, was, to all outward appearance, anything but a mob. A more respectable-looking congregation of worshippers I never witnessed in any church. There was not, so to speak, (and more the pity,) a single meanly-dressed person in the church, which, towards the middle of the service, was crowded in the body, and nearly filled in the galleries, and must, therefore, I am told, have contained about 2,000 people. No act of personal violence was resorted to; yet there was a moral display of resistance to practices quite unusual, if not illegal, in the conducting of the worship of our Church, (the purport of which demonstration could not but have been understood by the officiating clergyman,) and by a discreet relinquishing of which it was apparent peace might have been then restored.‡

---

* Now twenty years, and my opinion is still the same. (1878.)

† It will be borne in mind that the Letters were written before the grosser acts of profanation which subsequently took place.

‡ "The beginning of strife is as when one letteth out water: therefore leave off contention, before it be meddled with."—Prov. xvii. 14.

Then comes the question of intoning and chanting—met on the part of the congregation by loud *saying*—the prayers and psalms. Is the former method of conducting this part of the service, it will be asked, to be given up at the cry of a " lawless and irreligious mob ? " I think it very possible that this point would not have been so vehemently objected to had it not been carried to a needless excess, and taken in connexion with the other manifest indications of a leaning towards Rome. The one has a kind of precedent in the immemorial custom of our cathedrals—(a custom, I would say, more honoured in the breach than the observance);* the other has none, that I am aware of. But, be that as it may, surely the minister of so important a parish as that of St. George's-in-the-East, with its population of 20,000, might have discovered that such a mode of conducting the service in his church was not calculated to win souls in those parts, however attractive it might be to the fashionable residents in the neighbourhood of Margaret Street or Belgravia. And one would have thought that common sense, not to say Christian charity, would have dictated the expediency of giving up one's own feelings in such a matter, (supposing one to think ever so strongly upon it,) to the wishes or even prejudices of so numerous and unenlightened a flock.

Finding, however, that such was not the case, nor likely to be so;—that private remonstrance, an empty church, repeated letters, both signed and anonymous, articles in almost all the papers, and, finally, a pastoral interview with his bishop,† had no effect whatever in diverting the rector from his determination to "win the day," and to establish,

---

* This is part of the " Petrifaction of Religion." See p. 370.

† One of the Rector's letters to his Bishop, bearing date Dec., 1860, concludes thus: " Even you, my lord, can scarcely be sanguine enough to imagine that I shall respect the acts of your late illegal aggression upon my return to my charge."—*Public protest, by the Rev. Bryan King.*

quo jure quâve injuriâ, his own ideal of public worship in this parish,—I cannot say that I was surprised, nor can I say that I was sorry—and I believe I speak here but as the echo of thousands (expressed by a small female voice which I heard in the gallery, "It *must* be put down, and it *shall*")—I cannot say that I was sorry that the congregation resorted to the dreadful, but only remaining, expedient of meeting will by will, obstinacy by obstinacy, and (so far as was within their power) force by force.

What, let me ask, would have been the alternative had they not done so? had they contented themselves, as, unfortunately, too many would have done in like circumstances, with a shrug of the shoulder, a systematic absence from their lawful church,* and a mere negative protest against that which they might have easily represented as no affair of theirs, or one, at least, where they were powerless to interfere for any good? These men thought otherwise, and acted otherwise, and, at the risk, nay, the certainty, of much misrepresentation, have stepped forward to prove that such things cannot be done, *and shall not be done*, with impunity in this free country of England.

No Popery, no semi-Popery, shall be tolerated here.† These men are not Puritans, as they have been called; they have no more sympathy with Geneva than they have with Rome. What they want, and what they will have,—these men of St. George's-in-the-East, and with them concur the great bulk of the people of England,—is the simple

---

* We regret to say that in other instances besides this, might be applied to the party, to which the Rector of St. George's-in-the-East belongs, the memorable saying of Galgacus respecting the *Romans* of *his* day:—
"Solitudinem faciunt, pacem appellant."
"They make a solitude, and call it peace."

† See "Scottish Episcopal Romanism, or Popery without a Pope," by the Rev. Richard Hibbs, M.A., pp. 48-9. Edinburgh, 1856.

Word of God plainly and intelligibly delivered, without the invention or the interpolation, the fancies or the follies, of man. They want, in short, and will have, religion, not priestcraft—the substance, not the shadow—the *spirit*, in short, not the *burlesque* of the Gospel. And are they for this to be branded as rioters, disturbers of the peace, outragers of the sanctity of the temple, profaners of the worship of God?—I trust not.

The alternative, I affirm without a moment's hesitation, would have been a fearful precedent for other ministers of religion (and they are unfortunately not wanting) to go and do likewise, after the approved and sanctioned fashion of St. George's-in-the-East.*

---

* It is *operæ pretium* to read the following letter, which appeared in one of the London papers in November, 1861:—

ST. PAUL'S CHURCH, BRIGHTON.

To the Editor of the Daily News.

SIR,—During a visit to Brighton, in October last, I was attracted to St. Paul's Church by the tolling of the bell at 7 o'clock, in the expectation of hearing the morning service, instead of which I found it was the celebration of what is called the holy Eucharist. To say nothing of the gaudy decorations and the candles burning on "the altar" (although not necessary for the purpose of affording light, and therefore reprehensible), I saw precisely what I have occasionally observed in a Popish chapel. The altar (not "the Lord's table," as prescribed by the Rubric) was covered with a richly embroidered cloth, and the officiating priest, with a scarlet scarf over the surplice, was kneeling before the altar, with his back towards the congregation, not "standing at the north side of the table," as prescribed also by the Rubric. Behind him I observed *another person in a surplice, kneeling also, but not in holy orders*, as I afterwards discovered, being only an assistant of the priest. The officiating priest remained in the same kneeling position for some time. I observed *eight females with veils over their heads* leaning forward almost as if prostrate on the ground, and two males, one of whom I thought was a clergyman, *making up, together with myself, the whole of the congregation*. The elements, covered with a scarlet cloth, were brought by the assistant from what is called "a credence table" to the priest, who in Popish style placed them upon the altar. Having done so, he resumed the former position, kneeling before the altar, with his back to the congregation. What then took place no one, I should think, but himself knew.

Many a suburban church, many a country village, would have had its Bryan King and his acolytes; the plague-spot would have spread far and wide through the land; the Church would have become first deserted, then despised, by the more spiritual of its congregation; and in due time a state of religion would have been extensively propagated, which it would have required a fresh Reformation, with all its attendant evils, to correct or counteract.

I then saw what appeared to be *the elevation of the host*, such as I have seen it in a Popish chapel. The paten, containing, as I supposed, the bread—or, it might have been the consecrated wafer—*held up in a superstitious manner, as if for adoration*, over the priest's head for three or four minutes, and then the cup, as I supposed, containing the wine, held up in a similar manner—such mummery as I never expected to see practised in our Protestant Church of England. There was a considerable pause whilst this was doing, but *although I was near I could not hear the sound of a voice.* There was something very objectionable in the whole of what I saw and heard. I spoke to one of the females as she came out of the church, remonstrating with her for encouraging such Popish practices.

I have briefly described what I witnessed in St. Paul's Church, but surely I have stated enough to show that the corporeal presence in the consecrated elements is inculcated by the priest in this church. I need not remind your readers that many of the founders of our English Reformed Church, such as Bishops Hooper, Ridley, and Latimer, in the reign of our Queen Mary, suffered at the stake because they would not believe in the corporeal presence in the sacrament. And nothing can be plainer than what is stated on this point in Article XXVIII. as the doctrine of our Protestant Church of England:—"The body of Christ is given, taken, and eaten in the Supper only after an heavenly and spiritual manner." The foregoing is a brief account of what I witnessed in St. Paul's Church, Brighton, on Wednesday morning, Oct. 9, and this is only *a sample of what is taking place in many other parish churches*. The question naturally arises in my own mind, and I have no doubt too in the minds of many of your readers, "Are the bishops in their respective dioceses aware that such Popish practices prevail ? If not, they ought to be informed; but if they are aware of such practices, surely they are bound to interpose their episcopal authority as far as possible, and put a stop to such semi-popery, which ought not to be tolerated within the pale of our Protestant Church of England. With a view to inform your readers of what I myself witnessed at St. Paul's Church, Brighton, I have sent my present letter, hoping you will give it a conspicuous place in your journal.
—I am, &c., D. TUCKER, Rector.
Sandon Rectory, near Royston, Nov. 18, 1861.

From this cheerless prospect the so-called "lawless and irreligious mob" of St. George's has (as far as rests with them) delivered us and our children. And if they have not altogether succeeded in their object, they have effectually prevented the triumph of their opponents, and put a check, which will be long remembered, to the stealthy progress of a system which, up to that period, was rapidly gaining ground in the kingdom; and whose ultimate tendency is to assimilate the Protestant worship of our churches to the more attractive and sensuous but less spiritual character of those of France, Italy, and Spain.

We trust, in conclusion, that Parliament will shortly interfere by some legislative enactment in such a manner as to render a recurrence of the scenes at St. George's impossible,* and so relieve other congregations from the painful position of either submitting to a form of worship which is hateful in their sight, or of being branded as disturbers of the peace, and enemies to religion, if they take measures to resist it.

I remain, Sir, yours, &c.,
November 18*th*, 1859. "INGOLDSBY."

LETTER LXV.

THE MORNING SERVICE AT ST. GEORGE'S-IN-THE-EAST.

"Principiis obsta: sero medicina paratur
Cum mala per longas invaluere moras."—OVID.

SIR,—Believing, as I have elsewhere said, that the follies which have been enacted at St. George's-in-the-East

---

* Lord Shaftesbury did introduce a Bill with this object in the Session of 1860, but it was not proceeded with at that time; and the encouragement these practices have since met with in high quarters has made it more than ever difficult to grapple successfully with them.

for now nearly two years, till they have at length reached a culminating point, have mainly contributed to convince the public, if not the bishops, of the necessity for *some* revision of the laws by which our Church polity is directed,* I made it my business, being in London, on Sunday morning last, to pay a visit to the scene of so much unfortunate notoriety.

Various accounts of the proceedings at this church have from time to time appeared in almost all the papers; but I am not aware that any report has yet been furnished by a clergyman, *eo nomine;* who, by the nature of his office, is best able to give an exact detail of the points in which the practice of this church differs from the ordinary English service as conducted in our other places of worship, whether in town or country. I purpose, therefore, being very minute, but, to the best of my ability, strictly accurate, in my description of what took place last Sunday; in order that, if any alteration of our laws should result (as I think not impossible) from this forcing of the letter of the Rubric to, or rather beyond, its extreme interpretation, it may remain on record what were the principal matters at issue between the so-called Protestant and the so-called Romanising party in this parish (and to a certain extent throughout the entire kingdom), in the middle of the nineteenth century.

The service began at eleven, and was not over until a quarter before one, *though no part of the Litany was read,* and the Communion not administered. I notice this in refutation of those who maintain that the "permission" to read the Litany in the afternoon has set at rest the question of the "abridgment of the Morning Service,"*—also as, by the way, an answer to Bishop Graham's theory that the real

---

* This point is very strongly put in the Tract entitled "Quousque," to which reference has already been made in Letter LVIII.

† See Letters v. to VII., pp. 25—43.

remedy for the evil lies in "shortening the sermon;"* the sermon in this case being only twenty-five minutes long, without any prayer before or after it in the pulpit.

The congregation consisted of decently dressed persons, most of them having the appearance of gentlemen, or the first class of tradespeople. They were almost all males; I did not see above thirty females, out of a congregation which, though comparatively scanty at first, could not have numbered much less than 2,000 before the close of the service. From twelve to fifteen policemen of the K division were stationed about the church at equal distances;† and outside the church was a much larger number of these officers, who, I suppose, have thus, for the first time in the history of the Church, been called into requisition for the support of the minister in the ordinary discharge of his duties.‡

The officiating clergyman was the Rev. C. F. Lowder, formerly curate of St. Barnabas, and now of the Mission Home, Wellclose Square. The Rev. Bryan King, the rector, was understood to be absent from illness. Mr. Lowder wore the dress which has been adopted since the late arbitration of the Bishop of London upon this point; consisting of a surplice with stiff collar, black stole or scarf, and scarlet hood; this dress was not changed at any part of the service. The prayers were intoned from the chancel, where the clergyman remained during the whole ministration, except for the short period when he ascended the pulpit. Ten or a dozen chorister boys were ranged opposite each other in this chancel, or rather apse, in front of the "altar." This last had the appearance

---

* See Letter LXII., p. 373.
† These were afterwards increased to from three to four hundred.
‡ A similar demand for their services subsequently took place in consequence of the disturbances at the Rev. Arthur Tooth's church at Hatcham, which became, in consequence, almost as notorious as St. George's-in-the-East (1875).

of a large cubical box, and was either painted or covered with some variously-coloured silk or other stuff; it was elevated from the floor by two or three steps, after the fashion of the diagram of Bishop Andrews' altar, as given in Archbishop Laud's handwriting in 1623.* On it were *two enormous candles*,† not lighted; and over it were several crosses in various devices, the largest being about five feet long and three feet broad, all of them, however, as far as I could observe, level with, or very slightly projecting from, the east wall.

The psalms were chanted, the organ accompanying; but here such a jargon of sounds arose from the mixed voices of those who *said* and those who *sang*, that it was utterly impossible to distinguish a note or word from beginning to end; and the same remark applies to the Te Deum, Jubilate, and both creeds, all of which were chanted by the clergy and choristers from the chancel.

The lessons were read from a high reading-desk (placed parallel with the pulpit in front of the chancel) by one of the choristers, a youth of sixteen or seventeen years of age; and, I regret to say, were read very indifferently—one unvaried, feeble, and unimpressive tone being adopted throughout. No public demonstration was made at this portion of the service, though to my mind it was the most distressing of the whole, as showing a disregard to the due delivery of God's Inspired Word, while so much importance was attached to forms, attitudes, and ceremonies of mere human invention.

The prayers which followed were still intoned from the

---

* See "Cogent Reasons for Revising the Prayer-book," by William Peace. London: Partridge, 1859. P. 21; where an extract upon this subject is furnished from the diary of Archbishop Laud. A similar "altar" (as used at Cuddesdon) was published in the *Rock*, October, 1878.

† This practice I have seen adopted by a Rural Dean in the diocese of Salisbury, the candles, which were a yard long, being removed to the Rector's *drawing-room* during the week on *account of the bats!*

chancel, some of the congregation *saying*, and some *intoning* the AMEN; the effect of which (to speak with reverence) was the more ludicrous, owing to the sharp, rapid manner in which the word was pronounced by some, as contrasted with the measured drawl in which it was lengthened out by others. It might be observed that the "intoners" were mostly provided with red-edged Prayer-books, of an uniform type or fashion, while the "sayers" had either ordinary Prayer-books or gilt-edged Church Services.

At the end of the third collect the 94th hymn was given out from a "hymnal," which was the signal for considerable hubbub in the congregation, accompanied with much coughing, scraping of feet, and opening and shutting of doors, which tokens of displeasure were largely increased upon the clergyman, at the conclusion of the hymn, ascending the steps of the "altar," at the north-west end, turning his back rapidly upon the congregation,* dropping on one knee, and receiving something from one of the choristers who attended him, and with whom he exchanged a few words in a low voice. This dumb show continued for about half a minute, when the clergyman returned to his former place in the chancel, at the south-west end, where the remainder of the prayers were again intoned as before, ending with the Prayer of St. Chrysostom and "the Grace of our Lord;" no part of the Litany being read.

That portion of the 119th Psalm which begins at the 161st verse, was then given out, called in the Latin *Principes persecuti sunt*—in our version, "Princes have persecuted me without a cause." This was once more the prelude to much coughing and other discordant noises throughout the church; increased, as before, upon Mr. Lowder's again ascending the

---

* A practice justly denounced by Sydney Smith, as making religion a system of "postures and impostures, circumflexions and genuflexions, garments and vestures, ostentation and parade."—*Memoirs*, vol. ii., p. 459.

north-west angle of the "altar," where he knelt,* and said the first two prayers of the Communion office in a subdued voice, and with his back to the congregation. These ended, he rose, and, turning to the congregation, recited the Ten Commandments in a kind of monotone, *without book*, the choristers and organ responding; while the congregation persisted, as on all occasions of this kind, in *saying*, " Lord, have mercy upon us," &c. He then, still facing the people, *shifted his position, by a side-long motion, to the south-west angle of the altar*, from whence he gave out the Epistle, and read it with marked emphasis, the passage being Eph. vi. 10—"My brethren, be strong in the Lord, and in the power of his might," &c.

The Epistle ended, by a *reversal of his former action*, he removed to his original position at the north-west angle of the altar, and gave out the Gospel; which over, he suddenly presented his back to the people, and commenced the Nicene Creed in a rapid key-note, followed by the organ and choristers, the people *saying* it; the result being the greatest amount of confusion that had been produced throughout the whole of this unhappy exhibition.

At this point I could not help noticing the distressed appearance of the poor old clerk, whose occupation was evidently completely gone.† He was a highly respectable man in appearance, of about sixty-five years of age, and occupied the clerk's usual place under the reading-desk, but took no part in the service from beginning to end,—not even, to the best of my observation, repeating the clerk's immemorial *rôle* of "Amen." Whether he were under orders to be silent, or whether he had his own opinions, and did not like to give offence to either party by seeming to side with one or the other, I cannot

---

* The Rev. F. G. Lee, in a letter to the *Times* of February 8, 1860, states that, "in every particular, the services at St. George's were in strict accordance with the plain law of the Prayer-book." Is this so?

† This functionary subsequently resigned his office, and no wonder!

say; but the effect was singular, to say the least of it, and methought could not but excite the comments of the rate-payers, who, amongst other items of the annual collection, have to provide for the salary of the parish clerk.

Yours, &c.,

November 19*th*, 1859.   "INGOLDSBY."

LETTER LXVI.

MORNING SERVICE AT ST. GEORGE'S-IN-THE-EAST.
(*Continued.*)

"Infelix, utcunque ferent ea faĉta minores."—VIRGIL.

"I pray you, in your letters,
When you shall these unlucky deeds relate,
Speak of me as I am; nothing extenuate,
Nor set down aught in malice: then must you speak
Of one, *acting not wisely.*"—*Othello.*

SIR,—My desire to relate minutely, though with strict adherence to facts, what took place on Sunday morning, the 13th inst., at St. George's-in-the-East, has necessitated the division of my subject into two letters; a circumstance which I think the occasion sufficiently justifies, the *facts* being thus put permanently on record, let the inference from them be what it may.

It is for this reason that I hope to stand excused in the judgment of all sensible men for departing for once in my life from the more congenial employment of a portion of the day of rest, and the solemn worship of our Common Maker. The question having now become a trial of strength, between the obstinacy of a few misguided individuals on the one hand, resolved to have all their own way, and the fixed determination of the vast mass of the British public, on the other, to arrest the stealthy inroads of Popery, under whatever guise,—any one who contributes by his evidence to put an end to this unseemly conflict can hardly be *neglecting* his Master's service, even if he be not thereby materially promoting it.

The Nicene Creed ended, Mr. Lowder published, from the N.W. end of the "altar," facing the people, the banns of marriage between some eight or ten couples.* Now we are told by Mr. Davis, in his last work on Liturgical Revision,† that "the publication of banns was ordered to take place *after the Second Lesson, instead of immediately before the Offertory,* by the Act of 26 George II., cap. 33," in accordance with which regulation the Rubric in my copy of the Prayer-book runs as follows:—" The banns of all that are to be married together must be published in the church three several Sundays, during the time of Morning Service, or of Evening Service (if there be no Morning Service), *immediately after the Second Lesson;*" and so have I always, *without a single exception,* heard them published for as long as my memory will serve me for a witness. The Rubric also following the Nicene Creed, as I have it, runs thus:—" Then the Curate shall declare unto the people what Holy Days or Fasting Days are, in the week following, to be observed. And then also (if occasion be) shall notice be given of the Communion; and Briefs, Citations, and Excommunications read," but no mention is made of banns of marriage. It would seem, therefore, in this instance at any rate, that the curate was clearly acting at variance with the law of the land, and, as far as appears from the Prayer-book, not in accordance with the law of the Church.‡

---

* It is lamentable to think that this farce (for farce it is in the way in which it is done) should still be continued in large towns—the High Church Manchester, and the Mother Church at Leeds and Halifax, for example.

† London: Seeley and Jackson, Fleet Street, 1859, p. 8.

‡ In another Prayer-book, however, bearing date 1820, I find a Rubric still standing at the Form of Solemnization of Matrimony, ordering the banns to be read "*immediately before the sentences for the Offertory.*" An unanswer-

The publication of banns ended, the clergyman turned round to the "altar," and bowed, *presenting his back to the people*, who received the action with mingled hisses and groans.* Upon this he walked straight into the pulpit, in the same surplice, stole, and scarlet hood he had hitherto worn, followed by an attendant, who placed a tumbler of water behind him on the ledge of the pulpit; and without kneeling, or saying any other preliminary prayer than "In the name of the Father, and of the Son, and of the Holy Ghost, Amen," (which was greeted with a loud and continued cough by the congregation,) he gave out the text thus —"It is written in the 14th of St. John, 27th verse, 'Peace I leave with you; my peace I give unto you: not as the world giveth, give I unto you. Let not your heart be troubled, neither let it be afraid;'" upon which he delivered a sermon of twenty-five minutes' length without book.

It is no part of my business to give an analysis of the discourse. I will only, therefore, state that it was of a very common-place description, plentifully interlarded with a repetition of the text, and the words "dear brethren," "my dear brethren," "my Christian brethren;"—words which, with all charity, I could not help feeling (as I am convinced must have done the bulk of the congregation) came with a bad grace from the lips of one who could hardly be unconscious that he was doing all that lay in his power to promote a breach of that very "peace" of which he was speaking, and which it surely should be one of the first objects of Christ's ministers to maintain. †

---

able argument, surely, in favour of *rubrical* revision, when even the Rubric is thus at issue with itself. "If the trumpet give an uncertain sound, who," &c.?

* See Letter xiv., p. 95.

† Bishop Wilberforce, however, appears to think differently. See his Speech in reply to Lord Ebury, May 27th, 1862, *Times* Report. "The noble

The key in which he delivered the sermon was one unvaried plaintive note, as of a much-injured Christian martyr, his posture being once only relieved by his turning round to take a draught from the tumbler of water, and his tone once only varied by his entering momentarily upon the causes of the late disturbances in the parish, "*quorum* (it was most evident) *pars magna fuit;*" but being met here by a concentrated volley of coughs, he desisted, and fell back upon his former vein of harmless platitudes.

Being an amateur phrenologist, I could not help noticing at this point the peculiar conformation of the skull of one who seemed, by the self-satisfied complacency of his countenance, and the transient smile that played on his upper lip, to take an evident delight in the painful position which, in the eyes of every beholder, he was occupying. Suffice it to say, that the head, which was thinly clad with hair, showed an exaggerated organ of Firmness, and Self-esteem, considerable Veneration and Conscientiousness, moderate Benevolence, and small Ideality, with marked narrowness in the regions of Constructiveness, Caution, and Causality. I may add, that a precisely similar organisation once before came under my own observation, being that of a young layman, a devoted adherent of the Oxford School of Theology, and who, alas! ended his days, not in a Monastery (for which he was eminently fitted), but in a Lunatic Asylum!

The sermon abruptly ended, the preacher, without any prayer or benediction audibly pronounced, turned his *back*

---

lord promised the effect of his system would be *harmony;* but there was something better than *harmony*, and that was TRUTH—truth objective in what we hold, and truth subjective in what we believe." The Bishop seems to forget that it is possible to *unite* these; and by no means necessary, in these days, whatever may have been the case 200 years ago, to

"Prove your doctrine orthodox
By Apostolic blows and knocks."

suddenly upon the congregation, and *stood in that posture for a few seconds, with his head inclined to the east*, amidst the loud coughing, hissing, and hooting of the people.

He then descended to the "altar," whence he read one or two of the offertory sentences, while a collection was being made from seat to seat, with apparently small success, in little silken bags tied to the end of long wands or sticks. The book from which he read had all the appearance of a richly illuminated Romish Missal.

The alms being presented, he *again turned his back on the people*, as he stood at the north-west angle of the "altar," and read the prayer for the Church Militant, not one syllable of which could have been heard by the congregation, except the words, "We also bless Thy holy name for all Thy servants *departed this life* in Thy faith and fear," which he delivered with a marked emphasis, having made a distinct pause for some seconds upon arriving at them. I need not remind my readers that in the first Liturgy of Edward VI. a long commendatory *Prayer for the Dead* occupied this place —removed in the Second Book, upon the exceptions of Bucer and Calvin, and subsequently replaced by the above sentence at the last review.*

This, and the following prayer, "Grant, we beseech Thee" (which was read in the same attitude and place), were concluded under the usual struggle between the *intoners* and the *sayers* of "Amen." Mr. Lowder then turned his face to the congregation, and pronounced the benediction with clasped hands, until arriving at the clause "And the blessing

---

* The question of the orthodoxy of offering up prayers for the dead in the Protestant Church has been recently brought under discussion by a controversy in the diocese of Ripon, upon the erection of a tombstone bearing the words, *Ora pro anima*, &c., which was removed by order of the Bishop (Bickersteth). The Rev. Joseph Oldknow, of Bordesley, in a letter to the *Birmingham Gazette*, July, 1861, defended the practice as not inconsistent with our present Liturgy. This I unhesitatingly deny.

of, &c.," when he unclasped them, *deliberately raising his right hand with open palm extended towards the people*, as those who have visited Rome may have seen done by the Pope when blessing his votaries from the Vatican.

This ended, he *again turned his back upon the congregation*, and dropped on one knee for a moment before the "altar;" whence he carefully raised the book, or Missal, and *holding it horizontally before him*, marched down the central aisle of the church, preceded and followed by the choristers in mockery of a procession; the police gathering hurriedly from all sides, and so escorting him in safety to the west end of the church, through the crowd pressing upon him in every direction, the organ loudly playing to drown the remarks which now issued not unsparingly from the dispersing congregation.

A middle-aged respectably-dressed female, who had sat near me in the gallery, here gave vent to her suppressed feelings, saying in a clear and determined voice, "It *must* be put down, and it *shall!*" Persons who were reporting for the newspapers might be seen shutting up their note-books, as at the close of a public meeting. In fact, anything less partaking of the nature of a religious service could hardly be conceived; not one word having been delivered for "the use of edifying" from beginning to end, except, possibly, the sermon, which, had it been preached by a Paul or an Apollos, must have fallen without effect upon minds so justly exasperated at the silly apings of Popery which had been previously exhibited by the preacher.

Having now finished my tale, I must apologise for the length to which it has been carried; but as I have never witnessed the like scene before in a church, and trust never to witness it again, I thought it due to those who are espousing one side or the other in this unseemly strife, to put on record a true and faithful account of what was done, and what was left undone, by the officiating clergyman on this occasion; in order that each looker-on may judge for himself of the merits and demerits of the respective parties in this nineteenth century enactment of a Sacred War.

I remain, Sir, yours, &c.,
November 30th, 1859.   " INGOLDSBY."

POSTSCRIPT.

As an important argument in favour of a Revision of the Prayer-book is the mode in which divine service is, *or ought to be*, conducted in our Church, I feel justified in reproducing the following notice of the preceding letters from the Journal where they were first published*:—

We beg to call particular attention to the two letters of our much-esteemed correspondent "Ingoldsby," on the subject of the disturbances at St. George's-in-the-East. Those who have read the many contributions to our paper, which have from time to time appeared under that *nom de plume*, will be prepared to see this matter treated by him with clearness, moderation, and a great admixture of common sense, at the same time without party or sectarian prejudice. Such a witness, therefore, on this occasion, is extremely valuable; and we do not think there was any occasion for him to make the apology he does at the commencement of one of the letters for devoting a couple of hours on the Lord's-day to doing this particular service at this trying moment to the cause of religion and good order.

It must be quite evident, to the most casual observer, that matters cannot go on much longer as they have done. The very idea of public worship being conducted, Sunday after Sunday, for weeks together, under awe of the policeman's baton, is absurd; and one wonders at the infatuation that can so blind the eyes of the sticklers for a revived Popish ceremonial, as to prevent their seeing, what must strike every one else, that they are thus effectually proclaiming to the world the unpopularity, and therefore the untenableness, of their silly practices.

"Ingoldsby" gives, with his peculiar skill when he has to separate the ridiculous from the grave, a phrenological analysis of the development of the most conspicuous actor in this painful drama; and compares

---

* The *Christian World*, Nos. 138 and 139.

his organisation to that of a young Oxonian, or Oxford theologian (which it does not exactly appear, nor does it much signify), who ended his days in a Lunatic Asylum, in default of a Monastery, where he might have indulged his propensities in harmless solitude. But unfortunately the circumstances are altered when they come to be applied to the case of a minister of God, filling the responsible situation of rector or curate to some 20,000 souls in the most ignorant and depraved quarter of this vast metropolis. We do not say that Messrs. Bryan King, Lowder, Lee, Purchas, and the like, are not acting conscientiously; but as the learned Professor Sedgwick once observed at Cambridge on a somewhat similar occasion,* "Of all mischievous men a wrongheaded *conscientious* man is one of the most dangerous;" certainly, if not dangerous, it may be truly said, most injurious to the Church to which he is unhappily attached in place of authority.

Whether a Revision of the Prayer-book as advocated by "Ingoldsby," Lord Ebury, and the London Association, be the *right* remedy for the present evil or not, there may be some difference of opinion. For ourselves, we think MUCH might be done in that way, but not ALL that is needed. That the bishops, as a body, should oppose such a revision, and yet make complaint that they *can do nothing* to stop the growing mischief, is so inconsistent, that if their lordships do not look well to their footing they may chance to stumble while they think they stand. Certain it is the public will not much longer tolerate a form of worship that requires for its sustentation an armed force of two or three hundred Bow Street officers; and if, as "Ingoldsby" remarks, it has come to a trial of strength between the conflicting parties in this warfare, it needs no wizard to tell us to which side the victory will ultimately incline.†

---

* This was in reference to the so-called "conscientious" exercise of the office of Proctor for the University in 1859. It is hardly too much to say of such misguided men, that—

"Hypocrisy and nonsense
Have got th' advowson of their conscience;
Still so perverse and opposite,
As if they worshipp'd God for spite."

† The following resolution was agreed to by the vestry of St. George's-in-the-East, October, 1860, and presented to the Bishop of London:—"This vestry regrets that the following innovations are still retained in the services at the parish church, namely, surpliced choristers, chanting instead of reading the prayers of the day, preaching in a surplice, Popish hymnals, communion-table elevated on steps, super-altar and embroidered altar-cloth, candlesticks with candles, and credence-table, all which this vestry is of opinion are distasteful to the parishioners at large, and deter many from betaking

LETTER LXVII.

LITURGICAL REVISION, *Illustrated and Vindicated on Orthodox Principles.* By the Rev. C. H. DAVIS. With an Introduction by LORD EBURY. Seeley, 1859.

"Prove all things; hold fast that which is good."—1 THESS. v. 21.

SIR,—I am too old a controversialist not to be fully alive to the delicacy of acting as an honest reviewer of the work now before me. But as Lord Ebury, with his characteristic good-nature, has not shrunk from connecting his name with the present treatise, who am I that I should flinch from bearing my share in the invidious task?

Of the Author of the volume suffice it to say, in his own words as applied to another, " His numerous works are too well known to need specific reference." But were they not so, a recapitulation of them is given on the cover, to which I beg to direct the attention of all who may require such information—of whom indeed it may be said, in reference to this indefatigable Revisionist,

"Not to know him argues themselves unknown."

For the contents of the volume, they are partly new, partly a *réchauffé* of the author's previous works. But that is immaterial, provided the dish before us be to our taste. The proof, they say, of the pudding is in the eating; and the readers of this treatise will doubtless here judge for themselves.

---

to their parish church, or connecting themselves with its services; and this vestry is further of opinion that a return to the old form of worship, as it was when the Rev. Bryan King became rector, and as it is now performed at the other three churches in the parish,—viz., Christ Church, St. Mary's, and St. Matthew's,—is the only way to obtain the confidence of the parish."

Mr. Davis has his merits, but method and perspicuity unfortunately form no part of these.

"Non omnia possumus omnes."

One man has one virtue, another has another. A large amount of reading, considerable research, and an industrious comparison of the productions of former labourers in the field of Liturgical Amendment, are conspicuous elements in the present, as in all our author's works.

"Much learning" has, however, made him—not indeed "mad," but—certainly anything but lucid. He labours with his material like Vesuvius before an eruption. At last out it all comes—*disjecta membra*—cinders, stones, rubbish, lava, dirt, much smoke, a very little fire, and a great deal of noise. But when the first confusion has somewhat subsided, and we begin to look quietly and curiously (provided we have leisure and patience for the purpose), into the varied mass lying at our feet, we find it not without value; and only wish in vain for the spirit of Paley to come to the rescue, in reference to whose remarkable "organ of order" it has been justly observed, that "learning, passing through the alembic of his brain, came out *common sense.*"

The INTRODUCTION from the pen of Lord Ebury has, like his lordship's two Speeches on the subject of Revision, this greatest of all merits.* The misfortune is, that, like most other good things—from good sermons down to good jokes—it suffers from the sad defect of being too brief. One would think that Lord Ebury, when he penned these few lines, bore carefully in mind the much disregarded warning of Job, "Oh that my enemy would write a book!" and therefore confined himself to writing a *Preface,*—had we not

---

* The same may be said of the *third* Speech, delivered May 27th, 1862, and since published with his lordship's corrections. Hatchard, Piccadilly.

A A

proof that he *can* " write a book," by his *having written* one of the most unartificial accounts of a *séjour* in Germany that it ever fell to our lot to peruse.*

From this unpretending little volume I take the opportunity to make a short extract, as bearing on the subject we have in hand ; and as showing that a Revision of our Church Services, in one feature at least, is no new theory with his lordship, but has been in his mind for not less than ten years, and that at the most mature and reflecting age of man :—

"Why," he asks (chap. vi., p. 113), "Why is our Church so unbending that our services can never be accommodated to the wants of our people, and no *shorter selection from our Liturgy* ever permitted under any pretence in our churches, however suitable it may be to the requirements of particular populations?"

In the INTRODUCTION now before us Lord Ebury does not enter into any of the details of Liturgical Reform ; he contents himself with referring the reader to the pamphlet to which his notice is prefixed, guarding himself with statesmanlike caution from being held responsible for the contents of the volume. One cannot help wondering, as one reads, whether his lordship really "examined and approved" all that lies here before us ; whether he knows much, little, or nothing about the author; whether he is versed in the other productions of his pen ; whether he has ever seen them, or him ; whether he can read his handwriting,† or whether he leaves that disagreeable task to his private secretary ; or whether, finally, the letters he may receive

---

* LEAVES FROM MY JOURNAL, during the Summer of 1851. By Lord Robert Grosvenor. London : Murray, 1854. *Second Edition.*

† This, whatever else may be, is certainly not the Rev. C. H. Davis's forte. I wish it were not equally true of certain Bishops and Deans with whom the author has had occasional correspondence.

from him go straight to the waste-paper basket unopened and unread?

We are told in one of the numbers of the *Spectator* that there is a class of persons who can delineate the character of an individual by a sight of his handwriting. But what if they could not read it? What if it were like the "Mene, Mene, Tekel, Upharsin," equally unmanageable in the deciphering and the interpretation?

Let us suppose, however, in charity, that his lordship had only the labour of perusing these pages in *print*, and that the poor "devil" alone, (rightly so named,) had the misery of wading through the manuscript and correcting the proof-sheets. Coming, then, with his temper unruffled to the comparatively easy work of penning the Introduction, Lord Ebury tells us good-humouredly that "he can add nothing to the intrinsic value of the contents of the work;" that "the statements are clear"—so at least says my lord;—and that "much industry and learning have been brought to the task." This last encomium we are quite willing to endorse. "The work will further," his lordship hopes, "obtain favour on account of the small compass within which the author has managed to compress his matter."

But then what is *this matter?* Hear the Table of CONTENTS, and judge of the possibility of its condensation into 76 pp., with a considerable substratum and interlineation, after the author's peculiar fashion, of notes and references :—

INTRODUCTION BY LORD EBURY,—PREFACE.

PART I.—Discussion of the Subject—The Case as it is—Note on Chap. i.—Protestant-Comprehension-Scheme Revision—Necessary Proliminaries—Suggestive Table, &c.—Practical Illustrations.—Chapp. i. ii., secs. 1, 2, 3.

PART II.—Vindication of Liturgical Revision—Omission of the Romish Feasts and Saints' Days—Substitution of "*Festival*" for "Feast"—Disuse of the Apocryphal Lessons—Disuse of the term "Priest."—Chapp. i.—iv., secs. 1, 2.

Designation of the Absolution—Substitution of "Hades" for "Hell" in the Creeds—The Athanasian Creed—Limited Application of its Damnatory Clauses—Omission of its Damnatory Clauses.—Chapp. v.—vii., secs. 1, 2.

Disuse of the Saints' Days as Holidays—The Communion Service—The Baptismal Service—Baptismal Regeneration indisputably open—The Sponsions—Omission of the Declaration of Deceased Infant's Salvation.—Chapp. viii.—x., secs. 1, 2, 3.

The Church Catechism—The Second Answer—The Fourth Answer—Definition of a "Sacrament"—Omission of the Question and Answer about "Two Parts in a Sacrament."—Chap. xi., secs. 1, 2, 3, 4.

Confirmation Service, Modification of its Collect—The Burial Service—The "Sure and Certain Hope" of the Resurrection—The Hearty Thanksgiving—The "Hope" of the Deceased's Salvation.—Chapp. xii. xiii., secs. 1, 2, 3.

The Commination—The Ordination Service—The Import of our Saviour's Words in John xx. 22, 23—The Disuse of our Saviour's Words in John xx. 22, 23.—Chapp. xiv. xv., secs. 1, 2.

Omission of the Absolution of the Sick—A Larger Catechism.—Chapp. xvi. xvii.

PART III.—Conclusion.

(And *after the Conclusion*, "a few more last words," as we hear occasionally from an indifferent preacher.)

APPENDIX A.—Insufficiency of the Present Law for Shorter Services with Sermons.

APPENDIX B.—The Thirty-nine Articles of Religion, &c.—!!—High Churchman's Candid Admissions.

APPENDIX C.—Comparative View of English Episcopate.

APPENDIX D.—Form of Prayer, &c.

And (as if this were not sufficient) ADDENDA!!

This one would think enough for a pamphlet of less than five sheets, but, unfortunately, we cannot release our readers even here; for we are told by Lord Ebury, at the close of his Introduction, that "the Author is ready to follow up this publication with *another, more complete and not less practical.*"

"Visions of Nailsworth, spare my aching sight;
Ye unborn pages, crowd not on my soul!"

Happily, however, our readers have only to deal with seventy-six of these, to the study of which we recommend them to address themselves without delay, as we can assure them of finding much valuable information on the subject of Revision in this *olla podrida*, of which our time and space permit us to present them only with the *carte*.

I am, Sir, yours, &c.,
Dec. 7, 1859. " INGOLDSBY."

LETTER LXVIII.

CHURCH QUESTIONS. By the Rev. C. ROBINSON, LL.D., Incumbent of Holy Trinity Church, Blackburn. London: Hatchard & Co., 1859.*

THE UNFEIGNED ASSENT AND CONSENT TO ALL AND EVERYTHING.

"This the clergy readily complied with; for you know that sort of men are taught rather to obey than understand, and to use the learning they have to justify, not to examine, what their superiors command."—LOCKE.

"A public Liturgy should contain as few controverted propositions as possible."—PALEY.

SIR,—We have no personal acquaintance with the writer of the above treatise; his existence was unknown to us (*valeat quantum*) until we received a copy of his pamphlet. The *English Churchman*, however, a disinterested witness in this case, tells us that "he has two full choral services on Sundays, with a surpliced choir,"—let us hope conducted in a more seemly manner than those it was our lot to witness a month ago at St. George's-in-the-East,†—and that "there are indications in his pamphlet of a higher and more liberal Churchmanship than that of the Puritan or ultra-Protestant party of the present day."

---

* A Second Series of Church Questions was published by the same author in 1861, after which the oracle appears to have become dumb.

† See Letter LXIV., p. 381.

This being all we know of the antecedents of the Rev. C. Robinson, it is with some diffidence that we call attention to his little volume, the contents of which are as follows :—

1. Practical Method of an Abridged Morning Service.
2. A New Occasional or Third Service.
3. A Revision of the Liturgy.
4. The Restoration of Dissenters.
5. Church Rates.
6. Royal Commission, Convocation, National Council, &c.

Now, bearing in mind what we said, in our last, of Mr. Davis and his 76 pp., it will be easily imagined that we are of opinion that scant justice can be done to any two or three of the above "Church Questions" in the 72 pages of which Dr. Robinson's book consists. The author is aware of this himself; and, modestly enough, puts forth his remarks (as has been done lately by another writer on the subject)* in a kind of tentative manner, rather with a view to elicit other people's sentiments, than to declare his own; his object being professedly " not the relief of his own conscience, but that of others."

For his own part, he "is READY AGAIN" to give his "*entire assent and consent*† to *all* and *everything* contained in the Book of Common Prayer; and to subscribe to the Articles, in a plain, literal, and grammatical sense."

Now, upon the first of these paragraphs we take leave to join issue with our reverend author. With the Articles we have never pretended to meddle; our business is, and has been throughout, with the "Book of Common Prayer;" for a

---

* See CHURCH ORDERS, with a Few Practical Suggestions on the Present Wants of the Church. By Rev. George Venables, of Friesland, near Manchester, at one time an indefatigable workman in the cause of Revision; but now, alas! like one or two others, fallen away from his former creed.

† See Letter XII., p. 80.

Revision of which we call (and shall continue to call), in common with the other supporters of Lord Ebury, whether coming under the *English Churchman's* "Rubrical" or "Doctrinal" classification of Revisers.

We have vividly before our eyes the *Quarterly Reviewer's* taunts against Canon Wodehouse of Norwich, some five-and-twenty years ago, for accepting *fresh* preferment, and therefore a *second time* giving his "unfeigned assent and consent to all and everything." Nevertheless,—not to re-open a wound, which we trust has long since healed over, and which ought never to have been inflicted,—we hesitate not to express it as our deliberate opinion that it is most *unfair*, not to say most *unwise*, to exact this said "assent and consent to *all* and *everything*," in the present age, from all persons originally accepting, or exchanging, preferment in the Church.*

What is the inevitable result of the persistence in such a Draconian proceeding? Is it not notoriously to make men either hypocrites, or worse? †

Just look for a moment at the Prayer-book as it is; with all its minute rules and Rubrics;—many of them obsolete from time; some of them impracticable; a few contradictory; ‡—its damnatory clauses of the Athanasian Creed, which even an

---

* The Nonconformists of 1662 state, in their reasons for refusing to accept this test, "that such a declaration was as much as could be desired concerning the Bible itself; and *more than ought to be made concerning any copy of it now extant*." (Nonconformist Memorial, vol. i., p. 39.)

† "What was the aim of all, but to settle impositions, which in all ages have been greedily swallowed by men of looser principles, while they have been snares to the most conscientious?" (Palmer, Introduction, p. 35.)—In the words of Archdeacon Hare, this test acted as a net to "cast out many of the best fish, while all the bad, careless, unscrupulous, and unprincipled were at liberty to remain in it unmolested." This precise test is now (thanks, probably, to this agitation) somewhat modified, and merely *assent, without the consent*, required! (1878.)

‡ See "The Necessity for Liturgical Revision Demonstrated from Canonical Subscription." By the Rev. D. Nihill, of Fitz, Salop. London. Bosworth and Harrison, 1859.

archbishop "wished we were well rid of;"—its "sure and certain hope,"* which 4,000 clergy lately prayed to be relieved from reading over *all* the departed; and of which 4,000, not less than six or seven are now, or have been, bishops, including the present Bishop of Lincoln (now of London), Dr. Jackson.†

Is, then, a man of high education, and of a thoughtful and pious mind, to be deterred for ever from entering into Holy Orders, because he not so much *cannot*, as that he honestly *will* not, on the spur, and once for all, give his "unfeigned assent and consent" to *every syllable of this*, and more?—or, being already in Holy Orders, and holding some poor benefice or curacy, is he, though a most active minister, able preacher, and zealous Christian, to be debarred thenceforth from rising to any higher rank in his elected line of life because that now having at his leisure looked into, and inquired maturely of, these things for himself, he *cannot* conscientiously—not to say that he *will not*—repeat (or, in Dr. Robinson's words, be "*ready again* to give") that *entire* assent and consent to *all* and *everything* contained in the Prayer-book, which he gave some ten, twenty, or thirty years ago, when but just emerging from the leading-strings of his Alma Mater, and barely acquainted with the very rudiments of his profession?

We say, and we say it deliberately, that if Lord Ebury does nothing more than call public attention to this glaring thraldom‡ inflicted upon the English clergyman, and,

---

* In the Conference with the Puritans in 1661 the Bishops conceded that these words might be omitted. (Cardwell, p. 345.)

† This statement is made on the authority of the Rev. C. H. Davis, in his treatise on Liturgical Revision, p. 13.

‡ There can be no doubt that the signatures of many of the celebrated "Ten Thousand" are traceable to the narrowing effects upon the mind of this tyrannical and wholly unwarrantable exaction.

thereby, upon the whole English nation,* he is doing an act of service to our Church, for which he will deservedly earn the thanks of her truest and most thoughtful sons.†

Mr. Davis, indeed, at the close of his late pamphlet, observes that "there are some clergymen who oppose all proposals to alter the Prayer-book by authority, but who yet take the law into their own hands, and systematically alter it for themselves *without authority ;*—for example, by the habitual disuse of the Apocryphal Lessons; the mutilation of the Marriage Service; the omission of the Athanasian Creed; the disuse of the Commination on Ash-Wednesday; the non-observance of such days as the Circumcision, Epiphany, and Ascension-day; the ignoring of saints' days, &c., &c." With such, says Mr. Davis, he "has no sympathy; and while the Prayer-book remains *as it is*, he does his best honestly to carry out in practice its obvious provisions, and to conform to the Liturgy as it is now by law established."

How far such a course of proceeding is consistent with a systematic agitation, carried on for now some ten or twelve years, and through a series of tracts, numbering not less than eight or nine, from the pen of this most laborious writer, I leave others to judge. But for my own part, wishing earnestly as I do for a revisal of the oppressive and now all but inoperative Act of 1662‡—wishing to widen,

---

* Since the Toleration Act of William III., and subsequent removal of restraints on Nonconformity, the Act of 1662 has ceased to apply to the nation generally, and has become simply operative upon the clergy, *if even upon them.*

† We were glad to hear this meed of well-deserved praise tardily bestowed upon Lord Ebury, in the face of the opposition of the Right Rev. Bench, by Earl Russell, in the debate of May 27th, 1862.

‡ "An Act as disastrous in its consequences as cruel in its intention." —*Bishop Baring, Charge of,* Sept. 1860. Of this Act the Rev. Charles Girdlestone observes in a recent pamphlet, entitled "Black Bartholomew's

not to narrow the portals of our Church—wishing for some such a "Protestant-Comprehension-Scheme Revision," as that for which the industrious Nailsworth Author is so strong an advocate on paper—I should think the best way to promote it would be *not* to take pains to "teach the laity rightly to understand the few phrases of *doubtful* import in the Prayer-book,"* but to urge them to join heart and hand with Lord Ebury and others in their efforts to get that which is "doubtful" made plain, that which is crooked straightened, that which is obsolete removed, that which is imperfect carried onward to perfection.

Even Acts of Parliament must in time wear out;† and there are some laws which are more honoured in the breach than the observance;‡ and, "when we add to all this," as Lord Ebury observed in his first speech in the House of Lords, and has never been contradicted, "that those who ought to set us the highest and most scrupulous example of obedience to the laws are compelled to break the Act of Uniformity; that there is not a single Right Reverend Prelate sitting upon the Bench who has not broken that Act of Parliament hundreds of times, and will not be com-

---

Day," p. 7: "Never had the Church of England such an opportunity of expressing regret for the past, by repealing or *amending the objectionable clauses* in the *Act of Uniformity*. On no day could a liberal amendment of that Act, involving a judicious *adaptation* of the *formularies of the Church* to the *wants* of the *present generation*, come into effect with half so good a grace, or so great a probability of conciliating opponents, as on *August* 24, 1862." W. J. Johnson, Fleet Street, 1862.

* This was in vain attempted by Dr. C. J. Vaughan in his Tract on the Revision of the Liturgy. 1860.

† The Bishop of London (Tait), on the other hand, would seem to think that 200 years of its existence gives the weight of authority to the oppressive Act of 1662. See his Lordship's Speech in reply to Lord Ebury, May 27th, 1862.

‡ We are happy in believing that there is now a growing disposition in all parts of the kingdom to consider rather the spirit than the letter of some of the rules governing the Church. (1878.)

pelled to break it for the rest of his life,"*—I think most people will be of opinion that the time has at length arrived when either this Act, and the Sealed Book attached to it, should undergo a careful revision and amendment, or at least that *meanwhile* the stringency of the words "assent and consent to *all* and *everything*" should be modified or explained by a special Act of Parliament.†

I cannot ask you to devote more space at present to the details of Dr. Robinson's book, but beg earnestly to recommend it to the perusal of all interested in this question, and feel assured it will contribute not a little to throw light upon the various difficult points the author has undertaken to notice.

I am, Sir, yours, &c.,

Dec. 27, 1859. "INGOLDSBY."

LETTER LXIX.

APOLOGY FOR THE INGOLDSBY LETTERS.

"Let none object my lingering way;
I gain, like Fabius, by delay:
Fatigue and weaken every foe
By long attack, secure though slow."—GAY.

HAVING arrived at the close of another campaign in this protracted war,‡ it may be well to take this opportunity of explaining more at large, than we have hitherto thought necessary to do, our reason for adopting the method we have resorted to in carrying on the contest.

---

* See "First Speech of Lord Ebury," Fourth Edition, 1861; p. 16.

† Such was the object of Lord Ebury's Bill of May 27th, 1862, and in this at least he has succeeded, though to a very limited extent, by the passing of the new Subscription Act of 1865.

‡ Dating the present agitation for a Revision of the Prayer-book from the year 1857, when it was first made a Parliamentary question.

That the war is likely to be an internecine one, may be gathered from a late article in the *Morning Post ;** accompanied by a manifesto under the signatures of Dean Trench, of Westminster (now Archbishop of Dublin) ; Archdeacon Denison, of Taunton ; the Rev. W. J. E. Bennett, of Frome; the Hon. and Rev. R. Liddell, of St. Paul's, Knightsbridge ; and seventy other clergymen not equally known to fame.†

---

* See *Morning Post* of Dec. 12, 1859. The following also, from the pen of Archdeacon Denison, which appeared in the *Guardian* of Dec. 14th, will give some idea of the conciliatory spirit in which *any* amendment of the Prayer-book is likely to be received by a certain party in the Church:—" If Lord Ebury wants a new Prayer-book *for us all*, he *must not have it*, nor any machinery for making it. If he wants a new Prayer-book for *some of us*, he *must not have it*, nor any machinery for making it ! The last is the danger we have to guard against, because it is the only *possible* issue."—East Brent, Dec. 8, 1859. The *Literary Churchman* of Dec. 2nd, 1861, observes that "the Ingoldsby gilding leaves the Ebury pill as objectionable as ever."

† In reference to the above, the following letter by the Rev. C. H. Davis appeared in the *Record* of Dec. 16th, 1859 :—

"The gentlemen who have formed this new coalition merely echo the Bishop of London's remark, that it is well *quieta non movere ;* and so they ' express their conviction that *any attempt* at the present time to alter the Book of Common Prayer would be attended with great danger to the peace and unity of the Church.' In reply to this I merely ask, Are things quiet ? Is the Church at peace or in unity ? And does the present Prayer-book act as a bond of peace and union ? Did not Archdeacon Denison throw the Church into confusion by his doctrine on the Real Presence, asserted to be drawn from the present Prayer-book ? Did not the Rev. W. J. E. Bennett leave London under a cloud in 1850 ? Did not the Rev. R. Liddell defend the Rev. A. Poole, and challenge the Bishop of London to try himself in the Court of Arches ? And did not this same Mr. Liddell taunt his Evangelical opponents (and let those who now coalesce with him mark it well) with unfaithfulness in habitually mutilating the notice of the Communion ?

"The Rev. F. C. Massingberd, in the *Journal of Convocation*, No. iv., p. 191, gravely proposes *two* Burial Services—one for communicants, and one for non-communicants ! Some years back, I read that Canon Stowell had publicly declared that he never had read, and never would read, a lesson from the Apocrypha. Of course he will now uphold the *Union* people in trying to get into use ' Our Lady,' because the Prayer-book in the Table of Lessons, as it is, once sanctions it.

"Then, as to ' peace ' and ' unity '—from 1843 (when the Rev. C. Benson urged revision of the rubric during the London and Exeter surplice riots), to

These gentlemen, following the Bishop of Oxford, or his chaplain, the Dean (which is much the same thing), give out that "the Prayer-book shall not be revised at this present time."* It becomes, therefore, a matter not of choice, but of duty, with ourselves and all who differ in opinion from the memorialists, to persevere in proclaiming, on the other hand, that our views are equally unaltered, that the Prayer-book *ought to be revised;* and that *the present time is* as fit as any other for the purpose.†

We contemplated, in the first instance, nothing more in these Letters than a Reply to the bishops who took part in the debate on the Revision of the Liturgy in the Upper House of Convocation in February, 1858, when the Bishop of Oxford, though not indeed the first, nor the only speaker, was clearly the leading spirit of the movement in opposition to all Revision. In carrying out, however, our original intention, we found the subject (which is indeed of world-wide interest) grow unexpectedly upon our hands; so much so, that even now that we have discharged, to the best of our ability, the invidious task we reluctantly undertook (chiefly because no one else was willing to do so), we hardly seem nearer the end of our journey than we were at first setting out;—an end of which it may be said, as of the horizon, that it

"Allures from far, but as we follow flies."

Our duty, meanwhile, is to pursue and to pursue, as

1859, when St. George's-in-the-East is protected by the police—has the Prayer-book, I ask, as it is, effected 'unity,' or promoted 'peace?' If not, what meaneth this manifesto? The Church's 'peace and unity' are destroyed; and therefore is this cry for revision."

* See Lord Ebury's speech of May 8th, 1860. Hatchard. Third Edition.

† The Dean of Norwich (Pellew) truly observed in his speech before Convocation, 1861, p. 6: "I hold that the most suitable time for making improvements is whenever the opportunity arises. When the want is felt, and the public loudly calls, as at present, for a remedy, that is the time to apply it."

long as any prospect of success is before us.* And as we are persuaded the prospect is much brighter than it was when the first of these Letters saw the light,† so we have no reason to regret having written them, or to alter the style in which they were originally conceived. That the Letters have already run to some threescore and ten in number, is not our fault, but our misfortune.‡ It has arisen wholly from the nature of the case; and should it be necessary to double the number,§ we hope it will not be imputed to any desire on our part to make a profit of the occasion, or to acquire a temporary notoriety at the expense of truth.

So far from *profit*, either present or prospective, being any part of our scheme, it will be admitted by most, that the road we are travelling is not the *shortest one to preferment*, even if it be not *in exactly the opposite direction;* ‖ and in any other way it would be equally hard to prove how the person who devotes so much time, labour, and expense to a matter, in which he is only interested in common with every other member of the Church, is likely to be individually a gainer. Truly might the writer of these Letters apply to

---

* Supposing always that we are in the *right track*, which we have hitherto seen no reason to doubt. (1878.)

† An Archbishop and a Bishop had not then come forward to charge their respective clergy in favour of Revision, as we have seen done in 1860; and two of the Prelates and a Minister of the Crown had not spoken favourably to the question, as we have witnessed in 1862.

‡ Any one who has ever undertaken the agitation of a great public question knows from experience the value of the proverb,

"Gutta cavat lapidem non vi sed sæpe cadendo."

§ The letters ran finally to No. cxxviii. Even Sisyphus, I suppose, tired at last of his thankless task, and so it was with INGOLDSBY. (Feb., 1863.)

‖ As time and the event have fully proved (1878). All advocates for Revision may well apply to themselves the Psalmist's observation, " Promotion (for them at least) cometh neither from the east, nor from the west, nor yet from the south," nor even from the North, as it did towards the end of the last century. " The man who is in advance of his age, and writes for future generations, must not expect to be paid by this."—*Pycroft's English Reading.*

himself (if it did not savour of ostentation to do so) the well-known lines of our English satirist :—

"You ask me if I ever knew
Court chaplains thus the lawn pursue.
They know great cars are over-nice,
And never shock their patron's vice.
But I this hackneyed path despise;
'Tis my ambition not to rise."*

And as for notoriety—the only notoriety he can promise himself is that of being called by no very civil names, after the approved fashion of the Anti-Liturgical Revisionists of the day, who, for lack of argument, resort to that comparatively easy, and with some, more "telling" mode of warfare.†

"Aude aliquid brevibus Gyaris et carcere dignum,
  Si vis esse aliquis,"

says the poet;—but the Laudian days are unhappily over, and a man has small chance of incurring the honours of martyrdom in this nineteenth century by any amount of "audacity"‡ in thought or speech. The fact is, the author had no alternative. He has embarked on an undertaking which admits of but one solution –to be, or not to be. It

---

* The Biographer of Erasmus observes that "the publication of the 'Praise of Folly' destroyed all chance of preferment. How *could* a man who had said such sharp things against the Church be put into high office in it? Such is not the stuff of which bishops or even deans are made. In our own days it seems impossible to promote a man who has in any way attacked or dissented from any part of the Church doctrine or discipline, or even run counter to popular opinion in these matters; and assuredly great offence would have been taken had any special favour been shown to the author of the *Moria*."—*Drummond's " Life of Erasmus,"* vol. i., p. 239.

† The blows have fallen heaviest on the head of Lord Ebury, but the more obscure Ingoldsby has come in for his full share, even to the extent of being called names by a bishop! See Bishop Wilberforce on "The Stridulous Grasshopper," Vol. II., Letter xcvi.

‡ See the Bishop of Oxford's remarks in reply to Lord Ebury in the House of Lords, May 27th, 1862.

is not that he strives for victory; it is not that he cares for defeat. But being firmly persuaded that the best interests of the Church, of which he is an attached member, are involved in the successful issue of this struggle; and being equally convinced that if not successful *now* (humanly speaking), the attempt will not be repeated again in this generation;* he feels it due to those who are engaged with him in the same pursuit never to desert it, even though the obstacles to be overcome present greater difficulties then they have hitherto done.†

That the question has progressed largely in public opinion within the last few years, can be denied by none. That it will receive its solution, in some form or other, in due time, is almost an equal matter of certainty.‡ But should a different result ensue, the author has still that confidence in the overruling Providence of God, as to feel no hesitation in again cheerfully buckling on his armour, through evil report and good report (of which last he gets but little), for fresh and fresh exertions in the cause.

One word as to our adopted *nom de plume* of INGOLDSBY.

---

* Never were truer words spoken than the following oft-quoted ones of Archdeacon Paley (Works, vol. iii., page 313; Edit. 1825): "As the man who attacks a flourishing establishment writes with a halter round his neck, few will ever be found to attempt alterations but *men of more spirit than prudence*, of *more sincerity than caution*, of *warm, eager, and impetuous tempers*. If, consequently, we are to wait for improvement till the cool, the calm, the discreet part of mankind begin it; *till church governors solicit*, or *ministers of state propose it;* I will venture to pronounce, that, without His interposition with whom nothing is impossible, we may remain as we are till the renovation of all things."

† The "difficulties," whose name once was Legion, have now resolved themselves into *one* phasis, "THIS IS NOT THE TIME," or "THIS IS NOT THE WAY," to do it. Even the *Clerical Journal* went so far as to admit that "the Prayer-book is far from perfect, and only requires the *proper authority* for its amendment;" Jan. 30, 1862.

‡ No doubt matters are progressing in this direction, but on the *festina lente* principle, and the next generation will probably reap some fruit from the seed now sown by the advocates for Liturgical Revision. (1878.)

That *concealment* was from the first no part of our object in writing under a feigned signature, has been already sufficiently declared,* and to that declaration we adhere; and are quite willing to bear whatever odium or damage to our private character, or position in the Church, may be incurred by anything we have written.

Acting, however, as we do, not on our individual judgment, in agitating this question, and being fully aware how extensive are the interests it involves, we thought from the first (and continue to think) that it was not becoming in one, occupying the humble position of a plain Country Clergyman, to appear week after week, for two or three years together, in his own name, as the Reviewer of the speeches and writings of others, many of them of talents and acquirements superior to his own, and for the most part occupying stations whose exalted nature must have either deterred, or materially checked and embarrassed personal criticism.

The author, therefore, of the "Ingoldsby Letters," under an assumed but not unwarranted† title, claims for himself no other privilege than that of any unknown writer in the *Times* or the *Edinburgh Review*, who by reason of his concealment is supposed to express the sentiments of *others* rather than his own, using for the purpose the mysterious but omnipotent little particle WE.

If this explanation is not satisfactory to those who prefer openness at all times, (as indeed do we ourselves as a general rule,) let them bear in mind that the course we have adopted is at least as defensible as that of the anonymous writers hostile to Revision, who from time to time spit their miserable

---

* See Letter XVII., p. 118.

† As the Rector of a parish in Lincolnshire bearing the same name as the far-famed LEGENDS published under the *sobriquet* of THOMAS INGOLDSBY, Esq.

venom at Lord Ebury and his supporters, under the dark titles of ORUS, ANTI-REVISIONIST, PRESBYTER ANGLICANUS, PHILIP PLAINSPOKEN,* and the like.

Such articles remind one painfully of the controversy, carried on so fiercely two hundred years ago upon this identical subject, in which Martin Mar-Prelate and his opponents appear so little to their respective credit. The men who are now venting their spleen in bootless malignity, under shadow of the two or three journals that give admission to their wretched twaddle, are indeed worthy descendants of the authors of " A Pappe with an Hatchet," " An Almond for a Parrot," " Hay any Worke for Cooper," " An Epistle to the Terrible Priests of the Con-Focation House," and other effusions of the seventeenth century.†

From such advocates may our cause be long delivered, as it has hitherto been.—*Non tali auxilio!*—And if in the course of this protracted struggle we have said anything unbecoming the character of a Christian gentleman, or clergyman, we hereby express our regret for it, and our readiness to recall it when pointed out. We have all along had no other aim than, by a little harmless satire (hurting, we sincerely trust, no one but ourselves ‡), to expose what we consider the extremely weak position of our opponents; and to bring public opinion

---

* This last-named gentleman was generally understood to be the Rev. Philip Freeman, afterwards Archdeacon of Exeter, and who came to an untimely end by an accident on the railway. We are happy, however, to say that this description of correspondence after a while almost ceased; though leading articles of a personally abusive character from time to time continued to disgrace one or two of the London papers.

† See " Puritan Discipline Tracts." John Petheram. London, 1844.

‡ Most honestly do we believe that the well-known line of the poet may be with equal truth adopted as our own motto on this occasion—

" Nec quenquam nostri *nisi nos* laesere libelli."

Certainly no other has been our desire, however we may be judged by our readers. The truth, the whole truth, and nothing but the truth, has been our one aim throughout.

to bear with its irresistible sway upon the untenable arguments, and almost childish timidity, of the advocates for retaining all things *as they are,* merely because alteration is sometimes attended with danger, and that it is *possible* to change for the worse.

Ingoldsby Rectory, Dec. 31, 1859.

REVIEW OF THE INGOLDSBY LETTERS.

("DUBLIN UNIVERSITY MAGAZINE.")

[THE following Review of the Ingoldsby Letters appeared in the *Dublin University Magazine,* shortly after the publication of the First Edition, and is reprinted here as an additional apology, if any were needed, for the peculiar style adopted by the author, which he is aware has been called in question by some of the more rigid opponents of Revision :—]

On the 6th of November, 1630, Archbishop Laud made the following entry in his diary, relating to Dr. Leighton, one of the Puritans who had, through Laud's instigation, been condemned in the Star Chamber :—

November 6th.
First, he was severely whipt before he was set in the pillory.
Second, being set in the pillory, he had one ear cut off.
Third, one side of his nose was slit up.
Fourth, he was branded on the cheek with a red-hot iron.
On that day se'nnight, his sores upon his back, ear, nose, and face being not yet cured, he was whipt again at the pillory in Cheapside, cutting off the other ear, slitting the other side of his nose, and branding the other cheek.

In December, 1858, appears a volume containing the highly-amusing, but sharply-cutting letters of "Ingoldsby," in reply to the speeches against a Revision of the Liturgy, delivered by the Bishops in Convocation the preceding February, and also in the House of Lords, on Lord Ebury's motion on the same subject.

These Letters, as we have remarked, are sharply-cutting, and yet, as far as we know, the writer of them remains unscarred, both nostrils sound, and his ears not even pulled; although, possibly, some of the bishops on whom he has passed his strictures would like to do as much, whilst others of them might think he deserved a portion cut off. We can hardly imagine any of them wishing for a whole ear; they are too kind-hearted for that. But, does he not richly deserve punishment? some of the bishops will say—does he not, sir? some of the chaplains, with more indignation, will reiterate. On this point there may be a difference of opinion; but, even if he should, we, for our part, would rather live in the mild days of John Bird Sumner, than in those of William Laud. We would rather live in days, when men may write pungently and sarcastically, at no greater risk than being replied to in their own terms, than in the days of old, when a man could not call his nose his own, if he chanced to differ in opinion from those above him.

In case, however, this sentiment should not be agreeable to some of our readers, who, on opening the pages of "Ingoldsby," begin to wax wroth with him, and wish for the pillory-and-slitting-of-noses days to come back again, we would beg them to stop before they proceed further, and read the seventeenth Letter first. This will show them that "Ingoldsby" has no guile in his composition, and will also furnish them with the reason for his adopting his present style. They will learn that "Ingoldsby," having found their lordships the bishops perfectly unimpressible under the heavy style of writing which had been hitherto used in treating the subject of Liturgical Revision, was induced to adopt a lighter and more piquant method,* in the hope that this sort might be more effective, according to his motto—

---

* Even the *Clerical Journal* was fain to admit that "the Ingoldsby Letters have the merit of some wit, and have managed to throw a little of

"Ridiculum acri
Fortius et melius magnas plerumque secat res."
"For Ridicule will frequently prevail,
And cut the knot where graver Reasons fail."

Whilst wishing, however, to put those who may peruse his letters in good humour with him, and prevent their longing for the Laudian days to return, we must candidly admit that he would have given us individually more satisfaction had he not been quite so jocose upon the bishops and their speeches; and many probably will be disposed to agree with us. However, against this charge it will be but fair to let "Ingoldsby" speak for himself; and to enable him so to do, and at the same time to show the raciness and cheerfulness of his style, and likewise his close arguing (for his letters are far more logical than many duller compositions on the Revision question), we will proceed to give some extracts from the letter to which we have alluded :—

"I have no wish to be severe. My object is, and has been throughout, 'the truth,' which the Bishop of Oxford lays such stress upon—the whole truth, and nothing but the truth. And if you are a scholar, which I have no means of ascertaining except from the internal evidence supplied by your letter,* which shows that *paulo majora* is not Greek to you :— if, I say, you are a scholar, I ask,

——'Ridentem dicere verum
Quid vetat?'

Why may not my argument be carried on as well with a smiling as a frowning face? It is true, a man *may* 'smile,

---

the gay and pleasant round a subject somewhat ghastly and destructive in its character and aims."—*Clerical Journal*, January 30th, 1862.

* The letter from which the above is quoted was a reply to an anonymous writer who objected to the satirical tone of Ingoldsby's strictures on the bishops. It must be noticed that bishops too can descend to sarcasm and personality when it suits their purpose; witness the Bishop of Oxford in reply to Lord Ebury in the House of Lords, May 27th, 1862.

and smile, and smile, and be a villain,' as said (the late) Lord Derby on a memorable occasion to, or of, a certain right reverend prelate. But I hope every man who smiles is not to be so set down. I would live, if I could, under the sunbeam of a perpetual smile."

And again—

"And now for the clergy and the people. Have they not been assailed with solid arguments for the last quarter of a century till their stomach rises at the sight of such indigestible food? It is like the boiled beef in the Knightsbridge barracks; they sigh for the garlic of Egypt, a little allspice, something piquant and pungent, curry powder, cayenne, and the like. Have not all the writers on Liturgical Reform, from 1834 to 1858, plied them with solid arguments, thick and hard and cold as hailstones? Riland with an i, and Ryland with a y; Powys, Hon. and Rev., and Powys, Rev., but not Hon.; Archdeacon Berens, now in his eighty-third year, and 'holding the same sentiments with failing eyesight,' which he published to the world above thirty years ago; Tyndale the same, in his eightieth year, &c. &c.; and last, not least, the learned barrister in the north, Mr. J. C. Fisher; —have not all of these, in their several ways, and according to their 'peculiar views of truth,' tried the force of solid arguments in every diversity of expression, till they have exhausted the vocabulary, and rung the changes upon Liturgical Revision to the last conceivable variation? and *cui bono?* to what effect?—Why, that when their eyes are waxed dim with writing, and their natural strength abated from waiting so long upon the bishops, they have the satisfaction of hearing that their lordships have declared, through their mouthpieces in their own proper House, that the Prayer-book shall remain UNTOUCHED and UNALTERED in their day."

These Letters, though they are written in a satirical and

lively style, are close and logical in argument, and teem with most apposite and choice quotations. We never remember to have met with the like in the course of our reading. Sydney Smith was felicitous beyond compare in the combination of his ideas; but he does not abound with quotations, and very rarely indulges in classical allusions. With these "Ingoldsby" is full to overflowing, and they are not the hackneyed aphorisms mouthed out in Parliament, and understood in these days by learned ladies and middle-class graduates; but the most refreshing *morceaux* from the fountain-head of classic lore, as well as from our own standard writers, and such as are not every day sounded in our ears. Horace's advice has not been lost upon him—

"Nocturna versate manu, versate diurna."

The quotations seem part of himself, and flow naturally from him. There is no force-pumping, no recourse to indices or book-shelves. Illustrations appear to come up just as he wants them. They stand, like obedient imps, at his elbow as he writes along. At a hint they fall into their ranks and fit— the right man in the right place. There is no occasion to say, "Attention! dress!" They suit where they stand, and look well, clad in uniform, the uniform of appropriateness and applicability. With the qualities we have mentioned, the Letters will prove to many an intellectual treat; and, though they may be too peppery for some of their lordships' stomachs, and be apt to disagree with their digestion, yet to others, who are blessed with stronger gastric juice, or less irritable mucous membranes, they will afford excellent nourishment, and even cause them to smack their lips and wish for more. Only let them read the seventeenth Letter first; for the perusal of it, we feel confident, will ensure their regarding with favour their literary *cuisinier*.

But, joking apart, for the sake of the important subject on which the Letters treat, we wish much the bishops *would* read them, although the writer has not spared some of the right reverend bench.* We, indeed, cannot help repeating our wish that " Ingoldsby " had been somewhat more merciful. Each of their lordships will probably say, with deep feeling, " *Homo sum ;* " and each knowing the plague of his own heart, mourns doubtless over it more than " the inferior clergy " are apt to think. Some bishops who offer two fingers to a wretched curate, when they should offer the whole hand, feel ashamed of themselves afterwards; and others, who whirl about with the wind, resolve, it may be, over and over again, to remain more firm for the future. The wonder is that bishops are not spoilt more than they are by titles and palaces, obsequious chaplains, and fawning expectants. Still we must repeat the wish that their lordships would read, for the subject's sake, these powerful Letters, though at the risk of getting angry, and inwardly thinking that, though Laud went too far in his operative surgery, it would be very desirable to administer some homœopathic globules of chastisement to that " naughty boy, Ingoldsby."

Revision of the Liturgy, Ingoldsby's gravamen, it cannot be denied, is being demanded far and wide.† Timely con-

---

* Having had the opportunity (while these pages were going through the press) of reading the very interesting Autobiography of the Archdeacon of Taunton, I am happy to be able to quote here a sentiment of so marked a controversialist in which I cordially concur,—though differing, I regret to say, from many of the conclusions of that venerable authority:—

" Is it said, these are hard words? I know they are hard words; but I know nothing in the law of nature, or of Grace, or of both, to tell me not only that I may not use hard words in denouncing false principles, but to acquit me if, knowing the principles to be false, *I do not denounce them. In this case hard words become a duty.*"—*Notes of my Life,* by G. A. DENISON, chap. v., p. 85.

What I have said " hardly " of Bishops Wilberforce and Thirlwall, (and I am not aware of having done so of any other of the Right Rev. Prelates,) I consider (after the interval of nearly twenty years) fully justified by the premises; and I see no reason to modify or retract any of the expressions, however seemingly severe.—INGOLDSBY. (1878.)

† The difficulty is to find an advocate sufficiently at leisure, and sufficiently

cession on this point would tend, we are persuaded, to bring ultimate peace to the Church, and increase the number within her fold. Whereas we fear, if no relief be granted, disunion will go on increasing, and the number of dissentients from the Church become greater than even now.

That the bishops, in the end, will have to give way, there cannot be a shadow of doubt. It would be well if their lordships would lay this thought to heart, and, instead of opposing anything like alteration, would use their weight and influence to bring about this desirable and needful reform. "Ingoldsby" would then relinquish his humble though useful office of *cuisinier*, and become their faithful squire, their *avant-courier*, proclaiming joyfully before them, "Oyez, oyez! listen to the voice of authority speaking wisely in high places." For though he may seem to dissent from the views of some two or three of their number, it is clear from the general tone of his letters that he respects the order on the whole, and has only written as he has done with the intention of holding up a mirror to eyes a little blinded by flattery; has only whispered a few wholesome syllables in ears too rarely reached by naked and simple TRUTH.

We hope, when Lord Ebury next brings on his motion, he will *divide* the House. Not that we expect to find his Lordship in a majority, or anything like it; but it will serve to separate the chaff from the wheat, and enable the public to see who are the real obstructives in this case. The Jew Bill was not carried till after some score of hostile divisions; so the friends of Liturgical Reform have no cause to fear a second or a third defeat,—they have only to persevere steadily, and the victory is certain in the long run.

---

well informed on the subject, to bring and keep it continually before the eyes of the public and the Legislature.

APPENDIX A.

THE RITUAL COMMISSION, 1867-70.

"Parturiunt montes: en exit ridiculus mus!"
"What is the use of a Commission, which leaves a chief blot just where it found it?"—*Notes of my Life*, by G. A. DENISON, chap. ii., p. 31.

As allusion has been more than once made, in the course of the previous Letters, to the Ritual or Rubrical Commission of 1867-70, it may be as well to put on record here an *abstract of the principal items in their Report*, as published in the papers in the autumn of the latter year, but never put legally in force from that time to the present (1878); such is the progress of ecclesiastical legislation!

1. Upon *week days*, instead of the whole Order for Morning and Evening Prayer, such selections from the same may be used as shall be approved by the Ordinary. Nevertheless, in Cathedral and Collegiate Churches the whole Order for Morning and Evening Prayer shall be said daily.

2. Upon occasions to be approved by the Ordinary other Psalms may, *with his consent* (!), be substituted for those which are appointed in the Psalter.

3. The Morning Prayer, the Litany, and the Order for the Administration of the Lord's Supper or Holy Communion, may be used together, or as separate services, at the discretion of the minister; and when the Morning Prayer is said alone, a sermon may follow the third Collect or the end of the service. . . . . At *Morning Prayer*, upon days other than Sundays and holy-days, the minister may at his discretion proceed at once to the General Confession.

4. The Athanasian Creed.—The existing rubric is retained, but at the end is added—"*Note*, That the condemnations in

this Confession of Faith are to be no otherwise understood than as a solemn warning of the peril to those who wilfully reject the Catholic faith."

5. In the Communion Service.—*Revised Rubric.* Then shall follow one of these two Collects for the Queen (except when the Queen has been prayed for in the service immediately preceding).

6. Wafer bread forbidden at the celebration of the Holy Communion; and the address to the whole rail at once sanctioned, in the case of there being many communicants.

7. Public Baptism.—One sponsor sanctioned when two or three cannot be conveniently obtained; and parents to stand for their children.

8. The Burial Service.—It shall be lawful for the minister, on sufficient cause, to read one or both of the Psalms, together with one of the following Lessons, and the four sentences appointed to be said while the corpse is made ready to be laid into the earth, concluding with the Lord's Prayer and the Grace at the end of the office: provided always, that the office thus allowed be *not used without the permission of the Ordinary* (!); but that if from want of time this permission cannot be obtained, then the minister shall notify in writing within seven days to the Ordinary the use of the shortened service, and the reasons for his having so used it (!) The following are the alternative lessons given: Matthew xxiv. 35—42; Mark v. 35—41; Luke vii. 11—16; John xi. 30—44; 1 Thess. iv. 13—18.

These are really the *only material* suggestions in the Report, which said Report two of the Commissioners declined to sign! and from *parts of which* almost all of them signified some dissent, or entered some protest against it!

It seems scarcely credible that nearly three years should have been consumed in the discussion of this matter, with such a miserable and almost ludicrous result.

APPENDIX B.

THE "TIMES" NEWSPAPER ON CONVOCATION: JUNE 12, 1872.

"No man putteth new wine into old bottles: else the new wine doth burst the bottles, and the wine is spilled, and the bottles will be marred: but new wine must be put into new bottles."—MARK ii. 22.

THE following article, which appeared in the *Times* on the day mentioned above, so entirely coincides with the views repeatedly expressed by the Author in the body of this work,[*] that he is glad to give it a more permanent position than the columns of a daily newspaper afford:—

"Some sanguine persons took the trouble to hold a meeting yesterday evening in order to advocate the Reform of Convocation. There can be no doubt that such a process is greatly needed if Convocation is to be permitted to assume real powers of action, but this was a point with which the speakers did not seem to think it necessary to trouble themselves. The attendance at the meeting, however, must have somewhat enlightened them respecting the probability of any such permission being granted. It was a significant illustration of the practical interest taken by the public in this subject. If Convocation were felt to exert any real influence, a proposal for its Reform could not fail to command attention. Yet the small room in King Street was half empty at the commencement of the proceedings, and a mere handful of listeners lingered to the close. Even of the speakers, who were announced, some did not appear to think it worth while to come, and one solitary Bishop discharged the Episcopal function of discussing the difficulties of innovation.

"This singular indifference cannot be supposed to arise

---

[*] See INDEX in Vol. II., under head, CONVOCATION.

from any general satisfaction with the existing constitution of Convocation; it can be interpreted only as a profound indifference to Convocation itself; and if, as Lord Lyttelton considers, we have paid more attention of late to the proceedings of that body, it seems evident that we have given ourselves needless trouble. There appears, moreover, no sign of progress in the movement. It was almost pathetic to hear speaker after speaker recounting how he had made a speech, or written a pamphlet, advocating the representation of the laity twenty years or more ago. The quarter of a century or so has elapsed, and speeches and pamphlets have passed away with it. At the end of the time the Bishop of Ely, after much hesitation and mediæval research, has just got back to his old position, and Lord Lyttelton has occasion to speak his old speeches over again. The cause seems a dead horse, which cannot be flogged into vitality. A few curious philosophers may lift it on to its legs for a few moments, but as soon as their hands are removed it tumbles down.

"The truth is that the slight prominence recently obtained by Convocation is due to circumstances which are totally independent of the influence of that body itself. The activity of the Church at large *and the altered necessities of the public had gradually produced a general desire for certain improvements in the public Services.* The excesses of the Ritualists rendered it necessary to appoint a Royal Commission, and the Ministry of the day took the opportunity to direct the consideration of these reforms. The Commission accordingly prepared the new Lectionary, and suggested those amendments to the Act of Uniformity which the Bill of this Session carries into effect. According to precedent, it was presumed to be requisite that Convocation should be consulted before any such legislation was submitted to Parliament, and it was at least thought desirable to obviate formal objections. For this reason alone Letters of Business were issued, and the Convocations of the two Provinces were compelled to discuss subjects of real public interest. But it is always to be remembered that *Convocation was so far from promoting or assisting these reforms that, on the contrary, the Revised Lectionary obtained its sanction by a scanty and doubtful majority*, and it has since absolutely refused to entertain a proposal with respect to the Athanasian Creed *which the vast majority of Churchmen have deeply at heart.*

"Convocation has been debating for twenty years, but the only practical result of its proceedings, so long as it was left to itself, was an ineffectual alteration in an obsolete Canon. It is no answer to these facts to urge, as one of the speakers did yesterday, that Convocation was inactive only because it had no powers of action. *It never displayed any practical disposition for action.* The readiness with which the proposals of the Ritual Commission were accepted proved that the Church at large was looking anxiously for some guidance and impulse; and if Convocation had really deserved and commanded confidence, it would have anticipated *the suggestions to which it tardily gave a grudging assent.* It had the power of speech, and that in these days is a good deal. Had it used that power well, and exhibited an inclination to moderate and useful reforms, it might have been granted further powers, and might by this time have helped to solve many practical problems. The Royal Commission had no power of action, but simply a power of consultation and recommendation. Yet it turned this modest opportunity to very good effect, and we owe to it the only useful reform introduced into the Church since the Reformation. *Convocation had its opportunity and failed,* and the formal necessity of consulting it before submitting the recent legislation to Parliament cannot alter the public judgment of its proceedings. We have ceased to expect any help from it, and that is the reason why the speakers of yesterday addressed a half-empty room.*

"Lord Lyttelton argues that if the Church possesses a real vitality, it must have some means of 'self-regulation and self-development.' We shall not dispute the position, or deny that the abeyance of all power of development in the Anglican Church for 300 years is a singular anomaly. But if these questions are to be effectually raised, they will touch far more important matters than the reform of Convocation. For good or for harm, the absence of any independent action on the part of the Church has been the inevitable result of its intimate relations with the State; and the statement of the first Resolution yesterday, that 'the Reform of Convocation is essential to the stability of the Church of England as an Establishment,' would probably be more accurate if qualified by the judicious insertion of a negative (!) *So long as the Church of England is an Establishment, the less of Convocation the better;* and if once the Church of England ceases to be an Establishment, some totally different body will have to be called into existence for the purpose of its self-government. *Convocation is the relic of an ecclesiastical order which has long passed away.* The acute statesmen of the Reformation, who took care to cover all their strong acts with the shield

---

* On the subject of *Reform of Convocation*, see Life of G. A. Denison (already quoted), chap. iv., p. 65:—"Many good friends of mine keep deluding themselves and others with the hope of what is called 'Reform of Convocation'"—meaning, as I am able to understand it, some better adjustment of the Lower House. Well, supposing this were got, *the real grievance would remain just where it was before;* namely, that with a reformed Synod you would be just as unreal, and just as powerless, as you now are. *The House of Commons is not going to allow* Convocation to 'do' anything to make an *Imperium de Imperio.*" See also *the same*, chap. ix., p. 280, &c.

I feel disposed to remark upon this very true observation of the irrepressible Archdeacon,—"ΕΤ ΤΥ, ΒΡΥΤΕ!" I hope I shall not be accused of using "hard words." (See p. 424.)

of legality, induced it to assist them in rendering its action obsolete.

"The friends of Convocation are fond of appealing to those precedents, and if they wish its powers to be revived for the purpose of performing more completely a similar 'happy despatch,' no one will have the least objection to gratify them. But if the independent action of the Church is to be revived, some new and more appropriate instrument will have to be created.

"The Bishop of Ely very pertinently observed that primitive bishops were personages of a very different character from bishops in the present day. They were independent realities, they actually represented their flocks; and clerical assemblies, instead of being in antagonism to the laity, were the ultimate expression of lay as well as of clerical opinion. Convocation has come down to us from a time when these wholesome conditions of religious life had been entirely destroyed, and *it is of no avail trying to put new wine into so old a bottle.* Before any healthy action is aroused in the Church, it would be necessary to get rid of the obsolete forms and the obstructive traditions of which Convocation is the refuge. The principal speakers themselves were very careful to explain that they did not at present attempt to define what their contemplated Reforms should be. Perhaps when they come to consider this rather important question they will find that it is too large to be solved by the existing materials of Convocation. They may be perfectly right in their vague impression that something must soon be done; but if they would attempt to make up their minds what this should be, they would at once find themselves entangled in problems which last night could conveniently be ignored."

SELECTIONS FROM

Messrs. Cassell, Petter, Galpin & Co.'s Publications.

The Life and Work of St. Paul.
By the Rev. F. W. FARRAR, D.D., F.R.S., Late Fellow of Trinity College, Cambridge; Canon of Westminster; and Chaplain in Ordinary to the Queen. Two Volumes, demy 8vo, cloth, 24s.; morocco, £2 2s.

THE NEW BIBLE COMMENTARY.

A New Testament Commentary for English Readers. Edited by C. J. ELLICOTT, D.D., Lord Bishop of Gloucester and Bristol.

Volume I., price 21s., contains—

ST. MATTHEW	By Rev. E. H. PLUMPTRE, D.D.
ST. MARK	By Rev. E. H. PLUMPTRE, D.D.
ST. LUKE	By Rev. E. H. PLUMPTRE, D.D.
ST. JOHN	By Rev. H. W. WATKINS, M.A.

Volume II., price 21s., contains—

THE ACTS OF THE APOSTLES ...	By Rev. E. H. PLUMPTRE, D.D.
ROMANS	By Rev. W. SANDAY, M.A., D.D.
CORINTHIANS I.	By Rev. T. T. SHORE, M.A.
CORINTHIANS II.	By Rev. E. H. PLUMPTRE, D.D.
GALATIANS	By Rev. W. SANDAY, M.A., D.D.

Volume III., price 21s., contains—

EPHESIANS	By Rev. Canon BARRY, D.D.
PHILIPPIANS	By Rev. Canon BARRY, D.D.
COLOSSIANS	By Rev. Canon BARRY, D.D.
THESSALONIANS I. and II. ...	By Rev. Canon MASON, M.A.
TIMOTHY I. and II.	By Rev. Canon SPENCE, M.A.
TITUS	By Rev. Canon SPENCE, M.A.
PHILEMON	By Rev. Canon BARRY, D.D.
HEBREWS	By Rev. W. F. MOULTON, D.D.
ST. JAMES	By Rev. E. G. PUNCHARD, M.A.
ST. PETER I.	By Rev. Canon MASON, M.A.
ST. PETER II.	By Rev. A. PLUMMER, M.A.
ST. JOHN: Epistles I., II., and III.	By Rev. W. M. SINCLAIR, M.A.
ST. JUDE	By Rev. A. PLUMMER, M.A.
THE REVELATION	By Rev. W. B. CARPENTER, M.A.

"We have here less notice of disputes and discrepancies—far more attention to the bearings of the holy words of Christ and the incidents of His Divine life upon thought and practice, upon prayer and duty. We think this work in many ways more delicate and anxious than that which belongs to the commentaries of a different order; and we must heartily congratulate Bishop Ellicott on the success of his fellow-labourers."—*Guardian.*

"This is a work by thorough scholars and exegetes, intended for the use of those unable to read the sacred text in its original language, and to put them in possession of its exact sense, at the same time carefully maintaining that higher exegesis that no mere grammatical analysis can supply—the development and exhibition of the inner life and meaning of the sacred writers."—*British Quarterly Review.*

Cassell, Petter, Galpin & Co.: Ludgate Hill, London; Paris; and New York.

Selections from Messrs. Cassell, Petter, Galpin & Co.'s Publications (continued).

The Bible Educator.
Edited by the Rev. E. H. PLUMPTRE, D.D., assisted by some of our most eminent Scholars and Divines, containing about 400 Illustrations and Maps. Complete in Four Vols., cloth, 6s. each; or Two Double Vols., cloth, 21s.; half-calf, 31s. 6d.

The Family Bible.
With 900 ILLUSTRATIONS, References, Concordance, Critical and Explanatory Notes, &c. Printed on Fine Toned Paper, leather, gilt edges, £2 10s.; morocco, £3 10s.; best morocco, £3 15s.

The Guinea Bible.
With 900 ILLUSTRATIONS. Royal 4to, 1,476 pages. Cloth gilt, gilt edges, 21s.; or 25s. strongly bound in leather.

The Half-Guinea Illustrated Bible.
With 900 Original Illustrations, executed specially for this Edition. Printed in clear type, with References, &c. &c. 1,248 pages, crown 4to, cloth, 10s. 6d. **** *Can be also had in Leather Bindings in great variety, specially suitable for Presentation.*

The Doré Bible.
ROYAL 4to EDITION. Complete in Two Vols., with 220 Illustrations by GUSTAVE DORÉ. Plain morocco, £4 4s.; best morocco, £6 6s.

The Bible Dictionary.
With nearly 600 ILLUSTRATIONS. 1,100 pages, imperial 8vo. One Volume, cloth, 21s.; morocco, 40s.; or Two Volumes, cloth, 25s.

Matthew Henry's Commentary.
NEW EDITION. With Annotations consisting of Supplementary Original Notes by eminent Biblical Scholars of the present day. Complete in Three Vols., royal 4to, £3 10s.

The Child's Bible.
With 200 ILLUSTRATIONS, especially designed for Children. Being a Selection from the Holy Bible, in the Words of the Authorised Version. 120*th Thousand.* Cloth, gilt edges, £1 1s.; with clasps and rims, £1 10s.

Daily Devotion for the Household.
Containing a Short Prayer, with Hymn and a Portion of Scripture for Every Morning and Evening in the Year. Illustrated. Royal 4to, leather, £1 15s.

Family Prayers.
Prepared by a Committee of the Upper House of Convocation of the Province of Canterbury, and published by Authority of the House. Cloth, 1s.

The Family Prayer Book.
Edited by the Rev. Canon GARBETT, M.A., and the Rev. SAMUEL MARTIN. Demy 4to, 398 pages, cloth, 7s. 6d.; cloth, gilt edges, 9s.; morocco, £1 1s.

Cassell, Petter, Galpin & Co.: Ludgate Hill, London; Paris; and New York.

Selections from Messrs. Cassell, Petter, Galpin & Co.'s Publications (continued).

The Quiver.
An Illustrated Religious Magazine. Yearly Volumes, 7s. 6d.; also Monthly Parts, 6d.

The History of the English Bible.
By the Rev. F. W. MOULTON, M.A., D.D. Reprinted, with Additions and Corrections, from "The Bible Educator." Cloth, 3s. 6d.

Christ Bearing Witness to Himself.
By the Rev. G. A. CHADWICK, B.D. Being the Donnellan Lectures for 1878-9. Crown 8vo, cloth, 5s.

The Doré Scripture Gallery of Illustrations.
Containing 250 Drawings of Scripture Subjects, by GUSTAVE DORÉ, with Text by EDMUND OLLIER. Two Vols., £5 10s.

The History of Protestantism.
By the Rev. J. A. WYLIE, LL.D. Complete in Three Vols., containing upwards of 600 ILLUSTRATIONS. Extra crown 4to, cloth, 27s.

Keble's Christian Year.
With Illustrations on nearly every page. Reprinted from the Original Edition. Cloth, 7s. 6d.; cloth, gilt edges, 10s. 6d.

A Preacher's Legacy to his Congregation and their Children.
By the Rev. H. MARTYN-HART, M.A. Price 5s.

Some Difficulties of Belief.
By the Rev. T. TEIGNMOUTH SHORE, M.A., Incumbent of Berkeley Chapel, Mayfair. Post 8vo, cloth, 6s.

The Life of the World to Come, and other Subjects.
By the Rev. T. TEIGNMOUTH SHORE, M.A., Incumbent of Berkeley Chapel, Mayfair. Cloth, 5s.

Pilgrim's Progress and Holy War.
With 200 Wood Engravings and 12 Chromo Plates. Demy 4to, cloth, gilt edges, £1 5s.

Bunyan's Pilgrim's Progress.
With 100 ILLUSTRATIONS by SELOUS and PRIOLO. Cloth, 7s. 6d.

Bunyan's Holy War.
With 100 ILLUSTRATIONS by SELOUS and PRIOLO. Cloth, 7s. 6d.

The Ingoldsby Letters on the Revision of the Book of Common Prayer.
By Rev. J. HILDYARD, B.D. Revised and Enlarged. Two Vols., 12s.

The Young Man in the Battle of Life.
By the Rev. Dr. LANDELS. Cloth, 3s. 6d.

The True Glory of Woman.
By the Rev. Dr. LANDELS. Cloth gilt, gilt edges, 3s. 6d.

Cassell, Petter, Galpin & Co.: Ludgate Hill, London; Paris; and New York.

Selections from Messrs. Cassell, Petter, Galpin & Co.'s Publications (continued).

The Life of Christ.
By the Rev. F. W. FARRAR, D.D., F.R.S., Canon of Westminster, and Chaplain in Ordinary to the Queen.

LIBRARY EDITION (24th Edition), complete in Two Volumes, demy 8vo, cloth, 24s.; morocco, £2 2s.

ILLUSTRATED EDITION. With about 300 Illustrations, Coloured Map and Steel Title, extra crown 4to, cloth, gilt edges, 21s.; calf or morocco, £2 2s.

"No thoughtful mind will rise from the perusal of this book without feeling that it reveals a beautiful and an harmonious conception. It will serve to raise the mind from mere objections in detail to a comprehensive view of the who'e subject, and it will at least assist candid objectors to do justice to the Christian tradition."—*Times.*

"It is impossible, in the space at our disposal, to do justice to what we feel the most valuable element of Dr. Farrar's work—the ar', namely, with which he places us in the presence of the Great Teacher, and enables us not merely to follow the trains of His thought, but often to detect their subtle source, or trace them in their secret working upon the minds of friendly or hostile listeners."—*Quarterly Review.*

"We have in every page the result of an intimate acquaintance with the literature bearing upon his gr at subject."—*Guardian.*

"A scholarly yet popular Life of Christ was much wanted by the thousands who teach in our schools, and by the tens of thousands who now read and study the Gospels for themselves. This want has been met, fully and admirably, by the Life now before us."—*Nonconformist.*

"Stands among modern Lives alone for its deep piety, its reverent spirit, and especially its wealth of illustration and splendour of rhetoric.'—*New York Church Journal.*

"Many of the illustrations are extremely beautiful; all of them serve a distinct purpose. Considering the beauty and number of the illustrations, this admirably printed volume is likely to prove one of the most attractive gift books of the year."—*Pall Mall Gazette.*

The Patriarchs.
By the Rev. W. HANNA, D.D., and the Rev. Canon NORRIS, B.D. With Coloured Map. Reprinted, with Revisions, from "The Bible Educator." Cloth, 3s. 6d.

The Music of the Bible.
With an Account of the Development of Modern Musical Instruments from Ancient Types. By JOHN STAINER, M.A., Mus.Doc. Reprinted, with Revisions, from "The Bible Educator." Cloth, 3s.

Flowers from the Garden of God.
A Book for Children. By Rev. GORDON CALTHROP, M.A. Cloth, 2s.6d.

The Voice of Time.
By JOHN STROUD. *New Edition.* Cloth gilt, 1s.

Shall We Know One Another?
By Rev. CANON RYLE, M.A. *New Edition.* Cloth gilt, 1s.

Peace or War?
A Sermon by the Rev. E. H. PLUMPTRE, D.D. 6d.

Who is Sufficient?
A Sermon by the Rev. E. H. PLUMPTRE, D.D. 6d.

COMPLETE CATALOGUES of
MESSRS. CASSELL, PETTER, GALPIN & CO.'S PUBLICATIONS,
CONTAINING A LIST OF
EDUCATIONAL WORKS, DICTIONARIES, FINE-ART VOLUMES, CHILDREN'S BOOKS, HISTORIES, NATURAL HISTORY, HOUSEHOLD AND DOMESTIC TREATISES, HANDBOOKS AND GUIDES, SCIENCE, TRAVELS, &c. &c., *together with a Synopsis of their numerous* ILLUSTRATED SERIAL PUBLICATIONS, *sent post free on application to* CASSELL, PETTER, GALPIN & Co., Ludgate Hill, London.

Cassell, Petter, Galpin & Co.: Ludgate Hill, London; Paris; and New York.